Religion in Sociological Perspective

Essays in the Empirical Study of Religion

The Wadsworth Series in Sociology

General Editors

Travis Hirschi   University of California, Davis
Rodney Stark   University of Washington

The Black Family: Essays and Studies
Robert Staples, Howard University

Research Methods: Issues and Insights
Billy J. Franklin, University of Iowa
Harold W. Osborne, Baylor University

Deviant Behavior: A Social Learning Approach
Ronald L. Akers, University of Washington

Survey Research Methods
Earl R. Babbie, University of Hawaii

Religion in Sociological Perspective

Essays in the Empirical Study of Religion

From the
Research Program in Religion and Society
Survey Research Center
University of California, Berkeley

Edited by
Charles Y. Glock
with contributions by

Earl R. Babbie
Bruce D. Foster
Charles Y. Glock
Jeffrey K. Hadden
Phillip E. Hammond
Travis Hirschi
John Lofland
Gary T. Marx

Armand L. Mauss
Robert E. Mitchell
Donald W. Peterson
Harold E. Quinley
Raymond C. Rymph
Rodney Stark
Stephen Steinberg
Robert Wuthnow

Wadsworth Publishing Company, Inc.
Belmont, California

Designer: R. Kent

Editor: Sandra Craig/Kevin Gleason

ISBN-0-534-00216-1
L. C. Cat. Card No. 72-87021
Printed in the United States of America

1 2 3 4 5 6 7 8 9 10 — 77 76 75 74 73

In Memory of
Sydney S. Spivack

Contents

Not since the turn of the century has religion generated as much attention from sociologists as it is now receiving. The revival has not assumed mammoth proportions and a gap remains between the significant questions which might be examined and those which are examined, but there has been a substantial increase both qualitatively and quantitatively in the output of empirical research on religion paralleled by a similar growth in macrotheoretical-historical work. Within slightly more than the last decade there has also been an increase in the number of channels for reporting the results of such work. Today more journals are devoted wholly or substantially to presenting results of sociological inquiry on religion than to any other subject matter in the discipline. Other signs of the resurgence are the spate of national and international sociology of religion congresses, the proliferation of courses in the subject in colleges and universities, and the burgeoning memberships in specialized professional societies.

That religion is exciting sociologists once again and at this particular time is not surprising. The accelerated erosion of traditional faith and the institutions it has spawned has made urgent their documentation and the assessment of their meaning for the future not only of religion but of all social life. Also, there is the tendency in times of major social change to reflect on social institutions associated with more stable times and to address old questions about them from a fresh perspective. Then too times of social change are also times when men address religious questions anew. Almost inevitably new answers have social meanings to which sociologists, when they are alert, pay attention.

This book is intended as a demonstration of what the new sociology of religion is about, especially in its empirical thrust. We believe that this will interest the general reader whose literary taste combines an intellectual interest in religion with wonderment about its survival—indeed, sometimes its remarkable vitality. We also had in mind those who are professionally engaged in religion, because they have a personal stake in being informed about its present course.

Finally, and fundamentally, the book is addressed to young social scientists who are still in training and who could still decide to make empirical sociological work on religion an area of specialization.

We have brought together exemplary empirical essays from the Research Program in Religion and Society of the Survey Research Center at the University of California, Berkeley. This program, launched in the early sixties, is the most sustained and comprehensive attempt in America and perhaps in the world to subject contemporary religious phenomena to empirical scientific scrutiny. Its work is a rich source of material with which to illustrate the kinds of questions about religion empirically oriented social scientists are asking and the answers they are beginning to produce.

There are innumerable ways to order the sociological (and social psychological) questions which can be asked about religion. At the outset it is useful to distinguish simply between questions about the religion of individuals, of groups, and of larger entities—for example, nation-states, cultures—and the book is organized to report serially on work done at these different levels of analysis.

The most elementary observation which can be made about the religion of individuals is its great variety. People differ enormously in the way in which they are religious (or irreligious or a-religious) and in the degree to which they are devout. The simple fact of variety is the stimulus to an almost insatiable curiosity about man's religion. Once the variety is recognized, it begs description and conceptual order. In what myriad of forms does man express himself religiously? What is the nature of these forms, their frequency, their distribution? Variety has also generated a drive toward explanation. How is the variety to be understood? What leads some people to be religious and others not to be religious? Curiosity about the sources of religious commitment leads inexorably to questions about the consequences of commitment. What differences are caused in individual behavior and the quality and character of social life by the ways religion is expressed in a society and by whom it is expressed?

Such questions have been central to the empirical study of religion in its individual manifestations, and they have informed much of the work of the Berkeley program. From that work we have chosen for this volume first a set of essays addressed to the questions of what being religious can signify and what leads people toward or away from religion. These are presented in part 1, On Being and Becoming Religious. Part 2, On the Effects of Religion, comprises a second set of essays exemplifying what is being learned about religion's impact on man's attitudes, values, and behavior.

The observations so far have been concerned with the man in the street rather than those who are engaged in religion professionally. With some modification, questions which are relevant to the former also apply to the latter. In the present era it cannot be taken for granted what the religious orientations of clergy are. To find out and to be able to identify the changes that are taking place and their causes are empirical questions of inherent importance to understanding the contemporary religious scene. Moreover, any assessment of the direction that religious institutions may take and what new forms of religious consciousness may evolve must necessarily take the condition of the religious professional into account.

Empirical sociological research on the clergy has a short history. Most of the work has been done in the past three decades, and more has been in the most recent decade than in the two previous decades combined. Part 3, On Conformity and Rebellion among the Professionally Religious, indicates the content of this work.

Beyond the individual, the religious group — whether it is a cult, sect, denomination, church, or ecclesia—is the next analytic level at which the potential for empirical work has been demonstrated. Here, as at the individual level, there is the initial matter of typologizing the variety; of putting it into conceptual order. Underlying the attempts at classification is a theoretical concern about the sources of the variety—about the conditions which give rise to new religious movements and which shape their character. Questions about etiology follow naturally from questions about origins. What courses do different religious movements follow? What determines the course? What are the implications of different outcomes for society?

The emergence of so-called new religions, particularly in the United States and Japan, has been a special stimulus to recent empirical work, although new analyses of more established groups and movements continue to appear. We have sought in part 4 to illustrate the old and the new in essays On the Origin and Evolution of Religious Movements.

Perhaps the largest question being asked by sociologists of religion these days is what the present period of general social unrest portends for the future of religion. Are the changes so profound as to signify a whole new start in the form and content of man's religious consciousness? Or is there no more in the cards than a modification of existing religious arrangements? Part 5, On the Future of Religion, is devoted to such larger questions in the contemporary study of religion. The essays are intended to demonstrate the contributions which the microscopic examination of religious phenomena may contribute to informed theorizing about the macroscopic issues.

Part One

On Being and Becoming Religious

Making the individual the unit of analysis seems at first glance a more fitting undertaking for the psychology than the sociology of religion. Psychology, after all, seeks to understand the working of the individual psyche and presumably those elements therein which might be defined as religious. Sociologists ordinarily legitimatize their participation by pointing out that there are social psychological as well as purely psychological questions to be addressed in studying the religion of individuals. Variations in individual religiosity, for example, cannot be understood adequately without taking social variables into account.

Sometimes overlooked or even denied is the fact that focusing on individuals is also a means for more purely sociological inquiry into religion. Propositions to the effect that "religion is the opiate of the masses," or that religion is society's principal agent of social control, or that the so-called Protestant ethic was a necessary condition for the rise of capitalism have been generated out of macroscopic inquiry into religion. Subjecting such propositions to test, however, cannot be accomplished by remaining at the macro level. They are assertions about the attitudes, values, or behavior of individuals, and in the end research on individuals is required to determine the validity of the propositions.

Whether informed by social psychological or sociological concerns, empirical inquiry into religion must begin with the tasks of definition, conceptualization, and measurement. What is to indicate religiousness or its absence, and what is to be excluded? How is variation in religious expression to be ordered? Does it fall on a single plane, so that degree of religiousness is all that needs to be measured? Or is the variation multi-dimensional, calling for measurement in kind as well as in degree?

Surprisingly, such questions have only recently commanded the attention of sociologists. Until well into the 1950s little effort was devoted to trying to precisely conceptualize religiosity. Empirical studies of religion were few in any case, and those that were undertaken by and large used essentially everyday distinctions to categorize subjects by religion. The primary basis of distinction was whether individuals identified themselves as Protestant, Catholic, or Jew. On the rare occasions when finer distinctions were attempted, they went no further than to separate regular from irregular churchgoers or believers in God from nonbelievers.

Why the problem of conceptualization was taken more seriously beginning in the late fifties and early sixties is not entirely clear. Undoubtedly the fact that some reasonably substantial resources became available to undertake research on religion was one motivating factor. Another was probably the previously mentioned resurgence of interest in the study of religion, which brought a larger number of qualified sociologists to such inquiry. In any case, over the last decade the field has witnessed a widespread, sustained effort to devise sophisticated ways to define and measure religion that are applicable within and across cultures.

The Berkeley Research Program in Religion and Society has been a sustained contributor to the drive for more adequate conceptualization. Our book opens with four chapters from this work. Chapter 1 was the program's first attempt to tackle the conceptualization problem. It demonstrates the need to conceive of religion in multidimensional rather than in unidimensional terms—that is, to take into account distinctions in the way religion may be expressed as well as in the degree to which it may be practiced. Subsequent work on conceptualization in the Berkeley program has been devoted largely to delineating how these distinctions in kind might be specified fruitfully. Chapters 2 through 4 illustrate how complex this task can become.

The complexity arises partly because sociologists of religion do not agree about what to include and what to exclude in a definition of religion. There is widespread disaffection with limiting conceptions to institutionalized forms of religion, but there is disconsensus about how far to stretch the parameters. These difficulties are exemplified in chapter 2, which is addressed to finding some common ground for conceptualizing not all but simply one of the dimensions of religion—religious belief.

Another factor that complicates the task of conceptualization is the somewhat belated recognition that as there are various ways to be religious there are also alternatives for not being religious. Now that we appear to be in a period of increasing secularization, finding a way to order religious defection looms as an increasingly urgent problem. In chapter 3, Armand Mauss advances a possible solution.

Accuracy in conceptualization is also made difficult because of the ambiguity in religious terms as they are used in everyday language. A by now classic case is what it means for someone to identify himself as Jewish. In chapter 4 Stephen Steinberg demonstrates the variety of meanings which are encompassed in the designation and the difficulties of defining the term so as to make it useful for scientific research.

Taken in sum, these first four selections say something about the variation which exists in the way people may or may not be religious and about the conceptual and measurement problems this situation generates. The next two chapters in part 1 attempt to explain the variation. It might seem strange that such explanation should have high priority among students of religion. To know why and by what processes people become the way they are religiously seems absolutely essential to gaining a comprehensive understanding of the phenomenon. Yet very little research has been undertaken, and we remain relatively ignorant on this vital topic. At Berkeley the topic has been on the agenda, but as elsewhere, the research undertaken until now falls far short of comprehending the complex factors that lead people toward or away from religious commitment. Still, the work is a start and can be used to illustrate some of the possibilities.

Two rather different approaches have been adopted in the research done at Berkeley on the sources of religious commitment. One approach, exemplified in chapter 5, by John Lofland and Rodney Stark, involved participant observation of a religious group to try to learn the social processes underlying changes in religious status. Lofland and Stark report on their discoveries about how people are converted to a deviant religious perspective.

Survey research procedures have been used to try to identify through quantitative analysis the social conditions under which various forms of religious expression are maximized and minimized. Studies in this mode have proved useful to test commonsense assumptions about what makes people religious as well as more theoretical hypotheses. The mode is illustrated in chapter 6, in which Rodney Stark explores a number of widely held notions about the role of age in generating various forms of religious commitment and departures from commitment.

Additional Reading

On Being Religious

James, William. *The Varieties of Religious Experience*, New York: Modern Library. Originally published by Longmans, Green and Co., 1902. The classic treatment of variations in the modes of religious consciousness.

Stark, Rodney. "A Taxonomy of Religious Experience," *Journal for the Scientific Study of Religion* 5:1 (Fall 1965). Stark does for religious experience what was tried in chapter 2 for religious belief.

Journal for the Scientific Study of Religion 6:2 (Fall 1967). Ways to conceptualize the religious variable are the subject of about half the articles in this special issue. Contributers are Morton King, Russell O. Allen, Bernard Spilka, and Larry Shiner, with commentary by James E. Dittes. King also contributes a useful bibliography.

On Becoming Religious

Demerath, N. J. III: *Social Class in American Protestantism*, Chicago: Rand McNally, 1965. Demerath successfully tackles the difficult problem of sorting out the conflicting evidence on the relationship between social class and religious style, and in the process he breaks some new ground in elaborating a typology of religiousness.

Stark, Rodney. "Social Contexts and Religious Experience," *Review of Religious Research* 7:1 (Autumn 1965). This is a follow-up on Stark's conceptual treatment of religious experience (see above). Here he addresses the social sources of religious experience.

Glock, Charles Y.; Ringer, Benjamin B.; and Babbie, Earl R. *To Comfort and to Challenge*, Berkeley and Los Angeles: University of California Press, 1967. A report on a national study of Episcopalians, this book develops and tests a model to explain why parishioners vary in the extent of their involvement in the church. The effects of differential involvement are also examined.

Chapter One

The Dimensions of Religious Commitment*

Charles Y. Glock

What it means to be "religious" is not the same to all men—either in modern complex societies or in even the most homogeneous primitive groups. Even within a single religious tradition, many variations can be found. This simple fact scarcely needs documentation. Evidence that people think, feel and act differently when it comes to religion is all around us.

In the face of this diversity, the student of the individual and his religion is faced with the formidable task of deciding how to conceptualize the phenomenon of religiousness and how to distinguish people in terms of their degrees of religious commitment. These are not, certainly, questions that have been entirely ignored by students of religion. There have been attempts to distinguish people religiously and to discover what leads people to be religious or not. But the efforts have been surprisingly few and, on careful examination, incomplete. All things considered, the task of constructing a conceptual framework for the systematic study of differential commitment to religion still lies ahead of us.

The present chapter is an effort to move closer to that goal. It considers the question of what is required for a comprehensive and operationally useful definition of religiousness. The intrinsic importance of religion in the life of man would be enough to justify the study of individual religiosity. But having a way to measure differential commitment to religion would do more than simply satisfy our curiosity. It is a prerequisite to moving on to the more compelling questions of what are the sources and the consequences of religious involvement—both for individuals and for societies.

A first and obvious requirement if religious commitment is to be comprehensively assessed is to establish the different ways in which individuals

*Excerpted from Charles Y. Glock, "On the Study of Religious Commitment." Research Supplement to *Religious Education* 57, no. 4 (July-August 1962). Reprinted with the permission of *Religious Education*.

can be religious. With some few exceptions, past research has curiously avoided this fundamental question. Investigators have tended to focus upon one or another of the diverse manifestations of religiosity and to ignore all others. Thus, in one study, attention will be confined to studying religious belief, and, in another, to studying differences in religious practices. The particular aspect of religion being studied is rarely, if ever, placed within the broader context of its relations to other expressions of religiousness. Nor is the question raised of whether commitment manifested in one way has anything to do with its being expressed in other ways.

If we examine the religions of the world, it is evident that the details of religious expression are extremely varied; different religions expect quite different things of their adherents. Catholics and Protestants, for example, are expected to participate regularly in the Christian sacrament of Holy Communion. To the Moslem such a practice is alien. Similarly, the Moslem imperative to undertake a pilgrimage to Mecca during one's lifetime is alien to the Christian.

In the midst of the great variation in detail, there nevertheless exists among the world's religions considerable consensus as to the more general areas in which religiosity ought to be manifested. These general areas may be thought of as the core dimensions of religiosity. Five such dimensions can be distinguished; within one or another of these dimensions all of the many and diverse manifestations of religiosity prescribed by the different religions of the world can be ordered. We shall call these dimensions the *experiential*, the *ritualistic*, the *ideological*, the *intellectual*, and the *consequential*.

The *experiential dimension* gives recognition to the fact that all religions have certain expectations, however imprecisely they may be stated, that the religious person will at one time or another achieve direct knowledge of ultimate reality or will experience religious emotion. Included here are all of those feelings, perceptions, and sensations which are experienced by an actor or defined by a religious group as involving some communication, however slight, with a divine essence, i.e., with God, with ultimate reality, with transcendental authority. The emotions deemed proper by different religions or actually experienced by different individuals may vary widely—from terror to exaltation, from humility to joyfulness, from peace of soul to a sense of passionate union with the universe or the divine. The emphasis placed on religious feeling as an essential element of religiosity may also vary widely; even within Christianity, groups differ widely in their evaluation of mysticism or in the importance they attach to the experience of conversion. Nevertheless every religion places some value on subjective religious experience as a sign of individual religiosity.

The *ideological dimension* is constituted, on the other hand, by expectations that the religious person will hold to certain beliefs. The content and scope of beliefs will vary not only between religions but often within the same religious tradition. However, every religion sets forth some set of beliefs to which its followers are expected to adhere.

The *ritualistic dimension* encompasses the specifically religious practices expected of religious adherents. It comprises such activities as worship, prayer, participation in special sacraments, fasting, and the like.

The *intellectual dimension* has to do with the expectation that the religious person will be informed and knowledgeable about the basic tenets of his faith and its sacred scriptures. The intellectual and the ideological dimensions are clearly related since knowledge of a belief is a necessary condition for its acceptance. However, belief need not follow from knowledge nor, for that matter, does all religious knowledge bear on belief.

The *consequential dimension*, the last of the five, is different in kind from the first four. It encompasses the secular effects of religious belief, practice, experience, and knowledge on the individual. Included under the consequential dimension are all those religious prescriptions which specify what people ought to do and the attitudes they ought to hold as a consequence of their religion. The notion of "works," in the theological meaning of the term, is connoted here. In the language of Christian belief, the consequential dimension deals with man's relation to man rather than with man's relation to God.

It is the nature of the consequential dimension of religiosity that it cannot be studied apart from the other dimensions. Attitudes and behavior in secular areas of life can be used as measures of religious commitment only where they are grounded in religious conviction—where they follow from religious belief, practice, experience, and knowledge.

The mere identification of the different ways in which religious commitment may be expressed turns out to be useful in a number of respects. It provides a perspective for locating the gaps in past and present research. It clarifies some of the discrepancies in what has been observed and reported about religiosity. And it establishes, at least roughly, the requirements to be met if we are to study the phenomenon of religion comprehensively.

Chapter Two

On the Study of Religious Beliefs and Non-Belief*

Charles Y. Glock

The starting point for the study of any phenomenon is a way to conceptualize it so that it may be subjected to sustained inquiry. This task has not been accomplished for the study of religious belief and non-belief. So far, at any rate, confusion and ambiguity rather than clarity and precision have characterized usage of the terms.

Part of the difficulty has been to establish the boundaries for inquiry. Belief can characterize a wide spectrum of the human experience; there can be belief in God, in astrology, in free will, in birth control; indeed, in virtually anything. What boundaries, if any, ought to be imposed and how are they to be determined?

A second problem is one common to all attempts at conceptualization: arriving at a formula at once culture-free and sensitive to variations within and between different cultures. It has yet to be settled whether this criterion can be met for religious belief or, if it can be met, by what means.

Ambiguity has also arisen out of the tendency to associate belief and non-belief with religion. There has been controversy about whether such an association is warranted as well as about how religious beliefs and non-beliefs are to be distinguished from non-religious ones. What constitutes religious belief when there is no religious institution has also been a source of contention, and some have suggested that the concept of non-belief has meaning only where religion is institutionally separated.

It is probably not possible to remove all ambiguity or to obtain agreement from everyone—social scientists, churchmen, theologians, philosophers, the man

*Excerpted from Charles Y. Glock, "The Study of Unbelief: Perspectives on Research," in *The Culture of Unbelief*, ed. Rocco Caporale and Antonio Grumelli (Berkeley and Los Angeles: University of California Press, 1971). Reprinted with the permission of the author and the publisher.

in the street—on any one definition. But unless a formalization of the concept can be produced about which some degree of consensus coalesces, it is doubtful that religious belief can be raised to the level of a scientific concept or become a subject of fruitful inquiry.

The starting place for conceptualization is with the boundary problem—with trying to pinpoint just what it is we mean to include as belief. The choices seem virtually infinite; yet it is evident from the way "belief" is used in both ordinary and scientific discourse that we do not think of the options as being so varied. Whether there is belief or non-belief in birth control or in free love or in evolution or in a myriad of other things is not decisive in making the identification. Ordinarily, it is one connotation, rather than a variety, which comes to mind.

The connotation will be expressed in very different ways. The man in the street will probably verbalize it as belief in Christ or God or Allah or Krishna. For others, belief will be belief in any higher power, whether conceived in deistic, theistic, or pantheistic forms. Paul Tillich equated belief with the presence of a sense of ultimate concern. Sociologists sometimes associate it with the absence of anomie.

These ideas are at once very different and very alike. Their common theme is that belief is constituted by an experience of the "sacred" and by feeling—indeed being—subject to its authority. Where the ideas diverge is in their vision of the "sacred"; but even here, the differences are apparent as well as real.

There is agreement, I would suggest, that the central problem to which the "sacred" is addressed is that of the meaning of being. The "sacred" provides a perspective on life which transforms it into something beyond, as Robert Bellah has put it, "the literateness of everyday life."[1] There is also agreement that whatever the nature of the "sacred," it is transcendent of self. Whether thought of as God, as Nirvana, as ultimate reality, as the divine essence in all of us, or as the experience of personal meaning and authenticity, the "sacred," when believed, is an authority beyond self with the power to constrain self.

There is a distinction to be made, however, between supernatural and simply transcendent or natural conceptions of the source of "sacred" authority. In supernatural conceptions, the "sacred" is ordained by an otherworldly power to which this world is subject. The power may be held to reside in an anthropomorphic God or gods. It may also be a law of creation without deity, such as the Hindu idea of Nirvana or the ancient Chinese notion of a natural harmony of order in the universe. Indeed, modern science offers its own version of a harmony of order to which we may be said to be subject. In natural conceptions, an atheistic or agnostic position is taken on the existence of the supernatural. In this the authority of the "sacred" is internal to the beliefs themselves; one is captured by them, beholden to them, but there is no God or law of creation to say that this is the way it must be.

Supernatural conceptions of the "sacred" may be, borrowing Bellah's terms,

[1] Robert Bellah, "The Historical Background of Unbelief," in *The Culture of Unbelief*, ed. Rocco Caporale and Antonio Grumelli, (Berkeley and Los Angeles: University of California Press, 1971).

objectivist or subjectivist; so may natural conceptions.[2] We may speak, then, of four types of belief: objectivist supernatural, objectivist natural, subjectivist supernatural, and subjectivist natural.

Objectivist supernatural belief is constituted by literal acceptance and internalization of a supernatural interpretation of meaning set forth and objectified in doctrine, dogma, and creed by an institution (usually a Church), by a person, or by tradition. The doctrines of the Roman Catholic Church, the claims of a Father Divine, the Hindu law of karma, primitive conceptions of mana, all qualify as referents for objectivist supernatural belief. They all contain a supernatural vision of the "sacred" and are set forth objectively, so that they may be accepted or rejected by those exposed to them.

Objectivist natural belief is essentially similar to objectivist supernatural belief except that the source of the interpretation of meaning is not supernatural. An orthodox Marxist would be an objectivist natural believer, as would a National Socialist in Nazi Germany. Existentialists would also be so classified, as would those who accept any naturalistic philosophy or religion set forth and objectified by an institution, by a person, or by tradition.

Subjectivist supernatural belief includes a conception of a supernatural working out for himself a meaning for his life which transcends everyday experience. Such elements of objectivist belief as may be contained in subjectivist faith are privatized interpretations rather than literal acceptance of objectified doctrines or creeds. Subjectivist belief is, or is close to being, unique to the individual, whereas objectivist belief is generally common to some group. This does not necessarily mean that there will be as many subjectivist beliefs as there are subjectivist believers; working independently, it is quite possible that people may arrive at the same conclusions. This, however, is a matter for empirical resolution and we shall have to have data before we can decide whether subjectivist beliefs can be meaningfully ordered.

Subjectivist supernatural belief includes a conception of a supernatural entity—not a conventional entity, but one worked out by the individual for himself. The supernatural may be conceived of in theistic, deistic, or pantheistic terms, but it is always some force beyond this worldly comprehension to which this world and specifically, the subjectivist, supernatural believer is subject. For the subjectivist believer the supernatural functions as warrant for what he holds to be "sacred." The subjectivist natural believer needs no such warrant. It is enough for him to feel that what he believes is specifically unalterable for himself; he is incapable of brooking an alternative.

Logically the system allows for only one definition of nonbelief—namely, the failure to score as a believer in any of the four belief categories. Non-belief may also be defined, however, from the perspective of each belief category; thus, one may speak of objectivist supernatural believers and non-believers, objectivist natural believers and non-believers, and so on. Additional definitions of non-belief may stem from narrower conceptions of objectivist belief. Thus, from the perspective of Christian belief, a non-Christian would be a non-believer, as

[2]*Ibid.*

would a non-Communist from a Marxist perspective. Consensus around any one of these definitions of unbelief cannot be expected, of course; nor is it necessary for research. Given this range of definitions, it is possible through research to test all of them to determine which one or combination is the most fruitful in illuminating sociological inquiry. It may turn out that considerably greater significance attaches to whether a person is an objectivist supernatural believer or not than whether he fits into any belief category or not. It is also possible and perhaps likely that we will find the determining factor to be, not whether or not a person is a believer, but what kind and how strong a believer he is.

It is clear that the proposed conceptualization only begins to order the alternatives and that considerable refinement of categories and the introduction of subcategories will be required to operationalize it and make it subject to measurement. Extensive empirical investigation will be required, obviously, for this to be done. What I have sought simply to do here is clarify the conceptual confusion which has plagued us in the past.

Chapter Three

Dimensions of Religious Defection*

Armand L. Mauss

It is probably indicative of a bias in social science that religious *commitment* is considered a research problem, but religious *defection* is not—or so it would seem from the paucity of available research literature on the subject of religious defection. A recently published and very comprehensive bibliography of social science literature in the field of religion not only has no topical section on defection, but it does not even list a single book or article devoted to that topic.[1] An extensive search through various important works in the sociology and psychology of religion failed to uncover more than an occasional oblique mention of religious defection in connection with some other topic, but not even a paragraph on defection *per se*.[2]

*Excerpted from Armand L. Mauss, "Dimensions of Religious Defection," *Review of Religious Research* 10, no. 3 (Spring 1969). Reprinted with the permission of the author and the *Review of Religious Research*.

[1]Morris I. Berkowitz and J. Edmund Johnson, *Social Scientific Studies of Religion: A Bibliography* (Pittsburgh: University of Pittsburgh Press, 1967).

[2]Among the works consulted were: Gordon Allport, *The Individual and His Religion* (N.Y.: Macmillan, 1950); Charles Y. Glock and Rodney Stark, *Religion and Society in Tension* (Chicago: Rand McNally, 1965); Charles Y. Glock *et al.*, *To Comfort and To Challenge* (Berkeley: University of California Press, 1967); William James, *The Varieties of Religious Experience* (New York: Modern Library); Gerhard Lenski, *The Religious Factor* (N.Y.: Doubleday, 1961); Thomas F. O'Dea, *The Sociology of Religion* (Englewood Cliffs, N.J.: Prentice-Hall, 1966); Joachim Wach, *Sociology of Religion* (Chicago: University of Chicago Press, 1944); and Max Weber, *The Sociology of Religion* (trans. by Ephraim Fischoff) (Boston: Beacon Press, 1964). Also consulted were all the articles so far published in the *Journal for the Scientific Study of Religion*, and all articles whose titles seemed the least bit relevant from the indexes of the *American Journal of Sociology* and the *American Sociological Review*. (This was all *in addition to*—and by way of double-checking—the bibliographical work listed above in fn. 1). The most explicit and direct references that I found in the literature on this general topic were these three: (a) Joseph H. Fichter, S.J.,

There is, of course, no *scientific* reason that religious defection should be any less interesting or important than, say, political defection, or, for that matter, dropping out of school. Religious "drop-outs" may not present the kind of critical societal problem that school "drop-outs" do, or the kind of interesting political problem presented by the "switchers" and "cop-outs" from various political movements, but as a scientific problem, religious defection offers at least as much potential yield as these other kinds. For one thing, the incidence and the variety of religious defectors might give us clues as to the nature and consequences of *change* within religious cultures and organizations; they might also provide an important source of *recruits* to various *new* social and religious movements, cults, and sects. From the point of view of the religionist, moreover, there is, of course, the additional potential gain of an insight into the causes and types of religious defection that can lead to effective programs of prevention and reactivation.

The work here reported is mainly of a theoretical kind, offered in the hope that it will be heuristically suggestive. It should be made clear at the outset that the term "defection" will be used herein to refer to the withdrawal from fellowship or activity by church members *who have had some history of regular attendance and involvement in the church*, not merely nominal affiliation; nor will the term refer to the simple "denominational switching" that is sometimes associated with mixed marriages, social mobility, and the like (although, of course, "defectors" might join other denominations subsequent to their defection). The term "defection," as I use it, will be more or less synonymous with "disaffection" (or, more colloquially, "dropping out"); or, it might just as well be considered "disinvolvement," to indicate that it is an opposite or counterpart to the concept of religious "involvement" employed by Glock, Lenski, and others.[3]

Social Relations in the Urban Parish (Chicago: U. of Chicago Press, 1954), pp. 56-79, where Fichter introduces a typology of parish members, including the categories "marginal," "dormant," and "dead"; these would seem collectively to correspond somewhat to what I am here calling "defected" or "disinvolved," although Fichter stops at the descriptive level and attempts no analytical elaboration upon his categories. (b) David O. Moberg, *The Church as a Social Institution* (Englewood Cliffs, N.J.: Prentice-Hall, 1962), pp. 405-413 (where Moberg discusses Fichter's typology somewhat), and pp. 430, 436, 438, 441, and 478. In these latter pages Moberg is concerned mainly with the question of *conversion*, but he comments upon some of the factors which might lead to "backsliding" or "defection" on the part of converts, and he emphasizes in particular the importance of *social ties* in maintaining the conversion experience. (c) Martin E. Marty's *Varieties of Unbelief* (New York: Holt, Rinehart, Winston, 1964) also bears upon my topic somewhat, but Marty's focus is largely theological, rather than sociological, and is more upon subjective, personal experiences of *un*belief, whereas my focus is more upon certain objective concomitants of *dis*involvement. (See also fn. 5 below.)

[3]Glock and Stark, *op.cit.*, Chapter 2; Glock, *et al., op.cit.*, Chapter 1; and Lenski, *op.cit.*, pp. 17-22. (It has been suggested to me that my definition of "defector" might not take due account of what might be called the "de facto defector," who may have ceased to believe, but who continues anyway to participate for some reason or another. Though I recognize that such church members may indeed exist, I do not include them in my definition, mainly because of the difficulty in identifying them empirically.)

The Three Dimensions of Religious Defection

The identification of religious defection as a general phenomenon, however, is only the beginning of a study of this topic, for we must expect to find different dimensions of religious *dis*involvement, just as we find different dimensions of *involvement*. Charles Glock has discussed in Chapter One five theoretical dimensions of involvement, and Morton King, in a recent article, uses a very elaborate empirical process to identify *nine* such dimensions.[4] We should probably not expect religious *dis*involvement to be any less complex.

One dimension of disinvolvement or defection that is perhaps best known to academicians is what we might call the *intellectual dimension* (this would be the negative counterpart to Glock's "ideological dimension"). This dimension refers to the kind of disinvolvement that is based upon disbelief of certain central tenets of a religion accompanied, presumably, by a belief in rival secular doctrines. Atheism and agnosticism are perhaps the most common expressions of this dimension of disinvolvement, although there are many possible indicators, some of which would be unique to certain denominations. *Indicators* that might be used for this dimension would be: expression of disbelief in any kind of God, or in the literal divinity of Jesus; a belief in evolution of the species; a belief in the merely palliative function of religion; reading habits that center on books and journals of secular "high culture," rather than on religious literature, etc. We might expect intellectuals and academics to be particularly exemplary of the intellectual dimension of defection, since there is evidence (though not conclusive) that higher education in many academic fields, especially in the social sciences and humanities, is generally incompatible with religious commitment. Stark suggests that this incompatibility is inherent in the differences of approach, method, and premises between religion and these secular fields; Greeley claims that the relatively low level of religiosity among academicians is only the result of selective recruitment to academic life; and Thalheimer presents evidence that intellectual defection from religion begins to take place well before the college years.[5] In any case, it seems well established, both from research and from common experience, that the intellectual dimension is one dimension of defection that we can quite readily identify. (It should be added here in passing that one need not be an academician, or even

---

[4]Glock and Stark, *loc. cit.*; Morton King, "Measuring the Religious Variable: Nine Proposed Dimensions." *Journal for the Scientific Study of Religion*, VI:2 (Fall, 1967), pp. 173-185. (The latter article is followed by an excellent bibliography of works on religious involvement.)

[5]Rodney Stark, "On the Incompatibility of Religion and Science: A Survey of American Graduate Students," *Journal for the Scientific Study of Religion*, III:1 (Fall, 1963), pp. 3-20; exchanges between Andrew Greeley, Rodney Stark and others on the same subject in *JSSR* III:2 (Spring, 1964), pp. 239-243; Andrew Greeley, "The Religious Behavior of Graduate Students," *JSSR* V:1 (Fall, 1965), pp. 34-40; Fred Thalheimer, "Continuity and Change in Religiosity: A Study of Academicians," *Pacific Sociological Review*, 8:2 (1965), pp. 101-108. (This "intellectual dimension" of defection seems closest to what Martin E. Marty is concerned with in his work mentioned at the end of fn. 2 above.)

highly educated, to experience this kind of defection; and conversely, that there are, of course, such things as religious intellectuals and academicians.)[6]

Turning from matters of belief, let us consider religious disinvolvement on the strictly *social dimension*. The importance of the various social functions of religious involvement is, of course, a classical concept in the sociology of religion, central to the thought of such early theorists as Durkheim.[7] More recently Lenski has identified two varieties of social involvement in religion, a "communal," or primary group involvement, and an "associational" or secondary group involvement.[8] Glock has shown the importance for religious involvement that various social factors have, including social class, family status, and life cycle, and he has hypothesized "social deprivation" in the secular world as one of the determinants of involvement in religious organizations.[9] In an article on Mormons, Photiadis has shown how involvement or participation in the church on the *social* level functions to produce overt conformity to church norms, independently of the *intellectual* (or belief) dimension.[10] Hagburg has shown how the level of participation in an organization is dependent upon the primary group satisfactions which members receive from participating, and he suggests that churches, labor unions, and other organizations are functional counterparts or equivalents in offering such satisfactions to their members.[11]

If, as all such literature suggests, social ties and social integration of the individual are so important in producing religious *involvement*, then we might plausibly infer that *dis*involvement or defection can occur as a consequence either of the disintegration of social bonds, or of unsatisfying social experiences,

[6]In fact, there may well be another expression of intellectual defection altogether, besides that seen in the rejection of traditional theological concepts; that is the intellectual (or ideological) defection that occurs *because of a perceived lack* of metaphysical or other-worldly orientation or theology in some of the more liberal denominations. An allusion to the possibility of this kind of intellectual defection was made recently by Rabbi Arthur Hertzberg of Temple Emanuel, Englewood, N.J., who was quoted in the *New York Times* (Sunday, March 10, 1968, p. 33). Among his remarks were the following excerpts:

". . . What people come to religion for is an ultimate metaphysical hunger, and when this hunger is not satisfied, religion declines. . . Beneath their involvement (in secular social issues), people are not very happy with any of our answers. They are worried about something more than Dow Chemical and napalm. They are worried about what's it all for. They are worried about—dare I say it? immortality, what their lives are linked to."

[7]See e.g., Emile Durkheim, *The Elementary Forms of Religious Life* (trans. by Swain) (N.Y.: Collier Books, 1961), pp. 393-434.

[8]Lenski, *loc. cit.*

[9]Glock and Stark, *loc. cit.*; Glock *et al.*, *loc. cit.*

[10]John D. Photiadis, "Overt Conformity to Church Teaching as a Function of Religious Belief and Group Participation," *American Journal of Sociology*, 70:4 (1965), pp. 423-428.

[11]Eugene C. Hagburg, "Correlates of Organizational Participation," *Pacific Sociological Review*, 9:1 (1966), pp. 15-21. It might be interesting to note that the concept of social "disinvolvement" or "defection" in the context of institutional religion is rather akin to the concept of "disengagement," associated with aging. This idea is developed in Chapters XII and XIII of Elaine Cumming and William E. Henry, *Growing Old: The Process of Disengagement* (New York: Basic Books, 1961). Paralleling my own interests, the authors here are especially interested in the *social* genesis of role-withdrawal on the part of the aged.

or of the formation of strong social ties outside the church. Empirical *indicators* of disinvolvement on the social dimension might be: loss (or lack) of close friends in the church; relatively low social status *compared to* the congregation generally; personal acquaintance with few, if any, church workers, lay leaders, or clergy; little or no participation in church auxiliary or social activities; marriage to a devout member of another faith; and perceptions of "coolness" or "cliques" among members of the congregation.

Any of us who has discussed religion with very many defectors, however, has heard expressions of disaffection that have little to do with lack of social ties, or with conscientious intellectual problems: charges that regular church-goers are hypocrites, that the churches are interested only in money, and that religion was forced on one as a child, are among the most common cliches heard in the company of the defected. Given the human capacity for rationalization and other ego defense mechanisms, one wonders whether to take such charges at face value as the "real reasons" for the defection. The experiences upon which such charges are based have surely occurred in the lives of many who have *not* defected, so there is nothing automatic about the defector's reaction to such experiences. It is proposed here that charges of this kind might be considered *symptoms* of this kind of defection that occurs on the *emotional dimension*, which is the third of our three dimensions of defection, and which religionists might prefer to call the *spiritual* dimension.[12] There are some passing references to this kind of dimension in psychological literature.

Gordon Allport discusses briefly the common phenomenon of youthful rebellion against parental religion and points out that many youngsters drift away from religion ". . . not because of intellectual doubts, but because of a gnawing sense of guilt and shame, due perhaps to sex conflicts."[13] Allport also identifies a kind of "acute negativism" toward religion that he regards as "emotionally over-determined," perhaps as a reaction to some kind of earlier *trauma* (such as when religion seemed ineffectual in the face of unhappiness or tragedy), or, perhaps as a symptom of repressed animosity toward one's father, in accordance with the Freudian conception.[14] Writing in a somewhat similar vein, Richard McCann sees the "seed for future agnosticism" sown in unhappy, unsatisfying, emotionally deprived, or rigid family environments, especially in the more fundamentalist homes.[15]

The purport of such observations is not, of course, to suggest that the emotional problems that people have with religion are not real problems, but only that they are more deep-seated ones than would be apparent from the rationalizations offered by the emotionally defected. Such rationalizations can

---

[12]For a defense of the use of such concepts as "spiritual" by social scientists, as well as by religionists, see David O. Moberg, "The Encounter of Scientific and Religious Values Pertinent to Man's Spiritual Nature," *Sociological Analysis*, 28:1 (Spring, 1967), pp. 27-28.

[13]Allport, *op.cit.*, pp. 32-33.

[14]*Ibid.*, p. 103.

[15]Richard McCann, "Developmental Factors in the Growth of a Mature Faith," in Richard D. Knudten (ed.), *The Sociology of Religion* (N.Y.: Appleton-Century-Crofts, 1967), p. 210.

be regarded, however, as perhaps the most readily available empirical *indicators* of emotional defection. It would be premature at this stage of the work to attempt a comprehensive catalogue of all the emotional conditions and symptoms that are related to the emotional dimension of defection. This dimension is perhaps the most elusive and subjective of the three, in the sense that objective empirical indicators of it are much harder to identify than is the case with the intellectual and social dimensions. The assistance of psychologists would be very helpful at this point. Perhaps what has been offered above, however, is sufficient *prima facie* evidence for the existence of this emotional dimension.

The Typology Deriving from the Three Dimensions

Having identified, hopefully, three discrete dimensions which appear among religious defectors, I hasten to make the obvious but necessary observation that not all defection is purely on one dimension or another. These three dimensions must be combined into a hypothetical typology which will reflect the various *combinations* of defection derived from these dimensions. The result is the 8-celled typology represented in Figure 1. Cell 1 represents the "total

Figure 1.   *A Hypothetical Typology of Religious Defection*

		High on Emotional Defection		Low on Emotional Defection	
		Social Defection		Social Defection	
		High	Low	High	Low
Intellectual Defection	High	1	2	5	6
	Low	3	4	7	8

1 = Total defectors	4 = Emotional	7 = Social
2 = Psychological (Int. & Em.)	5 = Cultural (Soc. & Int.)	8 = Circumstantial
3 = Alienated (Soc. & Em.)	6 = Intellectual	

defectors," those who are high on *all three* dimensions of defection; those in Cell 2 we might call the "psychological defectors," since their defection is both intellectual and emotional, but not social; in Cell 3 we have the "alienated defectors," who may not have intellectual problems, but they are both socially unintegrated and emotionally distressed; Cell 4 would contain the purely "emotional defectors." Turning to the half of the typology that is without the emotional dimension, we have the "cultural defectors" of Cell 5, so called because they are high on both the social and intellectual dimensions; Cell 6 has the purely "intellectual defectors," and Cell 7 the purely "social defectors." Cell 8 is a residual category representing those who have become disinvolved in church, but not for any generic reason. Such people are not offended or disaffected about anything; they are simply taken away from church activities, by such circumstances as going away to military service, and have not yet overcome the inertia in order to become reinvolved. These I call "circumstantial defectors." All such terminology is, of course, tentative at this point, and the eight names that have been used for these cells might have more poetic than empirical value.

From a scientific point of view, a typology of the kind proposed here might have considerable heuristic value, not only for its more obvious taxonomic function, but also as a guide in the study of *change*. The different types of defectors from various denominations over time ought to tell us something about the changes taking place in the relations between those denominations and secular social institutions. Defectors of various types, furthermore, often become recruits or converts to different kinds of *new* social movements or religious sects. While this typology does not tie directly into an existing body of scientific theory, it has many indirect ties to much of the work done on religious commitment or involvement, since it involves negative counterparts to several ideas that have been advanced on the subject of commitment, as indicated throughout the preceding discussion.

Chapter Four

The Anatomy of Jewish Identification*

Stephen Steinberg

The perennial question—are Jews a race, a religion, a nationality, or a culture?—itself reveals a good deal about the ambiguity and complexity of Jewish identification. The question would not be asked, and asked so often, if not for the fact that Jewish identity takes such a wide range of forms and expressions. What it means to be a Jew is clearly not the same in Israel as in America; in California as in New York; in Shaker Heights as in Forest Hills.

Not only do different Jews identify in different ways, but for any individual it becomes possible to distinguish various dimensions underlying his identity. Once these dimensions are identified and measured, the anatomy of Jewish identification can be systematically studied. What is the range and frequency of different patterns of identity? How do they vary among different segments of the Jewish population? To what extent are different patterns of identity associated with different outcomes, such as experiencing anti-semitism, achieving high social status, and holding liberal political values?

This chapter outlines a number of core dimensions of Jewish identification. It is hoped that these distinctions will be useful in future research, both in the formulation of research questions and in the analysis of data.

The Tribal Dimension

The most fundamental mode of identification for any ethnic group involves a consciousness of kind or a sense of peoplehood.[1] Ethnic cohesion is typically formed out of such objective conditions as a common ancestry, a common past,

*Excerpted from Stephen Steinberg, "The Anatomy of Jewish Identification: A Historical and Theoretical View," *Review of Religious Research* 7, no. 1 (Fall 1965). Reprinted with permission of the author and the *Review of Religious Research*.

[1] For a discussion of these and other concepts of ethnicity, see Milton M. Gordon, *Assimilation in American Life* (New York: Oxford University Press, 1964), pp. 23-30.

and common traditions and values. But these conditions would be of little significance without the subjective feelings that normally accompany them. Indeed, these subjective feelings often take on a life of their own, and perpetuate themselves even after the objective conditions that produced them no longer exist in their original form.

Tribal sentiments range from a self-conscious nationalism to a vague sense of group belonging that may remain hidden in the subconscious. Freud described his own subliminal attachments to Judaism as follows:

> What bound me to Jewry was (I am ashamed to admit) neither faith nor national pride, for I have always been an unbeliever and was brought up without any religion. . . . Whenever I felt an inclination to national enthusiasm I strove to suppress it as being harmful and wrong, alarmed by the warning examples of the peoples among whom we Jews live. But many other things remained to make the attraction of Jewry and Jews irresistible—many obscure emotional forces, which were the more powerful the less they could be expressed in words, as well as a clear consciousness of inner identity, the safe privacy of a common mental construction.[2]

Of course, whenever such feelings are latent or actively suppressed, problems of measurement become acute. One potentially fruitful approach is suggested by Jewish history. How secularized Jews react to the persecution of other Jews (or more recently by threats to Israel) has often been the acid test of Jewish identity. For example, at the end of the nineteenth century Reform Jews went so far as to formally renounce the concept of Jewish nationalism; that is, they rejected the idea that Jews were a nation in exile with loyalties that transcended national boundaries. But as Nathan Glazer points out, these same Jews were surprised by their own strong reaction to the pogroms in Russia, and eventually abandoned their anti-nationalist position.[3] Inasmuch as tribal sentiments surface most clearly during periods of crisis, this suggests a line of questioning or observation that might produce sensitive indicators of the tribal dimension.

The Religious Dimension

Religion, of course, constitutes another basis for identity. While traditional Judaism does not always distinguish between the religious and the secular, for our purposes it is crucial to impose this distinction and to analyze religion narrowly as an independent category of behavior. Once this is done, it will be possible to explore the relation between this and other dimensions.

Even when considered apart from other dimensions, however, the religious dimension encompasses a wide range of behavior. Glock has delineated five

---

[2] Quoted in Eric H. Erikson, "The Concept of Identity in Race Relations: Notes and Queries," *Daedalus*, Vol. 95 (Winter 1966), p. 148.

[3] Nathan Glazer, *American Judaism* (Chicago: University of Chicago Press, 1957), p. 55.

dimensions of religious commitment that can usefully be incorporated into the present conceptual scheme.[4] They are, it will be recalled:

1 The ideological dimension: the extent to which individuals adhere to basic tenets of faith. Past studies indicate that Jews typically score low on this dimension, at least as compared to Protestants and Catholics. However, problems of comparability arise when the same questions are employed to measure belief in such different religious systems. Future research should devise questions that are especially tailored to the unique character of Jewish belief.

2 The ritualistic dimension: the extent to which individuals observe prescribed rituals and practices. Given the legalistic nature of Judaism, this dimension assumes special importance. To what extent are different rituals observed in different segments of the Jewish population? And what significance does ritualistic observance have for other modes of identity?

3 The experiential dimension: the extent to which individuals report deeply moving religious experiences. These may range from moments of religious inspiration to feelings of personal contact with the divine. In the case of Jews it would be interesting to look for traces of Jewish mysticism.

4 The intellectual dimension: the extent to which individuals are knowledgeable about their religion. This raises questions about the effects of religious education both for future religious commitment and for secular forms of identification.

5 The consequential dimension: the extent to which religion influences behavior in the secular sphere. For example, do more religious Jews show a tendency to enter certain vocations, to have more stable marriages, to hold certain political values?

The Communal Dimension

The synagogue in America has been a resilient institution. Threatened by a decline of religion among secularized Jews, the synagogue responded by expanding its activities into larger social spheres. The result has been a proliferation of social organizations, many of which are only marginally connected with religion as such. According to one description:

> Contemporary American synagogues and temples . . . offer a wide variety of age-graded activities in addition to worship services; afternoon Hebrew schools, Sunday schools, young people's groups, Temple Brotherhoods and Sisterhoods all offer opportunities for Jewish education and Jewish "activities." Jewish Community Centers, sometimes connected with a synagogue, more often not, together with Jewish "Y's". . . offer programs of education and recreation with Jewish cultural content for children, youth, and adults.[5]

[4] See Chapter One.

[5] Gordon, *op. cit.*, pp. 175-76.

Zionist groups, charitable and philanthropic organizations, and defense agencies extend this list even further.

Thus another dimension of Jewish identification refers to the extent of involvement in these communal structures. In this case measurement is a fairly simple procedure. A more formidable question concerns the significance of communal involvement for more basic forms of identity. To what extent do communal institutions simply provide outlets for social activity and recreation, and to what extent are they vehicles for the preservation of Jewish culture and identity?

The Secular Dimension

This question applies with even greater force to the next dimension, which is represented by the Jew who rejects most of religious and communal life but who continues to identify with Judaism. He typically does so by associating with other Jews and by giving expression to such selected elements of traditional culture as Yiddish words, Jewish food, Jewish humor, and a Jewish world view. Although he is in many ways similar to the Jew who participates in the communal culture, his main distinction is that he gains reinforcement for and expresses his Jewishness through interpersonal relationships that occur outside the organized Jewish community. In this sense he is a "secularist."

The secular dimension lends itself to a further distinction: relationships may be either associational or sociometric, depending on whether they occur within a formal or an informal social context. Thus a Jew who belongs to a predominantly Jewish country club may be said to identify along the associational subdimension since he 1) identifies with other Jews, 2) in a formal social structure that 3) exists outside the organized Jewish community. In the case of the sociometric subdimension, identification with other Jews assumes a relatively unstructured form, as in the case of friendship or marriage. The number of formal and informal relationships with Jews outside the organized Jewish community would provide a crude index to the *degree* of strength of this *kind* of identification.

The Intellectual Dimension

A fifth dimension of Jewish identification is the intellectual dimension. Religious knowledge already has been considered under the religious dimension. Aside from this, however, individuals differ in the extent of interest in and knowledge about Jewish affairs—Israel, for example. Taken by itself such knowledge is not likely to be significant, but in combination with other factors, it may be important for stable identification.

Conclusion

This paper has suggested that it is useful to think of Jewish identification in terms of its underlying dimensions, and to treat it as a phenomenon that varies in kind as well as degree. Herein lies the key to understanding the survival of

Jewish life in America. By constructing new institutional forms and new modes of identity, Jews succeeded in eluding some of the forces that led to the destruction of other immigrant cultures. However, it is not enough to point out that new forms of identification have evolved to replace outmoded ones. It is crucial to ask whether the new forms are equally valid and equally enduring.[6]

The problem is one of authenticity. The accommodations of second generation Jews were not achieved without cost. The third generation is, to be sure, firmly committed to Judaism, but it is also a generation largely cut off from its moorings in Jewish culture and religion. It is hardly a formidable bulwark to the ultimate assimilation that Robert Park and his colleagues predicted. Contemporary sociologists have perhaps been too hasty in rejecting the assimilation model. The modifications of Jewish identity may not have guaranteed the survival of Jewish life, but only prolonged its demise. No longer grounded in religion, ethnic identity and involvement in community are less secure. No longer steeped in tradition, Jewish values have become atrophied. The revised modes of identification may be only reflections of a culture that is rapidly losing its depth.

6 For a much neglected paper dealing with this question, see Herbert J. Gans, "American Jewry: Present and Future," *Commentary* Vol. 21, No. 5 (May 1956), pp. 422-30.

Chapter Five

Becoming a World-Saver: A Theory of Conversion to a Deviant Perspective*

John Lofland and Rodney Stark

All men and all human groups have ultimate values, a world view, or a perspective furnishing them a more or less orderly and comprehensible picture of the world. Clyde Kluckhohn remarked that no matter how primitive and crude it may be, there is a "philosophy behind the way of life of every individual and of every relatively homogeneous group at any given point in their histories."[1] When a person gives up one such perspective or ordered view of the world for another we refer to this process as *conversion*.[2]

Frequently such conversions are between popular and widely held perspectives—from Catholicism to Communism, or from the world view of an underdeveloped or primitive culture to that of a technically more advanced society, as from the Peyote Cult of the Southwest Indians to Christianity. The continual emergence of tiny cults and sects in western industrial nations makes it clear, however, that sometimes persons relinquish a more widely held perspective for an unknown, obscure and often, socially devalued one.

In this paper we shall outline a model of the conversion process through which a group of people came to see the world in terms set by the doctrines of one such obscure and devalued perspective—a small millenarian religious cult.

*John Lofland and Rodney Stark, "Becoming a World Saver: A Theory of Conversion to a Deviant Perspective," *American Sociological Review* 30, no. 6, December 1965. Reprinted with the permission of the authors and the *American Sociological Review*.

[1]Clyde Kluckhohn, "Values and Value-Orientations in the Theory of Action: An Exploration in Definition and Classification," in Talcott Parsons and Edward Shils (eds.), *Toward a General Theory of Action*, (New York: Harper Torchbooks, 1962), p. 409.

[2]The meaning of this term has been muddied by the inconsistent usage of Christian religious writers. Often they have used "conversion" to refer to an aroused concern among persons who already accept the essential truth of the ideological system, Yet, in keeping with the earliest Christian examples of conversion, such as that of St. Paul, they have also used the word to describe changes from one such system to another. These are very different events and ought to be indicated by different words.

Although it is based on only a single group, we think the model suggests some rudiments of a general account of conversion to deviant perspectives. But the degree to which this scheme applies to shifts between widely held perspectives must, for now, remain problematic.

Background

Our discussion is based on observation of a small, millenarian cult headquartered in Bay City,[3] a major urban center on the West Coast. This "movement" constitutes the American following of a self-proclaimed "Lord of the Second Advent," a Mr. Chang, who has attracted more than 5,000 converts in Korea since 1954. The "Divine Precepts," the doctrine Chang claims was revealed to him by God, concerns a complete "Restoration of the World" to the conditions of the Garden of Eden by 1967. The message was brought to this country by Miss Yoon-Sook Lee, a graduate of Methodist seminaries, and a former professor of social welfare at a large, church-supported, women's college in Seoul.

In 1959 Miss Lee arrived in a university town (here called Northwest Town) in the Pacific Northwest, and, in two years gained five totally committed converts to the Divine Precepts (hereafter referred to as the D.P.). In December, 1960, after difficulties with local clergymen and public opinion, largely touched off when two female converts deserted their husbands and children, the group moved to Bay City.

By mid-1963, 15 more converts had been gained and by the end of 1964 the cult numbered more than 150 adherents. Converts were expected to devote their lives to spreading "God's New Revelation" and preparing for the New Age theocracy which God and a host of active spirits were expected to create on earth shortly. Typically the converts lived communally in a series of houses and flats, contributed their salaries from menial jobs to the common treasury, thus supporting Miss Lee as a full-time leader, and gave all their spare time to witnessing and otherwise proselytizing.

In this brief report, analysis will be limited to the single problem of conversion.[4] Under what conditions and through what mechanisms did persons come to share the D.P. view of the world, and, conversely, who rejected this perspective?

The logical and methodological structure of the analysis is based on a "value-added"[5] conception. That is, we shall offer a series of seven (more or less) successively accumulating factors, which in their total combination seem to

[3] All names that might compromise converts' anonymity have been changed.

[4] Other aspects of the cult's formation, development, maintenance and proselytization procedures are analyzed in John Lofland, *Doomsday Cult*, Englewood Cliffs, N.J.: Prentice-Hall, 1966.

[5] Neil J. Smelser, *Theory of Collective Behavior,* (New York: The Free Press of Glencoe, 1963), pp. 12-21. See also Ralph Turner, "The Quest for Universals in Sociological Research," *American Sociological Review*, 18 (1953), pp. 604-611.

account for conversion to the D.P. All seven factors seem necessary for conversion, and together they appear to be sufficient conditions.

The sequential arrangement of the seven conditions may be conceived in the imagery of a funnel; that is, as a structure that systematically reduces the number of persons who can be considered available for recruitment, and also increasingly specifies who is available. At least theoretically, since the mission of the cult was to "convert America," all Americans are potential recruits. Each condition narrows the range of clientele: ultimately, only a handful of persons responded to the D.P. call.

Typically, and perhaps ideally, the conditions develop as presented here, but the temporal order may vary. The ordering principle is *activation*, rather than temporal occurrence alone: the time of activation is the same whether a condition exists for a considerable time prior to its becoming relevant to D.P. conversion or only develops in time to accomplish conversion.

Data were gathered through participant observation in the cult from early 1962 to mid-1963. Further information was obtained from interviews with converts, their acquaintances, families, and work-mates; with persons who took some interest in the D.P. but were not converts; and with a variety of clergymen, officials, neighbors, employers and others in contact with the adherents. Less intensive observation was conducted through mid-1964.

Although complete data pertinent to all seven steps of the conversion model were not obtainable for all 21 persons who were classified as converts by mid-1963, full information on all seven factors was available for 15 converts. All the available data conform to the model. In presenting biographical information to explicate and document the model, we shall focus on the most central of the early converts, drawing on material from less central and later converts for illustrations. The converts were primarily white, Protestant, and young (typically below 35); some had college training, and most were Americans of lower middle-class and small-town origins.

Conversion Operationally Defined

How does one determine when a person has "really" taken up a different perspective? The most obvious evidence, of course, is his own declaration that he has done so. This frequently takes the form of a tale of regeneration, about how terrible life was before and how wonderful it is now.[6] But verbal claims are easily made and simple to falsify. Indeed, several persons who professed belief in the D.P. were regarded as insincere by all core members. A display of loyalty and commitment, such as giving time, energy, and money to the D.P. enterprise, invariably brought ratification of the conversion from all core members, but to require such a display as evidence of "actual" conversion overlooks four persons who made only verbal professions but were universally regarded as converts by core members. To avoid this difficulty two classes or degrees of conversion may

[6]Peter Berger has given us a delightful characterization of the reconstructive functions of such tales. See his *Invitation to Sociology*, (New York: Doubleday Anchor, 1953), Ch. 3.

be distinguished: *verbal converts*, or fellow-travelers and followers who professed belief and were accepted by core members as sincere, but took no active role in the D.P. enterprise; and *total converts*, who exhibited their commitment through deeds as well as words.

Up to a point, the same factors that account for total conversion also account for verbal conversion and initially we shall discuss the two groups together. Later we shall attempt to show that verbal conversion is transformed into total conversion only when the last stage in the conversion sequence develops.

A Model of Conversion

To account for the process by which persons came to be world-savers for the D.P., we shall investigate two genres of conditions or factors. The first, which might be called *predisposing conditions*, comprises attributes of persons *prior* to their contact with the cult. These are background factors, the conjunction of which forms a pool of potential D.P. converts. Unfortunately, it has become conventional in sociology to treat demographic characteristics, structural or personal frustrations, and the like, as completely responsible for "pushing" persons into collectivities dedicated to protest against the prevailing social order. These factors are not unimportant, but a model composed entirely of them is woefully incomplete. The character of their incompleteness is expressed by a Meadian paraphrase of T. S. Eliot: "Between the impulse and the act falls the shadow." The second genre of conditions is this shadowed area, the situational contingencies.

Situational contingencies are conditions that lead to the successful recruitment of persons predisposed to the D.P. enterprise. These conditions arise from confrontation and interaction between the potential convert and D.P. members. Many persons who qualified for conversion on the basis of predisposing factors entered interpersonal relations with D.P. members, but because the proper situational conditions were not met, they did not become converts.

With these two classes of factors in mind, we may turn to a discussion of the first and most general of predisposing conditions.

1. Tension

No model of human conduct entirely lacks a conception of tension, strain, frustration, deprivation, or other version of the hedonic calculus. And, not surprisingly, even the most cursory examination of the life situations of converts before they embraced the D.P. reveals what they at least *perceived* as considerable tension.[7]

This tension is best characterized as a felt discrepancy between some

---

[7]We conceive this tension as subjective to avoid judgments about how tension-producing the "objective" circumstances actually were, attending instead to the way these circumstances were experienced.

imaginary, ideal state of affairs and the circumstances in which these people saw themselves caught up. We suggest that acutely felt tension is a necessary, but far from sufficient condition for conversion. That is, it creates some disposition to act. But tension may be resolved in a number of ways (or remain unresolved); hence, that these people are in a tension situation does not indicate *what* action they may take.

Just as tension can have myriad consequences, its sources can also be exceedingly disparate. Some concrete varieties we discovered were: longing for unrealized wealth, knowledge, fame, and prestige; hallucinatory activity for which the person lacked any successful definition; frustrated sexual and marital relations; homosexual guilt; acute fear of face-to-face interaction; disabling and disfiguring physical conditions; and—perhaps of a slightly different order—a frustrated desire for a significant, even heroic, religious status, to "know the mind of God intimately," and to be a famous agent for his divine purposes.[8]

Brief life histories of a few central believers will indicate concretely what bothered them as pre-converts. The case of Miss Lee, the "Messiah's" emissary in America, illustrates the aspiration to be an important religious figure.

Miss Lee was born and raised in Korea and converted to Chang's cult in 1954 when she was 39. During her early teens she was subject to fits of depression and used to sit on a secluded hilltop and seek spirit contacts. Shortly she began receiving visions and hearing voices—a hallucinatory pattern she was to maintain thereafter. Her adolescent mystical experience convinced her she had a special mission to perform for God and at the age of 19 she entered a Methodist seminary in Japan. She was immediately disenchanted by the "worldly concern" of the seminarians and the training she received, although she stuck out the five-year course. Prior to entering the seminary she had become engrossed in the Spiritualistic writings of Emmanuel Swedenborg, who soon began to appear to her in visions. Her estrangement from conventional religious roles was so great that upon graduating from seminary she, alone among her classmates, refused ordination. She returned to Korea at the start of World War II, and by 1945 was professor of social welfare at a denominational university in Seoul. In 1949 the Methodist Board of Missions sent her to a Canadian university for further theological training. There she wrote her thesis on Swedenborg, who continued to visit her in spirit form. In Canada, as in Japan, she was bitterly disappointed by the "neglect of things of the spirit," caused concern among the faculty by constantly hiding to pray and seek visions, and occasionally stole away to Swedenborgian services. Her spirits continued to tell her that she was a religious figure of great importance. Returning to her academic life in Korea she fell ill with chronic diarrhea and eventually nephritis, both of which resisted all medical treatment. After two years of this, her health was broken and she was completely bedridden. At this time her servant took her to see Chang.

[8]It is currently fashionable to reduce this last to more mundane "real" causes, but it is not necessary here to pre-judge the phenomenology.

Thus is summarized a portrait of a desperately estranged maiden lady, with secret convictions of grandeur, frequent "heterodox" hallucinations, and failing health, who felt herself badly entangled in the mundane affairs of modern religious bureaucracy.

Although the cultural context is rather different, the cases of *Bertha* and *Lester* follow lines rather similar to Miss Lee's, but include an important sexual theme.

Bertha, 29 at conversion, was the daughter of German immigrants and was raised in a suburban town. After high school she attended a modeling school, the kind operated in large cities for naive, fame-hungry girls, regardless of suitability. She returned to marry a local boy who was employed as a stereotyper in a printing plant. On her wedding night she spent two hours locked in their hotel bathroom, and subsequently did not improve her evaluation of sexual intercourse. Later the couple separated briefly, reunited, and after five years of marriage had their first child (1955). The second came in 1957, and they moved to the West Coast. There Bertha began having private religious hallucinations, including "sanctification"—being made holy and free of all sin. She went to various ministers to tell of her marvelous experiences, but was not warmly received; indeed, most advised psychiatric help. She began, then, to tell her husband that one day she would be very important in the service of the Lord. Following a homosexual episode with a neighbor woman, Bertha demanded to be taken elsewhere and the family went to Northwest Town in April 1959. There they settled in rural Elm Knoll, a collection of half a dozen houses about seven miles from town. This was soon to be the scene of the initial formation of the cult group, and here she came to know two neighbors, Minne Mae and Alice. These young housewives drew the attention of other neighbors by spending many hours hanging around the nearby general store, sometimes drinking beer and often complaining a good deal about their husbands. During this period, Bertha attended churches of various denominations and continued to have frequent ecstatic religious experiences, mostly while sitting alone in a clump of bushes near her house, where she was also reported to have spent a good deal of time crying and moaning.

Like Miss Lee, *Lester* (25 at conversion) went to a seminary (Lutheran) after a series of hallucinatory, spiritualistic experiences and aroused a good deal of curiosity and opposition among his fellows and the faculty. He left after an abortive part-time year to take up full-time graduate work in linguistics at a large state university in the same Bay City as the seminary. He remained convinced he was destined to be a one-man revitalization movement in the church. He took an extremely active role in campus student religious programs, meanwhile increasing his preoccupation with spiritualism and his own psychic experiences. For his first full-time year of graduate school he was awarded a Woodrow Wilson fellowship. But he was much more concerned about his religious life, and a new interest: he went to live with a young Hungarian ex-aristocrat, well-known in the area as a practicing homosexual. The young Hungarian led Lester to organized Spiritualism, where his religious preoccupations and hallucinations were greatly reinforced and increased, but Lester found these groups wanting. They contented themselves with very mundane affairs and seemed uninterested in speculations on larger theological matters. In addition, Lester was very ambivalent about his homosexuality, unable to explain it, unable to accept it, and unable to quit it. Then he met Miss Lee.

Bertha's friend, *Minnie Mae*, did not aspire to significant status, religious or otherwise. She pined, rather, for the more modest goal of marital satisfaction.

Minnie Mae (27 at conversion) was born in Possum Trot, Arkansas, of hillbilly farmers. She was one of 11 children, began dating at 12, and married at 15, having completed only rural elementary school. She and her young husband left Arkansas for lack of jobs and settled in Northwest Town. Her husband took a job as a laborer in a plywood factory. Although the young couple did not join a church, they came from a religious background (Minnie Mae's mother was a Pentecostal lay preacher), and they began attending tent meetings near Northwest Town. During one of these Minnie Mae began speaking in "tongues" and fell into a several-hour trance. After this her husband discouraged church activities. The couple had three children at roughly two year intervals, and until 1960 Minnie Mae seems to have spent most of her time caring for these children and watching television. She reported tuning in a local channel when she got up in the morning and keeping it on until sign-off at night. In 1958 the couple built a small house in Elm Knoll. Here, in her behavior and conversations with neighbors, she began to reveal severe dissatisfactions in her marriage. She repeatedly complained that her husband only had intercourse with her about once a month, but she also reported being very afraid of getting pregnant again. Furthermore, she wanted to get out and have some fun, go dancing, etc., but her husband only wanted to watch TV and to fish. She wondered if she had let life pass her by because she had been married too young. And, often, she complained about her husband's opposition to fundamentalist religious activities.

Merwin and *Alice* followed quite a different pattern. Theirs was not an intensely religious concern, indeed their grandiose ambitions were for fortune.

Merwin (29 at conversion) was raised in a Kansas hamlet where his father was the railroad depot agent. After high school he tried a small Kansas junior college for a year, did poorly, and joined the Marines. Discharged in 1952, he spent one year at the University of Kansas majoring in architecture, and did well, so he transferred to what he felt was a better school in Northwest Town. Here he didn't do well and adopted a pattern of frequently dropping out, then going back. Estranged and alone, he bought a few acres in Elm Knoll with a small ramshackle cottage and took up a recluse's existence—he rarely shaved or washed, brewed his own beer, and dabbled in health foods, left-wing political writings, and occult publications, while supporting himself by working in a plywood plant. Next door, about 20 yards away, lived Alice, her two children and her husband, also a plywood plant worker. Alice's husband, however, worked a swing shift, while Merwin worked days. The result was that Aliced filed for divorce and moved over to Merwin's. The husband departed without undue resistance. After their marriage, Merwin began to put his plans for financial empires into action. He considered a housing development, a junkyard, and finally bought a large frame house in Northwest Town to convert into a boarding house for students. After he had bought furniture and made other investments in the property, the city condemned it. Merwin filed bankruptcy and returned to Elm Knoll to lick his wounds and contemplate his next business venture. Merwin had long been disaffected with the established religions, had considered himself an agnostic, but was also interested in the occult. These interests were developed by his work partner, Elmer, whom we shall meet in a moment.

Alice, also a small town girl, had traded for what she felt was a better man, one who was "going places," but these hopes seemed to be fading after the bankruptcy. She still bragged to Minnie Mae and Bertha that Merwin would be a big man someday, but there was little evidence to support her.

Elmer's case illustrates yet another kind of frustrated ambition, that of attaining status as a man of knowledge and invention.

Elmer was born on a farm in North Dakota but his parents fled the drought and depression for the West Coast during the late thirties and settled on a farm near Northwest Town. Elmer, 26 at the time of his conversion, was slightly built with something of a vacant stare. After high school, he flunked out of the university after one semester and spent the next two years in the army where he flunked medical technician school. After the army he enrolled in a nearby state college and again lasted only one semester. He then returned to his parents' farm and took a job in the plywood factory. Elmer conceived of himself as an intellectual and aspired to be a learned man. He undertook to educate himself, and collected a large library toward this end. Unfortunately, he was virtually illiterate. In addition to more conventional books (including much of the Random House Modern Library), he subscribed to occult periodicals such as *Fate, Flying Saucers, Search*, etc. He also viewed himself as a practical man of invention, a young Thomas Edison, and dreamed of constructing revolutionary gadgets. He actually began assembling materials for a tiny helicopter (to use for herding cattle) and a huge television antenna to bring in stations hundreds of miles away. On top of all this, Elmer was unable to speak to others above a whisper and looked constantly at his feet while talking. Furthermore, he had great difficulty sustaining a conversation, often appearing to forget what he was talking about. But despite his "objective" failures at intellectual accomplishment, Elmer clung to a belief in his own potential. The consequences of failure were largely to make him withdraw, to protect this self image from his inability to demonstrate it.

These case histories provide a concrete notion of the kinds of things that bothered pre-converts. These problems apparently are not qualitatively different from the problems presumably experienced by a significant, albeit unknown, proportion of the general population. Their peculiarity, if any, appears to be that pre-converts felt their problems were quite acute, and they experienced high levels of tension concerning them over rather long periods.

From the point of view of an outside observer, however, their circumstances were not extraordinarily oppressive; in the general population, many persons undoubtedly labor under tensions considerably more acute and prolonged. Perhaps the strongest qualitative generalization supported by the data is that pre-converts felt themselves frustrated in their rather diverse aspirations. Most people probably have some type of frustrated aspiration, but pre-converts *experienced* the tension rather more acutely and over longer periods than most people do.

Explanation cannot rest here, for such tensions could have resulted in any number of other resolutions, and in fact they usually do. Thus, these unresolved problems in living are part of the necessary scenery for the stage, but the rest of the props, the stage itself, and the drama of conversion remain to be constructed.

2. Type of Problem-Solving Perspective

Since conversion to the D.P. is hardly the only thing people can do about their problems, it becomes important to ask what else these particular people could have done, and why they didn't. Because people have a number of conventional and readily available alternative definitions for, and means of coping with, their problems, there were, in the end, very few converts to the D.P. An alternative solution is a perspective or rhetoric defining the nature and sources of problems in living and offering some program for their resolution. Many such alternative solutions exist in modern society. Briefly, three particular genres of solution are relevant here: *the psychiatric, the political* and *the religious.* In the first, the origin of problems is typically traced to the psyche, and manipulation of the self is advocated as a solution. Political solutions, mainly radical, locate the sources of problems in the social structure and advocate reorganization of the system as a solution. The religious perspective tends to see both sources and solutions as emanating from an unseen and, in principle, unseeable realm.

The first two secular rhetorics bear the major weight of usage in contemporary society. No longer is it considered appropriate to regard recalcitrant and aberrant actors as possessed of devils. Indeed, modern religious institutions tend to offer a secular, frequently psychiatric, rhetoric concerning problems in living. The prevalence of secular definitions of tension is a major reason for the scarcity of D.P. converts. Several persons, whose circumstances met other conditions of the model, had adopted a psychiatric definition of their tensions and failed to become converts. In one exaggerated instance, an ex-GI literally alternated residence between the D.P. headquarters and the psychiatric ward of the veterans' hospital, never able to make a final decision as to which rhetoric he should adopt.

All pre-converts were surprisingly uninformed about conventional psychiatric and political perspectives for defining their problems. Perhaps those from small towns and rural communities in particular had long been accustomed to define the world in religious terms. Although all pre-converts had discarded conventional religious outlooks as inadequate, "spiritless," "dead," etc., prior to contact with the D.P., they retained a *general propensity to impose religious meaning on events.*

Even with these restrictions on the solutions available for acutely felt problems, a number of alternative responses still remain. First, people can persist in stressful situations with little or no relief. Second, persons often take specifically problem-directed action to change troublesome portions of their lives, without adopting a different world view to interpret them. Bertha and Minnie Mae might have simply divorced their husbands, for instance, and presumably, Lester could have embraced homosexuality. Clearly many pre-converts attempted such action (Merwin *did* start a boarding house, Elmer *did* attend college, etc.) but none found a successful direct solution to his difficulties.

Third, a number of maneuvers exist to "put the problem out of mind." In general these are compensations for or distractions from problems in living: e.g., addictive consumption of the mass media, pre-occupation with child-rearing, or immersion in work. More spectacular examples include alcoholism, suicide, promiscuity, and so on. Recall, for example, that Minnie Mae, Alice and Bertha "hung around" the general store during the day getting high on beer during the summer of 1959. Had they done this in a more urban setting, in bars with strange men available, their subsequent lives might have been different.

In any event, we may assume that many persons with tensions not only explore these possible strategies, but succeed in some cases in "making it," and hence, are no longer potential D.P. recruits.[9]

---

[9]Our analysis is confined to isolating the elements of the conversion sequence. Extended analysis would refer to the factors that *in turn* bring each conversion condition into existence. That is, it would be necessary to develop a theory for each of the seven elements, specifying the conditions under which each appears. On the form such theory would probably take, see Ralph Turner's discussion of "the instrusive factor," *op. cit.*, pp. 609-611.

3. Seekership

Whatever the reasons, pre-converts failed to find a way out of their difficulties through any of the strategies outlined above. Their need for solutions persisted, and their problem-solving perspective was restricted to a religious outlook, but all pre-converts found conventional religious institutions inadequate as a source of solutions. Subsequently, each came to define himself as a religious seeker, a person searching for some satisfactory system of religious meaning to interpret and resolve his discontent, and each had taken some action to achieve this end.

Some hopped from church to church and prayer group to prayer group, pursuing their religious search through relatively conventional institutions. A male convert in his early twenties recounted:

> My religious training consisted of various denominations such as Baptist, Methodist, Congregationalist, Jehovah's Witnesses and Catholicism. Through all my experiences, I refused to accept ... religious dogma ... because it was Truth I was seeking, and not a limited belief or concept.

Others began to explore the occult milieu, reading the voluminous literature of the strange, the mystical and the spiritual and tentatively trying a series of such occult groups as Rosicrucians, Spiritualists and the various divine sciences.

> In April, 1960, my wife and I ... [began] to seek a church connection. [We] began an association with Yokefellow, a spiritual growth organization in our local church. My whole religious outlook took on a new meaning and a broader vision. I grew emotionally and spiritually during the next two and one half years.
>
> However, as I grew, many spiritual things remained unanswered and new questions came up demanding answers which Yokefellow and the Church seemed not to even begin to touch upon. . . . My wife and I became interested in the revelation of Edgar Cayce and the idea of reincarnation which seemed to answer so much, we read searchingly about the Dead Sea Scrolls, we decided to pursue Rosicrucianism, we read books on the secret disclosures to be gained from Yogi-type meditation. The more we searched the more questions seemed to come up. Through Emmet Fox's writings I thought I had discovered a path through Metaphysics which through study would give me the breakthrough I longed for.

Or, the seeker might display some amalgam of conventional and unusual religious conceptions, as illustrated by a male convert's sad tale:

> I was reared in a Pentecostal church and as a child was a very ardent follower of Christianity. Because of family situations, I began to fall away and search for other meanings in life. This began ... when I was about 12 years old. From that time on, my life was most of the time an odious

existence, with a great deal of mental anguish. These last two years have brought me from church to church trying to find some fusion among them. I ended up going to Religious Science in the morning and fundamentalist in the evening.

Floundering about among religions was accompanied by two fundamental postulates that define more specifically the ideological components of the religious-seeker pattern. Although concrete pre-convert beliefs varied a good deal, all of them espoused these postulates about the nature of ultimate reality.

First, they believed that spirits of some variety came from an active supernatural realm to intervene in the "material world." Such entities could, at least sometimes, "break through" from the beyond and impart information, cause "experiences" or take a hand in the course of events.

Second, their conception of the universe was teleological, in the sense that beyond all appearances in the "sensate world" exists a purpose for which every object or event is created and exists. The earth is as it is to meet the needs of man, for example, and man manifests the physical structure he does to do the things he does. More important, man himself as a phenomenon must "be on earth" because, somewhere, sometime, somehow, it was decided that *homo sapiens* should "fulfill" a purpose or purposes. Accordingly, each person must have been "put on earth" for some reason, with some sort of "job" to perform.

Beliefs were typically no more specific than this. The religious seeking itself was in terms of finding some more detailed formulation of these problematically vague existential axes.

A few words on the general question of the importance of prior beliefs in effecting conversion are necessary at this point. A number of discussions of conversion have emphasized congruence between previous ideology and a given group's "appeal,"[10] while others treat the degree of congruence as unimportant so long as the ideology is seen as embodied in what appears to be a successful movement.[11] Both views seem extreme.[12]

Our data suggest that only the two gross kinds of congruence that make up the ideology of religious seekership are necessary for conversion to the D.P. Presumptively important items, such as fundamentalist Christianity, millenarian expectations, and hallucinatory experience were far from universal among pre-converts. Most pre-converts believed in a vaguely defined "New Age" that would appear gradually, but they *became* apocalyptic pre-millenarian only upon conversion.

The role of these gross points of congruence is suggested in the substantive D.P. appeals to pre-converts. Active spirits were rampant in their view of reality.

[10]E.g., H. G. Brown, "The Appeal of Communist Ideology," *American Journal of Economics and Sociology*, 2 (1943), pp. 161-174; Gabriel Almond, *The Appeals of Communism*, (Princeton: Princeton University Press, 1954).

[11]E.g., Eric Hoffer, *The True Believer*, (New York: Mentor, 1958 [copyright 1951]), p. 10.

[12]Cf. Herbert Blumer, "Collective Behavior" in Joseph B. Gittler (ed.), *Review of Sociology* (New York: Wiley, 1957), pp. 147-148.

Converts lived with an immediate sense of unseen forces operating on the physical order (e.g., the weather) and intervening in human affairs—in relations among nations, in the latest national disaster, and in their own moment-to-moment lives. Nothing occurred that was not related to the intentions of God's or Satan's spirits. For persons holding a teleological conception of reality, the D.P. doctrine had the virtue of offering a minute and lawful explanation of the whole of human history. It systematically defined and revealed the hidden meaning of individual lives that had lacked coherence and purpose, and of course, it explained all hallucinatory behavior in terms of spirit manifestations. These spirits had been preparing the pre-convert to see the truth of the D.P.

Although acute and enduring tensions in the form of frustrated aspirations is not an ideological component, in the sense of being a more abstract postulate about the nature of reality, it should be noted here, in relation to the matter of congruence, that the D.P. also offered a proximate and major solution. Converts were assured of being virtual demi-gods for all eternity, beginning with a rule over the restored and reformed earth in the immediate future. By 1967 God was to impose the millennium upon earth, and those who converted early, before the truth of this message became self-evident, would occupy the most favored positions in the divine hegemony. Converts particularly stressed this advantage of conversion in their proselytization: "those who get in early," as one member often put it, "will be in on the ground floor of something big."

Religious seekership emerges, then, as another part of the path through the maze of life contingencies leading to D.P. conversion. It is a floundering among religious alternatives, an openness to a variety of religious views, frequently esoteric, combined with failure to embrace the specific ideology and fellowship of some set of believers.[13] Seekership provided the minimal points of ideological congruence to make these people available for D.P. conversion.

4. The Turning Point

The necessary attributes of pre-converts stated thus far had all persisted for some time before the pre-converts encountered the D.P.; they can be considered "background" factors, or predispositions. Although they apparently arose and were active in the order specified, they are important here as accumulated and simultaneously active factors during the development of succeeding conditions.

We now turn to situational factors in which timing becomes much more significant. The first of these is the rather striking circumstance that *shortly* before, and *concurrently* with their encounter with the D.P., all pre-converts had reached or were about to reach what they perceived as a "turning point" in their

---

[13] For further suggestive materials on seekers and seeking see H. T. Dohrman, *California Cult* (Boston: Beacon, 1958); Leon Festinger, Henry Riecken and Stanley Schacter, *When Prophecy Fails* (Minneapolis: University of Minnesota Press, 1956); Sanctus De Santis, *Religious Conversion* (London: Routledge and Kegan Paul, 1927), esp. pp. 260-261; H. Taylor Buckner, "Deviant-Group Organizations," Unpublished M.A. Thesis, University of California, Berkeley, 1964, Ch. 2. For discussion of a generally similar phenomenon in a different context, see Edgar H. Schein, *Coercive Persuasion* (New York: Norton, 1961), pp. 120-136, 270-277.

lives. That is, each had come to a moment when old lines of action were complete, had failed or been disrupted, or were about to be so, and when they faced the opportunity (or necessity), and possibly the burden, of doing something different with their lives.[14] Thus, Miss Lee's academic career had been disrupted by long illness from which she recovered upon meeting Chang; Bertha was newly arrived in a strange town; Lester was disaffected from graduate studies after having quit the seminary; Minnie Mae no longer had a pre-school child at home to care for; Merwin had just failed in business after dropping out of school; and Elmer had returned to his parents' farm after failing in college for the second time.

Turning points in general derived from recent migration; loss of employment (a business failure in Merwin's case); and completion, failure, or withdrawal from school. Perhaps because most converts were young adults, turning points involving educational institutions were relatively frequent. Illustrations in addition to the cases described above are a graduate student who had just failed his Ph.D. qualifying examinations, two second-semester college seniors who had vague and unsatisfying plans for the future, and a seventeen year-old who had just graduated from high school. Recovery from or the onset of an illness, marital dissolution and other changes, extant or imminent, such as Minnie Mae's new freedom, were relatively infrequent. The significance of these various turning points is that they increased the pre-convert's awareness of and desire to take some action about his problems, *at the same time giving him a new opportunity to do so.* Turning points were situations in which old obligations and lines of action were diminished, and new involvements became desirable and possible.

5. Cult Affective Bonds

We come now to the contact between a potential recruit and the D.P. If persons who go through all four of the previous steps are to be further drawn down the road to full conversion, an affective bond must develop, if it does not already exist, between the potential recruit and one or more of the D.P. members. The development or presence of some positive, emotional, interpersonal response seems necessary to bridge the gap between first exposure to the D.P. message and accepting its truth. That is, persons developed affective ties with the group or some of its members while they still regarded the D.P. perspective as problematic, or even "way out." In a manner of speaking, final conversion was coming to accept the opinions of one's friends.[15]

[14]Everett C. Hughes, *Men and Their Work* (Glencoe: Free Press, 1958), Ch. 1; Anselm Strauss, "Transformations of Identity," in Arnold Rose (ed.), *Human Behavior and Social Processes* (Boston: Houghton Mifflin, 1962), pp. 67-71. Cf. the often-noted "cultural dislocation" and migration pattern found in the background of converts to many groups, especially cults.

[15]Cf. Tamatsu Shibutani, *Society and Personality*, (Englewood Cliffs, N. J.: Prentice-Hall, 1961), pp. 523-532, 588-592. Schein (*op. cit.*, p. 277) reports that "the most potent source of influence in coercive persuasion was the identification which arose between a prisoner and his more reformed cellmate." See also Alan Kerckhoff, Kurt Back and Norman Miller, "Sociometric Patterns in Hysterical Contagion," *Sociometry*, 28 (1965), pp. 2-15.

Miss Lee's recollections of her conversion provide a graphic illustration:

> In addition to this change [her recovery from illness] I felt very good
> spiritually. I felt as if I had come to life from a numb state and there was
> spiritual *liveliness and vitality within me by being among this group.* As
> one feels when he comes from a closed stuffy room into the fresh air, or
> the goodness and warmth after freezing coldness was how my spirit
> witnessed its happiness. *Although I could not agree with the message
> intellectually I found myself one with it spiritually.* I reserved my
> conclusions and waited for guidance from God. [Italics added.]

Miss Lee further revealed she was particularly attracted to Mr. Chang and resided
in his dwelling to enjoy the pleasure of his company, until, finally, she decided
his message was true. Her statement that she "could not agree with the message
intellectually' is particularly significant. Other converts reported and were
observed to experience similar reservations as they nevertheless developed strong
bonds with members of the group. Thus, for example, Lester, the most highly
intellectual of the converts, displayed an extremely strong attachment to the
middle-aged Miss Lee and manifested the "intellect problem" for some weeks
after he had turned his life over to her. At one point late in this period he could
still reflectively comment to an observer:

> I have not entirely reconciled [the D.P. world view] with my intellect, but
> [Miss Lee] keeps answering more and more questions that are in my mind
> so I am beginning to close the holes I have found in it.

It is particularly important to note that conversions frequently moved
through *pre-existing* friendship pairs or nets. In the formation of the original
core group, an affective bond first developed between Miss Lee and Bertha (the
first to meet Miss Lee and begin to espouse her views). Once that had happened,
the rest of the original conversions were supported by prior friendships. Bertha was
part of the housewife trio of Minnie Mae and Alice; Merwin was Alice's
husband, and Elmer was Merwin's friend and workmate. Subsequent conversions
also followed friendship paths, or friendships developed between the pre-convert
and the converts, prior to conversion.

Bonds that were unsupported by previous friendships with a new convert
often took the form of a sense of instant and powerful rapport with a believer.
Consider, for example a young housewife's account of her first view of Lester
while attending an Edgar Cayce Foundation retreat:[16]

> I went to [one of the] Bible class[es] and saw [Lester] in our class—I had
> seen him for the first time the night before and had felt such love for
> him—he was my brother, yet I had not met him. He looked as if he were

[16]Lester was at this retreat precisely for the purpose of meeting potential converts.
Attendance at religious gatherings in the masquerade of a religious seeker was the primary
D.P. mode of recruiting.

luminous! After the class I wanted to talk to him—but our project group had a discipline that day—complete silence—I did not want to break it, yet I felt such a need to talk to him. I prayed and asked God what He would have me do—I received such a positive feeling—I took this as an answer and sought out [Lester]. When I found him, I did not have anything to say—I just mumbled something—But he seemed to understand and took me to the beach where he told me "He is on earth!" Oh, what joy I felt! My whole body was filled with electricity.

The less-than-latent sexual overtones of this encounter appeared in a number of other heterosexual attachments that led to conversion (and quite a few that did not). Even after four years of cult membership Elmer could hardly hide his feelings in this testimonial:

> Early in 1960, after a desperate prayer, which was nothing more than the words, "Father if there is any truth in this world, please reveal it to me," I met [Miss Lee]. This day I desire to never forget. Although I didn't fully understand yet, I desired to unite with her. . . .

Although a potential convert might have some initial difficulty in taking up the D.P. perspective, given the four previous conditions *and* an affective tie, he began seriously to consider the D.P. and to accept it as his personal construction of reality.

6. Extra-Cult Affective Bonds

One might suppose that non-D.P. associates of a convert-in-process would not be entirely neutral to the now immediate possibility that he would join the D.P. group. We must inquire, then, into the conditions under which extra-cult controls are activated through emotional attachments, and how they restrain or fail to restrain persons from D.P. conversion.

Recent migration, disaffection with geographically distant families and spouses and very few nearby acquaintances made a few converts "social atoms"; for them extra-cult attachments were irrelevant. More typically, converts were acquainted with nearby persons, but none was intimate enough to be aware that a conversion was in progress or to feel that the mutual attachment was sufficient to justify intervention. Thus, for example, Lester's social round was built primarily around participation in religious groups. Although he was well-known and appreciated for his contributions, he was not included in any local circles of intimacy. Many people knew him, but no one was a *personal* friend. Further, Lester's relations with both parents and stepparents manifested considerable strain and ambivalence, and his homosexual liaison was shot through with strain.

In many cases, positive attachments outside the cult were to other religious seekers, who, even though not yet budding converts themselves, encouraged continued "investigation" or entertainment of the D.P. rather than exercising a countervailing force. Indeed, such an extra-cult person might be only slightly behind his friend in his own conversion process.

In the relatively few cases where positive attachments existed between conventional extra-cult persons and a convert-in-process, control was minimal or absent, because of geographical distance or intentional avoidance of communication about the topic while the convert was solidifying his faith. Thus, for example, a German immigrant in his early thirties failed to inform his mother in Germany, to whom he was strongly attached, during his period of entertainment and only wrote her about the D.P. months after his firm acceptance. (She disowned him.)

During the period of tentative acceptance, and afterwards, converts, of course, possessed a rhetoric that helped to neutralize affective conflicts. An account by a newly converted soldier in Oklahoma conveys the powerful (and classic) content of this facilitating and justifying rhetoric:

> I wrote my family a very long detailed but yet very plain letter about our movement and exactly what I received in spiritual ways plus the fact that Jesus had come to me himself. The weeks passed and I heard nothing but I waited with deep trust in God.
>
> This morning I received a letter from my mother. She . . . surmised that I was working with a group other than those with the "stamp of approval by man." She . . . called me a fanatic, and went on to say: "My fervent constant prayer is that time will show you the fruitlessness of the way you have chosen before it consumes you entirely. A real true religion is deep in the heart and shines through your countance for all to see. One need not shout it to the house tops either."
>
> At first it was the deepest hurt I had ever experienced. But, I remember what others in [the D.P.] family have given up and how they too experienced a similar rejection. But so truly, I can now know a little of the rejection that our beloved Master experienced. I can now begin to understand his deep grief for the Father as he sat peering out of a window singing love songs to Him because he knew that the Father would feel such grief. I can now begin to feel the pain that our Father in heaven felt for 6,000 years. I can now begin to see that to come into the Kingdom of heaven is not as easy as formerly thought. I can now see why many are called but few are chosen. I began to understand why men will be separated, yes even from their families. I begin to see the shallowness of human concern for God as a Father and their true blindness. Oh my heart cries out to Our Father in greatful [sic] praise and love for what He has given.
>
> [In the words of Miss Lee:] "As we get close to the Father the road shall become more difficult"; "Only by truly suffering, can we know the Leader and the heart of the Father"; "You shall be tested." "He will come with a double-edged blade." Only now am I beginning to realize the deep significance of these words. Only now am I beginning to know the heart of the Father and the great suffering of our Lord.

When there were emotional attachments to outsiders who were physically present and cognizant of the incipient transformation, conversion became a "nip-and-tuck" affair. Pulled about by competing emotional loyalties and discordant versions of reality, such persons were subjected to intense emotional strain. A particularly poignant instance of this involved a newly-wed senior at the local state university. He began tentatively to espouse the D.P. as he developed strong ties with Lester and Miss Lee. His young wife struggled to accept, but she did not meet a number of the conditions leading to conversion, and in the end, seemed nervous, embarrassed, and even ashamed to be at D.P. gatherings. One night, just before the group began a prayer meeting, he rushed in and tearfully announced that he would have nothing further to do with the D.P., though he still thought the message was probably true. Torn between affective bonds, he opted for his young bride, but it was only months later that he finally lost all belief in the D.P.

When extra-cult bonds withstood the strain of affective and ideological flirtation with the D.P., conversion was not consummated. Most converts, however, lacked external affiliations close enough to permit informal control over belief. Affectively, they were so "unintegrated" that they could, for the most part, simply fall out of relatively conventional society unnoticed, taking their co-seeker friends, if any, with them.

7. Intensive Interaction

In combination, the six previous factors suffice to bring a person to *verbal conversion* to the D.P. but one more contingency must be met if he is to become a "deployable agent,"[17] or what we have termed a *total convert*. Most, but not all, verbal converts ultimately put their lives at the disposal of the cult. Such transformations in commitment took place, we suggest, as a result of intensive interaction with D.P. members, and failed to result when such interaction was absent.

Intensive interaction means concrete, daily, and even hourly accessibility to D.P. members, which implies physical proximity to total converts. Intensive exposure offers an opportunity to reinforce and elaborate an initial, tentative assent to the D.P. world view, and in prolonged association the perspective "comes alive" as a device for interpreting the moment-to-moment events in the convert's life.

The D.P. doctrine has a variety of resources for explicating the most minor everyday events in terms of a cosmic battle between good and evil spirits, in a way that placed the convert at the center of this war. Since all D.P. interpretations pointed to the imminence of the end, to participate in these explications of daily life was to come more and more to see the necessity of one's personal participation as a totally committed agent in this cosmic struggle.[18]

---

[17]On the concept of the "deployable agent" or "deployable personnel" in social movements see Philip Selznick, *The Organizational Weapon* (New York: The Free Press, 1960 [copyright 1952]), pp. 18-29.

[18]Cf. Schein, *op. cit.*, pp. 136-139, 280-282.

Reminders and discussion of the need to make other converts, and the necessity of supporting the cause in every way, were the main themes of verbal exchanges among the tentatively accepting and the total converts, and, indeed, among the total converts themselves. Away from this close association with those already totally committed, one failed to "appreciate" the need for one's transformation into a total convert.

In recognition of this fact, the D.P. members gave highest priority to attempts to persuade verbal converts (even the merely interested) to move into the cult's communal dwellings. During her early efforts in Northwest Town, Miss Lee gained verbal conversions from Bertha, Minnie Mae, Alice, Merwin, and Elmer, many months before she was able to turn them into total converts. This transformation did not occur, in fact, until Miss Lee moved into Alice and Merwin's home (along with Elmer), placing her within a few dozen yards of the homes of Minnie Mae and Bertha. The resulting daily exposure of the verbal converts to Miss Lee's total conversion increasingly engrossed them in D.P. activities, until they came to give it all their personal and material resources.[19] Recalling this period, Minnie Mae reported a process that occurred during other verbal converts' periods of intensive interaction. When one of them began to waver in his faith, unwavering believers were fortunately present to carry him through this "attack of Satan."

Most verbally assenting converts were induced out of this tenuous state, through contrived or spontaneous intensive interaction, within a few weeks, or more typically, a few months. In a few instances the interval between assent and total commitment spanned a year or more. When the unmarried older sister of the German immigrant mentioned above came to entertain the D.P. perspective, some 11 months of subtle and not-so-subtle pressures were required to get her to leave her private apartment and move into the communal dwelling. Within two months she went from rather lukewarm belief to total dedication and subsequent return to Germany as a D.P. missionary. The following ecstatic testimonial given during her second month of cult residence contrasts sharply with her previously reserved and inhibited statements:

> In the beginning of May I moved into our center in [Bay City]. A complete new life started for me. Why had I not cut off my self-centered life earlier! Here under [Miss Lee's] care and guidance I felt God's power and love tremendously and very soon it became my only desire to wholeheartedly serve our Father. How fortunate I am being a child and student of our beloved mother and teacher, [Miss Lee]. She reflects in all her gestures, words and works the love and wisdom of our Lord and Master.

[19]Although a number of our illustrative cases are drawn from the period of the group's formation, the process of cult formation itself should not be confused with the analytically distinct process of conversion. The two are merely empirically compounded. Cult formation occurs when a network of friends who meet the first four conditions develop affective bonds with a world-view carrier and collectively develop the last two conditions, except that condition seven, intensive interaction, requires exposure *to each other* in addition to the world-view carrier. (For a different conception of "subculture" formation see Albert K. Cohen, *Delinquent Boys*, [Glencoe, Ill.: The Free Press, 1955, Chp. 3].)

Thus, verbal conversion and even a resolution to reorganize one's life for the D.P. is not automatically translated into total conversion. One must be intensively exposed to the group supporting these new standards of conduct. D.P. members did not find proselytizing, the primary task of total converts, very easy, but in the presence of persons who reciprocally supported each other, such a transformation of one's life became possible. Persons who accepted the truth of the doctrine, but lacked intensive interaction with the core group, remained partisan spectators, who played no active part in the battle to usher in God's kingdom.

Summary

We have presented a model of the accumulating conditions that appear to describe and account for conversion to an obscure millenarian perspective. These necessary and constellationally-sufficient conditions may be summarized as follows:

For conversion a person must:
1. Experience enduring, acutely felt tensions
2. Within a religious problem-solving perspective,
3. Which leads him to define himself as a religious seeker;
4. Encountering the D.P. at a turning point in his life,
5. Wherein an affective bond is formed (or pre-exists) with one or more converts;
6. Where extra-cult attachments are absent or neutralized;
7. And, where, if he is to become a deployable agent, he is exposed to intensive interaction.

Because this model was developed from the study of a small set of converts to a minor millenarian doctrine, it may possess few generalizable features. We suggest, however, that its terms are general enough, and its elements articulated in such a way as to provide a reasonable starting point for the study of conversion to other types of groups and perspectives.

A closing *caveat*. The D.P. had few competitive advantages, if any, over other unusual religious groups, in terms of the potential converts' predispositions. In terms of situational conditions the D.P. advantage was simply that they were on the scene and able to make their "pitch," develop affective bonds and induce intensive interaction. We hope our effort will help dispel the tendency to assume some "deep," almost mystical, connection between world views and their carriers. Like conceptions holding that criminals and delinquents must be "really different," our thinking about other deviants has too often assumed some extensive characterological conjunction between participant and pattern of participation.

Chapter Six

Age and Faith: A Changing Outlook or an Old Process?*

Rodney Stark

Man's ubiquitous fear of death has long been judged a mainspring of Christian commitment. From its earliest days, Christian proselytization has stressed the promise of life everlasting as the central and glorious message of the New Testament—"O death, where is thy sting? O grave, where is thy victory" (I Corinthians 15:55, A.V.). Indeed, for centuries the major spokesmen of Christianity have deemed it unthinkable that the faith would have any relevance to the human condition without the promise of immortality. According to the Apostle Paul, "If in this life only we have hope in Christ, we are of all men most miserable" (I Corinthians 15:19). As one might expect, Martin Luther expressed these sentiments in earthier language: "If you believe in no future life, I would not give a mushroom for your God."[1] More recently, Harry Emerson Fosdick wrote that "The goodness of God is plainly at stake when one discusses immortality, for if death ends all, the Creator is building men like sand houses on the shore, caring not a whit that the fateful waves will quite obliterate them."[2] In this he echoed Tennyson's line, "If immortality be not true, then no God but a mocking fiend created us."[3]

This centrality of the "victory over death" in Christian teaching is connected with a basic tenet of conventional wisdom: men become more pious as they grow older and begin to fear the imminence of their death. "Beads and prayer-books are the toys of age," wrote Alexander Pope in *An Essay on Man*.

---

*Rodney Stark, "Age and Faith: A Changing Outlook or an Old Process?" *Sociological Analysis* 29, no. 1 (Spring 1968). Reprinted with the permission of the author and *Sociological Analysis*.

[1]Quoted in Radoslav A. Tsanoff, *The Problem of Immortality* (New York: Macmillan Co., 1924), p. 245.

[2]*The Assurance of Immortality* (New York: Association Press, 1926), p. 100.

[3]Quoted in A. Seth Pringle-Pattison, *The Idea of Immortality* (London: Oxford University Press, 1922), p. 184.

Of course, as is always the case with conventional wisdom, there is an opposing minority view that the young, not the old, fear death most. Indeed, as George Herbert put it, "Old men *go* to death; death *comes* to young men."[4] Still, the stereotype of piety in old age seems very credible and is continually reinforced by stories of death-bed conversions.

Past research has provided a smattering of data on the relationship between age and piety. Studies by Fichter,[5] Gorer,[6] Cauter and Downham,[7] and Glock, Ringer, and Babbie[8] have shown that weekly church attendance is slightly higher among older people than among younger people. In addition, Gorer found slight differences in belief in life after death between older and younger persons.[9] However, all these findings are subject to a major problem of interpretation. Each is based on differences between younger and older persons at a single point in time. None charted changes in the same persons over time. Consequently, we cannot say whether these differences represent changes over age or whether they show instead that recent generations are simply less religious than earlier ones. This is a most vexing difficulty, for if there is strong reason to predict increases in religious commitment as persons age there are equally persuasive reasons to expect that secularization has been occurring in modern society and thus that the young are less religious.

A second inadequacy of previous research is that the data have been exceedingly skimpy—handicapped by poor samples and few indicators of religious commitment. Indeed, nearly all these findings are based on nothing more than church attendance. But as chapters 1 through 4 have demonstrated, religious commitment is a complex phenomenon requiring a variety of measurements. Thus, at present we really know very little about the empirical relationship between age and faith.

In this chapter I examine this relationship and attempt to resolve the question of whether differences are attributable to aging or to changes in the religious commitment of society, which is reflected in lower religiousness among the younger generations.

The data were collected from a random sample of the church-member population of four West Coast counties centered on San Francisco. All

4 *Jacula Prudentum*, 1651; italics added.

5 Joseph H. Fichter, "The Profile of Catholic Religious Life," *American Journal of Sociology* 58 (July 1952): 145-49.

6 Geoffry Gorer, *Exploring English Character* (London: Cresset, 1955).

7 T. Cauter and J. S. Downham, *The Communication of Ideas* (London: Reader's Digest and Chatto and Windus, 1954).

8 Charles Y. Glock, Benjamin B. Ringer, and Earl Babbie, *To Comfort and To Challenge: A Dilemma of the Contemporary Church* (Berkeley and Los Angeles: University of California Press, 1967).

9 *Op. cit.* In addition, Vacan and his associates found slight increases in the proportion believing in life after death as age increased; the study, however, was restricted to persons over sixty. For lack of denominational controls, and because of the small and somewhat inconsistent difference, it is difficult to say what, if anything, these data mean. R. S. Cavan, et al., *Personal Adjustment in Old Age* (Chicago: Science Research Associates, 1949).

Protestant and Catholic congregations in the four counties were included in the sampling frame. Congregations were selected randomly, each having the number of chances for selection equal to its total membership. After drawing congregations, random samples of members were drawn from the church rolls. Each respondent selected was sent a lengthy mail questionnaire—approximately 500 items were included—and 73 percent of the Protestants and 54 percent of the Roman Catholics returned completed documents. Telephone interviews were conducted with random samples of both Protestant and Roman Catholic nonrespondents to assess what biases may have operated in the return rate. These findings indicate that the data were remarkably representative of the population sampled. With the data finally gathered, 2,326 Protestants and 545 Roman Catholics had returned questionnaires.[10]

Orthodoxy[11]

The argument that secularization is taking place in America depends on evidence that the young are less likely to hold the traditional tenets of Christian orthodoxy than are the old. But it is also supposed that persons are more likely to hold these beliefs as they get older. Yet these are not in fact exactly similar predictions, and the pattern of the data in table 1 seems to permit the hypothesis of secularization, but not that of increasing orthodoxy with age.

If orthodoxy increases with age we would expect this to be a systematically cumulative process. Thus, we would expect some persons to respond to this process in their forties, to be joined by more persons during their fifties, and more again in their sixties and so on, so that each older group would show a higher proportion of believers than the next younger group. However, a secularization hypothesis need not assume such cumulative changes. A major change could have occurred at some point in recent history, and all the subsequent generations could show this new lower level of piety without becoming successively less pious. Furthermore, age changes should operate in all Christian groups, Protestants as well as Catholics, and among liberal Protestants as well as among moderate and conservative ones. But the data shown in table 1 indicate that there seem to be no meaningful differences with age among the liberal Protestants or among the Roman Catholics. We shall return to this point in a moment. Furthermore, age differences among moderate and conservative Protestants are not the cumulative increases over age required by a theory of

[10]Full details on sampling and data collection are reported in Charles Y. Glock and Rodney Stark, *Christian Beliefs and Anti-Semitism* (New York: Harper and Row, 1966).

[11]Four items were scored to create the orthodoxy index. These measured firm belief in a personal God, in the divinity of Jesus Christ, in the authenticity of biblical miracles, and in the existence of the Devil. Respondents received one point for each of these in which they believed without doubt. Respondents who expressed doubt or disbelief on an item were scored zero. Persons who failed to answer any of the four were not scored. The initial index thus ranged from a high of four through a low of zero. As used here *high* indicates a score of three or four on the index. A full account of construction and validation of the index may be found in Rodney Stark and Charles Y. Glock, *American Piety* (Berkeley and Los Angeles: University of California Press, 1968), ch. 3.

belief increasing as people get older. Instead, the only meaningful shift in orthodoxy with age occurs between the forty-year-olds and the fifty-year-olds in both the moderate and conservative Protestant groups. Above 50 there are no meaningful increases, nor are there any meaningful decreases below 40. This shift is marked by a broken line in the table.

Table 1.   *Age and Orthodoxy*

	Percent High on Orthodoxy Index			
Age:	Liberal Protestants	Moderate Protestants	Conservative Protestants	Roman Catholics
Under 20	5 (19)	29 (15)	a (12)	a (9)
20-29	10 (91)	26 (95)	75 (89)	64 (89)
30-39	10 (243)	27 (203)	79 (101)	66 (141)
40-49	9 (262)	28 (244)	78 (102)	48 (124)
Postwar generations				
Prewar generations				
50-59	11 (157)	40 (134)	94 (67)	61 (83)
60-69	14 (80)	49 (79)	89 (43)	73 (41)
70 and over	27 (40)	45 (51)	100 (19)	64 (15)

aToo few cases for stable percentages

What can we conclude from this? It seems more than coincidental that the age at which fewer persons adhere to traditional religious beliefs occurs precisely at the age that separates the pre-World War II generations from the postwar generations. Persons who were from forty to forty-nine in 1963, the time these data were collected, were from seventeen to twenty-six at the time the war broke out. These people, and those born after them, have been most shaped by the emergence of an America of mobile city dwellers who inhabit a fast, technical, mass society. World War II was a watershed between this new world and the older America of parochial small-town and rural society. While all the persons in this sample live today in this new America, those past fifty *did not grow up in it*. The data strongly suggest that in this new America traditional Christian orthodoxy is less powerful.

But why do there seem to be no similar shifts among the liberal Protestants and the Roman Catholics? It appears in the table as if the liberal Protestants have been unaffected by recent social changes, but this is partly produced because there are very few orthodox believers of any age in these denominations. Consequently, only very small differences in the proportions of highly orthodox persons between the prewar and postwar generations *could* have occurred. However, if we examine instead the proportions who scored zero or one on orthodoxy, and thus were the least possible orthodox believers, we find that slightly more than half (52 percent) of those from postwar generations received such scores, while only 40 percent of those in prewar generations did so. Thus, the younger generations show an increased tendency to reject traditional orthodoxy in the liberal denominations too.

The resistance of Roman Catholics to the postwar changes in religious perspectives may be based on the fact that the new urban America is not so new to the Catholics. They have historically been citydwellers in this country, and the great changes of recent decades only seem to be extreme when viewed from the perspective of an earlier agrarian America, not when viewed from the city. For the cities have not changed so much; it is rather that Protestants have moved to town. Thus Catholicism perhaps long ago adjusted to maintaining faith in urban society; however, it may also be that the younger Catholics have undergone changes in their religious perspective which are simply not reflected by the tenets making up this measure of orthodoxy.

Fortunately data are available to pursue this possible explanation. As can be seen in table 2, the younger generations of Catholics do show a drop in commitment to several specifically Catholic beliefs. The first of these, shown in

Table 2.   *Age and Beliefs about Birth Control and Papal Infallibility among Roman Catholics*

Percent who thought that "practicing artificial birth control" would "definitely prevent" salvation			
Age:	Percent	N	
Under 20	20	10[a]	
20-29	20	88	
30-39	23	142	
40-49	18	122	Postwar generations
50-59	38	80	Prewar generations
60-69	38	39	
70 and over	38	16	

Percent who thought it "completely true" that "the pope is infallible in matters of faith and morals"			
Age:	Percent	N	
Under 20	40	10[a]	
20-29	69	91	
30-39	69	142	
40-49	69	121	Postwar generations
50-59	75	85	Prewar generations
60-69	80	44	
70 and over	89	18	

[a]Too few cases for stable percentages, shown for descriptive interest only.

the upper half of the table, asks about the relevance of practicing artificial birth control for gaining salvation. Roughly 20 percent of Catholics under fifty think this would "definitely prevent" salvation, whereas 38 percent of those over fifty think this is the case. Above fifty there are no differences among the age groups; below fifty there are no significant differences either. These data precisely match the prewar/postwar shifts seen among Protestants in table 1.

The second specifically Catholic belief shown concerns the infallibility of the pope in matters of faith and morals. Here again the major shift in the proportions who think it "completely true" that the pope is infallible is between the prewar and postwar generations. Ignoring data on those under twenty years of age (because the percentage is based on too few cases to be trustworthy), there are no differences in the proportion accepting papal infallibility among the postwar generations. Above the broken line a slight increase from one age group to the next is suggested. However, the main effect seems to be a slight shift away from this belief by the younger generation.

These data show that Catholicism has not been impervious to the secularizing forces of the new America. However, the impact so far seems to have been confined to tenets which are exclusively Catholic—beliefs which separate Rome from the rest of Christianity—while the universal tenets of Christianity seem so far unaffected among Roman Catholics. These and all other relationships reported in this section were independent of sex or social class.

We have seen that commitment to Christian orthodoxy does not appear to be related to the process of getting old. However, belief in life after death is not one of the four basic beliefs making up the orthodoxy index. These four are belief in God, in the divinity of Jesus, in the authenticity of biblical miracles, and in the existence of the Devil.[12] Unwavering commitment to these tenets does not seem related to aging, but belief in immortality, because of its special relevance for the elderly, might increase systematically with age. And surprising as this may seem, table 3 clearly shows that this is the case among Protestants.

For example, only 38 percent of the liberal Protestants who are less than twenty years old felt that the existence of life after death was "completely true," whereas this proportion rises to 51 percent among those in their fifties and up to 70 percent of those seventy and over. (The several small reversals are probably only random fluctuations.)

Among moderate Protestants these proportions increase from 56 percent of those less than twenty to 75 percent of those in their fifties and 88 percent of those seventy and over. Belief in life after death also increases with age among conservative Protestants; however, here the extraordinarily large proportions at all age levels who believe in immortality make it impossible for very large differences to obtain.

The pattern among Roman Catholics is not altogether clear. The data suggest that belief is high among the very young and slowly falls—perhaps as younger

[12]Analysis of the relationship between each of these items and age showed patterns identical with that produced by the index.

adults shrug off their childhood training, and then begins to increase again at about age fifty.

In any event it is clear that although commitment to Christian orthodoxy in general does not increase as people age, belief in survival beyond the grave *does*

Table 3.   *Age and Belief in Life after Death*

	Percent who think it "completely true" that "there is a life beyond death"			
Age:	Liberal Protestants	Moderate Protestants	Conservative Protestants	Roman Catholics
Under 20	38% (21)	56% (16)	87% (15)	90% (10)[a]
20-29	41 (95)	62 (99)	90 (89)	84 (93)
30-39	47 (249)	65 (205)	92 (105)	78 (145)
40-49	44 (278)	69 (251)	90 (103)	70 (122)
50-59	51 (169)	75 (149)	99 (68)	80 (87)
60-69	75 (91)	86 (92)	96 (45)	81 (47)
70 and over	70 (52)	87 (59)	100 (20)	78 (18)

[a]Too few cases for a stable percentage, presented for descriptive interest only.

increase among Protestants. What are we to make of this? James B. Pratt anticipated such an empirical finding in his theoretical study of the psychology of religion published in 1928.[13] He wrote that

> as the belief in miracles and special answers to prayer and in the interference of the supernatural with the natural has gradually disappeared, almost the only pragmatic value of the supernatural left to religion is the belief in a personal future life.[14]

Be that as it may, further examination of many other belief questions contained in the data revealed none on which there were cumulative increases with age. Thus it is necessary to conclude that changes in the religious perspective of American society are revealed by comparisons between church members of different ages, but that people do not get more orthodox or conservative in their religious beliefs as they get older, except that they do increasingly become certain of the existence of life beyond death. In general, then, people do not become more pious with age, insofar as piety means belief in God, the divinity of Jesus, and similar bedrocks of Christian theology. There is of course nothing in these tenets that is more relevant to the aged than to the young. However, where Christian belief does assume special relevance for the existential anxieties of aging—in its doctrine of victory over death—the aging process does seem to produce increased belief.

[13] *The Religious Consciousness* (New York: Macmillan Co., 1928).

[14]*Ibid.*, p. 253.

Ritual Participation[16] and Private Devotionalism[17]

If the aged do not express increasing piety in terms of adherence to the theology of Christianity (aside from immortality), perhaps they do become increasingly engrossed in the ritualistic and devotional aspects of religious commitment. Table 4 allows a test of this hypothesis.

Table 4. *Public Ritual Involvement, Private Devotionalism, and Age*

Age:	Liberal Protestants	Moderate Protestants	Conservative Protestants	Roman Catholics
	Percent High on Index of Public Ritual Involvement			
Under 20	19 (21)	38 (16)	36 (14)[a]	30 (10)[a]
20-29	23 (97)	40 (99)	73 (89)	46 (92)
30-39	38 (247)	45 (208)	73 (107)	47 (146)
40-49	28 (282)	46 (258)	75 (104)	46 (129)
50-59	24 (168)	41 (146)	83 (65)	43 (94)
60-69	24 (95)	47 (90)	75 (43)	54 (46)
70 and over	54 (54)	53 (60)	90 (21)	41 (22)
	Percent High on Index of Private Devotionalism			
Under 20	37 (19)	29 (14)[a]	64 (14)[a]	56 (9)[a]
20-29	34 (90)	35 (97)	62 (87)	58 (93)
30-39	41 (237)	43 (204)	75 (105)	63 (142)
40-49	35 (268)	46 (246)	79 (104)	62 (125)
50-59	48 (163)	58 (148)	88 (68)	74 (91)
60-69	51 (94)	71 (93)	93 (45)	77 (47)
70 and over	68 (53)	81 (57)	96 (21)	75 (20)

[a]Too few cases for stable percentages, presented for descriptive purposes only.

The relationship between age and public ritual participation, as shown in the upper half of the table, seems very slight. Among Protestants it appears that persons seventy and over are more inclined to ritual commitment than those below seventy. However, there are no interpretable differences among the below-seventy age groups, except for the possibility that persons under twenty are a bit less likely to be involved in ritual than are those over twenty. This

[16]The index of ritual involvement consists of answers to two questions: (1) the frequency of church attendance and (2) the frequency of saying table grace. Persons who *both* attended church every, or nearly every, week and who said grace at least once a week were classified as high on the index. Persons who did either this frequently were scored as medium. Persons who did neither this often were scored as low. A full account of index construction and validation can be found in Stark and Glock, op. cit., ch. 4.

[17]The index of private devotionalism was based on the frequency of private prayer and the importance the individual placed on private prayer. Scored high were those who said prayer was "extremely" important and who pray privately at least once a week. Those scored medium met one of these criteria. Those scored low met neither. A full account of index construction and validation can be found in Stark and Glock, op. cit., ch. 5.

difference is uncertain, however, because of the small number of cases on which the percentages are based. Among Roman Catholics, aside from the possibility that those under twenty are less likely to be involved in ritual than the rest, there appears to be no interpretable relationship between age and ritual involvement.

This lack of any important connection between age and ritual involvement may stem from the fact that although older persons do become more engrossed in religion, the difficulties of attending worship services because of ill health and disability work against an increase in their attendance. However, this would not apply to saying table prayers, or grace, and this item, which is included in the index, shows no connection with age either.

Looking at the lower half of the table, it is apparent that private devotionalism increases greatly with age. Among liberal Protestants only 34 percent of those in their twenties scored high on private devotionalism, whereas 48 percent of those in their fifties and 68 percent of those seventy and over did so. Among moderate Protestants these same proportions are 35 percent, 58 percent, and 81 percent, and among conservative Protestants 62 percent, 88 percent, and 96 percent. A similar increase can be seen among Roman Catholics, from just more than half scoring high in the younger age groups up to about three-fourths scoring high in the older groups.

The systematic way in which these proportions increase, although it does not preclude an explanation based on social change, strongly suggests that aging accounts for the changes. Thus, the effect of age seems to be not so much in what one believes but in what one does about what he believes. The elderly do not shift their image of God from a "higher force" to a kindly man with a white beard, but they begin praying a good deal more to whatever conception of God they hold.

Religious Experience[18]

How does aging affect the propensity to have religious experiences? The data shown in table 5 indicate that the tendency to have religious experience does not increase with age except among the conservative Protestant groups. Indeed, there is some suggestion in the data that in the other Protestant bodies and among Roman Catholics younger persons might be slightly more prone to such experiences than older persons. Because of small case bases in the under-twenty group, this suggestion must be taken with caution; still, it is also supported by contrasts between persons in their twenties and those in their thirties, where the case bases are quite large. It may be that in the moderate and liberal Protestant

[18]Three items constitute the religious experience index: "A sense of being saved in Christ," "A feeling that you were somehow in the presence of God," and "A feeling of being punished by God for something you had done." Those scored high on the index at least thought they had experienced all three. Those scored medium thought they might have had one or two of these experiences. Those scored low were certain they had not had any of these experiences. A full account of index construction and validation can be found in Stark and Glock, op. cit., ch. 6.

bodies, where the churches do not formally attempt to produce such experiences, they are mainly associated with the impressionability of youth—a suggestibility and naiveté that is outgrown (albeit some would wish to call it an innocence that is lost).

Table 5. *Age and Religious Experience*

	Percent High on Index of Religious Experience			
Age:	Liberal Protestants	Moderate Protestants	Conservative Protestants	Roman Catholics
Under 20	67 (18)	70 (10)[a]	79 (14)	78 (9)[a]
20-29	53 (89)	63 (95)	83 (83)	62 (84)
30-39	44 (227)	53 (191)	89 (100)	60 (127)
40-49	39 (231)	51 (218)	89 (84)	48 (99)
50-59	39 (129)	66 (116)	91 (58)	60 (63)
60-69	41 (66)	65 (63)	96 (28)	60 (30)
70 and over	36 (25)	59 (34)	100	50 (10)[a]

[a]Too few cases for stable percentages, presented for descriptive interest only.

However, among conservative Protestants, whose churches maintain organized social situations aimed at producing such religious encounters, the proportions who "succeed" in fulfilling this expectation rise with age. While 79 percent of those under twenty and 83 percent of those in their twenties scored high on the index of religious experience, 96 percent of these in their sixties and 100 percent of those seventy and over scored high.

Thus, the effect of age on religious experience depends on the nature of the religious expectations of the denomination to which one belongs. Where religious experiences are fostered, the propensity for this form of commitment increases with age. Where it is not greatly or formally encouraged, it seems to occur more commonly among the very young.

Finally, an examination of the relationship between age and religious knowledge revealed no patterns to indicate either social change or a connection with aging.

These data force the conclusion that the primary outlet provided by religion for the anxieties and deprivations of old age is in personal devotional activities—that is, the increasing piety of the elderly is manifested through prayer. Church members seemingly are more likely to believe in the doctrine of immortality as they get older, but in no other way does their theological outlook change or become more conservative. Nor are the aging more likely to undergo religious experiences (indeed, the opposite may be the case) or to take part in ritual activities or to be more informed about religion.

Thus the widespread notion that men become increasingly pious as a means to overcome the ravages of time is true only if piety is carefully defined as private devotionalism and belief in an immortal soul. It is not true if the word *piety* is used as a synonym for religious commitment in its other aspects.

Part Two

On the Effects of Religion

The idea that being religious has consequences is a common feature of all the world's religions. Religions differ of course about what it means to be properly religious, but each religion expects that being so on its terms will transform individual lives and in the process, presumably, the character of social life.

Sociological research on religious effects has been devoted partly to testing the claims of religion—for example, that religiousness is a source of moral virtue. By and large, however, there has been considerably more interest in trying to identify latent consequences of religion, effects which the faithful neither claim nor foresee—for example, that different religions produce different attitudes toward work or that particular theologies have the unanticipated result of generating prejudice.

The social sciences have yet to produce a comprehensive theory of religious effects. Indeed, nowhere has there been an attempt even to catalog what the possible effects might be. Nevertheless, probably no other topic has generated as much research in the sociology and social psychology of religion. Religion has been studied as a source of rigidity and flexibility, of narrow-mindedness and open-mindedness, of tolerance and bigotry, of mental illness and mental health, of social solidarity and social disintegration, of social stability and social change, of an entrepreneurial spirit and a bureaucratic one.

Research on religious effects has been attended by a considerable amount of controversy. Social scientists and religionists have frequently been in conflict about the validity of research that reveals religion to be other than beneficent. Among social scientists there has also been considerable disagreement, most often about whether causality has been established in particular studies.

At Berkeley studies have been done to test both for anticipated and unanticipated effects of religion and to try slowly to build an empirical base on which a general theory of religion's effects might be developed. To this end special attention has been given to establishing the conditions under which religion does and does not have attitudinal and behavioral consequences.

In making the selections on religions effects for this volume we sought to convey a sense of the range of topics on which research has been done, to illustrate varying processes through which unanticipated effects are produced, and to inform the reader about some of the controversy which has characterized this area of research.

We begin with two selections addressed to testing an age-old assumption about religion—namely, that by generating conformity to existing social arrangements, religion functions as one of society's major agents of social control. Gary Marx in chapter 7 tests whether the assumption explains differential participation by blacks in civil rights protest. In chapter 8 Travis Hirschi and Rodney Stark test to see whether religion helps to account for the incidence of delinquent behavior among youth.

Chapter 9 is a summary of the extensive work done within the Berkeley program on religion and prejudice, and chapter 10 is a first report on Stephen Steinberg's current investigation of the impact of religion on recruitment to and performance in higher education. Finally, in chapter 11, also published for the first time in this volume, Robert Wuthnow summarizes what we know, and have still to discover about the impact of religion on political thought and behavior.

Additional Reading

Lenski, Gerhard. *The Religious Factor: A Sociological Study of Religion's Impact on Politics, Economics, and Family Life.* Garden City, N.Y.: Doubleday, 1961; revised for Anchor paperback edition, 1963. This latter-day attempt to test some of the effects of religion postulated by Max Weber in *The Protestant Ethic and the Spirit of Capitalism* finds that the "ethic" still has power in the modern world.

Schuman, Howard. "The Religious Factor in Detroit: Review, Replication, and Reanalysis." *American Sociological Review* 36:1 (February 1971). This is Lenski reexamined about ten years later—a rare replication in the sociology of religion. See also in the same issue of *ASR* Lenski's commentary, "The Religious Factor in Detroit: Revisited."

Glock, Charles Y., and Stark, Rodney. *Christian Beliefs and Anti-Semitism.* New York: Harper and Row, 1966. Done in the Berkeley style, this study finds that anti-Semitism continues to have religious roots in contemporary life.

Stark, Rodney; Foster, Bruce D.; Glock, Charles Y.; and Quinley, Harold E. *Wayward Shepherds: Prejudice and the Protestant Clergy.* New York: Harper and Row, 1971. This is another replication, this time of the aforementioned *Christian Beliefs and Anti-Semitism.* The authors check to see whether the earlier discoveries on the religious sources of contemporary anti-Semitism among laymen are repeated among clergy.

Lipset, Seymour M. "Religion and Politics in the American Past and Present." In *Religion and Social Conflict*, ed. Robert Lee. New York: Oxford University Press, 1964. An extended historical look at the role religion has played in American politics.

Alford, Robert R. *Party and Society: The Anglo-American Democracies.* Chicago: Rand McNally, 1963. A study of the patterns of voting behavior in four Western democracies in which the religious factor is given sensitive attention.

Chapter Seven

Religion: Opiate or Inspiration of Civil Rights Militancy Among Negroes?*

Gary T. Marx

The relationship between religion and political radicalism is a confusing one. On the one hand, established religious institutions have generally had a stake in the status quo and hence have supported conservatism. Furthermore, with the masses having an otherworldly orientation, religious zeal, particularly as expressed in the more fundamentalist branches of Christianity, has been seen as an alternative to the development of political radicalism. On the other hand, as the source of universal humanistic values and the strength that can come from believing one is carrying out God's will in political matters, religion has occasionally played a strong positive role in movements for radical social change.

This dual role of religion is clearly indicated in the case of the American Negro and race protest. Slaves are said to have been first brought to this country on the "good ship Jesus Christ."[1] While there was occasional controversy over the effect that religion had on them it appears that most slave-owners eventually came to view supervised religion as an effective means of social control. Stampp, in commenting on the effect of religion, notes:

> ... through religious instruction the bondsmen learned that slavery had divine sanction, that insolence was as much an offense against God as against the temporal master. They received the Biblical command that servants should obey their masters, and they heard of the punishments

*Gary Marx, "Religion: Opiate or Inspiration of Civil Rights Militancy Among Negroes?" *American Sociological Review* 32, no. 1 (February 1967). Reprinted with the permission of the author and the *American Sociological Review*.

[1]Louis Lomax, *When the Word is Given* (New York: New American Library, 1964), p. 34.

awaiting the disobedient slave in the hereafter. They heard, too, that eternal salvation would be their reward for faithful service. . .[2]

In discussing the period after the Civil War, Myrdal states that ". . . under the pressure of political reaction, the Negro church in the South came to have much the same role as it did before the Civil War. Negro frustration was sublimated into emotionalism, and Negro hopes were fixed on the after world."[3] Many other analysts, in considering the consequences of Negro religion from the end of slavery until the early 1950's, reached similar conclusions about the conservatizing effect of religion on race protest.[4]

However, the effect of religion on race protest throughout American history has by no means been exclusively in one direction. While many Negroes were no doubt seriously singing about chariots in the sky, Negro preachers such as Denmark Vesey and Nat Turner and the religiously inspired abolitionists were actively fighting slavery in their own way. All Negro churches first came into being as protest organizations and later some served as meeting places where protest strategy was planned, or as stations on the underground railroad. The richness of protest symbolism in Negro spirituals and sermons has often been noted. Beyond this symbolic role, as a totally Negro institution, the church brought together in privacy people with a shared problem. It was from the church experience that many leaders were exposed to a broad range of ideas legitimizing protest and obtained the savoir faire, self-confidence, and organizational experience needed to challenge an oppressive system. A recent commentator states that the slave churches were "the nucleus of the Negro protest" and another that "in religion Negro leaders had begun to find sanction and support for their movements of protest more than 150 years ago."[5]

Differing perceptions of the varied consequences religion may have on protest

[2]Kenneth Stampp, *The Peculiar Institution*, (New York: Alfred A. Knopf, 1956), p. 158.

[3]Gunnar Myrdal *et al., An American Dilemma* (New York: Harper, 1944), pp. 851-853. About the North he notes that the church remained far more independent "but on the whole even the Northern Negro church has remained a conservative institution with its interest directly upon other-worldly matters and has largely ignored the practical problems of the Negro's fate in this world."

[4]For example Dollard reports that "religion can be seen as a mechanism for the social control of Negroes" and that planters have always welcomed the building of a Negro church on the plantation but looked with less favor upon the building of a school. John Dollard, *Caste and Class in a Southern Town* (Garden City: Doubleday Anchor, 1957), p. 248. A few of the many others reaching similar conclusions are, Benjamin E. Mays and J. W. Nicholson, *The Negro's Church* (New York: Institute of Social and Religious Research, 1933); Hortense Powdermaker, *After Freedom* (New York, Viking Press, 1939), p. 285; Charles Johnson, *Growing Up in the Black Belt* (Washington, D.C.: American Council of Education, 1941), pp. 135-136; St. Clair Drake and Horace Cayton, *Black Metropolis* (New York: Harper and Row, 1962), pp. 424-429; George Simpson and Milton Yinger, *Racial and Cultural Minorities* (New York: Harper, rev. ed., 1958), pp. 582-587. In a more general context this social control consequence of religion has of course been noted throughout history from Plato to Montesquieu to Marx to Nietzsche to Freud to contemporary social theorists.

[5]Daniel Thompson, "The Rise of Negro Protest," *Annals of the American Academy of Political and Social Science*, 357 (January, 1965).

have continued to the present time. While there has been very little in the way of
empirical research on the effect of the Negro church on protest,[6] the literature
of race relations is rich with impressionistic statements which generally
contradict each other about how the church either encourages and is the source
of race protest or inhibits and retards its development. For example, two
observers note, "as primitive evangelism gave way to a more sophisticated social
consciousness, the church became the spearhead of Negro protest in the deep
South,"[7] while another indicates "the Negro church is a sleeping giant. In civil
rights participation its feet are hardly wet."[8] A civil rights activist, himself a
clergyman, states: ". . . the church today is central to the movement . . . if there
had been no Negro church, there would have been no civil rights movement
today."[9] On the other hand, a sociologist, commenting on the more involved
higher status ministers, notes: ". . . middle class Negro clergymen in the cities of
the South generally advocated cautious gradualism in race activities until the
mid-1950's when there was an upsurge of protest sentiment among urban
Negroes . . . but most of them [ministers] did not embrace the more vigorous
techniques of protest until other leaders took the initiative and gained
widespread support."[10] Another sociologist states, "Whatever their previous
conservative stance has been, the churches have now become 'spearheads of
reform.' "[11] still another indicates: ". . . the Negro church is particularly
culpable for its general lack of concern for the moral and social problems of the
community . . . it has been accommodating. Fostering indulgence in religious
sentimentality, and riveting the attention of the masses on the bounties of a
hereafter, the Negro church remains a refuge, and escape from the cruel realities
of the here and now."[12]

[6]The empirical evidence is quite limited. The few studies that have been done have focused
on the Negro minister. Thompson notes that in New Orleans Negro ministers constitute the
largest segment of the Negro leadership class (a grouping which is not necessarily the same as
"protest leaders") but that "The vast majority of ministers are primarily interested in their
pastoral role . . . their sermons are essentially biblical, dealing only tangentially with social
issues." Daniel Thompson, *The Negro Leadership Class* (Englewood Cliffs, New Jersey:
Prentice-Hall, 1963), pp. 34-35. Studies of the Negro ministry in Detroit and Richmond,
California also stress that only a small fraction of Negro clergymen show any active concern
with the civil rights struggle. R. L. Johnstone, *Militant and Conservative Community
Leadership Among Negro Clergymen,* Ph.D. dissertation, University of Michigan, Ann
Arbor, 1963, and J. Bloom, *The Negro Church and the Movement for Equality*, M.A. thesis,
University of California, Berkeley, Department of Sociology, 1966.

[7]Jane Record and Wilson Record, "Ideological Forces and the Negro Protest," *Annals, op.
cit.,* p. 92.

[8]G. Booker, *Black Man's America* (Englewood Cliffs, N.J.: Prentice-Hall, 1964), p. 111.

[9]Rev. W. T. Walker, as quoted in William Brink and Louis Harris, *The Negro Revolution in
America* (New York: Simon and Schuster), 1964, p. 103.

[10]N. Glenn, "Negro Religion in the U.S." in L. Schneider, *Religion, Culture and Society*
(New York: John Wiley, 1964).

[11]Joseph Fichter, "American Religion and the Negro," *Daedalus* (Fall, 1965), p. 1087.

[12]E. U. Essien-Udom, *Black Nationalism* (New York: Dell Publishing Co., 1962), p. 358.
    Many other examples of contradictory statements could be offered, sometimes even in
the same volume. For example, Carleton Lee stresses the importance of religion for protest
while Rayford Logan sees the Negro pastor as an instrument of the white power structure
(in a book published to commemorate 100 years of emancipation). Carleton Lee, "Religious

Thus one faces opposing views, or at best ambiguity, in contemplating the current effect of religion. The opiating consequences of religion are all too well known as is the fact that the segregated church is durable and offers some advantages to clergy and members that might be denied them in a more integrated society. On the other hand, the prominent role of the Negro church in supplying much of the ideology of the movement, many of its foremost leaders, and an institution around which struggle might be organized—particularly in the South—can hardly be denied. It would appear from the bombings of churches and the writings of Martin Luther King and other religiously inspired activists that for many, religion and protest are closely linked.

Part of this dilemma may lie in the distinction between the church as an institution in its totality and particular individual churches within it, and the further distinctions among different types of individual religious concern. This chapter is concerned with the latter subject; it is an inquiry into the relationship between religiosity and response to the civil rights struggle. It first considers how religious denomination affects militancy, and then how various measures of religiosity, taken separately and together, are related to civil rights concern. The question is then asked of those classified as "very religious" and "quite religious," how an "otherworldly orientation"—as opposed to a "temporal" one—affects militancy.

In a nationwide study of Negroes living in metropolitan areas of the United States, a number of questions were asked about religious behavior and beliefs as well as about the civil rights struggle.[13] Seven of the questions dealing with civil rights protest have been combined into an index of conventional militancy.[14] Built into this index are a number of dimensions of racial protest such as impatience over the speed of integration, opposition to discrimination in public facilities and the sale of property, perception of barriers to Negro advancement, support of civil rights demonstrations, and expressed willingness to take part in a demonstration. Those giving the militant response to five or more of the questions are considered militant, those giving such a response to three or four of the questions, moderate, and fewer than three, conservative.[15]

Roots of Negro Protest," and Rayford Logan, "Educational Changes Affecting American Negroes," both in Arnold Rose, *Assuring Freedom to the Free* (Detroit: Wayne University Press, 1964).

[13]This survey was carried out in 1964 by the Survey Research Center, University of California, Berkeley. A non-Southern metropolitan area probability sample was drawn as well as special area samples of Negroes living in New York City, Chicago, Atlanta and Birmingham. Since the results reported here are essentially the same for each of these areas, they are treated together. More than 90% of the interviews were done with Negro interviewers. Additional methodological details may be found in Gary Marx, *Protest and Prejudice: A Study of Belief in the Black Community* (New York: Harper & Row, 1967).

[14]Attention is directed to conventional militancy rather than to that of the Black Nationalist variety because a very small percentage of the sample offered strong and consistent support for Black Nationalism. As in studying support for the KKK, the Birch Society or the Communist Party, a representative sample of normal size is inadequate.

[15]Each of the items in the index was positively related to every other and the index showed a high degree of internal validity. The index also received external validation from a number

Denomination

It has long been known that the more fundamentalist sects such as the Holiness groups and the Jehovah's Witnesses are relatively uninterested in movements for secular political change.[16] Such transvaluational movements with their otherworldly orientation and their promise that the last shall be first in the great beyond, are said to solace the individual for his lowly status in this world and to divert concern away from efforts at collective social change which might be brought about by man. While only a minority of Negroes actually belong to such groups, the proportion is higher than among whites. Negro literature is rich in descriptions of these churches and their position on race protest.

In Table 1 it can be seen that those belonging to sects are the least likely to be militant; they are followed by those in predominantly Negro denominations. Ironically those individuals in largely white denominations (Episcopalian, Presbyterian, United Church of Christ, and Roman Catholic) are those most likely to be militant, in spite of the perhaps greater civil rights activism of the Negro denominations. This pattern emerged even when social class was held constant.

Table 1.   *Proportion Militant (%) by Denomination* *

Denomination	% Militant
Episcopalian	46 (24)
United Church of Christ	42 (12)
Presbyterian	40 (25)
Catholic	40 (109)
Methodist	34 (142)
Baptist	32 (658)
Sects and Cults	20 (106)

*25 respondents are not shown in this table because they did not specify a denomination, or belonged to a non-Christian religious group, or other small Christian group.

In their comments members of the less conventional religious groups clearly expressed the classical attitude of their sects toward participation in the politics of the secular world. For example, an Evangelist in the Midwest said, "I don't believe in participating in politics. My church don't vote—they just depends on the plans of God." And an automobile serviceman in Philadelphia stated, "I, as a Jehovah's Witness, cannot express things involving the race issue." A housewife

---

of additional questions. For example, the percentage belonging to a civil rights organization went from zero among those lowest in militancy to 38 percent for those who were highest, and the percentage thinking that civil rights demonstrations had helped a great deal increased from 23 percent to 58 percent. Those thinking that the police treated Negroes very well decreased from 35 percent to only 2 percent among those highest in militancy.

[16]Liston Pope, *Millhands and Preachers* (New Haven: Yale University Press, 1942), p. 137. J. Milton Yinger, *Religion, Society, and the Individual* (New York: The Macmillan Company, 1957, pp. 170-173).

in the Far West ventured, "In my religion we do not approve of anything except living like it says in the Bible; demonstrations mean calling attention to you and it's sinful."

The finding that persons who belong to sects are less likely to be militant than the non-sect members is to be expected; clearly this type of religious involvement seems an alternative for most people to the development of radicalism. But what of the religious style of those in the more conventional churches which may put relatively less stress on the after-life and encourage various forms of secular participation? Are the more religiously inclined within these groups also less likely to be militant?

Religiosity

The present study measured several dimensions of religious involvement. Those interviewed were asked how important religion was to them, several questions about orthodoxy of belief, and how frequently they attended worship service.[17] Even with the sects excluded, irrespective of the dimension of religiosity considered, the greater the religiosity the lower the percentage militant. (See Tables 2, 3 and 4.) For example, militancy increases consistently from a low of only 29 percent among those who said religion was "extremely important" to a high of 62 percent for those who indicated that religion was "not at all important" to them. For those very high in orthodoxy (having no doubt about the existence of God or the devil) 27 percent were militant while for those totally rejecting these ideas 54 percent indicated great concern over civil rights. Militancy also varies inversely with frequency of attendance at worship service.[18]

Each of these items was strongly related to every other; when taken together they help us to better characterize religiosity. Accordingly they have been combined into an overall measure of religiosity. Those scored as "very religious" in terms of this index attended church at least once a week, felt that religion was extremely important to them, and had no doubts about the existence of God

[17]These dimensions and several others are suggested in chapter 1 of this volume. For another measure of religious involvement, the number of church organizations belonged to, the same inverse relationship was noted.

[18]There is a popular stereotype that Negroes are a "religious people." Social science research has shown that they are "over-churched" relative to whites, i.e., the ratio of Negro churches to the size of the Negro population is greater than the same ratio for whites. Using data from a nationwide survey of whites, by Gertrude Selznick and Stephen Steinberg, some comparison of the religiosity of Negroes and whites was possible. When these various dimensions of religiosity were examined, with the effect of education and region held constant, Negroes appeared as significantly more religious *only* with respect to the subjective importance assigned to religion. In the North, whites were more likely to attend church at least once a week than were Negroes; while in the South rates of attendance were the same. About the same percentage of both groups had no doubts about the existence of God. While Negroes were more likely to be sure about the existence of a devil, whites, surprisingly, were more likely to be sure about a life beyond death. Clearly, then, any assertions about the greater religiosity of Negroes relative to whites are unwarranted unless one specifies the dimension of religiosity.

Table 2.   *Militancy by Subjective Importance
Assigned to Religion**

Importance	% Militant
Extremely important	29 (668)
Somewhat important	39 (195)
Fairly important	48 (96)
Not too important	56 (18)
Not at all important	62 (13)

*Sects are excluded here and in all subsequent tables.

Table 3.   *Militancy by Orthodoxy*

Orthodoxy	% Militant
Very high	27 (414)
High	34 (333)
Medium	39 (144)
Low	47 (68)
Very low	54 (35)

Table 4.   *Militancy by Frequency of Attendance
at Worship Services*

Frequency	% Militant
More than once a week	27 (81)
Once a week	32 (311)
Once a month or more but less than once a week	34 (354)
Less than once a month	38 (240)

and the devil. For progressively lower values of the index, frequency of church attendance, the importance of religion, and acceptance of the belief items decline consistently until, for those scored "not at all religious," church is rarely if ever attended, religion is not considered personally important and the belief items are rejected.

Using this measure for non-sect members, civil rights militancy increases from a low of 26 percent for those labeled "very religious" to 30 percent for the "somewhat religious" to 45 percent for those "not very religious" and up to a high of 70 percent for those "not at all religious."[19] (Table 5.)

[19]When the sects are included in these tables the results are the same. The sects have been excluded because they offer almost no variation to be analyzed with respect to the independent variable. Since virtually all of the sect members scored as either "very religious" or "somewhat religious," it is hardly possible to measure the effect of their religious involvement on protest attitudes. In addition the import of the relationships shown in these tables is considerably strengthened when it is demonstrated that religious involvement inhibits militancy even when the most religious and least militant group, the sects, are excluded.

Table 5.   *Militancy by Religiosity*

Religiosity	Very Religious	Somewhat Religious	Not Very Religious	Not at All Religious
% Militant	26	30	45	70
N	(230)	(523)	(195)	(36)

Religiosity and militancy are also related to age, sex, education, religious denomination and region of the country. The older, the less educated, women, Southerners and those in Negro denominations are more likely to be religious and to have lower percentages scoring as militant. Thus it is possible that the relationship observed is simply a consequence of the fact that both religiosity and militancy are related to some third factor. In Table 6 it can be seen, however, that even when these variables are controlled the relationship is maintained. That is, even among those in the North, the younger, male, more educated and those affiliated with predominantly white denominations, the greater the religiosity the less the militancy.

Table 6.   *Proportion Militant (%) by Religiosity, for Education, Age, Region, Sex, and Denomination*

	Very Religious	Somewhat Religious	Not Very Religious	Not at All Religious
Education				
Grammar school	17 (108)	22 (201)	31 (42)	50 (2)
High school	34 (96)	32 (270)	45 (119)	58 (19)
College	38 (26)	48 (61)	59 (34)	87 (15)
Age				
18-29	33 (30)	37 (126)	44 (62)	62 (13)
30-44	30 (53)	34 (180)	48 (83)	74 (19)
45-59	25 (71)	27 (131)	45 (33)	50 (2)
60+	22 (76)	18 (95)	33 (15)	100 (2)
Region				
Non-South	30 (123)	34 (331)	47 (159)	70 (33)
South	22 (107)	23 (202)	33 (36)	66 (3)
Sex				
Men	28 (83)	33 (220)	44 (123)	72 (29)
Women	26 (147)	28 (313)	46 (72)	57 (7)
Denomination				
Episcopalian, Presbyterian, United Church of Christ	20 (15)	27 (26)	33 (15)	60 (5)
Catholic	13 (15)	39 (56)	36 (25)	77 (13)
Methodist	46 (24)	22 (83)	50 (32)	100 (2)
Baptist	25 (172)	29 (354)	45 (117)	53 (15)

The incompatibility between piety and protest shown in these data becomes even more evident when considered in light of comments offered by the respondents. Many religious people hold beliefs which clearly inhibit race protest. For a few there was the notion that segregation and a lowly status for

Negroes was somehow God's will and not for man to question. Thus a housewife in South Bend, Indiana, in saying that civil rights demonstrations had hurt Negroes, added "God is the Creator of everything. We don't know why we all dark-skinned. We should try to put forth the effort to do what God wants and not question."[20]

A Negro spiritual contains the lines "I'm gonna wait upon the Lord till my change comes." For our respondents a more frequently stated belief stressed that God as the absolute controller of the universe would bring about change in his own way and at his own time, rather than expressing segregation as God's will. In indicating her unwillingness to take part in a civil rights demonstration, a Detroit housewife said, "I don't go for demonstrations. I believe that God created all men equal and at His appointed time He will give every man his portion, no one can hinder it." And in response to a question about whether or not the government in Washington was pushing integration too slowly, a retired clerk in Atlanta said: "You can't hurry God. He has a certain time for this to take place. I don't know about Washington."

Others who desired integration more strongly and wanted immediate social change felt that (as Bob Dylan sings) God was on their side. Hence man need do nothing to help bring about change. Thus a worker in Cleveland, who was against having more civil rights demonstrations, said: "With God helping to fight our battle, I believe we can do with fewer demonstrations." And in response to a question about whether Negroes should spend more time praying and less time demonstrating, an Atlanta clergyman, who said "more time praying," added "praying is demonstrating."[21]

Religion among the Militants

Although the net effect of religion is clearly to inhibit attitudes of protest it is interesting to consider this relationship in the opposite direction, i.e., observe religiosity among those characterized as militant, moderate, and conservative with respect to the civil rights struggle. As civil rights concern increases, religiosity decreases. (Table 7.) Militants were twice as likely to be scored "not very religious" or "not at all religious" as were conservatives. This table is also of interest because it shows that, even for the militants, a majority were scored either "very religious" or "somewhat religious." Clearly, for many, a religious orientation and a concern with racial protest are not mutually exclusive.

[20]Albert Cardinal Meyer notes that the Catholic Bishops of the U.S. said in their statement of 1958: "The heart of the race question is moral and religious." "Interracial Justice and Love," in M. Ahmann, ed., *Race Challenge to Religion* (Chicago: H. Regnery, 1963), p. 126. These data, viewed from the perspective of the activist seeking to motivate Negroes on behalf of the civil rights struggle, suggest that this statement has a meaning which Their Excellencies no doubt did not intend.

[21]A study of ministers in Richmond, California notes that, although almost all questioned were opposed to discrimination, very few had taken concrete action, in part because of their belief that God would take care of them. One minister noted, "I believe that if we all was as pure . . . as we ought to be, there would be no struggle. God will answer my prayer. If we just stay with God and have faith. *When Peter was up, did the people march to free him? No. He prayed, and God did something about it.*" (Bloom, *op. cit.*, italics added.)

Table 7. *Religiosity by Civil Rights Militancy*

	Militants	Moderates	Conservatives
Very religious	18%	24%	28%
Somewhat religious	48	57	55
Not very religious	26	17	16
Not at all religious	8	2	1
Total	100	100	100
N	332	419	242

Given the active involvement of some churches, the singing of protest spirituals, and the ideology of the movement as it relates to Christian principles of love, equality, passive suffering,[22] and the appeal to a higher moral law, it would be surprising if there were only a few religious people among the militants.

A relevant question accordingly is: Among the religious, what are the intervening links which determine whether religion is related to an active concern with racial matters or has an opiating effect?[23] From the comments reported above it seemed that, for some, belief in a highly deterministic God inhibited race protest. Unfortunately the study did not measure beliefs about the role of God as against the role of men in the structuring of human affairs. However, a related variable was measured which would seem to have much relevance—the extent to which these religious people were concerned with the here and now as opposed to the after-life.

The classical indictment of religion from the Marxist perspective is that by focusing concern on a glorious after-life the evils of this life are ignored. Of course there are important differences among religious institutions and among individuals with respect to the importance given to otherworldly concerns. Christianity, as with most ideologies, contains within it, if not out-and-out contradictory themes, then certainly themes which are likely to be in tension with one another. In this fact, no doubt, lies part of the explanation of religion's varied consequences for protest. One important strand of Christianity stresses acceptance of one's lot and glorifies the after-life;[24] another is more concerned

[22]Non-violent resistance as it relates to Christianity's emphasis on suffering, sacrifice, and privation, is discussed by James W. Vander Zanden, "The Non-Violent Resistance Movement Against Segregation." *American Journal of Sociology*, 68 (March, 1963), pp. 544-550.

[23]Of course, a most relevant factor here is the position of the particular church that an individual is involved in. Unfortunately, it was difficult to obtain such information in a nationwide survey.

[24]The Muslims have also made much of this theme within Christianity, and their militancy is certainly tied to a rejection of otherworldly religiosity. The Bible is referred to as a "poison book" and the leader of the Muslims states, "No one after death has ever gone any place but where they were carried. There is no heaven or hell other than on earth for you and me, and Jesus was no exception. His body is still . . . in Palestine and will remain there." (As quoted in C. Eric Lincoln, *The Black Muslims in America* [Boston: Beacon Press, 1961]. p. 123.)

However, while they reject the otherworldly theme, they nevertheless rely heavily on a deterministic Allah; according to E. U. Essien-Udom, this fact leads to political inactivity.

with the realization of Judeo-Christian values in the current life. King and his followers clearly represent this latter "social gospel" tradition.[25] Those with the type of temporal concern that King represents would be expected to be higher in militancy. A measure of temporal vs. otherworldly concern has been constructed. On the basis of two questions, those interviewed have been classified as having either an otherworldly or a temporal orientation.[26] The evidence is that religiosity and otherworldly concern increase together. For example, almost 100 percent of the "not at all religious" group were considered to have a temporal orientation, but only 42 percent of the "very religious." (Table 8.) Those in predominantly white denominations were more likely to have a temporal orientation than those in all-black denominations.

Table 8. *Proportion (%) with Temporal (as against Otherworldly) Concern, by Religiosity*

Religiosity	% with Temporal Concern
Very religious	42 (225)
Somewhat religious	61 (531)
Not very religious	82 (193)
Not at all religious	98 (34)

Among the religious groups, if concern with the here and now is a relevant factor in overcoming the opiating effect of religion then it is to be anticipated that those considered to have a temporal religious orientation would be much higher in militancy than those scored as otherworldly. This is in fact the case. Among the otherworldly religious, only 16 percent were militant; this

He notes, "The attainment of black power is relegated to the intervention of "Almighty Allah" sometime in the future . . . Not unlike other religionists, the Muslims too may wait for all eternity for the coming of the Messiah, the predicted apocalypse in 1970 notwithstanding." E. U. Essien-Udom, *Black Nationalism, op. cit.*, pp. 313-314.

[25]He states: "Any religion that professes to be concerned with the souls of men and is not concerned with the slums that damn them, the economic conditions that strangle them, and the social conditions that cripple them is a dry-as-dust religion." He further adds, perhaps in a concession, that "such a religion is the kind the Marxists like to see—an opiate of the people." Martin Luther King, *Stride Toward Freedom* (New York: Ballantine Books, 1958), pp. 28-29.

John Lewis, a former SNCC leader and once a Baptist Divinity student, is said to have peered through the bars of a Southern jail and said, "Think not that I am come to send peace on earth. I came not to send peace, but a sword." (Matthew 10:34.)

[26]The two items used in this index were: "How sure are you that there is a life beyond death?"; and "Negroes should spend more time praying and less time demonstrating." The latter item may seem somewhat circular when observed in relation to civil rights concern. However, this is precisely what militancy is all about. Still it would have been better to measure otherworldly vs. temporal concern in a less direct fashion; unfortunately, no other items were available. Because of this the data shown here must be interpreted with caution. However it does seem almost self-evident that civil rights protest which is religiously inspired is related to a temporal religious outlook.

proportion increases to almost 40 percent among those considered "very religious" and "somewhat religious" who have a temporal religious outlook. (Table 9.) Thus it would seem that an important factor in determining the effect of religion on protest attitudes is the nature of an individual's religious commitment. It is quite possible, for those with a temporal religious orientation, that—rather than the effect of religion being somehow neutralized (as in the case of militancy among the "not religious" groups)—their religious concern serves to inspire and sustain race protest. This religious inspiration can, of course, be clearly noted among some active civil rights participants.

Table 9.   *Proportion Militant (%) by Religiosity and Temporal or Otherworldly Concern*

Concern	Very Religious	Somewhat Religious
Temporal	39 (95)	38 (325)
Otherworldly	15 (130)	17 (206)

Conclusion

The effect of religiosity on race protest depends on the type of religiosity involved. Past literature is rich in suggestions that the religiosity of the fundamentalist sects is an alternative to the development of political radicalism. This seems true in the case of race protest as well. However, in an overall sense even for those who belong to the more conventional churches, the greater the religious involvement, whether measured in terms of ritual activity, orthodoxy of religious belief, subjective importance of religion, or the three taken together, the lower the degree of militancy.

Among sect members and religious people with an otherworldly orientation, religion and race protest appear to be, if not mutually exclusive, then certainly what one observer has referred to as "mutually corrosive kinds of commitments."[27] Until such time as religion loosens its hold over these people or comes to embody to a greater extent the belief that man as well as God can bring about secular change, and focuses more on the here and now, religious involvement may be seen as an important factor working against the widespread radicalization of the Negro public.

However, it has also been noted that many militant people are nevertheless religious. When a distinction is made among the religious between the "otherworldly" and the "temporal," for many of the latter group, religion seems to facilitate or at least not to inhibit protest. For these people religion and race protest may be mutually supportive.

[27]Rodney Stark, "Class, Radicalism, and Religious Involvement," *American Sociological Review*, 29 (October, 1964), p. 703.

Thirty years ago Donald Young wrote: "One function which a minority religion may serve is that of reconciliation with inferior status and its discriminatory consequences ... on the other hand, religious institutions may also develop in such a way as to be an incitement and support of revolt against inferior status."[28] The current civil rights struggle and the data observed here certainly suggest that this is the case. These contradictory consequences of religion are somewhat reconciled when one distinguishes among different segments of the Negro church and types of religious concern among individuals.

[28]Donald Young, *American Minority Peoples*, New York: Harper, 1937, p. 204.

These data are also consistent with Merton's statement that it is premature to conclude that "all religion everywhere has only the one consequence of making for mass apathy" and his insistence on recognizing the "multiple consequences" and "net balance of aggregate consequences" of a given institution such as religion. Robert Merton, *Social Theory and Social Structure* (Glencoe: Free Press, 1957, revised edition), p. 44.

Chapter Eight

Hellfire and Delinquency*

Travis Hirschi and Rodney Stark

From time to time judges advise juvenile offenders to attend church for periods of months or years. Such "sentences" are not intended as punishment.[1] Because the judge assumes that religious training and commitment produce moral character, he assumes such attendance may lead to repentance and reform. This view is widespread in law enforcement circles. As J. Edgar Hoover tells us:

> Invariably when you analyze the reasons for such [criminal] actions, certain facts stand out stark and revealing—the faith of our fathers, the love of God, and the observance of His Commandments have either been thrust aside or they never existed in the heart of the individual transgressor. . .[2]

It is hardly surprising that this position is supported by clergymen. Religious leaders traditionally blame "rising crime and immorality" on a decline in religious conviction, and many argue that religious commitment is the *only* secure basis for moral behavior. In the writings of religious scholars, again and again we encounter the same syllogism:

Most acts of delinquency are amoral, and the roots of morality are either

---

*Travis Hirschi and Rodney Stark, "Hellfire and Delinquency," *Social Problems* 17, no. 2 (Fall, 1969). Reprinted with permission of the authors and The Society for the Study of Social Problems.

[1]Don J. Hager in "Religion, Delinquency, and Society," *Social Work*, 2, July 1957 reports that the judge's advice may in effect become a requirement and nonattendance considered a violation of probation or parole.

[2]Quoted by John Edward Coogan, "Religion a Preventive of Delinquency," *Federal Probation*, 18 (December, 1954), pp. 29-35.

principally or exclusively religious. Delinquents, therefore, should be lower
than nondelinquents in religiosity or religiousness.[3]

Such notions are congruent with the social scientific view that religious
sanctioning systems play an important role in ensuring and maintaining
conformity to social norms.[4] Drawing heavily on the work of Emile Durkheim,
the way in which religion performs this role is usually summarized as follows:[5]
(1) through its belief system religion legitimates social and individual values; (2)
through its rituals it reinforces commitment to these values; (3) through its
system of eternal rewards and punishment, religion helps to insure the
embodiment of values in actual behavior.

It is hard to challenge the idea that persons often do have internalized ethics
which sometimes govern their actions. But does religion, at least in
contemporary society, have much to do with developing or sustaining such
personal ethics? Indeed, is the Christian sanctioning system of hellfire for sinners
and heavenly glory for the just, able to deter unlawful behavior even among
those who are firm believers?

By implication these questions bear on present concerns over the relevance of
religion in modern life. Many clergymen have come to doubt the ability of the
faith to move men on moral questions. These doubts have arisen mainly around
such matters as prejudice, peace, poverty, and various political abominations.
However, the relation between religiousness and delinquency seems to offer an
especially critical test of the relevance of religion. For if religion proves
immaterial here, in an area where it has always concentrated its efforts to
influence the ways in which men act, then its failure would seem acute. Evidence
on this question is mixed. Against the pronouncements of the theoretical
sociologist, the lawman, the layman, and the clergy, a few criminologists have
stood firm. In their view, the allegedly intimate connection between religiosity
and noncriminality is not obvious. Teeters only slightly overstates the position
of this group when he writes:

If there are any studies whatsoever that show up the value of religious
training as a deterrent to crime, delinquency, immorality, or unethical
conduct, this writer has never seen them.[6]

But there is by no means unanimity on this point among criminologists, and the

---

[3]Juan B. Cortes, "Juvenile Delinquency: A Biosocial Approach," in Angelo D'Agostino, ed.,
Family, Church, and Community (New York: P. J. Kenedy & Sons, 1965), pp. 114-115, and
122.

[4]See, e.g., Kingsley Davis, *Human Society* (New York: The Macmillan Company, 1948), pp.
73-74, 371-373.

[5]See: J. Milton Yinger, *Religion, Society and the Individual* (New York: Macmillan, 1957).

[6]Negley K. Teeters, "Reply," *Federal Probation,* 16 (September, 1952), p. 41. Teeters is
replying to an article by John Edward Coogan (" 'The Myth Mind in an Engineers' World,' "
Federal Probation, 16 [March, 1952]) in which criminologists are taken to task for ignoring
the impact of religion.

usual problems arise when one attempts to reach a firm conclusion from past research. Much of this research does not meet minimum standards of adequacy: for example, many of the studies cited in typical review articles do not even have comparison groups.[7] But there is a further and somewhat unusual problem: interestingly enough, accusations of bias, either for or against religion, are common.[8] And, indeed, there does seem to be a relation between the findings and the religiosity of the researcher. While most studies conducted by criminologists suggest that religion has little or no effect, research by religionists tends to indicate that religion is just what it has always been thought to be, a powerful "aid to the sword" in the maintenance of conformity, a factor in delinquency at least equal to the variables traditionally considered important by criminologists.[9]

Given these conflicting claims, given the sociological view of the functions of religious institutions, and given the more narrowly practical question of the relevance of religion to man's day-to-day behavior, we propose to examine again the question of the relation between religiosity and delinquency.

Sample and Data

The sample on which our study is based was drawn from students entering the public junior and senior high schools of Western Contra Costa County, California, in the Fall of 1964. This population was stratified by race, sex, school, and grade, and random samples drawn from each substratum.[10] Of the 5,545 students drawn in the original sample, 4,077 or 74 percent eventually completed a lengthy questionnaire.[11] School records on the entire original

[7]See, e.g., George Edward Powers, "Prevention Through Religion," in William E. Amos and Charles F. Wellford, *Delinquency Prevention: Theory and Practice* (Englewood Cliffs, N.J.: Prentice-Hall, 1967), pp. 99-127).

[8]"There seems to be a bias in favor of religious influence as an aid to good behavior whenever the investigator is a religious leader." *Ibid.*, p. 106. Compare: "Many research persons are . . . definitely antireligious in their approach to the crime problem." Mabel A. Elliott, *Crime in Modern Society* (New York: Harper and Brothers, 1952), p. 835. For expansion of the latter view, see Coogan, " 'The Myth Mind . . .'," *op. cit.*

[9]". . . the difference in religiosity was extremely significant. There was no other variable which discriminated better between (delinquents and nondelinquents)" (Cortes 1965:123).

[10]Sampling was disproportionate by race and sex: 85 percent of Negro boys, 60 percent of Negro girls, 30 percent of white boys, and 12 percent of white girls were selected. These percentages were selected in each grade in all schools *except* where the sampling fraction would not produce at least 25 students in each school, in which case the entire population of the school was included. When race and sex are held constant, as in the present analysis, the original sample is therefore unbiased—except for a very slight over-representation of Negroes from predominantly white schools.

[11]In previous analyses of these data, adjustment has been made for differences among the substrata in the proportion actually completing the questionnaire. Such weighting procedures were not available for the present analysis. In most cases, however, comparison with previous results is possible, and the conclusions do not differ from one procedure to the other.

sample, and police records on all boys in the original sample are also available.[12]

Measures of delinquency

Delinquency was measured both by self-reports and by examination of police records. The self report index of delinquency was constructed from these items:

1. Have you ever taken little things (worth less than $2) that did not belong to you?

2. Have you ever taken things of some value (between $2 and $50) that did not belong to you?

3. Have you ever taken things of large value (worth over $50) that did not belong to you?

4. Have you ever taken a car for a ride without the owner's permission?

5. Have you ever banged up something that did not belong to you on purpose?

6. Not counting fights you may have had with a brother or sister, have you ever beaten up anyone or hurt anyone on purpose?

All of these acts are violations of law. In legal terms, they represent petty and grand larceny, auto theft, vandalism, and assault. Since the students reported when they had committed each of the acts listed, index scores were constructed simply by counting the number of separate offenses the student had committed in the year prior to administration of the questionnaire.

The measure of official delinquency is a count of the number of offenses known to the police over the period of about three years prior to examination of police records. Among white boys, the correlation between the self-report and official measures is .27. Rather than concern ourselves with the relative validity of these measures, we shall conduct parallel analyses using both the self-report and official measures of delinquency.

Measures of religiosity

If delinquency research is subject to dismissal on the ground that its findings bear only tangentially on the real phenomenon of delinquency, research on religiosity is doubly vulnerable to this charge. We shall not here be concerned with what religiosity really is. Instead, we shall take for granted the view that religiosity is many things; that these things should not be inextricably bound to

[12] All of which gives unusually detailed information on the extent of non-response bias in the "questionnaire" sample. For analysis of the extent and effect of nonresponse bias, see Alan B. Wilson, Travis Hirschi, and Glen Elder, "Technical Report # 1: Secondary School Survey," (Berkeley: Survey Research Center, University of California, 1965), pp. 3-21, and Travis Hirschi, *Causes of Delinquency* (Berkeley: University of California Press, 1969).

each other by definition, but may be linked to each other by conjecture and hypothesis.[13]

The usual beginning point in studies of the effects of religion on delinquency is a measure of church attendance. In our opinion, this is as it should be. The view that church attendance should reduce delinquency is accepted by sociologists, layman, and the clergy, not because it keeps the child off the streets for a few hours each week, but because participation in religious activities is believed to promote: (1) the internalization and/or acceptance of moral values, the belief that one's fellows deserve fair and just treatment; (2) acceptance of the legitimacy of legal authority, of the law and its agents; (3) belief in the literal existence of a supernatural world, and therefore the belief that one may be punished in the world to come for violations in the here and now.

We begin by examining the effects of church attendance on the attitudes and beliefs that in this view *link* such attendance to conformity with conventional codes of conduct.

Religion and Moral Values

Sociological theorists have been generally unwilling to see in delinquency evidence of immorality. In fact, sociologists have become so leery of "morality" as a concept that they are likely to stress the view that "illegality" and "immorality" are not the same thing, and, by extension, have little to do with one another. The clergyman, in contrast, has remained steadfast in the belief that morality and delinquency are intimately related, that most illegal acts are also immoral, and that the church has therefore an important role to play in the prevention of delinquency. Therefore, we must first ask: Is church attendance related to morality as the latter is traditionally defined by the church?

Two items on the questionnaire seem particularly appropriate as measures of morality. The students were asked whether they agreed or disagreed with these statements:

To get ahead, you have to do some things that are not right.
Suckers deserve to be taken advantage of.

Table 1 shows the relations between these items and church attendance. Although seven of the eight relations are in the direction favoring the view that attendance at religious services promotes acceptance of moral values, in all cases but one the relations are miniscule. For all intents and purposes, then, church attendance does not affect acceptance of the moral values assumed to be important deterrents of delinquency. Students who attend church are as likely as non-attenders to believe that those unable to defend themselves from

[13]Rodney Stark and Charles Y. Glock, *American Piety: The Nature of Religious Commitment* (Berkeley and Los Angeles: University of California Press, 1968), pp. 11-21.

exploitation deserve such exploitation; they are as likely to believe that success in worldly terms requires, and by implication justifies, the breaking of the moral law.

Table 1.   *Percent Accepting Amoral Statements, by Church Attendance, Race, and Sex*

	Church Attendance					
	Once a Week	2-3 Times a Month	Once a Month– Holidays	Hardly Ever	Never	Gamma[a]
Suckers deserve to be taken advantage of						
White Boys	25 (610)	29 (187)	30 (220)	27 (360)	32 (211)	−.04
Negro Boys	43 (525)	41 (191)	43 (121)	53 (124)	40 (40)	−.03
White Girls	16 (363)	17 (82)	23 (79)	19 (115)	19 (36)	−.03
Negro Girls	36 (541)	37 (147)	46 (46)	25 (60)	32 (19)	.01
To get ahead, you have to do some things that are not right						
White Boys	26 (610)	30 (187)	35 (220)	28 (360)	35 (211)	−.08
Negro Boys	49 (525)	48 (191)	60 (121)	50 (124)	52 (40)	−.04
White Girls	20 (363)	18 (82)	16 (79)	24 (115)	31 (36)	−.09
Negro Girls	31 (541)	38 (147)	28 (46)	57 (60)	58 (19)	−.14[b]

[a] In all tables presented, gamma was computed before the table was collapsed to its present form. For example, there were originally three categories of response to "Suckers deserve to be taken advantage of"–agree, undecided, disagree. The double- and triple-negative problems make straightforward interpretation of the sign of the relation difficult. In the table on this page, the minus sign means literally that as non-attendance increases agreement with the statement declines.

[b] χ^2 significant at one percent level.

Religion and Acceptance of Worldly Authority

Sutherland has said that persons become criminal because of an excess of definitions favorable to violation of law.[14] Although Sutherland did not specify the content of these attitudes and values conducive to law violation, attitudes toward the law itself and toward the agents of the legal system, especially the police, are obviously relevant. Once again, then, we are led to expect a relation

[14]Edwin H. Sutherland and Donald R. Cressey, *Principles of Criminology* (6th ed.) (Philadelphia: J. B. Lippincott, 1960), p. 78.

between religiosity and non-criminality, for the religious-moral laws advocated by the churches are largely incorporated in legal restraints. Most crimes, in other words, are also violations of the teachings of the church.[15] Furthermore, the churches strongly encourage respect for the law and cooperation with legal authorities.

The items used to determine the efficacy of the church in promoting such respect are straightforward. Students were asked to respond to the following statements:

> It is all right to get around the law if you can get away with it.
> I have a lot of respect for the (local) police.

Table 2 shows that students who attend church frequently are very slightly more likely than infrequent attenders to express respect for the police, and are slightly less likely to agree that law violation is okay if you don't get caught.

Table 2. *Respect for Law and Respect for the Police by Church Attendance, Race, and Sex*

Percent agreeing all right to get around the law	Church Attendance					
	Once a Week	2-3 Times a Month	Once a Month– Holidays	Hardly Ever	Never	Gamma
White Boys	10 (542)	8 (179)	18 (211)	9 (343)	17 (207)	$-.13^a$
Negro Boys	21 (407)	20 (169)	28 (105)	32 (102)	28 (36)	$-.10$
White Girls	6 (333)	6 (78)	7 (75)	5 (112)	3 (31)	$-.09$
Negro Girls	18 (477)	20 (133)	35 (43)	20 (54)	47 (19)	$-.22^a$
Percent expressing respect for the police						
White Boys	65 (610)	63 (187)	62 (220)	60 (360)	49 (211)	$.09^a$
Negro Boys	62 (525)	65 (191)	56 (121)	49 (124)	37 (40)	$.09^a$
White Girls	73 (363)	76 (82)	62 (79)	69 (115)	56 (36)	$.08$
Negro Girls	65 (541)	62 (147)	67 (46)	62 (60)	52 (19)	$.05$

[a] Significant at the five percent level (x^2).

15 Elliott, *op. cit.*, p. 364.

Seven of the eight relations are in the direction predicted from the assumption that exposure to religious teachings fosters acceptance of the legitimacy of worldly authority. In this case, four of the seven relations are statistically significant. We would conclude, then, on the basis of these data, that church attendance has some, very weak, effect on the development of attitudes apparently favorable to obedience to law.[16]

Religion and Supernatural Sanctions

Sociologists are as likely as churchmen to stress the fear of supernatural sanctions in the maintenance of conformity. According to Ross,[17] for example, Christianity has made the doctrine of a future life "a deterrent influence of the strongest kind." The idea is simple: In the life beyond death, the lot of each man will be at least in part determined by his thoughts and actions during his worldly existence. Since crimes unseen by worldly authorities are seen by watchers in another world, the fear of hell operates silently and efficiently to assure conformity to conventional, worldly norms.

It would appear obvious that participation in organized religious activities contributes to belief in the existence of a life beyond death populated by spirits or persons capable of punishing one for wrongdoings while on earth. Since we have already seen cases where obvious relations were nonexistent, however, in Table 3 we show the relation between church attendance and an index of belief in supernatural sanctions. The index was constructed from responses to two items: "There is a life beyond death," and, "The devil actually exists." Among all groups except Negro girls (where belief in the devil and a life beyond death is

Table 3. *Percent High on Index of Belief in Supernatural Sanctions by Church Attendance, Race, and Sex*

	Church Attendance					
	Once a Week	2-3 Times a Month	Once a Month– Holidays	Hardly Ever	Never	Gamma
White Boys	49 (505)	28 (162)	23 (194)	19 (334)	12 (187)	−.40
Negro Boys	50 (357)	34 (149)	30 (98)	21 (94)	32 (31)	−.30
White Girls	49 (327)	34 (79)	23 (74)	19 (108)	31 (32)	−.34
Negro Girls	42 (447)	40 (126)	36 (39)	42 (50)	53 (15)	−.07

[16]Other analysis shows that respect for the law and for the police decline rather markedly with age in the present sample. Although church attendance also declines with age, the relations in Table 2 survive when age is held relatively constant.

[17]Edward A. Ross, *Social Control* (New York: The Macmillan Company, 1920), p. 131.

common even among those who do not attend church) differences by church attendance are marked. Those attending church with some frequency are much more likely to believe in the literal existence of a supernatural realm than those only rarely attending church.

To this point we have examined three presumed consequences or correlates of religious activity thought by many to be important in the prevention of delinquency. One of the three routes by which religion might affect delinquency has been to all intents and purposes closed: those attending church are not more likely than those not attending church to accept moral and ethical principles opposed to the commission of illegal acts.[18] A second possible route from religiosity to non-delinquency remains only partially open: students attending church are only slightly more likely to have attitudes favorable to law and the police. If religiosity does affect delinquency, its major path of influence must be through its effect on belief in the existence of other-worldly sanctions, for it is only here that differences by church attendance are in any way pronounced.

We have seen the effect of church attendance on the variables through which it presumably affects delinquency. Are those variables themselves actually related to delinquency? According to Table 4, that set of variables unrelated to church attendance, which we have called measures of acceptance of moral values, *is* indeed related to delinquency. Students agreeing that suckers deserve what they get, that in order to achieve success in life one must occasionally sacrifice what one considers right, are much more likely than students disagreeing with these statements to have committed delinquent acts, by both self-report and by official measures.

According to Table 5, respect for the law and for the police, while only weakly related to church attendance, are both strongly negatively related to the commission of delinquent acts, again by both the self-report and official measures, and within all race-sex categories.

But when we turn to the one intervening variable strongly influenced by church attendance, the pattern reverses: *Students who believe in the Devil and in a life after death are just as likely to commit delinquent acts as are students who do not believe in a supernatural world* (as Table 6 shows).

On the basis of what we know, then, there is very little reason to expect a relation between religious activity and delinquency. The beliefs such activity affects are essentially unrelated to delinquency; the beliefs and attitudes the church has been traditionally assumed to affect are in fact strongly related to delinquency, but, alas for the church, it does not influence these beliefs and attitudes. And, indeed, Table 7 shows that church attendance is essentially unrelated to delinquency. *Students who attend church every week are as likely to have committed delinquent acts as students who attend church only rarely or not at all.* None of the relations in Table 7 approaches statistical significance.

---

[18]The lack of relationship between church attendance and moral and ethical principles in these data is supported by the more general finding that commitment to the tenets of Christian ethicalism, such as "Love thy neighbor" or "Do good unto others," is not related to commitment to Christian orthodoxy, or to church attendance, praying or participation in church activities. See: Stark and Glock, *op. cit.* Ch. 9.

Table 4. *Percent Committing Two or More Delinquent Acts by Acceptance of Moral Values*

Suckers deserve to be taken advantage of

	Agree	Undecided	Disagree	Gamma
White Boys (SR)[a]	30 (440)	22 (324)	12 (824)	−.27
Negro Boys (SR)	26 (230)	28 (217)	17 (319)	−.12
White Girls (SR)	11 (74)	3 (131)	5 (411)	−.03
Negro Girls (SR)	14 (174)	6 (179)	7 (328)	−.21
White Boys (Off)[b]	12 (440)	10 (324)	6 (824)	−.20
Negro Boys (Off)	23 (240)	23 (231)	15 (330)	−.17

To get ahead, you have to do some things that are not right

	Agree	Undecided	Disagree	Gamma
White Boys (SR)[a]	27 (468)	26 (264)	13 (856)	−.26
Negro Boys (SR)	26 (254)	28 (159)	17 (327)	−.12
White Girls (SR)	11 (71)	11 (103)	3 (429)	−.29
Negro Girls (SR)	10 (154)	10 (135)	6 (388)	−.14
White Boys (Off)[b]	12 (468)	11 (264)	7 (856)	−.18
Negro Boys (Off)	22 (259)	22 (162)	18 (333)	−.09

[a] Self-reported delinquent acts.

[b] Official delinquent acts. The police records of girls were not available.

None of the differences is of theoretical or practical significance, nor were they affected by denominational controls. Participation in religious activities and belief in a supernatural sanctioning system have no effect on delinquent activity.

Further evidence for the same conclusion is provided by the lack of a relation between the mother's church attendance and delinquency, by the absence of important differences between those students who belong to a church and those who do not, and by the fact that the several measures of religiosity are unrelated to yet another form of unethical conduct, cheating on tests—thus replicating a finding that goes back almost forty years.[19]

[19]Hugh Hartshorne and Mark A. May, *Studies in Deceit* (New York: Macmillan, 1930), esp. pp. 357-362.

Table 5.   *Percent Committing Two or More Delinquent Acts by*
Respect for the Police and Respect for Law

It is all right to get around the law if you can get away with it

	Agree	Undecided	Disagree	Gamma
White Boys (SR)	44 (177)	29 (259)	13 (1081)	−.41
Negro Boys (SR)	33 (208)	27 (181)	16 (477)	−.18
White Girls (SR)	18 (38)	12 (76)	4 (528)	−.42
Negro Girls (SR)	15 (154)	9 (136)	5 (458)	−.25
White Boys (Off)	16 (183)	12 (264)	7 (1089)	−.33
Negro Boys (Off)	27 (212)	19 (187)	17 (482)	−.22

I have a lot of respect for the police

	Agree	Undecided	Disagree	Gamma
White Boys (SR)	13 (969)	23 (396)	39 (223)	.34
Negro Boys (SR)	15 (463)	32 (219)	33 (183)	.26
White Girls (SR)	4 (450)	9 (156)	14 (42)	.32
Negro Girls (SR)	6 (460)	7 (152)	15 (137)	.16
White Boys (Off)	5 (969)	10 (396)	22 (223)	.33
Negro Boys (Off)	17 (472)	19 (222)	30 (187)	.19

Discussion

There are, of course, studies showing weak relations between church attendance and non-delinquency. In fact, two of the most respected pieces of research in the field, those of Nye and of the Gluecks[20] show that children who attend church regularly are somewhat less likely than non-attenders to be delinquent. If we grant that Nye's and the Gluecks' data are as good as our own, it may appear that we have contributed merely to the inconsistency and inconclusiveness of delinquency research. In our opinion such a conclusion is not warranted. Neither Nye nor the Gluecks report anything beyond the fact of a

[20]F. Ivan Nye, *Family Relationships and Delinquent Behavior* (New York: Wiley, 1958), pp. 35-36. Sheldon and Eleanor Glueck, *Unraveling Juvenile Delinquency* (Cambridge: Harvard University Press, 1950), pp. 166-167.

Table 6. *Percent Committing Two or More Delinquent Acts, by Belief in Existence of Other-Worldly Sanctions, Race, and Sex*

| | Index of Belief in Supernatural Sanctions | | | |
	Low	Medium	High	Gamma
White Boys (SR)	19 (320)	20 (641)	16 (425)	−.03
Negro Boys (SR)	19 (91)	21 (363)	25 (300)	.09
White Girls (SR)	7 (127)	5 (257)	5 (234)	.11
Negro Girls (SR)	11 (81)	8 (314)	8 (275)	−.07
White Boys (Off)	8 (329)	9 (660)	8 (433)	.02
Negro Boys (Off)	16 (99)	22 (379)	17 (312)	−.07

Table 7. *Percent Committing Two or More Delinquent Acts by Church Attendance, Race, and Sex*

| | Church Attendance | | | | | |
	Once a Week	2-3 Times a Month	Once a Month–Holidays	Hardly Ever	Never	Gamma
White Boys (SR)	17 (545)	21 (186)	23 (210)	20 (346)	22 (206)	.02
Negro Boys (SR)	22 (424)	24 (172)	21 (112)	25 (114)	40 (38)	.10
White Girls (SR)	5 (337)	5 (79)	8 (79)	4 (112)	15 (34)	.01
Negro Girls (SR)	7 (488)	10 (137)	19 (43)	10 (59)	6 (18)	.11
White Boys (Off)	7 (554)	6 (187)	13 (220)	9 (360)	11 (211)	.06
Negro Boys (Off)	19 (445)	22 (191)	18 (121)	24 (124)	25 (40)	.08

small relation. Had they attempted to determine why church attendance is or is not related to delinquency in their samples, as we have done, they might very well have concluded that church attendance is not in fact *causally* related to delinquency. The fact that there are many reasons to expect a causal relation between church attendance and delinquency is not sufficient reason to accept an observed relation without further analysis.

This touches on a problem endemic in evaluations of social science research. Had our investigation shown that religion is a deterrent to delinquency, we would have been accused of demonstrating the obvious. But the point in testing common sense notions is demonstrated by the fact that this one, as with many others, is simply wrong. Unfortunately, when social science reports against common sense, it is too often accused of falsehood, inadequate methods, or plain stupidity. Whenever one does research on religion this problem becomes especially acute. A common response from religionists to findings they dislike is to dismiss them by redefining religiousness in a way that excludes all culpability.[21] Thus, some will be prompted to respond that delinquency *is* irreligiosity, and that no *truly* religious youths commit delinquent acts. Such assertions are irrefutable, for they are true by definition. But, if one grants that religiousness has several components, and that they are capable of varying to some extent independently of each other, then we may conclude on the basis of these data that such central aspects of religiosity as attendance at religious services and belief in the existence of a supernatural world are unrelated to the legality or, for that matter, the morality of behaviour.

This, of course, does not say anything about the prevailing level of law-abiding behavior or morality in American society. On the contrary, the roots of morality, of law-abiding conduct are probably much the same as they have always been: attachment to, or, if you will, love for one's neighbor and awareness of and concern for the real-life costs of crime. The church is irrelevant to delinquency because it fails to instill in its members love for their neighbors and because belief in the possibility of pleasure and pain in another world cannot now, and perhaps never could, compete with the pleasures and pains of everyday life.

21 Stark and Glock, *op. cit.*, Ch. 1.

Chapter Nine

Prejudice and the Churches*

Rodney Stark and Charles Y. Glock

Virtually every clergyman in America would agree that authentic religious commitment precludes racial and religious prejudice. But despite such unanimity, it is not at all clear what role religious convictions and religious institutions play in contemporary prejudice.

One is often tempted to accept the picture of the church suggested by the sight of priests, ministers, and nuns marching in Selma, Washington, and Chicago, or by the claims that clergymen such as Milwaukee's Father James Groppi are the vanguard of a "new breed" of Christians who are leading a crusade against sin, defined in social rather than personal terms.

But despite all these signs, one must not assume too readily that religion is always a powerful and reliable force against prejudice. For there are many discrepant indications that must also be considered. Indeed, clergymen have been forced from parishes for expressing even moderate views on racial and religious prejudice. And for every Father Groppi there always seems to be another clergyman who is willing to lead a counterdemonstration. For every minister who speaks out against prejudice there are a number of others who either do not want to get involved or fear that to do so would upset the laity. Furthermore, while it is obvious that many Christians are moved by their faith to regard all men as brothers, it is equally obvious that the majority of those who throw rocks at Negro marchers, who picket schools to prevent integration, or who become agitated about keeping Jews off their local school boards or out of their clubs, regard themselves as Christians. What is one to make of these contradictions?

*Rodney Stark and Charles Y. Glock, "Prejudice and the Churches," in *Prejudice, U.S.A.*, ed. Charles Y. Glock and Ellen Siegelman (New York: Praeger Publishers, Inc., 1969). Reprinted with permission of the authors and the publisher.

This chapter attempts to bring together what we have learned about the role of religion in contemporary prejudice from the Berkeley research program[1] and from similar studies of prejudice. First, the extent to which prejudice exists within the churches is assessed. The specifically religious factors that give rise to prejudice or that tend to reduce it are then considered. (Because of the limits of available data, we shall confine our attention to American Christian denominations.)

The Incidence of Prejudice

How much prejudice exists within the churches? The answer to this question depends very much on the level at which the churches are examined: at the official, or bureaucratic, level; among the general clergy; or at the level of the laity. At each level, it is important to assess religious prejudice, that is, prejudice against persons of other faiths or denominations; racial prejudice; and, finally, the view of the role of the churches in combatting prejudice.

The Official Churches

At the official level of churches—i.e., the national bureaucratic and organizational apparatus, consisting of church leaders, commissions, agencies, governing bodies, councils of bishops, and the like—there is virtual unanimity; nearly all the major denominations have spoken out forcefully and repeatedly against prejudice, both religious and racial. In the area of religious prejudice, all major denominations are officially opposed to anti-Semitism. Furthermore, while the recent Vatican Council statement condemning the widespread belief that Jews are collectively guilty for the Crucifixion received considerable publicity, similar statements had been made a good deal earlier by most American Protestant bodies. On religious prejudice against other non-Christian groups, the churches have been less specific, but there is a growing moral sensitivity. At its 1968 national convention, for example, the Lutheran Church in America adopted a position on religious liberty which explicitly includes atheists and agnostics.

On matters of racial prejudice, the churches have been even more unanimous and outspoken. All major denominations have issued sharp condemnations of racial prejudice and specifically opposed discrimination in schooling, housing, and jobs. In addition to noble words, church bodies have also done some impressive deeds—from rewriting Sunday school and devotional materials to developing agencies devoted to action to opposed prejudice and discrimination.

---

[1]Findings on the role of religion in prejudice have appeared in Charles Y. Glock and Rodney Stark, *Christian Beliefs and Anti-Semitism* (New York: Harper and Row, 1966), in Gary T. Marx, *Protest and Prejudice* (New York: Harper and Row, 1967), Chap. 4, and in Rodney Stark, Bruce Foster, Charles Y. Glock, and Harold Quinley, *Wayward Shepherds: Prejudice and the Protestant Clergy,* (New York: Harper and Row, 1971).

The Clergy

When we look behind the superstructure of the churches and consider the views of the entire clergy rather than only those of religious leaders, we must make some important qualifications to the picture we have just sketched. If the official churches unanimously denounce prejudice and are committed to an active role in opposing it, the clergy as a whole are not unanimous on these same matters; a substantial minority of the clergy displays religious and racial prejudice.[2] Furthermore, even among unprejudiced clergymen there is a minority that does not believe the church ought to take an active role in the struggle for brotherhood. Nevertheless, the majority have relatively enlightened attitudes toward persons of other religions and races and do support the official actions of the churches. To give substance to these general remarks, let us consider some relevant research findings.

As already mentioned, officially the churches denounced the notion of collective and continuing Jewish guilt for the Crucifixion. The majority of the clergy support the official denunciations, but a minority continue to accept even the extreme forms of these notions. A recent national study of Protestant clergymen, conducted by Jeffrey K. Hadden, revealed that 6 per cent of the Methodist, 7 per cent of the Presbyterian, 21 percent of the American Lutheran, 22 percent of the American Baptist, and 38 percent of the Missouri Synod Lutheran clergymen in his sample agreed with the statement that "The reason Jews have so much trouble is because God is punishing them for rejecting Jesus."[3]

As with attitudes toward Jews, clerical attitudes toward blacks are also mixed. Again, however, what data there are reveal that the majority of Christian clergy have fairly enlightened attitudes. For example, 80 per cent of the Protestant ministers in the Hadden study rejected the statement that "Negroes could solve many of their own problems if they were not so irresponsible and carefree about life," and only about one in ten opposed the civil rights movement. Among Roman Catholic diocesan priests, also about 10 percent disapprove of the civil rights movement, according to Joseph Fichter's recent study of America's priests.[4]

The clergy, by and large, also supports an active role for the church in the struggle against discrimination. Here again one finds a minority that denies that the church has any business trying to reform society. However, a substantial majority does support an activist role for the churches and the clergy.

More than 75 percent of the Protestant clergy in Hadden's samples agreed that "For the most part, the churches have been woefully inadequate in facing up to the civil rights issues." Similarly, large majorities favored direct action by the

---

[2]See Jeffrey K. Hadden, *The Gathering Storm in the Churches* (Garden City, N.Y.: Doubleday, 1969).

[3]Hadden, *op. cit.*

[4] See Joseph Fichter, *America's Forgotten Priests: What Are They Saying* (New York: Harper & Row, 1968).

churches on social and moral issues. Indeed, nearly 80 percent felt that if the church did not speak out on such matters, its very existence would be threatened. When direct action on the part of clergymen to protest racial injustice was considered, the clerical support was somewhat diminished. Still, a strong majority were in favor. As would be expected, such support declined considerably among Southern clergy and among clergy in conservative denominations such as the Missouri Synod.

Although somewhat marred, the picture that emerges from an examination both of church pronouncements on prejudice and of clerical attitudes is a hopeful one. It would appear that the churches ought to be able to play a significant role in the struggle against prejudice.

The Laity

When we turn to rank-and-file church members, we get an entirely different perspective. The facts are that Christian laymen, as a group, are a rather prejudiced lot. It is perfectly obvious that large numbers of people in the churches, for whom Christian ethics provide an important basis for love, understanding, and compassion, are not prejudiced. But the majority of church members are prejudiced; furthermore, they deny the right of the churches to challenge their prejudices.

Looking first at religious prejudice, the following picture emerges: from half to two-thirds of American Christians would deny civil liberties to a person who does not believe in God. They would bar him from holding public office and remove him from a teaching position in the public schools. Similarly, half of American Christians continue to blame the Jews for the Crucifixion despite official pronouncements to the contrary. Worse yet, 33 percent of American Christians score high and another 40 percent score medium-high on an index made up of strongly anti-Semitic statements.[5]

Religious prejudice varies from denomination to denomination. Catholics are a bit less prone to such prejudice than are Protestants, and conservative Protestant bodies are somewhat more prejudiced than liberal Protestant groups. Nevertheless, religious prejudice is sufficiently widespread among laymen in all Christian bodies to constitute an important problem.

Turning to racial prejudice, one sees no change in this depressing picture. Among white Protestant and Catholic church members in the San Francisco-Bay Area of California, nearly half say they would move if several Negro families moved into their block. A third think Negroes are less intelligent; nearly half blame Communists and other radicals for racial tension.[6] These data were collected in 1963 before any of the riots. Undoubtedly things are worse today. Indeed, a recent national survey conducted by the National Opinion Research

[5]For example, "Jewish boys were less likely than Christian boys to volunteer for service in the armed forces during the last war"; "Jews are more likely than Christians to cheat in business"; "Jews, in general, are inclined to be more loyal to Israel than to America." Glock and Stark, *op. cit.*, pp. 124, 202.

[6]Some of these findings appear in Glock and Stark, *op. cit.*

Center for Jeffrey Hadden, 1967, showed that 89 percent of the Christian laity felt that Negroes ought to take advantage of the opportunities society offers them and quit their protesting. And sadly, too, only those who rarely or never attended church dropped significantly below this proportion.[7] By way of contrast, only a third of Protestant clergy would support this view of Negro protest.[8]

This brings us to a final point about the contemporary Christian church member. Not only does he differ sharply from the official church and the clergy on the matter of his prejudice, he strongly opposes the role being played by the churches in overcoming discrimination. Thus, 70 percent of the laity in the Hadden study denounced clerical involvement in social issues, such as civil rights. Indeed, data from a variety of recent studies indicate that the majority of laymen want their church to tend to the private religious needs of its members and to stay out of such questions as peace, social justice, and human rights.[9]

It is obvious that what one decides about the role of the churches in the battle against prejudice depends greatly on the level at which he examines the churches. For a moment let us think of the churches as a system having three parts. if we think of the official level as formulating the intentions of the churches, and the clergy as the means for achieving these intentions, it follows that the laity are supposed to exhibit the fruit of these intentions. But it is clear that although the intentions and the means are there, the intended consequences have not been forthcoming. Most of the laity continue to bear ill-will toward other races and religions. They may claim to love their brothers, but they are very finicky about whom they will call "brother." Thus, the system by which the words of the official churches are supposed to be translated into the hearts of the laity simply fails to operate effectively. The critical question is: Why?

Religious Influences on Prejudice

It seems clear that many Christians are able to justify racial and religious prejudice despite the official opposition of the churches to which they adhere. Thus, one must ask if it is possible that the churches are perhaps unwittingly doing something that contributes to this ability to rationalize prejudice.

Broadly speaking we are concerned with two classes of factors that influence prejudice among the laity. The first of these is theological, i.e., teaching and doctrine that bear upon racial and religious prejudice and, in some aspects, seem to promote prejudice while in others appear to provide the churches with

---

[7]See Hadden, *op. cit.*

[8]See Hadden, *op. cit.*

[9]See Earl R. Babbie, "A Religious Profile of Episcopal Churchwomen," *The Pacific Churchman* (January, 1967); Charles Y. Glock, Benjamin B. Ringer, and Earl R. Babbie, *To Comfort and To Challenge* (Berkeley and Los Angeles: University of California Press, 1967). Findings from the Berkeley project which also support this tendency among laymen will appear in Rodney Stark and Charles Y. Glock, *The Poor in Spirit; Sources of Religious Commitment* (Berkeley and Los Angeles: University of California Press, forthcoming).

powerful means for overcoming it. The second class is represented by institutional constraints. These are features of the organization of the churches that affect the power of religious leaders to influence the views of the laity.

Theological Factors

The idea that Christian beliefs may be a source of prejudice is likely to be rejected out of hand by theologians and churchmen. Their view of the faith rules out the possibility of such a connection. Nevertheless, there can be a link between theology and prejudice, especially as doctrine is comprehended in the pew. Interpretations of the faith that are widespread among laymen are often not conducive to tolerance; they serve, instead, as a supporting dynamic for prejudice. This is true of both religious and racial prejudice, although the theological elements active in the two types are sometimes different.

Examining first the prejudice of Christian laymen toward persons of other faiths, such as Jews or Hindus, or even between Catholics and Protestants, a significant theological buttress for such prejudice is what we have called particularism—the notion that only one's own religion is true and legitimate and that others are therefore false.[10] In contemporary Christianity, particularism continues to flourish in interpretations of the doctrines that Christ offers the only way to salvation and that to reject him is to be condemned to eternal damnation. Unless such notions are held with a degree of sophistication that seems beyond the capacity of many laymen, they readily support prejudice. If others are seen as committed to a false religion and thus condemned to hell, it is but a short step to seeing them as inferior and immoral. Indeed, a commonly held particularistic doctrine holds that only through Christian teachings is morality made possible.

The greater the strength with which particularistic theological views are held by Christians, and the more narrowly they are defined, the greater the hostility Christians harbor toward persons they see as religious outsiders: for example, Jews, Hindus, Moslems, and, of course, atheists and agnostics. Indeed, particularism generates hatred between Catholics and Protestants, and even between some Protestant groups.

When particularism is combined with the belief that the Jews crucified Christ and thus called down on themselves a collective and eternal curse, Christians display considerable vulnerability to general anti-Semitic beliefs. A Christian who sees the Jews as religiously illegitimate finds it difficult to resist other negative images of Jews.

These days few, if any, theologians would advocate a narrow particularism that would deny all religious virtue to non-Christians, and so far as we know no church officially endorses such doctrines. Indeed, the statements on religious liberty issued by various churches in the past several years uniformly condemn intolerance toward persons of other faiths. Nevertheless, these actions have had little impact upon rank-and-file Christians. A great many laymen continue to

[10]See Glock and Stark, *Christian Beliefs and Anti-Semitism*, op. cit.

find theological support for their religious prejudices in such doctrines as the necessity of accepting Christ in order to be saved. Many feel that persons who refuse to accept the glad tidings have only themselves to blame for subsequent misfortunes.

Turning from religious to racial prejudice, the part played by theology is not so obvious. Christian particularism, while a potent source of prejudice toward Jews and other non-Christians, does not generate prejudice toward Negroes. Negroes by and large are Christian and not susceptible to the charge of rejecting Christ. Nor is any other theological rationale for racial prejudice immediately apparent. For example, only a few extremists argue that racial inferiority and segregation are proper Christian views, basing their view on certain interpretations of passages in the Old Testament.

In our initial investigations we failed to detect any very important relationships between customary measures of religious commitment and the considerable racial prejudice of church members. We found a higher incidence of racial prejudice among those who held conservative theological views, and among those who participated in church activities, private devotions, and the like. These relationships were weak, however, and did not reveal any theological factor that contributed significantly to racial prejudice. The evidence of widespread racial prejudice among professing and practicing Christians, however, and the opposition among parishioners to active church involvement in civil rights, seemed nevertheless to hint that a subtle theological factor might be at work despite appearances to the contrary. Thus, we pursued the matter. Our investigations are still not complete but, briefly, here is what we have discovered so far:

Underlying traditional Christian thought is an image of man as a free actor, as essentially unfettered by social circumstances, free to choose and thus free to effect his own salvation.[11] This free-will conception of man has been central to the doctrines of sin and salvation. For only if man is totally free does it seem just to hold him responsible for his acts, to punish him for his sins, and to demand repentance. Correspondingly, to the extent that a man's destiny is fixed by external forces, to that extent the notion of guilt is unjust. It has been widely recognized that this conception of human nature has been a mainspring in the development of Western civilization and has greatly influenced our attitudes on personal accountability and the ingredients of personal success. An image of man as free and responsible lies behind such notions as rugged individualism, the self-made man, and the justification of wealth on the basis of merit. In short, Christian thought and thus Western civilization are permeated with the idea that men are individually in control of, and responsible for, their own destinies. If I am really the "captain of my soul" and "the master of my fate," then I have no one but myself to thank or to blame for what happens to me.

In the modern world, of course, these radical notions of unfettered free will

---

[11]Our initial discussion of free-will doctrines appeared in Charles Y. Glock and Rodney Stark, *Religion and Society in Tension* (Chicago: Rand McNally, 1965), Chap. 15. See also Chap. 21 in this volume.

have been somewhat modified. Still, a great many persons adhere to them in relatively pristine form, and they serve as lenses through which these people view and judge the behavior of others. The significance of this for prejudice is that radical and traditional Christian images of man prompt those who hold them to put the blame for disadvantage upon the individuals who are disadvantaged. A radical free-will image of man makes for an inability to perceive the effect of those forces outside the individual which may utterly dominate his circumstances. Thus, efforts to change the condition of the disadvantaged through social reforms appear irrelevant at best. Instead, one is led to dismiss the misery of the disadvantaged as due to their own shortcomings.

In pursuing this line of thought in our empirical studies we found that such an image of man tends to prevail among more active Christian church members and is strongly reflected in their disproportionate commitment to conservative politics.

The results of our empirical analysis lend themselves to the following interpretation: a free-will image of man lies at the root of Christian prejudice toward Negroes and of negative attitudes toward the civil rights movement; it also underlies the rejection of programs underwritten by the church and the government to improve the situation of minorities. The simple fact seems to be that a great many church people, because they believe men are mainly in control of their individual destinies, think that Negroes are themselves largely to blame for their present misery. It is not that these Christians condone the social forces that deprive black people, but rather that they simply do not recognize the existence of such forces in the world. They do recognize that Negroes are collectively disadvantaged. But the conclusion that logically follows from their theology is that this disadvantage must be the result of a racial shortcoming. For how else can one explain such a widespread racial circumstance, if one sees the world in primarily individualistic terms?

The flavor of this perspective on reality is perhaps best conveyed by those who accept it. Here are several comments written at the end of our questionnaires by Christian church members who took part in one of our major studies.

These are the views of a Protestant dentist:

> When I see the pictures of the poverty of Negroes on the TV and in the press I feel as sorry as anyone. But I am more depressed by all the "social-engineering" schemes that are being proposed to improve the lot of Negroes and others. Not only will these schemes destroy our free-enterprise heritage, but they will take away the only chance for the Negroes to live better lives. They do nothing about the real problem. The Negro is lazy, and short-sighted. He does not save his money or work to the future. And this is the only way anyone ever betters himself. If we turn to socialism for the answer we will simply make it impossible for the Negro to ever be better off, because under socialism individual initiative is destroyed, not created. We will all live in slums. Will that make Negroes feel better?

A Catholic housewife wrote: "The Irish came to this country way after the Negro and had it just as tough. Today we have an Irish president of the United States. The difference is hard work and the blessings of religion."

To the extent that Christian theology and institutions support a radical view of individual freedom and accountability, their members can be expected to reject the very premises upon which the battle against prejudice and discrimination rests. For if the disadvantaged condition of minority groups is proof of their unworthiness, how can people be expected to support measures to help them? In the eyes of such Christian laymen the doctrines of the church and its efforts on behalf of human rights often seem contradictory.

As we shall see shortly, this seeming contradiction provides a source of conflict that appears to accelerate a growing alienation between the churches and the laity. Furthermore, the prevalence of such doctrines among black Christians similarly affects Negroes' definitions of their own circumstances. Gary Marx's recent study of militancy in the black community revealed a strong negative correlation between religious commitment and the desire for social justice and equality.[12] The more committed a Negro was to Christian beliefs and institutions the readier he was to see the lowly condition of Negroes as self-inflicted. Indeed, two-thirds of the urban Negroes in Marx's samples agreed that "Negroes who want to work hard can get ahead just as easily as anyone else," and about half agreed that "Before Negroes are given equal rights, they have to show that they deserve them."

Our analysis showed that the conception of man as wholly free was related to racial prejudice, but it was even more closely related to opposing social action to improve the lot of disadvantaged minorities. Most lay opposition to church and clerical participation in human rights activities stems from the conviction that people get what they deserve in this life and the next.

A second interpretation of Christian doctrine that reinforces opposition to efforts to improve the lot of the disadvantaged is what we call the "miracle motif." This is the belief, most prevalent among evangelical Protestants, that if all men are brought to Christ, social evils will disappear through the miraculous regeneration of the individual by the Holy Spirit.

Billy Graham exemplifies this theological posture in his response to the social evils of our day. Recently, in answering critics' charges of indifference, Graham claimed to be a revolutionary. He argued that far from being unresponsive to the growing crises in human affairs—war, annihilation, inequality, hatred, and despair—he is actively pursuing a complete reconstruction of society. He claimed that he differs with his critics primarily on means, not ends. For Graham, the means are a miraculous revolution through individual salvation.

The perhaps unintended consequence of a preoccupation with individual salvation is a suspicion of, and often a hostility to, social and political efforts for reform. So long as there are men who have not been won to Christ, a sinful society is inevitable. Therefore, any attempts to reform society that do not require conversion to Christ are doomed to failure.

12See Gary T. Marx, *op. cit.*

The power of Christian faith to transform individual lives is evidenced by Christian saints and martyrs of the past and present. There is less evidence, however, that faith applies wholesale and that the vast body of persons calling themselves Christians have been so transformed. Nonetheless, individual conversion is the orientation which many Christians feel the church should take in confronting the problems of secular society.

This view is highly consistent with a free-will image of man. Indeed, like those who see man as in control of his own destiny, those for whom individual salvation is the key to social reform are prone to close their eyes to social factors that affect the individual. They hold that man chooses social disadvantage, social disadvantage does not choose man.

Beyond the notion that social change comes only through individual salvation, the miracle motif has broader implications for social reform. For a great many religious people, God is an active agent in worldly affairs. He ordains certain arrangements, sends certain tests, and in His own time brings about deliverance. We typically associate the fatalism inherent in this view with Eastern faiths, but it is not uncommon in Christianity. As a consequence, many people who might otherwise support or even help bring about changes, wait for God to do it. In his study of the black community, Gary Marx uncovered a strong vein of such sentiment.[13] About a third of Northern urban Negroes and more than half of Southern urban Negroes agreed that "Negroes should spend more time praying and less time demonstrating." One Negro clergyman interviewed in Marx's study said, "Praying is demonstrating." Another said, "I believe that if we all were pure . . . as we ought to be, there would be no struggle. When Peter was up, did the people march to free him? No. He prayed, and God did something about it."

Clearly, it is not only blacks who take this view. In a recent study of Episcopalian parishioners, it was found that when asked what the church could do to oppose war, a two to one majority proposed purely religious means such as increased missionary activity or prayer.[14]

When the expectation of divine intervention becomes the sole response of many Christians to the problems of this world, it impedes the adoption of this-worldly solutions. The churches themselves do not officially hold that Christians should totally rely upon prayer as a means for social reform. And the very Christians who advocate waiting for God to solve the problems of discrimination would think a man insane who, wanting to learn algebra, only prayed and never studied. Thus, one wonders if there isn't a certain hypocrisy in the ease with which some Christians prescribe prayer and individual salvation as the answer to the immediate problems of discrimination. One is reminded of the young Negro who said, "Man, I've had that praying jazz. We prayed for 400 years. God helps him who helps himself."

Thus far we have concentrated on theological factors that seem to foster prejudice. Obviously this would be an extremely biased assessment if we did not also give attention to the capacities of theology to serve as a bulwark against

[13]Marx, *op. cit.*

[14]See Glock, Ringer, and Babbie, *op. cit.*

prejudice. Christian claims about the stimulus for brotherhood, compassion, and love provided by the teachings of Christ are hardly partisan distortions. Rather, the ethical and moral teachings of the New Testament are rightfully used as a basis for all official church pronouncements on brotherhood. In our culture, such central ethical notions as "Love thy neighbor" and "Do unto others . . ." are pre-eminently religious teachings. Consequently we have also investigated the power of commitment to Christian ethics as a bulwark against prejudice, both religious and racial. Our findings produce an ironic contradiction, a basis both for future hope and for present disillusion.

First of all we find that as one might both hope and expect, individual commitment to Christian ethics provides a powerful antidote for prejudice. Persons high on ethical commitment are much less likely than others to hold religious and racial prejudices. *But the contradiction arises from equally persuasive evidence that commitment to Christian ethics is not related to other forms of Christian commitment.* Thus, while the ethics taught by the churches are a potent weapon against prejudice, it is not at all clear that the churches can claim direct credit for this fact. Instead, we found that those church members who accepted the other doctrines of the church, or who more regularly attended church or participated in church activities, were somewhat less likely to accept Christian ethics than those who were less orthodox in their beliefs and less regular in their participation.[15] That is to say, *Christians who are somewhat poorer church members judged on other criteria were more likely to be committed to the ethical teachings of the New Testament than were those who were otherwise better and more active members.* Thus, one is faced with the fact that Christian ethics is a powerful weapon against prejudice, but it is not clear that the churches are presently playing an important role in wielding this weapon.

We must emphasize that a great many devout Christians do accept Christian ethical teachings and are undoubtedly thereby inspired in their resolve to oppose prejudice. One need not look far to find many splendid examples. But when the whole range of Christians is examined, ethical commitment is, seemingly, not the typical product of religious devotion. When the churches search for support for their ethical teachings they are slightly more likely to find it among their most dormant members than they are to find it among the most active. Thus, the churches have not been effective in getting ethical doctrines across.

In addition to Christian ethics, a final doctrinal consideration is what we call the "moral cliché." Moral clichés are statements of high principle that are nearly unanimously agreed to but that people fail to manifest in concrete behavior. Let us consider some examples. Ninety-one per cent of both Catholic and Protestant church members in our California samples agreed with the statement "Love thy neighbor means that we should treat all races the same." Virtually identical proportions also agreed that "Negroes ought to have the same rights and opportunities as others." Such unanimous sentiments certainly seem promising

---

[15]See Rodney Stark and Charles Y. Glock, *American Piety: The Nature of Religious Commitment* (Berkeley and Los Angeles: University of California Press, 1968).

for the future of race relations. But despite having proclaimed their Christian love and advocated equal rights for Negroes, these people contradict themselves as soon as they are asked to make concrete applications. On the very page of the questionnaire on which the overwhelming majority professed their commitment to Christian brotherhood in principle, more than 40 percent of these same Christians said they would move if several Negro families came to live on their block, and nearly a third said they did not want to have Negroes in their churches.[16]

This discrepancy between principle and behavior illustrates a major difficulty in the role of the churches in combatting discrimination. It does little good for men to hold high principles if they are unable to recognize when and how these principles relate to their affairs. The failure of the churches is partly reflected in this inability. Often the churches are not really in a position to draw out the concrete implications of the high principles they teach. Instead they often seem to feel they must settle for teaching the abstract principles and hoping that parishioners will manage to see the implications on their own. We shall now try to say something about why this is so. What are some of the structural constraints that prevent the churches from translating their official intentions into demonstrations of Christian witness, especially among the laity?

Structural Constraints upon the Role of the Church

The central structural problem for the modern church is the question of authority. Generally speaking, it appears that often the church knows where it wants to lead, but as we have seen, it is often unable to do so.

Perhaps the most severe constraint upon the authority of the official church resides in the composition of its lay clientele: the factors that today best provide the churches with their members' commitment work against church authority, especially in dealing with social rather than personal problems. In a recent study of church members, the church has been characterized as having two main functions: the comforting and the challenging.[17] The comforting function is to provide persons with inner peace, with the ability to cope with their various existential anxieties. The challenging function, on the other hand, refers to efforts of the churches to exert moral leadership, to arouse members' interest in matters larger than themselves.

It was also suggested that there may be a certain inherent tension between these two functions of the churches, that persons whose religious commitment is grounded on the comforts of faith may be reluctant to accept the challenges of faith.

Research has borne out this suspicion. People who seek comfort for personal disappointments and anxieties through religion are opposed to those aspects of the churches that are devoted to a challenging function.[18] *But perhaps even*

[16]See Glock and Stark, *Christian Beliefs and Anti-Semitism.*

[17]See Glock, Ringer, and Babbie, *op. cit.*

[18]See Glock, Ringer, and Babbie, *op. cit.*; and Babbie, *op. cit.*

more serious is the fact that comfort-seekers constitute the bulk of the most active Christian laity: it is their money and participation upon which contemporary Christian organizations rest. Thus, there is a built-in resistance to the challenge function in the churches. Efforts to confront these people with challenges lead to conflict and often to rebellion. Thus, the churches risk the strongest base of their member support by being too active. A possible solution, of course, might be to rekindle the religious commitment of those who are concerned with questions of social justice. At the present time, however, the more a person is concerned with these matters the less active he is in the churches, the less he attends, and the less he contributes.[19]

Resistance to change by the comfort-seeking majority in the churches is not always passive. It is hardly a secret that a good many pastors around the nation have been forced to resign for speaking out strongly on problems of prejudice or for becoming involved in activities aimed at achieving social justice for minority groups. It has been reliably reported in the press that the Episcopal Church in California suffered serious declines in contributions following its strong opposition to Proposition 14, the measure that repealed the State's Fair Housing Law. Indeed, a catalog of such events would be extremely lengthy.[20]

A wide-ranging reaction of the clergy to such threats is timidity. Rather than risk a major outbreak in their congregations, pastors have been conspicuously absent from the ranks of clerical activists. For example, Jeffrey K. Hadden's several recent studies of ministerial participation in civil rights protest have shown that parish pastors rarely take part.[21] The activist clergy occupy positions in the churches that are not directly exposed to lay pressure, being heavily drawn from among denominational administrators, seminary faculties, chaplains, and the like. Hadden's studies showed that clergy who demonstrate do not differ from clergy who do not in terms of attitudes or theology but apparently only in their freedom to participate.

Obviously, the extent to which pastors are immediately vulnerable to a lay rebellion differs from denomination to denomination. The vulnerability is greatest when the laity are the pastor's employers, when they can simply fire him by voting to do so. Correspondingly, pastors are somewhat less vulnerable when they can only be removed by their bishop. Still, harmony in a congregation is highly prized, especially by bishops, and in the long run the whole church is vulnerable to widespread withholding of funds or affiliation.[22]

In this sense, the contemporary churches are held captive by a comfort-seeking laity who want their pastor to devote all his time to private religious needs. As a consequence, some of the seeming discontinuity between the pronouncements of the official church and the outlook of the laity stems from the reluctance of many pastors to preach the official position from the

[19]See Stark and Glock, *American Piety.*

[20]See Hadden, *op. cit.*

[21]Hadden, *op. cit.* See also Chap. 13 of this volume.

[22]See, for example, Ernest Q. Campbell and Thomas F. Pettigrew, *Christians in Racial Crisis* (Washington, D.C.: Public Affairs Press, 1959).

pulpit. When national conferences of church leaders meet and issue their pronouncements, they are made up mainly of men who are not directly vulnerable to member opposition. In fact, studies have shown that the majority of laymen never even find out what policies their leaders enunciated.[23] Thus, admirable words are often spoken and deeds done with minimal risk. But when the risks are high, as in face-to-face confrontations with the laity, the actions are minimal. As constituted today, the churches do not have sufficient authority over their lay members greatly to alter their prejudiced views or even to speak too boldly about them unless they are willing to take some risks.

[23]See Glock, Ringer, and Babbie *op. cit.*

Chapter Ten

The Changing Religious Composition of American Higher Education*

Stephen Steinberg

Even the most casual observer has some notion about the intellectual prominence of Jews in higher education. However, like most such ideas, this one is subject to ambiguity and distortion. What does *Jewish prominence* in higher education consist of ? Since Jews constitute only 3 percent of the national population, they could hardly form more than a small part of faculty and students in the nation's 2,300 institutions of higher learning. *Jewish prominence* could refer to the high representation of Jews in the better institutions. But once again the small size of the Jewish population makes it improbable that Jews would constitute more than a small minority. The phrase could refer to a concentration of Jews in just a few leading institutions or in a few disciplines, in which case the meaning of *prominence* is seriously qualified. Finally, *Jewish prominence* could refer only to the fact that a disproportionate number of leading scholars and scientists have been Jewish, which would circumscribe the meaning of the term even more. Exactly what is meant by *Jewish prominence* is itself far from clear: different people mean different things, and the various meanings are often confused.

The confusion with respect to *Catholic underachievement* takes a somewhat different form. Surveys have shown Catholics to be poorly represented among scholars and scientists of distinction.[1] Other studies have documented the poor academic record of Catholic colleges.[2] Confusion sets in when these findings are used as a basis for generalizing about Catholic "anti-intellectualism." Catholics

[1]Harvey C. Lehman and Paul A. Witty, "Scientific Eminence and Church Membership," *Scientific Monthly* 33 (December 1931): 544-49.

[2]Robert H. Knapp and H. B. Goodrich, *Origins of American Scientists* (Chicago: University of Chicago Press, 1952); R. H. Knapp and J. J. Greenbaum, *The Younger American Scholar: His Collegiate Origins* (Chicago: University of Chicago Press, 1953).

could be broadly represented in the academic community even if they are underrepresented among scholars of distinction. And it is obviously invalid to make inferences about the academic record of Catholics in secular institutions on the basis of observations about Catholic colleges.

This chapter is addressed to establishing exactly what the facts are concerning the representation and distribution of Catholics and Jews in higher education. The data employed are derived from major surveys of faculty and students in the nation's universities and colleges. These surveys were conducted by the Carnegie Commission's National Survey of Higher Education in the spring and fall of 1969. Insofar as a central interest of this study is to analyze religious differences in the production of scholars and scientists, the faculty survey proved to be of greatest utility. Data on graduate students and undergraduates are used sparingly, usually to assess future trends among faculty.

The faculty sample consists of 60,028 faculty in 303 institutions of higher learning. Because high-quality universities were oversampled, it was necessary to apply weights to restore the overall representativeness of the sample. The weights also compensate for the failure of a few institutions to provide mailing lists (in the faculty sample only 7 of 303 institutions failed to do so). The raw figures reported in the tables are weighted projections to the total population. The actual number of cases is not reported, because the magnitude of the sample assures that there are enough cases in any given cell to yield stable percentages.

The data for the faculty survey were collected by mail questionnaires in the spring of 1969. The response rate was normal (60 percent), and an extensive analysis of nonrespondents did not reveal any significant differences between respondents and nonrespondents. There is every reason for confidence that the sample adequately represents the total population.[3]

The Religious Distribution in Higher Education: An Overview

According to the most reliable estimates, the religious distribution of the United States is as follows:[4]

Protestants	66 percent
Catholics	26 percent
Jews	3 percent
Other religions	1 percent
No religion	3 percent
Not reported	1 percent

This constitutes one standard for assessing the religious distribution in higher education. However, there is one important qualification: the mere fact that a

---

[3] Detailed information on these surveys can be found in Martin Trow et al., *Technical Report: National Surveys of Higher Education* (Berkeley, Calif.: Carnegie Commission on Higher Education, 1971).

[4] U.S. Bureau of the Census, *Current Population Reports*, series P-24, no. 79 (February 2, 1958).

religious group is overrepresented or underrepresented cannot be assumed to be the result of religion as such. Jews are disproportionately urban and middleclass, and these factors would produce higher rates of college attendance even if no distinctively religious factor were at work. Nevertheless, it is meaningful to inspect the basic religious distribution apart from the factors that might produce or explain it. It makes good descriptive sense to know how many Protestants, Catholics, and Jews there are at various levels of higher education, and to examine these figures against the overall religious distribution in the national population.

Table 1 shows the religious breakdown of faculty, graduate students, and undergraduates. Caution should be used not to make inferences about religious trends from these figures. The fact that the proportion of Catholics increases as one goes down the academic ladder could mean one of two things. It could mean that Catholics are increasingly going to college; if this were true, we might anticipate a rise in the proportion of Catholic faculty as undergraduates and graduates advance through the system. Or it could mean that Catholic undergraduates are less likely to go on to graduate school and that Catholic graduates are less likely to become faculty, in which case no such increase in Catholic representation would be in the offing. This issue will be ironed out once the basic distribution is examined.

Table 1.   *The Religious Distribution in the Nation and in Higher Education*

	Nation	Faculty	Graduates	Under-graduates
Protestant	66.2%	66.0%	57.6%	58.4%
Catholic	25.7	18.5	25.1	29.3
Jewish	3.2	8.7	10.0	5.3
Other	1.3	3.6	3.7	4.2
None	2.7	3.2	3.7	2.8
N (weighted) =	(119,333,000)	(434,104)	(974,987)	(907,131)
		Index of Representation		
Protestant	100	100	87	88
Catholic	100	72	98	114
Jewish	100	272	312	166

As table 1 shows, the proportion of Catholics steadily increases as one goes down the academic ladder: Catholics are 18 percent of faculty, 25 percent of graduate students, and 29 percent of undergraduates. Protestants are 66 percent of faculty—the same as their proportion in the national population—but are 58 percent of both graduate students and undergraduates. The proportion of Jews in each group is under 10 percent, an amount that is small in absolute terms but large in relation to the number of Jews in the general population.

The second half of table 1 shows the "index of representation" for each group. This is a ratio between the proportion in the national population and the proportion at a particular level in higher education. A ratio of 100 indicates an exact correspondence between these two figures. Ratios above 100 indicate the

extent of overrepresentation, ratios under 100 the extent of underrepresentation.

This measure shows that the proportion of Catholics among graduate students
roughly matches their proportion in the general population, whereas Catholics
are underrepresented among faculty and overrepresented among undergraduates.
Jews, on the other hand, are substantially overrepresented among all three
groups; their overrepresentation is greatest among graduate students, but this
only reflects their particularly heavy concentration in professional schools.
Finally, the proportion of Protestants among faculty is equal to their proportion
in the general population, but Protestants are slightly underrepresented among
graduate students and undergraduates.

Institutional Quality

The figures just examined give the impression that although Jews are
overrepresented in higher education, they are far from being numerically
important. Catholics, on the other hand, do not appear to be as
underrepresented as past discussions of "Catholic anti-intellectualism" would
suggest. However, both these impressions are qualified once institutional quality
is brought into the picture. Table 2 distinguishes between universities and
colleges of high, medium, and low rank and junior colleges.[5] Of primary interest
are the seventeen highest ranking universities, represented in the column on the
extreme left. The religious composition of faculty in these institutions is 60
percent Protestant, 13 percent Catholic, and 17 percent Jewish. Thus, in
comparison to their overall representation in higher education (column on the
extreme right), Protestants are slightly underrepresented in ranking universities,
Catholics are substantially underrepresented, and Jews are substantially
overrepresented. Persons who reported their religious background as "none" are
also overrepresented.

It is noteworthy that the extent of Catholic underrepresentation in the
ranking universities is not as great among students as among faculty. This is most
easily observed by computing the ratio between the proportion of Catholics in
ranking universities and the proportion in the total population of faculty or
students. Among faculty this ratio is only 71; among graduate students it
increases to 80; among undergraduates it increases again to 91. Thus not only
does Catholic representation increase at lower academic levels, but the extent of
underrepresentation in the better institutions also grows smaller.

The extent of Jewish concentration in higher ranking institutions is indeed
striking. In the ranking universities Jews constitute 17 percent of faculty, 16
percent of graduate students, and 20 percent of undergraduates. On the other
hand, in the lowest ranking colleges the proportion of Jews hardly exceeds their
proportion in the population: Jews are 3 percent of faculty, 5 percent of
graduate students, and 4 percent of undergraduates.

[5]The basis source of the quality rating is Jack Gourman, *The Gourman Report* (Phoenix,
Ariz.: The Continuing Education Institute, 1967). For further details, see Trow et al.,
Technical Report.

Table 2. *The Religious Distribution in Higher Education by Institutional Quality*

	Universities			Colleges			Junior Colleges	Total
	High	Medium	Low	High	Medium	Low		
Faculty								
Protestants	59.9%	63.1%	69.3%	64.7%	66.7%	67.1%	69.9%	66.0%
Catholics	13.2	14.7	16.7	13.4	22.7	23.8	20.5	18.5
Jews	17.2	14.8	7.2	13.2	6.3	3.3	3.4	8.7
Other	3.9	3.5	3.9	4.2	2.2	3.6	3.7	3.6
None	5.8	4.0	2.9	4.5	2.1	2.1	2.4	3.2
N (weighted) =	(54,399)	(78,796)	(68,522)	(24,648)	(47,646)	(97,055)	(63,042)	(434,104)
Graduate Students								
Protestants	53.7	54.3	61.0	48.4	62.8	61.3		57.6
Catholics	20.0	24.3	24.8	22.2	29.1	29.8		25.1
Jews	16.0	14.6	6.5	13.1	3.9	4.9		10.0
Other	4.5	3.3	4.7	10.5	1.5	1.3		3.7
None	5.9	3.5	3.1	5.8	2.6	2.7		3.7
N (weighted)=	(167,089)	(24,992)	(216,139)	(58,156)	(115,994)	(167,615)		(974,987)
Undergraduates								
Protestants	43.2	57.6	57.0	65.2	62.8	57.2	59.7	58.4
Catholics	26.7	26.0	29.8	17.6	29.6	33.7	28.2	29.3
Jews	20.1	10.9	7.9	10.1	4.0	3.7	2.6	5.3
Other	4.5	4.0	4.0	4.0	1.8	4.2	4.9	4.2
None	5.5	1.5	1.4	3.0	1.8	1.2	4.6	4.2
N (weighted) =	(34,369)	(80,224)	(113,068)	(26,810)	(86,253)	(223,359)	(341,176)	(907,131)

Also noteworthy is the high proportion of Protestants in the undergraduate bodies of high-ranking colleges (65 percent, as compared to just 43 percent in high-ranking universities). Most of these colleges are small, private institutions high in social prestige that have been traditionally Protestant both in numbers and in social character.

Table 2 raises two questions that warrant further analysis. The first concerns the reasons for the Jewish overrepresentation at every level of higher education. Does this indicate special academic aptitude or superior performance on the part of Jews, or does it reflect economic advantage or some other factor? The second question concerns the finding that the Catholic representation is greatest among undergraduates and smallest among faculty. Does this indicate a secular trend for Catholics to enter higher education in greater numbers, or does it reflect a tendency for Catholic students to avoid academic careers and to enter nonacademic occupations instead? Let us address the second of these questions first.

Religious Trends in Higher Education

As indicated above, the fact that the proportion of Catholics increases as one goes down the academic ladder could signify either success or failure: it could indicate a trend toward increased Catholic representation or it could mean that Catholics disproportionately terminate their academic careers at lower levels. This issue can easily be resolved by inspecting religious differences by age, as is done for faculty in table 3.

These data show a definite upward trend in Catholic representation among faculty. Catholics make up 15 percent of the oldest age group, and this figure increases with younger age to 17, 19, and 20 percent. Among graduate students who say they plan a career in college teaching, the figure again rises to 22 percent.

As the bottom half of table 3 shows, among the oldest age group for every 100 Catholics in the general population there were only 57 among faculty in higher education. With younger age, however, this ratio increases—from 57 to 66 to 75 to 80. Among graduate students with academic plans the ratio again increases to 86. In short, Catholics are rapidly reaching the point of being represented among faculty in the same proportion as in the nation as a whole.[6]

If Catholic underrepresentation is rapidly becoming a thing of the past, it is because the aspirations and career plans of Catholic students are not substantially different from those of students generally. The proportion of

---

[6]There is little or no distortion resulting from the fact that 1957 census figures are used as the basis for estimating Catholic representation in higher education at the present time. The birth rate of Catholics is presently only slightly higher than the national average, and could not significantly alter the overall religious composition of the nation in only a twenty-year period. This is also indicated by surveys conducted since 1957. For example, a 1964 national survey found that Catholics were 25.8 percent of the national population, as compared to 25.7 percent according to the 1957 census estimate. Gertrude J. Selznick and Stephen Steinberg, *The Tenacity of Prejudice* (New York: Harper and Row, 1969).

Table 3.   *Religion Raised by Age among Faculty in All Institutions*

Religion	Over 55	45-54	35-44	Below 34	Graduate Students Planning a Career in College Teaching
Protestant	75.7%	69.0%	63.2%	62.6%	57.8%
Catholic	14.8	16.9	19.2	20.5	22.2
Jewish	5.5	8.2	9.5	9.6	9.6
Other	2.1	2.9	4.4	3.9	4.5
None	1.9	3.0	3.7	3.4	5.9
N (Weighted)=	(61,258)	(95,639)	(135,666)	(140,391)	(257,000)

Ratio of Representation

Protestant	144	104	96	95	87
Catholic	57	66	75	80	86
Jewish	172	256	297	300	300

graduate students who said they plan a career in college teaching is 35 percent for Protestants, 31 percent for Catholics, and 33 percent for Jews.[7] In the ranking universities the proportions are higher, but there is even less difference by religion: 42 percent of Protestants have academic intentions, as compared to 44 percent of Catholics and 43 percent of Jews. In other words, not only are Catholics entering graduate schools in increasing numbers, but they are just as likely to plan careers as scholars.

In the undergraduate survey students were asked what was the highest degree they hoped to attain. The proportion aspiring to the Ph.D. degree is comparatively high for Jewish students—23 percent. However, the figures for Protestants and Catholics are similar; if anything the Catholic proportion is higher (15 percent as compared to 12 percent). Among students enrolled in ranking universities and colleges, Catholics have the highest proportion aspriring to a Ph.D. The figures are Protestants, 24 percent; Catholics, 30 percent; Jews, 24 percent. (The Jewish proportion is somewhat depressed because of the high number planning professional careers that do not involve a Ph.D.) Far from being underrepresented in higher education, in another generation the proportion of Catholics among the nation's faculty may well exceed their national average.

The representation of Jews among faculty has undergone a similar, though less dramatic, increase. Jews were already overrepresented among the oldest group of faculty, but the proportion continued to rise in successive age groups, from 5.5 percent to 8.2, 9.5, and 9.6. Among graduate students planning an academic career, the figure remains constant at 9.6 percent. Indeed, careful examination of the figures in table 3 indicates that the Jewish proportion in higher education may be tapering off. The major increase occurred immediately

[7]These figures are somewhat inflated because one-quarter of the sample did not answer the question concerning career plans. They are excluded from the percentage base.

after World War II (that is, between the two oldest age groups), and since then increases between age cohorts have steadily grown smaller.

As a matter of simple arithmetic, the increase of Catholics and Jews must involve a decrease of Protestants. Whereas the overwhelming majority—76 percent—of the oldest faculty are Protestant, this has gradually declined to 63 percent among the youngest faculty, and to 58 percent among graduate students with academic intentions. Indeed, the index of representation (table 3) shows that relative to their proportions in the general population, Protestants and Catholics are equally represented among graduate students who plan an academic career. Those in the Protestant establishment who in the early part of this century resisted the incursions of immigrants would probably see in these trends the realization of their worst fears. In point of fact, American higher education has ceased to be a Protestant institution.

It is important to examine these trends within the context of institutional quality. If the Catholic increase were characteristic only of lower-ranking institutions, then their greater numbers might not indicate an improvement in academic performance or productivity.

Such an interpretation receives no support from the data. Table 4 shows the religious distribution by age for the seventeen ranking universities. As observed earlier, Catholics are underrepresented in these institutions, and this holds true at every age level. However, the proportion of Catholics shows the same increase in the quality institutions as was observed for all institutions together. From the oldest to the youngest age group, the proportion increases from 10 to 11 to 13 to 16 percent, and among graduate students with academic intentions it is 20 percent. In short, although Catholics continue to be underrepresented in the quality institutions, they are rapidly closing the gap, just as in higher education as a whole. On the other hand, the Jewish proportion again shows signs of

Table 4.   *Religion Raised by Age among Faculty in the Seventeen Ranking Universities*

Religion	Over 55	45-54	35-44	Below 34	Graduate Students Planning a Career in College Teaching
Protestant	71.8%	64.1%	56.4%	55.2%	52.0%
Catholic	9.6	10.9	13.3	16.0	20.1
Jewish	12.1	15.7	19.4	18.5	15.8
Other	2.5	3.5	5.0	3.8	5.0
None	4.1	5.7	6.0	6.5	7.2
N (Weighted)=	(8,176)	(11,466)	(17,209)	(17,429)	(145,512)
Ratio of Representation					
Protestant	108	97	85	83	78
Catholic	37	42	52	62	78
Jewish	378	491	606	578	493

tapering off. One cannot place too much confidence in projections based on the graduates who say they plan an academic career, but it appears that Jewish representation in quality institutions has reached its peak and is now on the decline.

Jews in Quality Institutions: A Close View

Ordinarily the presence of disproportionate numbers of Jews in the better institutions is taken as another sign of Jewish academic excellence. Certainly this is plausible. Only the most cynical observer would question some correlation, however imperfect, between the quality of the institution and the quality of its faculty and students. Nevertheless, the issue is not so easily settled. Is attendance at a quality institution a function of the selection of the more able candidates? Or would it be more correct to say that the better institutions produce the better scholars? Let us take graduate students and the observed concentration of Jews in the better graduate schools as an example. Does this indicate superior performance on the part of Jewish students as undergraduates? Or do Jews attend the better schools in greater numbers for some other reasons? A simple explanation might be that Jews, more than others, happen to reside in states where the better schools are located. Or it is possible that Jews more often have the desire and the economic resources to travel to the better schools. Finally, it is possible that Jews start out in better institutions as undergraduates, and that this determines their future career line as graduate students and later as faculty.

The first two hypotheses can be promptly eliminated. The Jewish concentration in the quality institutions cannot be explained in terms of Jewish affluence. For one thing, there is little or no relation between the quality of an institution and the financial security of students or the economic status of their parents. Graduate students in lower-quality institutions are almost as likely to report that their finances are adequate and that their parents are financially well off as students in higher-quality institutions. Graduate schools select students who can absorb the costs of further education and delayed earnings, and this is as true of lower-quality institutions as of higher-quality institutions. For much the same reason there are only small differences in the economic status of Protestant, Catholic, and Jewish graduate students. The percentage saying that their parents were financially comfortable during the time they were growing up is 74 percent for Jews, 72 percent for Protestants, and 68 percent for Catholics. The percentages saying that their current finances are adequate are 78, 77, and 74 percent. Thus, despite the fact that in the national population Jews are better off economically than non-Jews, the differences among graduate students are very slight and could not explain the relative concentration of Jews in the ranking institutions.

The proposition that Jewish students are more willing to travel to the better institutions must also be discarded. The data show that the proportion who came as graduate students to the state in which their graduate institution is located is the same for all religious groups. Nor can it be said that Jews attend better graduate schools because they happen to live in states where the better schools are located. This factor cannot be ignored altogether, but data show that Jews are more likely to be in better graduate schools whether they grew up in the same state or not.

The next question is whether the relatively high representation of Jews in the ranking school reflects superior academic performance on the part of Jewish students. However imperfect, undergraduate grade point average is nevertheless a reasonable indicator of a student's academic performance. It might be assumed that Jewish students, given their relative success at attending better graduate schools, also have higher undergraduate grades. This is not the case, however (table 5). The proportion reporting an undergraduate grade point average of A is about the same for Jews as for non-Jews (17 versus 19 percent).[8] The overall grade point average for both groups is 3.0. If grades are any indicator of academic excellence, by this standard Jews do not excel over others.

Table 5. *Comparisons between Jewish and Non-Jewish Graduate Students on Undergraduate Grades and Attendance at Ranking Undergraduate and Graduate Institutions*

	Jews	Non-Jews
Percent in a ranking university as graduate student	27%	15%
Percent with an A undergraduate average	17	19
Percent in a ranking university as an undergraduate	21	10
Percent in a ranking college as an undergraduate	19	3
Total in a ranking university or college[a]	40	13
Percent with an A undergraduate average among:		
Those in a high ranking undergraduate university	23	21
Those in a high ranking undergraduate college	14	17
Percent attending a ranking university among those having attended:		
A high ranking undergraduate university	54	47
A high ranking undergraduate college	19	17
Percent attending a ranking university standardizing for undergraduate institutional quality	27	23

[a] The percentage base for these figures is the total number of Jewish and non-Jewish graduate students. However, the quality of the undergraduate institution is known only for 45 percent of the sample. Because of practical considerations, respondents were not asked their undergraduate institution. Instead they were given a list of 45 of the major Ph.D.-producing institutions. Undergraduate quality is also known if a respondent went to the same graduate and undergraduate institution.

This conclusion, of course, can be challenged on the grounds that grades are not a good measure of academic excellence, especially when they come from many different institutions. It could be argued that Jewish students have obtained their grades at higher-quality and more competitive undergraduate

[8]Protestants and Catholics are combined in this analysis because they are basically alike on the variables under examination. For example, 20 percent of Protestants report an A undergraduate grade point average, as compared to 17 percent of Catholics. The proportion who attended a high-ranking university or college is 24 percent in the case of Protestants; 20 percent in the case of Catholics.

colleges, and therefore their grade point averages, while nominally the same as those of non-Jews, nevertheless indicate a higher level of excellence.

It is true that on the whole Jewish graduate students received their undergraduate education at higher-ranking institutions. The differences are striking: 40 percent of Jewish students came from the highest-ranking colleges and universities, as compared to just 13 percent of non-Jews.[9] However, the important question is how Jews compare to non-Jews in the same institutions. Do they get better grades?

The data indicate that they do not (table 5). At both high-ranking universities and colleges the difference between Jews and non-Jews in their grade point averages is negligible. Thus even when compared to non-Jews in institutions of the same rank, Jewish students do not show a tendency to receive higher grades.

Nor are Jewish students in a given institution much more likely to go on to a high-quality graduate school than non-Jewish students in the same institution came from ranking undergraduate universities 54 percent of Jewish students went on to a ranking university in comparison to 47 percent of non-Jews. When the relation between religion and quality of graduate school is standardized for the quality of the undergraduate school, the Jewish tendency to attend ranking graduate institutions is no longer pronounced (table 5, bottom row). Put another way, if as many non-Jewish as Jewish graduate students attended quality undergraduate schools, there would be no difference between them in their representation at the quality graduate schools. The overrepresentation of Jews that we observe in the better graduate schools seems to be simply an extension of their overrepresentation in the better undergraduate schools.

Of course part of the reason for the Jewish overrepresentation in the better undergraduate schools may well be that they do better in high school. There is also evidence in the undergraduate data that on the whole Jewish students achieve higher grades and more often plan to go to graduate school than do their non-Jewish counterparts.[10] However, the self-selective process involved in the decision to go to graduate school appears to place Jewish and non-Jewish students on an equal footing. Thus when Jewish and non-Jewish graduate students are compared, we find that they are equally likely to have achieved high undergraduate grades and, once the quality of the undergraduate institution is taken into account, to enter a quality graduate school. Put another way, on the whole Jewish students enter graduate school with no better qualifications than non-Jewish students from comparable undergraduate institutions.

[9]In most cases information regarding undergraduate quality is available only for students who attended major universities (see footnote to table 5). While the descriptive figures are therefore not realistic, the relative differences between Jews and non-Jews should not be adversely affected by this problem.

[10]Among undergraduates in ranking universities, the proportion with an A grade point average is 13 percent for both Protestants and Catholics and 18 percent for Jews. The difference is larger in ranking colleges: 20 percent of both Protestants and Catholics report an A average compared to 37 percent of Jews. In terms of career aspirations, Protestants and Catholics are again alike: 12 percent of Protestants and 15 percent of Catholics said they hoped to get a Ph.D. Among Jews the figure rises to 23 percent.

On this question the crucial factor is that Jews more often begin their academic careers at quality undergraduate institutions. This seems to establish their future path to the better institutions, first as graduate students and later as faculty.

The Protestant Denominations

So far in this analysis Catholics and Jews have been compared to Protestants. As the majority group, both in the nation and in higher education, Protestants are a good benchmark against which other groups can be compared. However, there are also hazards in this, because in some respects *Protestant* is an inadequate analytical category. It embraces a wide assortment of denominations, different in theology and religious practice, in their social attitudes and ethical prescriptions, and in the social class and region of their members. At one end of the spectrum are Episcopalians, Presbyterians, and Congregationalists, whose adherents come largely from the urban East and from the upper strata of the education and social class. Studies show that these groups tend to replace traditional belief and practice with modern interpretations consistent with their education and social position.[11] At the other end of the spectrum are the fundamentalist denominations, especially Southern Baptists and Missouri Lutherans, whose religious attachments are much more traditional. Their adherents come largely from the lower social strata and geographically from the South and border states. It is thus of limited meaning to present figures showing this or that proportion of Protestants in higher education, when these overall figures obscure an uneven representation of the various Protestant denominations. With this in mind, let us examine the religious distribution *within* Protestantism.

Such data are available only for graduate students. Although this precludes an analysis of the historical trend among faculty, it does permit an assessment of the contemporary situation among the nation's graduate students and the likely religious distribution among the next generation of faculty.

Table 6 shows three sets of figures: the percentage share of each denomination among the nation's Protestants, the percentage share of each denomination among graduate students, and the percentage share of each denomination among graduate students in ranking universities. In order to avoid blurring denominational effects with those of race, figures are reported for whites only.

Baptists are the largest Protestant denomination, consisting of 24 percent of all white Protestants in the nation. However, they are only 16 percent of the nation's graduate students and 11 percent of graduate students in ranking universities. Methodists and Lutherans are represented among graduate students in roughly the same proportions as in the national population. Three denominations are substantially overrepresented among graduate students:

---

[11]Rodney Stark and Charles Y. Glock, *American Piety: The Nature of Religious Commitment* (Berkeley and Los Angeles: University of California Press, 1968).

Table 6.   *Distribution of Protestant Denominations in the Nation,*
among Graduate Students, and among Graduate Students in the
Ranking Universities
(Whites only)

	Nation[a]	All Graduate Students	Graduate Students in Ranking Universities
Baptists	24%	16%	10%
Methodists	21	25	21
Lutherans	12	13	11
Presbyterians	10	15	20
Episcopalians	5	9	13
Congregationalists	4	7	8
Other	24	15	17
N (Weighted) =		(516,322)	(82,731)

[a] U.S. Bureau of the Census, Current Population Reports, series P-20, no. 79 (February 2, 1958). Estimates for Episcopalians, Congregationalists and Unitarians are based on a 1964 national sample.

Presbyterians, Episcopalians, and Congregationalists. The representation of each is even higher in the ranking universities. For example, Episcopalians are only 5 percent of the nation's Protestants but 9 percent of the Protestant graduate students and 13 percent of Protestants in the ranking universities.[12]

In table 1 it was reported that for every 100 Protestants in the national population, there were 87 in the graduate student population. It now appears that some Protestant denominations are far less underrepresented than this figure would suggest, whereas others are heavily overrepresented. For example, the ratio of representation is only 67 for Baptists but is 180 for Episcopalians. Like Episcopalians, Presbyterians and Congregationalists are each represented among graduate students in proportions that far exceed their numbers in the general population. It is apparent that Jews are not the only religious group with a penchant for higher education.

As with Jews, however, it would be hasty to jump to a cultural theory to explain differences in academic achievement between liberal and fundamentalist denominations. It is true that the liberal denominations that are heavily overrepresented in higher education are the ones that most typify the Protestant ethic, with its emphasis on rationalism and utilitarianism. But it is also true that there are important differences between liberal and fundamentalist denominations with respect to social class and regional factors. No explanation of why liberal denominations are more heavily represented in higher education would be

---

[12]Just as the data show Protestant, Catholic, and Jewish graduate students to be alike in terms of their career plans, there are no differences to speak of among Protestant denominations. The proportion who say they expect to pursue a career in college teaching is as follows: Episcopalians, 34 percent; Presbyterians, 37 percent; Congregationalists, 28 percent; Methodists, 35 percent; Lutherans, 28 percent; Baptists, 38 percent; Southern Baptists, 36 percent; Missouri Lutherans, 35 percent. While religious background seems to influence the chances an individual will attend graduate school, it has little or no influence on whether they plan academic careers.

complete without reference to both types of factors. It is not simply a matter of separating out the effects of religious factors from those of background factors by means of statistical controls. It is equally important to understand the process whereby cultural values are anchored in social structure.

Religious Concentrations within Institutions

Most students attend institutions fairly close to home. In the graduate sample only 34 percent moved across state lines to attend their graduate institution; another 11 percent did so as undergraduates. A majority (56 percent) lived in the state in which their graduate school is located at the time they began college. This proximity factor means, among other things, that the religious composition of a particular institution is apt to reflect the religious composition of the state in which it is located. Because Catholics and Jews tend to be concentrated in the urban North, one would expect to find large religious concentrations in Northern graduate schools on this account alone.

The extent of Jewish concentration is indeed striking. Of all Jewish graduate students in the sample, 58 percent are found in just ten institutions. In comparison, these same ten institutions account for just 24 percent of all graduate students. Despite this high concentration, in only three institutions in our sample of 148 do Jews constitute a majority of the graduate enrollment.

Most of the heavily Jewish institutions are among those with high-quality ratings. Of the ten institutions with the greatest numbers of Jewish students, eight are among the ranking universities and colleges; only one is in the third rank. The concentration of Jews in some of the better institutions perhaps explains the association that is frequently made between Jews and academic prominence. What tends to be overlooked, however, is that even in the most heavily Jewish institutions Jews are usually in the minority. Moreover, as was seen earlier in this chapter, the academic record of Jewish graduate students is not substantially different from that of their non-Jewish classmates.

Although there are some Catholic colleges and universities included in our sample, most are very small and together account for only 5 percent of all Catholic graduate students. The ten institutions with the largest concentrations of Catholics (in terms of absolute numbers) account for 37 percent of all Catholic graduate students in the sample. Although it is smaller than the comparable figure for Jews (which was 58 percent), this figure nevertheless indicates a high degree of concentration. As with Jews, however, the Catholic concentration is rarely so great as to constitute a numerical majority.

In the case of Protestants the denominational split is such that, except for denominational schools, it is rare for any single denomination to predominate. However, there are some noteworthy denominational differences that correspond to regional and class variations. In some of the elite Eastern colleges Episcopalians, Presbyterians, and Congregationalists are found in large numbers. On the other hand, many of the institutions in the West and South have heavy concentrations of Protestants from denominations that are theologically and socially more conservative.

Faculty, of course, are more mobile than students. Nevertheless, there is a good deal of concentration along religious lines. Largely due to the existence of Catholic colleges, 30 percent of all Catholic faculty teach at institutions whose faculties are more than one-half Catholic. On the other hand, one-third teach at institutions that are less than 15 percent Catholic, a level far below average. In other words, Catholics tend to be found at institutions that have either very high or very low Catholic representations.

Although Jews are only 8 percent of all faculty, they tend to be concentrated in a relatively few institutions, just as was observed for graduate students. In fact, half of all Jewish faculty teach at institutions that are at least 20 percent Jewish. There are 27 such institutions in our sample of 303. Such concentrations are bound to give the illusion of greater numbers than is actually the case. A more important implication is that there are some institutions where Jews exist in large enough numbers to have a significant impact on the intellectual and political climate.

Chapter Eleven

Religious Commitment and Conservatism: In Search of an Elusive Relationship*

Robert Wuthnow

According to a well-known tenet of conventional sociological wisdom, people who are religious tend to be conservative in political, economic, and other social matters. A weighty balance of theoretical argument as well as an accumulated body of empirical "proof" underlies this tenet. Yet the relationship between religion and conservatism remains an elusive one: there are theoretical arguments which deny it or suggest major qualifications and empirical results which show negative as well as positive associations.

Widely divergent traditions of sociological theory have arrived at virtually identical conclusions regarding religion and conservatism. Marxian theory, of course, with its thesis of religion as opiate, associates all religion with political conservatism. Engels stated, "We see therefore: religion, once formed, always contains traditional material, just as in all ideological domains, tradition forms a great conservative force."[1] A contemporary spokesman, Herbert Marcuse, takes a similar tack in averring that religion is "quickly digested by the status quo as part of its healthy diet."[2]

Marxian thought has undoubtedly been a major source of the tendency to associate religion with conservatism, but it is by no means the only one. The functionalist position is akin in this respect to the Marxist one. The purpose of religion, according to one functionalist advocate, Kingsley Davis, "is to justify, rationalize, and support the sentiments that give cohesion to society."[3] This

[1]Friedrich Engels, "Ludwig Feuerbach and the End of Classical German Philosophy," in Reinhold Niebuhr, ed., *Marx and Engels on Religion* (New York: Schocken, 1964), p. 266.

[2]Herbert Marcuse, *One Dimensional Man: Studies in the Ideology of Advanced Industrial Society* (Boston: Beacon Press, 1964), p. 14.

[3]Kingsley Davis, *Human Society* (New York: Macmillan Co., 1948), p. 519.

view of religion has prevailed in functionalist thinking from the early Durkheimian notion of collective representations to the present Parsonian theory of consensus. Although not all functionalists agree that religion is always politically conservative, there is consensus that the tendency is in this direction.[4] A third theoretical tradition linking religion with conservatism is church-sect theory. Sects are conceived to be far right both religiously and politically, whereas churches are theologically more liberal and politically more progressive. Such ideas are evident in a recent analysis of religion and politics which identifies groups who stress biblical literalism, the authority of the scriptures, and personal pietism as tending "to be at once nativist, racist, and chauvinistic."[5] The cumulative impact of these three theoretical traditions has been substantial and has produced a widespread and frequently uncritical tendency to conceive of religion as inerrantly conservative in such diverse areas as politics,[6] economics,[7] race relations,[8] urban problems,[9] and moral-ethical issues.[10]

Not everyone is in agreement, however, that the relationship is as strong or consistent as these theories would have it. By now, sufficient criticisms have been raised to question, at least, the universality of the association. Marx's views on religion, for example, have been criticized increasingly of late for being overly simple.[11] Functionalists have been criticized for reducing religion to its social consequences[12] and are being pressed to recognize the limits of religion as an integrative force and to pay attention to its disruptive elements[13] and its latent functions. And church-sect theory has been confronted with the historical

---

[4]For example, C. Wright Mills, *The Sociological Imagination* (New York: Grove Press, 1959), p. 48, and Ralf Dahrendorf, "Out of Utopia: Toward a Reorientation of Sociological Analysis," *American Journal of Sociology* 64 (September 1958): 115-27.

[5]Murray S. Stedman, Jr., *Religion and Politics in America* (New York: Harcourt Brace Jovanovich, 1964), p. 129.

[6]Seymour Martin Lipset, *The First New Nation: The United States in Historical and Comparative Perspective* (New York: Basic Books, 1963), pp. 79-83; and J. Milton Yinger, *Religion, Society and the Individual* (New York: Macmillan Co., 1957), p. 273.

[7]J. Milton Yinger, *Religion in the Struggle for Power* (New York: Russell and Russell, 1961), p. 222.

[8]Barry N. Schwartz and Robert Disch, eds., *White Racism: Its History, Pathology, and Practice* (New York: Dell, 1970), p. 6; and Louis L. Knowles and Kenneth Prewitt, eds., *Institutional Racism in America* (Englewood Cliffs, N.J.: Prentice-Hall, 1969), p. 7.

[9]Gibson Winter, *The Suburban Captivity of the Churches* (New York: Macmillan Co., 1962); and Harvey Cox, *The Secular City* (New York: Macmillan Co., 1965).

[10]Peter L. Berger, *The Noise of Solemn Assemblies* (Garden City, New York: Doubleday, 1961); and Pierre Berton, *The Comfortable Pew* (New York: Macmillan Co., 1965).

[11]Reinhold Niebuhr, ed., *Marx and Engels on Religion* (New York: Schocken, 1964); and Robert Blauner, "Marxian Theory and Race Relations," unpublished paper, Department of Sociology, University of California, Berkeley, 1970.

[12]Robert N. Bellah, *Beyond Belief: Essays on Religion in a Post-Traditional World* (New York: Harper & Row, Publishers, 1970), p. 247.

[13]Pierre L. Van den Berghe, "Dialectic and Functionalism: Toward a Theoretical Synthesis," *American Sociological Review* 28 (October 1963): 695-705.

existence of radical *left*-wing religious sects (such as the Anabaptists or radical Cromwellian sects), the persistence of orthodox religious belief in politically liberal churches, and the confounding influence of socioeconomic status on sectarian conservatism. Finally, a growing body of theory suggests that due to an evolving structural differentiation between religion and other social institutions, religion and politics have no longer any necessary connections at all.[14]

On the basis of theoretical argument alone, then, it is obvious that the relationship between religion and conservatism is more elusive, more deceptive, and more difficult to grasp than is often imagined. To help clarify this ambiguity, in this chapter we examine existing empirical evidence on the matter.

Method

A summary of available empirical research was obtained by conducting a two-stage review of relevant literature: first, all major journals of sociology and social psychology for the last decade plus several book-length studies were surveyed to locate the research on religion and conservatism conducted during this period; second, all previous articles and books referred to in these studies were read and summarized. Only studies which employed one or more measures of religiosity were included; studies which merely considered differences between Protestants and Catholics, for example, were excluded. The sample was further limited to studies which related religious commitment to some measure of political, economic, or social conservatism. Finally, only quantitative research conducted on samples within the United States was included.

Because religion, according to considerable theoretical and empirical evidence, is multidimensional (see chapter 1), the studies were first classified according to which one or more of eight measures of religion they had used. Each of the measures provided a means to differentiate subjects religiously.[15] Based on the eight measures, then, the more religious people were judged to be:

1. Those who belonged to doctrinally conservative denominations (denominational conservatism).[16]

[14]Louis Schneider, *Sociological Approach to Religion* (New York: John Wiley and Sons, 1970), pp. 70-83.

[15]It was not self-evident for all measures which responses ought to be considered the more religious and which the less religious ones—for example, how was denominational membership to be classified. In ambiguous cases greater religiousness was attributed to conservative than to liberal modes of religious expression. In this way the opportunity to demonstrate that religion and conservatism are positively related was maximized. This would enhance the potential for prevailing theory to be confirmed, it was recognized. At the same time, disconfirmation under these circumstances would be all the more theoretically damaging.

[16]Rodney Stark and Charles Y. Glock, *American Piety: The Nature of Religious Commitment* (Berkeley and Los Angeles: University of California Press, 1968); and Benton Johnson, "Ascetic Protestantism and Political Preference," *Public Opinion Quarterly* 26 (Spring 1962): 35-46 and "Ascetic Protestantism and Political Preference in the Deep South," *American Journal of Sociology* 69 (January 1964): 359-66.

2. Those who subscribed to traditional tenets of Christian faith—for example, unqualified belief in divinity, in the virgin birth, in immortality, and so on (orthodox belief).[17]

3. Those who engaged in private prayer, table grace, Bible reading, and so forth more frequently (devotionalism).[18]

4. Those who have great knowledge of their faith (religious knowledge).[19]

5. Those whose primary friendships are with coreligionists (communalism).[20]

6. Those whose organizational energies are primarily spent in church-related groups (associational involvement).[21]

7. Those who attend church more frequently (church attendance).[22]

8. Those who exhibited greater religiousness on some combination of above (composite religiosity).[23]

After the studies were distinguished by measure of religion, they were then further classified according to the means by which they measured conservatism. Subjects were classified as *economically conservative* if they showed opposition to such things as welfare programs, labor unions, government control of business, and socialized medicine; as *politically conservative* if they so identified themselves or indicated that they had last voted Republican; and *socially conservative* if by one or another indicator they revealed themselves to be ethnocentric, prejudiced, opposed to civil rights, and so on.[24]

Sixty-six articles and books had been located in the original canvass, and in these were included a total of 266 independent efforts to examine the relationship between religion and conservatism. Studies varied in the number of relationships examined; consequently in our analysis some studies are weighted more heavily than others. Generally, however, studies reporting numerous

[17]Cox. op. cit.; Winter, op. cit.; Charles Y. Glock, Benjamin B. Ringer, and Earl R. Babbie, *To Comfort and To Challenge: A Dilemma of the Contemporary Church* (Berkeley and Los Angeles: University of California Press, 1967), pp. 205-10; Schwartz and Disch, op. cit.; and Knowles and Prewitt, op. cit.

[18]Stark and Glock, op. cit.

[19]Ibid.

[20]Gerhard Lenski, *The Religious Factor* (Garden City, New York: Doubleday, 1963), p. 328.

[21]Stark and Glock, op. cit.

[22]Berton, op. cit.; Berger, op. cit.; and Samuel A. Stouffer, *Communism, Civil Liberties, and Conformity* (Garden City, N.Y.: Doubleday, 1955), pp. 140-49.

[23]W. M. O'Neill and Daniel J. Levinson, "A Factorial Exploration of Authoritarianism and Some of Its Ideological Concomitants," *Journal of Personality* 22 (June 1954): 449-56; and Gordon Allport, *Religion in the Developing Personality* (New York: New York University Press, 1960).

[24]Seymour M. Lipset and Earl Raab, *The Politics of Unreason: Right-Wing Extremism in America, 1790-1970* (New York: Harper & Row, Publishers, 1970), pp. 428-83.

findings also appear to have utilized the more sophisticated designs and to have been conducted on the largest samples. The articles and books surveyed provide a comprehensive, but probably not totally exhaustive, summary of the available evidence on religion and conservatism.[25]

Results

Out of 266 relationships reported, a majority (163) show religion, contrary to expectations, either unrelated or negatively related to conservatism.[26] Forty-six percent of the relationships are neutral, 15 percent are negative, and 39 percent are positive (table 1). Political conservatism is positively related to religion in only 36 percent of the cases; economic conservatism, in 21 percent; and social conservatism, in 46 percent of the cases. When studies conducted on Protestant samples are compared with studies conducted on Catholic samples, no significant differences occur except that positive relationships between orthodox beliefs and conservatism are slightly more likely among Protestants than Catholics. Altogether 34 percent of the relationships for Protestant samples and 35 percent for Catholic samples are positive. From this evidence alone it is obvious that the relationship between religious commitment and conservatism, theoretical tradition notwithstanding, is far from simple.

Part of this complexity is due to the fact that the consistency of relationships varies considerably according to the dimension of religion examined. Of the eight measures, only two are positively related to conservatism a majority of the time. When each dimension is considered separately, the following results emerge.

Among unidimensional measures only communalism is related positively to conservatism a majority of the time. All four correlations between communalism and social conservatism and half of the eight correlations with political conservatism are positive. (Only one relationship—neutral—with economic conservatism is reported.) A typical interpretation of this relationship is that communalism stimulates "a lack of concern with the problems of groups other than one's own".[27] Although both social class and denomination are related to communalism and conservatism, the observed relationship remains in all four cases reported where social class and denomination were controlled.

---

[25]The findings included from each article are indicated in the bibliography at the end of the chapter with the following abbreviations: D (denominational conservatism), A (church attendance), B (orthodox belief), I (associational involvement), C (communalism), V (devotionalism), K (religious knowledge), R (composite religiosity): P (political conservatism), E (economic conservatism), S (social conservatism). Thus, for example, "(AS,2BP)" following an entry indicates that one relationship between church attendance and social conservatism and two relationships between orthodox belief and political conservatism were enumerated from that entry.

[26]Relationships were considered positive if statistically significant positive variation was shown in cross-tabulations or if correlations exceeded +.15. Negative relationships were judged according to converse criteria.

[27]Lenski, op. cit., p. 193.

Table 1. *Summary of Research Showing Positive, Negative and Zero Correlations between Religion and Conservatism*

Conservatism	Denominational Conservatism	Church Attendance	Orthodox Beliefs	Associational Involvement	Communalism	Devotionalism	Religious Knowledge	Composite Religiosity	Total
Political									
Positive	33%	30%	41%	14%	50%	a	25%	58%	36%
Unrelated	56	58	59	72	50		25	42	56
Negative	11	12	0	14	0		50	0	8
Number	(9)	(33)	(22)	(7)	(8)		(4)	(12)	(97)
Economic									
Positive	a	33%	22%	0%	a	a	a	40%	19%
Unrelated		67	67	100				20	71
Negative		0	11	0				40	10
Number		(6)	(9)	(6)				(5)	(31)
Social									
Positive	100%	30%	48%	22%	100%	0%	0%	61%	45%
Unrelated	0	57	33	33	0	63	17	27	35
Negative	0	13	19	45	0	37	83	12	20
Number	(4)	(30)	(27)	(9)	(4)	(8)	(7)	(49)	(138)
Total									
Positive	47%	30%	41%	14%	62%	0%	8%	59%	39%
Unrelated	47	58	48	64	38	72	25	29	46
Negative	6	12	11	22	0	28	67	12	15
Number	(15)	(69)	(58)	(22)	(13)	(11)	(12)	(66)	(266)

a Too few cases

The only dimension clearly negatively related to conservatism is religious knowledge. This association would appear to be a function of social class, because it is known that religious knowledge increases with education;[28] in two reported instances where social class is controlled, however, the negative relation remains.

Devotionalism is either unrelated or negatively related to conservatism. Lenski[29] concludes that devotionalism is related to acceptance of humanitarian causes except where they are collectivistic or coercive. This conclusion is supported by the finding of Campbell and Fukuyama[30] that devotionalism is positively related to acceptance of outgroups but only slightly related to support of civil rights activities. However, Vanecko, Schellenberg et al., and Martin and Westie[31] each used large random samples and found devotionalism unrelated to conservatism.

Associational involvement appears to be essentially unrelated to conservatism. One study indicates a slight tendency for the highly involved to vote Republican, and several studies suggest negative relationships with social conservatism, but in general both "number of religious activities" and "proportion of activities religious" show no association with measures of conservatism.

Denominational conservatism is associated with social conservatism in four studies, but three are conducted on either student or southern samples; only Lenski[32] demonstrates a clear relationship with a sample of northern adults. Only one study examined economic conservatism in relation to denomination, showing zero correlations. Voting Republican is shown to be negatively related to denominational conservatism,[33] but important specifications are suggested. When the minister's theological position is used as a measure of denominational conservatism, slight *positive* tendencies toward voting Republican have been considered, although these have largely been explained by controlling for social class.[34] Johnson[35] attempts to show that frequent attenders of liberal

[28]Jerry Willis, "Correlates of Bible Knowledge," *Journal for the Scientific Study of Religion* 7 (Fall 1968): 280-81.

[29]Lenski, op. cit., p. 205.

[30]Thomas Campbell and Yoshio Fukuyama, *The Fragmented Layman: A Study of Church Participation* (Philadelphia: United Church Press, 1970).

[31]James J. Vanecko, "Types of Religious Behavior and Levels of Prejudice," *Sociological Analysis* 28 (Summer 1967): 119-20; James Schellenberg, Leo Stine, Thomas Bayton, and Fred Silva, "Religiosity and Social Attitudes in an Urban Congregation," *Review of Religious Research* 6 (Winter 1964): 142-46; and J. G. Martin and Frank W. Westie, "The Tolerant Personality," *American Sociological Review* 24 (August 1959): 521-28.

[32]Lenski, op. cit., p. 397.

[33]Ibid.

[34]Benton Johnson, *op. cit.*; Donald N. Anderson, "Ascetic Protestantism and Political Preference," *Review of Religious Research* 7 (Spring 1966): 167-71; and Gene F. Summers, Doyle P. Johnson, Richard L. Hough, and Kathryn A. Veatch, "Ascetic Protestantism and Political Preference: A Re-examination," *Review of Religious Research* 12 (Fall 1970): 17-25.

[35]Johnson, ibid.

congregations tend to vote Democratic due to exposure to social gospel theology, but Summers et al[36] argue that this hypothesis has not been substantiated at statistically significant levels. The complexity of the results, therefore, obviates simple conclusions and suggests a need for more attention to denominational differences than has been given before. With the growing number of comprehensive denominational surveys,[37] comparative efforts in this regard could prove particularly fruitful.

The relationship between orthodox belief and conservatism shows mixed results. All studies using southern samples found positive relationships between orthodoxy and social conservatism. Only two out of eleven relationships among northerners are positive, however, and these are both among students. A similar pattern holds for political and economic conservatism. Five of seven findings among southerners show positive relationships between orthodoxy and political and economic conservatism, but among northerners only four of fourteen relationships are positive, and the only relationship holding for northern adults is a tendency for believers to vote Republican.

Church attendance shows similar results. Four of ten relationships reported for southern samples are positive, as are three of five relationships among northern students. Among northern adults, however, none of the six relationships reported are positive. The majority of these relationships are neutral, although closer inspection has generally uncovered curvilinear relationships, with frequent attenders and non-attenders less conservative than infrequent attenders.[38] On measures of political and economic conservatism no positive relationships are shown for adult samples between church attendance and attitudes toward foreign policy, war, or economic issues, and for student samples only a slight tendency toward hawkishness is evident. Among adults a relationship between church attendance in conservative congregations and voting Republican has been suggested, but available evidence is only tentative.[39]

Finally, measures of composite religiosity, which include early scales such as Allport's extrinsic religiosity scale,[40] the Allport-Vernon scale of religious values,[41] Levinson's religious conventionality scale,[42] and the Chave attitude toward the church scale,[43] are positively associated with conservatism in 60 percent of the cases. Studies using these early scales have undoubtedly been

[36]Summers et al., op. cit.

[37]Glock et al., op. cit.; Campbell and Fukuyama, op. cit.; and Lawrence K. Kersten, *The Lutheran Ethic: The Impact of Religion on Laymen and Clergy* (Detroit: Wayne State University Press, 1970).

[38]Gordon W. Allport and Michael J. Ross, "Personal and Religious Orientation and Prejudice," *Journal of Personality and Social Psychology* 5 (April 1967): 432-43.

[39]Summers et al., op. cit.

[40]Allport, op. cit., and Allport and Ross, op. cit.

[41]Gordon W. Allport and P. E. Vernon, "A Test for Personal Value," *Journal of Abnormal and Social Psychology* 26 (May 1931): 231-48.

[42]O'Neil and Levinson, op. cit.

[43]L. L. Thurstone and E. J. Chave, *The Measurement of Attitude* (Chicago: University of Chicago Press, 1929).

largely responsible for the belief that religiosity and conservatism go hand in hand. The validity of these scales has been called into question, however. Allport's extrinsity scale has been criticized for including both motives and consequences of religious commitment[44] and has been shown to be only slightly correlated with other measures of religiosity.[45] Moreover, Allport and Ross[46] found the most conservative of their respondents not among the extrinsically religious but among the "indiscriminately religious," who accept both extrinsic and intrinsic items. The Allport-Vernon religious values scale has failed to yield consistent results[47] and when subjected to factor analysis has revealed factors other than religiosity.[48] Levinson's religious conventionality scale has also failed to yield consistent results[49] and is admittedly a measure of "tradition and conformity to institutional forms" as well as religiosity.[50] Finally, the Chave attitude toward the church scale has been shown through item analysis to measure "a tendency toward concreteness (as opposed to abstractness) instead of religiosity."[51] It is hardly surprising then that these composite scales have been found positively related to conservatism. The difficulty of ascertaining precisely what is being measured makes these scales less than useful for deriving valid conclusions, however.

Conclusions

Three major conclusions are evident from this analysis: (1) facile assertions connecting religion and conservatism are misleading, (2) different dimensions of religion and conservatism are related in different ways, and (3) gross methodological inadequacies must be overcome if this relationship is to be understood more fully.

1. Facile assertions connecting religion and conservatism are misleading.

[44]Stark and Glock, op. cit., pp. 18-20.

[45]John D. Photiadis and Jeanne Bigger, "Religiosity, Education, and Ethnic Distance," *American Journal of Sociology* 67 (May 1962): 666-72.

[46]Allport and Ross, op. cit.

[47]Richard I. Evans, "Personal Values as Factors in Anti-Semitism," *Journal of Abnormal and Social Psychology* 47 (October 1952): 749-56; Marshall B. Jones, "Religious Values and Authoritarian Tendency," *Journal of Social Psychology* 48 (August 1958): 83-89; Bernard Pyron, "Belief Q-sort, Allport-Vernon Study of Values and Religion," *Psychological Reports* 8 (June 1961): 399-400; and Milton Rokeach, *The Open and Closed Mind: Investigations into the Nature of Belief Systems and Personality Systems* (New York: Basic Books, 1960).

[48]Hubert E. Brogden, "The Primary Personal Values Measured by the Allport-Vernon Test, 'A Study of Values,'" *Psychology Monographs*, 66:16 (1952), no. 348; and Richard A. Hunt, "The Interpretation of the Religious Scale of the Allport-Vernon-Lindzey Study of Values," *Journal for the Scientific Study of Religion* 7 (Spring 1968): 65-77.

[49]Cody Wilson, "Extrinsic Religious Values and Prejudice," *Journal of Abnormal and Social Psychology* 60 (March 1960): 286-88; and Daniel J. Levinson, "The Intergroup Relations Workshop: Its Psychological Aims and Effects," *Journal of Psychology* 38 (July 1954): 103-26.

[50]O'Neil and Levinson, op. cit.

[51]W. Edgar Gregory, "The Orthodoxy of the Authoritarian Personality," *Journal of Social Psychology* 45 (May 1957): 217-32.

Only a minority of the findings reviewed here are positive, and when studies using early composite scales are deleted, the proportion of positive relationships drops to *one-third*. In the best-designed studies and in the poorest, neutral and negative relationships as well as positive are typical findings. This evidence is overlooked by the frequent pronouncements, based on popular interpretations of functionalism or Marxism, which claim religion to be inevitably associated with conservatism. The relationship between religion and conservatism, in fact, is more complex than is usually recognized.

2. Different dimensions of religion and conservatism are related in different ways. Orthodoxy, in spite of being charged with legitimating the status quo, seems to be of little consequence for political and social views, at least outside the South and among adults. Only when orthodoxy is combined with "particularistic" or radically "fundamentalistic" views does it show frequent correlations with conservative secular attitudes. Evidence on church attendance also violates simplistic assertions regarding its conserving functions. Refined measures generally revealed a curvilinear relationship between church attendance and conservatism. Moreover, the effects of church attendance, as argued by Johnson and his colleagues, seem to depend somewhat on the type of congregation attended. Communalism is the only dimension that seems unambiguously related to conservatism, especially social conservatism—confirming the expectation that sustained in-group association is related to intolerance and ethnocentrism. The only dimension negatively related to conservatism, according to the available evidence, is religious knowledge. Devotionalism is unrelated or else negatively related insofar as issues are humanitarian and not collectivistic or coercive. Finally, associational involvement has yet to be clearly shown either positively or negatively related to conservatism. Part of the complexity of the relationship between religion and conservatism, then, is clarified when dimensions of religion are analyzed separately. This fact requires that assertions relating religion and conservatism specify clearly which aspect of religion is being discussed.

3. Gross methodological inadequacies must be overcome if this relationship is to be understood more fully. Even when dimensions are examined separately considerable ambiguity in the relationship between religion and conservatism remains, the greater portion of which must be attributed to methodological weaknesses, much in evidence in these studies. In fact, the majority fail to meet even minimum standards of scientific procedure. One recent assessment of research in the sociology of religion[52] discovered only 5 (out of 185) articles that conformed to standard canons of causality. Studies of religion and conservatism are no exception.

None of the sixty-six studies reviewed here employ a panel design to establish time-order causality, and only fourteen provide any basis for generalization by utilizing random samples drawn from predefined universes. Exactly half the samples are composed of college students, which is a particularly acute difficulty

[52] Gary D. Bouma, "Assessing the Impact of Religion: A Critical Review," *Sociological Analysis* 31 (Winter 1970): 172-79.

because findings from student samples and findings from adult samples often differ. As observed above, orthodoxy and church attendance are associated with conservatism with greater frequency among students than among adults. This may be due to greater cognitive consistency among students resulting from their educational exposure, to their minority group status which possibly forces them to identify with conservative non-student religious groups, or simply to methodological error resulting from "demand characteristic effects."[53] Unfortunately no systematic evidence has been collected regarding these questions. More recent studies have been less subject to problems of sampling and design, but as yet only seven studies have been conducted on nationwide samples, and only two claim to be representative of church members at large. Also, studies only recently have begun to conceptualize religion and conservatism appropriately to capture their multiple dimensions. Finally, in spite of the fact that both religion and conservatism are known to vary with other variables such as age, region, and social class, only fourteen of the sixty-six studies reviewed here employed any third variables as a guard against spuriousness, and many of these were unable to show "specifications" because correlation analysis was used or complete tables were not presented.

Of these methodological shortcomings, the latter—insensitivity to third variables—seems most serious, but it also suggests hope for untangling the connection between religion and conservatism. The effects of social class raise particularly crucial questions. Not only is social class associated with both religion and conservatism, it is associated with various dimensions differently. Church membership, church attendance, and organizational involvement are generally more characteristic of the upper and middle classes, whereas belief and devotionalism are more common among the lower classes.[54] Moreover, measures of conservatism vary by social class, with political and social conservatism more common among the lower classes and economic conservatism more common among higher classes. Finally, denominational conservatism further complicates the picture as an intervening variable between social class and other dimensions of religion. Only scant attention has been devoted to unscrambling the relations between these variables in studies of religion and conservatism.

Recent research by Lipset and Raab[55] is suggestive of the type of analysis which needs to be focused on this problem. By constructing a typology consisting of "rednecks" (socially conservative, economically liberal), "right radicals" (conservative on both), "consistent liberals" (liberal on both), and "old guard" (socially liberal, economically conservative), they have explored the sources of different combinations of liberalism and conservatism. Although a composite scale of religious commitment (composed of "orthodoxy,"

[53]Martin T. Orne, "On the Social Psychology of the Psychological Experiment: With Special Reference to Demand Characterstics and Their Implications," *American Psychologist* 17 (October 1962): 776-83.

[54]N. J. Demerath III, *Social Class in American Protestantism* (Chicago: Rand McNally, 1965).

[55]Lipset and Raab, op. cit., pp. 426-83.

"particularism," and "libertarianism") is used and denominational effects are not controlled, they derive several fruitful conclusions. With their techniques they are able to show that both religion and social class produce independent variations in conservatism, that religion tends to distinguish between liberalism and conservatism on the social more than on the economic dimension, and that right radicals are more responsive to religious commitment than are rednecks (table 2).

Table 2.   *Typology, by Religious Commitment and Education (Percent)*

Religious Commitment	8th Grade		High School		College	
	Percent	Number	Percent	Number	Percent	Number
			Rednecks			
High	30[a]	(138)	30	(227)	17	(66)
Low	14	(14)	8	(37)	3	(37)
			Right Radicals			
High	37	(183)	26	(227)	27	(66)
Low	7	(14)	5	(37)	0	(37)
			Consistent Liberals			
High	2	(183)	3	(227)	8	(66)
Low	14	(14)	10	(37)	42	(37)
			Old Guard			
High (1)	1	(183)	2	(227)	8	(66)
Low	14	(14)	16	(37)	24	(37)

Reproduced from Seymour Martin Lipset and Earl Raab, *Politics of Unreason* (New York: Harper & Row, Publishers, 1970), p. 471.

[a] Percentage of those who have an eighth-grade education or less and have a high religious commitment who are Rednecks.

If research is to advance toward understanding the relationship between religion and conservatism, it must bring evidence to bear on the joint effects of social class, denomination, and other religious dimensions on dimensions of conservatism. Particular attention should be paid to combinations of religious and conservative dimensions that vary in different ways with social class. Similar attention needs to be directed toward unscrambling the connection between age, region, religion, and dimensions of conservatism. Toward this end more precise dimensions of conservatism need to be conceptualized and relatively neglected dimensions of religious commitment, such as devotionalism, communalism, and religious knowledge, need to receive greater attention.

Until more systematic evidence is available, the relationship between religion and conservatism must be considered problematic. Even on the basis of existing research, assertions suggesting a simple, unconditional relationship should be treated with skepticism. In regard to the theoretical traditions surveyed at the first of this paper, old hypotheses must be reformulated and new approaches to religion and its social consequences must be sought if the elusive relationship between religion and society is to be adequately grasped.

List of Books and Articles Subjected to Analysis

Adorno, T. W.; Frenkel-Brunswick, E.; Levinson, D. J.; and Sanford, R. N. *The Authoritarian Personality*. New York: Harper, 1950. (AS)

Allen, Russell O. "Religion and Prejudice: An attempt to Clarify the Patterns of Relationship." Ph.D. dissertation, University of Denver. (2RS)

Allport, Gordon W., and Ross, Michael J. "Personal and Religious Orientation and Prejudice." *Journal of Personality and Social Psychology* 5 (April 1967): 432-43. (18RS)

Anderson, Charles H. "Religious Communality and Party Preference." *Sociological Analysis* 30 (Spring 1969): 32-41. (3CP)

Anderson, Donald N. "Ascetic Protestantism and Political Preference." *Review of Religious Research* 7 (Spring 1966): 167-71. (AP)

Angell, Robert C. "Preferences for Moral Norms in Three Problem Areas." *American Journal of Sociology* 67 (May 1962): 650-60. (AS)

Baer, Danial J., and Mosele, Victor F. "Political and Religious Beliefs of Catholics and Attitudes toward Lay Dress of Sisters." *Journal of Psychology* 74 (January 1970): 77-83. (BP)

Blau, Peter. "Orientations of College Students toward International Relations." *American Journal of Sociology* 59 (November 1953): 205-14. (3AP)

Blum, Barbara Sandra, and Mann, John H. "The Effect of Religious Membership on Religious Prejudice." *Journal of Social Psychology* 52 (August 1960): 97-101. (IS)

Brown, Daniel C., and Lowe, Warner L. "Religious Beliefs and Personality Characteristics of College Students." *Journal of Social Psychology* 33 (February 1959): 103-29. (BE)

Burnham, Kenneth E.; Connors, John F., III; and Leonard, Richard. "Religious Affiliation, Church Attendance, Religious Education, and Student Attitudes toward Race." *Sociological Analysis* 30 (Winter 1969): 235-44. (AS)

Campbell, Thomas, and Fukuyama, Yoshio. *The Fragmented Layman: A Study of Church Participation*. Philadelphia: United Church Press, 1970. (BP, 2AS, IP, 2IS, VP, 2VS, KP, 2KS)

Carney, Richard E. "Some Correlates of Religiosity." *Journal for the Scientific Study of Religion* 1 (October 1969): 143-44. (RS)

Comrey, A. L., and Newmeyer, J. A. "Measurement of Radicalism-Conservatism." *Journal of Social Psychology* 67 (December 1965): 357-69. (RP, RE, 2RS)

Connors, John F., III; Leonard, Richard C.; and Burnham, Kenneth E. "Religion and Opposition to War among College Students." *Sociological Analysis* 29 (Winter 1968): 211-19. (8AP)

DeJong, Gordon F., and Faulkner, Joseph E. "The Church, Individual Religiosity, and Social Justice." *Sociological Analysis* 28 (Spring 1967): 34-43. (3RS)

Eckhardt, Kenneth W. "Religiosity and Civil Rights Militancy." *Review of Religious Research* 11 (Spring 1970): 197-203. (BS, AS, RS)

Evans, Richard I. "Personal Values as Factors in Anti-Semitism." *Journal of Abnormal and Social Psychology* 47 (October 1952): 749-56. (RS)

Feagin, Joseph R. "Prejudice and Religious Types: A Focused Study of Southern Fundamentalists." *Journal for the Scientific Study of Religion* 4 (Fall 1964): 3-13. (2RS)

———— "Prejudice, Orthodoxy, and the Social Situation." *Social Forces* 44 (September 1965): 46-56. (BS)

Friedrichs, Robert W. "Christians and Residential Exclusiveness." *Journal for the Scientific Study of Religion* 15 (Fall 1959): 20-22. (AS)

Garrison, Karl C. "Worldminded Attitudes of College Students in a Southern University." *Journal of Social Psychology* 54 (June 1961): 147-53. (3DP, 2DE, DS, RP, RE, RS)

Glock, Charles Y.; Ringer, Benjamin B.; and Babbie, Earl R. *To Comfort and to Challenge: A Dilemma of the Contemporary Church*. Berkeley and Los Angeles: University of California Press, 1967. (2IP, 3IE, IS)

Gregory, W. Edgar. "The Orthodoxy of the Authoritarian Personality." *Journal of Social Psychology* 45 (May 1957): 217-32. (RP, RS)

Hadden, Jeffrey K. "An Analysis of Some Factors Associated with Religion and Political Affiliation in a College Population." *Journal for the Scientific Study of Religion* 2 (April 1963): 209-16. (2RP, RE)

————. *The Gathering Storm in the Churches*. Garden City, N.Y.: Doubleday, 1969. (2AS, 3BE)

Holtzman, Wayne H. "Attitudes of College Men toward Non-segregation in Texas Schools." *Public Opinion Quarterly* 20 (Fall 1956): 599-609. (2AS)

Johnson, Benton. "Ascetic Protestantism and Political Preference." *Public Opinion Quarterly* 26 (Spring, 1962): 35-46. (DP, 2AP)

————. "Ascetic Protestantism and Political Preference in the Deep South." *American Journal of Sociology* 69 (January 1964): 359-66. (DP, 2AP)

Jones, Marshall B. "Religious Values and Authoritarian Tendency." *Journal of Social Psychology* 48 (August 1958): 83-89. (RS)

Keedy, T. C. "Anomie and Religious Orthodoxy." *Sociology and Social Research* 43 (September-October 1958): 34-37. (BS)

Kelly, J. G.; Ferson, Jean E.; and Holtzman, W. H. "The Measurement of Attitudes toward the Negro in the South." *Journal of Social Psychology* 48 (December 1958): 305-17. (AS, DS)

Kerr, Willard A. "Untangling the Liberalism-Conservatism Continuum." *Journal of Social Psychology* 35 (February 1952): 111-25. (RP, RE, RS)

Kersten, Lawrence K. *The Lutheran Ethic: The Impact of Religion on Laymen and Clergy*. Detroit: Wayne State University Press, 1970. (3BP, 3AP, 3IP, 3CP, 3KP, BE, AE, IE, CE, KE, 2BS, 2AS, 2IS, 2CS, 2KS)

Kirkpatrick, Clifford. "Religion and Humanitarianism: A Study of Institutional Implications." *Psychological Monographs* 63, no. 9 (1949). (RS)

Lenski, Gerhard. *The Religious Factor.* Garden City, N.Y.: Doubleday, 1963. (2BP, 2AP, DP, 2CP, AE, 2BS, AS, DS, 2CS, VS)

Levinson, Daniel J. "The Intergroup Relations Workshop: Its Psychological Aims and Effects." *Journal of Psychology* 38 (July 1954): 103-26. (RP, RS)

Liu, William T. "The Community Reference System, Religiosity, and Race Attitudes." *Social Forces* 39 (May 1969): 324-28. (AS)

McGovern, Eileen M., "Political Orientation and Socialization Background." Ph.D. dissertation, St. Louis University, 1969. (AP)

Maranell, Gary M. "An Examination of Some Religious and Political Attitude Correlates of Bigotry." *Social Forces* 45 (March 1967): 356-62. (10BP, 10AP, 4AE, 4BE, 6BS, 6AS)

Martin, J. G., and Westie, Frank W. "The Tolerant Personality." *American Sociological Review* 24 (August 1959): 521-28. (AS, 2VS, RS)

Neol, Donald L., and Pinkney, Alphonso. "Correlates of Prejudice: Some Racial Differences and Similarities." *American Journal of Sociology* 69 (May 1964): 609-22. (AS)

O'Reilly, Charles T., and O'Reilly, Edward J. "Religious Beliefs of Catholic College Students and Their Attitudes toward Minorities." *Journal of Abnormal and Social Psychology* 49 (July 1954): 378-80. (3RS)

Pettigrew, Thomas F. "Regional Differences in Anti-Negro Prejudice." *Journal of Abnormal and Social Psychology* 59 (January 1959): 28-36. (4AS)

Photiadis, John D., and Bigger, Jeanne. "Religiosity, Education, and Ethnic Distance." *American Journal of Sociology* 67 (May 1962): 666-72. (BP, AP, RP, BS, AS, RS)

Pyron, Bernard. "Belief Q-Sort, Allport-Vernon Study of Values and Religion." *Psychological Reports* 8 (June 1961): 399-400. (RS)

Rosenblith, Judy F. "A Replication of 'Some Roots of Prejudice.' " *Journal of Abnormal and Social Psychology* 44 (October 1949): 470-89. (RS)

Salisbury, W. Seward. "Religiosity, Regional Subculture, and Social Behavior." *Journal for the Scientific Study of Religion* 2 (Fall 1969): 94-101. (2BS)

Sartain, James A. "Attitudes of Parents and Children towards Desegregation." Ph.D. dissertation, Vanderbilt University, 1966. (IS)

Schellenberg, James; Stine, Leo; Bayton, Thomas; and Silva, Fred. "Religiosity and Social Attitudes in an Urban Congregation." *Review of Religious Research* 6 (Winter 1964): 142-46. (IP, IE, VP, VE)

Sheatsley, Paul B. "White Attitudes toward the Negro." *Daedalus.* Winter 1966, p. 226. (RS)

Shinert, Gregory, and Ford, Charles. "The Relation between Ethnocentric Attitudes and Intensity of Religious Practice." *Journal of Educational Sociology* 32 (December 1958): 159-62. (IS)

Stouffer, Samuel A. *Communism, Civil Liberties, and Conformity.* Garden City, N.Y.: Doubleday, 1955. (AS)

Struening, E. L. "Antidemocratic Attitudes in a Midwestern University." In H. H. Renners, ed., *Anti-Democratic Attitudes in American Schools*, chap. 9. Evanston, Ill.: Northwestern University Press, 1963. (AS)

Strommen, Merton P. "Religious Education and the Problem of Prejudice." *Religious Education* 62 (January-February 1967): 52-59. (2BS)

Summers, Gene F.; Johnson, Doyle P.; Hough, Richard L.; and Veatch, Kathryn A. "Ascetic Protestantism and Political Preference: A Re-examination." *Review of Religious Research* 12 (Fall 1970): 17-25. (AP, DP)

Thiessen, Victor. "Who Gives a Damn? A Study of Charitable Contributions." Ph.D. dissertation, University of Wisconsin, 1968. (IS)

Tumin, Melvin M. "Readiness and Resistance to Desegregation: Social Portrait of the Hard Core." *Social Forces* 36 (March 1958): 256-63. (AS, DS)

Vanecko, James J. "Types of Religious Behavior and Levels of Prejudice." *Sociological Analysis* 28 (Summer 1967): 119-20. (3BS, AS, 3VS, 3KS)

Walker, John E., Jr. "Liberal-Conservative Differences among Selected College Groups." Ph.D. dissertation, University of Florida, 1968. (DP)

Weima, J. "Authoritarianism, Religious Conservatism, and Sociocentric Attitudes in Roman Catholic Groups." *Human Relations* 18 (August 1965): 231-39. (2RS)

Wiley, Norbert. "Religious and Political Liberalism among Catholics." *Sociological Analysis* 28 (Fall 1967): 142-48. (RP)

Williams, Robert L. "Psychological Efficacy of Religiosity in Late Adolescence." *Psychological Reports* 20 (June 1967): 926. (AS)

Wilson, W. Cody. "Extrinsic Religious Values and Prejudice." *Journal of Abnormal and Social Psychology* 60 (March 1960): 286-88. (2RS)

Zimmerman, Franklin K. "Religion: A Conservative Social Force." *Journal of Abnormal and Social Psychology* 28 (January-March 1934): 473-74. (BP, BS)

Part Three

On Conformity and Rebellion among Religious Professionals

There is no great tradition of research on the religious professional in the sociology of religion. Some of the classic writers on religion, notably Max Weber, found it fruitful to study religious elites as a means to characterize and compare the religious modes of different times and places. These early leads were not followed up systematically, however, and a cumulative body of sociological research on religious officialdom has not been produced. As a result we still know relatively little about the recruitment, training, and role performance of clergy or about the nature and extent of the authority they exercise.

There is now some prospect for the neglect to be remedied. Over the last decade a spate of new studies has been directed to finding out what is happening among those who are committed enough to religion to devote their professional lives to it. This abundance of research has been stimulated not so much by new interest in religion as a profession as by the recognition that the clergy afford a strategic practical vantage point from which to study what many are convinced is a period of profound religious change. Although a needed cross-national and longitudinal research tradition is not developing, the research being done is affording new insights into the nature of religious professions and is helping to chart the course of more general religious change.

The question about religious professionals that has most intrigued us at Berkeley is whether in the present period they are likely to be the source of any major transformation in the form and content of religion. Outward signs suggest a degree of rebellion among clergy that is strong enough to upturn current arrangements, and a number of studies have been undertaken to discover what the prospects really are. Although research so far has been limited to samples of Protestant clergy in the United States, the studies probably reveal more general processes which operate in religious organizations to determine the size and pace of change. The four selections included in this part illustrate the processes and how they operate.

The first two selections are concerned principally to identify and to describe how clergy activism is accommodated structurally within the church. In chapter 12 Phillip E. Hammond and Robert E. Mitchell advance and test a theory that the accommodation is made through the "segmentation of radicalism." Jeffrey K. Hadden and Raymond C. Rymph in chapter 13 approach the same problem from a different theoretical perspective and methodology to conclude as well that the accommodation is rooted in the church's social structure.

Chapter 14 assesses the extent of conformity and rebellion that prevails among parish clergy and investigates how much of the variation stems from theological rather than structural roots.

Finally, in chapter 15 Robert Wuthnow investigates the potential for clergy-stimulated religious change through an investigation of prevailing variations in religious consciousness among the next generation of clergy—those now preparing for the ministry.

Additional Reading

Hadden, Jeffrey K. *The Gathering Storm in the Churches*. Garden City, N.Y.: Doubleday, 1969. Hadden's study, based on interviews of a national sample of Protestant clergy, affords a penetrating examination of the variety of perspectives the Protestant umbrella encompasses.

Mitchell, Robert E. "When Ministers and Their Parishioners Have Different Class Positions." *Review of Religious Research* 7:1 (Autumn 1965); "Polity, Church Attractiveness, and Ministers' Careers." *Journal for the Scientific Study of Religion* 5:2 (Spring, 1966); "Age and the Ministry: Consequences for Minister-Parishioner and Minister-Minister Relations." *Review of Religious Research* 8:3 (Spring 1967). Reports on an earlier national study of Protestant clergy, whose contents are revealed satisfactorily by Mitchell's adroit titling; should be read in contrast with Hadden's later study.

Fichter, Joseph. *America's Forgotten Priests: What Are They Saying*. New York: Harper & Row, Publishers, 1968. A profile of the attitudes of American diocesan priests on a wide range of issues, including celibacy; perhaps already a bit out of date, but it is an important benchmark against which to measure future change.

Neal, Marie Ausgusta. *The H. Paul Douglass Lectures for 1970*. "Part I. The Relation between Religious Belief and Structural Change in Religious Orders: Developing an Effective Measuring Instrument." *Review of Religious*

Research 12:1 (Fall 1970); "Part II: The Relation between Religious Belief and Structural Change in Religious Orders: Some Evidence." *Review of Religious Research* 12:3 (Spring 1971). These are the first reports of a massive inquiry into prevailing attitudes and beliefs among members of Roman Catholic religious orders in the United States.

Chapter Twelve

Segmentation of Radicalism:
The Case of the Protestant Campus Minister*

Phillip E. Hammond and Robert E. Mitchell

In pursuit of their goals, all organizations face a dilemma: how to adapt to changing environments without sacrificing organizational integrity. The dilemma may be thought of as a problem in balancing the commitments of members to the purposes of the organization, on the one hand, and to (their roles in) the organization's structure, on the other. Too inflexible a commitment to the organizational structure by some members can result in the defection of other members who claim that the goals have been forsaken. Too inflexible a goal commitment, however, can produce insensitivity to changing pressures, with a resultant lowered ability to achieve the organization's goals.

Whether viewed as a conflict between means and ends or between idealism and compromise, the dilemma is real. Organizations grow, die, barely struggle along, or change into other entities; and each response reflects some degree of viability. Viability, as an attribute of any organization, refers therefore to its degree of stability in the face of change.

Church organizations do not escape the dilemma. They have goals to achieve and personnel variously committed to those goals. They have environments to adapt to and an identity to maintain. That many of their goals are otherworldly may make it difficult to define "adaptation" and "commitment," but viability is no less a property of religious organizations. Indeed, the voluminous literature on church and sect attests to the importance of the dilemma for these organizations. In general, it seems, there have been two responses, neither of which yields optimum viability: the sect response, which maximizes goal commitment at the expense of adaptation, and the church response, which adapts at the expense of goals.

*Philip E. Hammond and Robert E. Mitchell, "Segmentation of Radicalism—the Case of the Protestant Campus Minister," *American Journal of Sociology* 71, no. 2 (September 1965). © 1965 by the University of Chicago. Reprinted with the permission of the authors and the *American Journal of Sociology*.

Forces toward breakdown or disintegration can come, then, from the outside in the form of environmental pressures or from the inside in the form of redefined goals, changes in role commitment, or efforts to alter the organization's boundaries. Inside pressures for change might be called "radicalism," and agents for such change "radicals." In every instance they are potential threats to organizational integrity, but they may also anticipate needed adaptation. The viable organization, therefore, finds room for its radicals, but typically does so by segmenting them, thereby minimizing disruption that radicals might create without sacrificing their potential insights by excluding them altogether. A common feature of organizations is thus the differentiation of radicals—a social structure serving two functions: a "safety valve" function of draining off dissidence and a "leavening" function of providing a source of new ideas.

Many organizations have social structures that function in these two ways, whether recognized or not. They may be called "research-and-development groups" in industrial corporations, "institutes" at universities, or "war colleges" in the military. In churches, the safety valve and leavening functions are typically served by such structures as monasteries, seminaries, and special orders. Our purpose in this paper is to discuss another of these structures—the ministry to higher education. We shall argue that for Protestant churches the campus ministry serves as an organizational device for segmenting radicals. Although that is not its manifest purpose, it siphons off potentially disruptive personnel, thus serving the safety-valve function; and, especially, it contributes to organizational change, thus serving the leavening function.

The consequences are not automatic, however; the channels through which they flow can also be identified. Following a discussion of the organizational effects of the campus ministry, therefore, we shall comment on a number of structural mechanisms which permit segmentation to serve the organization.

The Churches' Dilemma

At least since Troeltsch's monumental work on the impact of religious ideology on church structure, the organizational importance of many mansions in the religious house has been recognized. It is now generally recognized that church organizations atrophy unless regularly renewed but that the forces for renewal may also destroy. An *organizational* problem for religion, no less than for other organizations, is therefore one of segmenting the radical element, thereby containing and using it. The medieval church, in Troeltsch's words, "controlled this [radical] tendency by allowing it to express itself in the formation of new Religious Orders and confraternities."[1] At the same time "from this ascetic class the primitive Christian energy once more radiates fresh vitality into all merely relative approximations to the Christian standard."[2]

[1]Ernst Troeltsch, *The Social Teachings of the Christian Churches*, trans. Olive Wyon (2 vols.; New York: Macmillan Co., 1931), p. 701. See also pp. 237-45, 700-703.

[2]Ibid., p. 272.

MacMurray, who goes so far as to claim that the two forces of modernity—the Renaissance and the Reformation—stem from the medieval pattern of monasteries, says of them:

> It is here that the creative forces of the spiritual life are to be found; and here that the ferment of Christianity is most powerful and most difficult to deal with. If the will to power in the church is to maintain itself, it must suppress the spiritual creativeness within its own bosom. . . . The function of the monastic system [therefore] is to segregate the creative forces which would seek to realize Christianity and in so doing destroy the dualist structure of society.[3]

The medieval church, in other words, is cited as an example of a viable religious organization. "The church of the thirteenth century was relatively successful in finding a place . . . for the expression of the radical-individualizing tendencies of Christianity."[4] But, as Yinger and other observers of church and sect are quick to point out, the *degree* to which religious organizations "contain and use" their radicals is variable. They differ in their provisions for meeting the safety valve and leavening functions.

> It is commonly observed, for example, that the proliferation of religious divisions is far more extensive under Protestantism, with its greater emphasis on individual experience . . . encouraged the development of *different* religious structures. Catholicism reflects the variations in religious needs *within* its pattern. [5]

The Campus Ministry as a Radical Segment in Protestantism

Though by no means the only Protestant social structure for segmenting radicals, the campus ministry is one that has consequences, we shall argue, which exceed its numerical size. Dating from the turn of the century as a self-conscious separate ministry, the churches' work on college campuses has grown steadily. Currently it contains about 1,300 full-time workers, which is about 1 per cent of the ministerial force of the ten denominations supporting almost all of the full-time campus clergy. Although many schools of higher education, especially junior colleges and teachers colleges, are without campus ministers, large private or state universities may have as many as a dozen, and increasingly the small liberal arts colleges are hosting chaplains. Some of these persons are employed by the school as worship leaders, religious counselors, and teachers. The great majority, however, are employed by a denomination (or a regional division thereof—and, as directors of "foundations" ringing the campuses, administer

[3]John MacMurray, *The Clue to History* (London: SCM Press, 1938), pp. 155-56.

[4]J. Milton Yinger, *Religion in the Struggle for Power* (Durham, N.C.: Duke University Press, 1946), p. 21.

[5]J. Milton Yinger, *Religion, Society and the Individual* (New York: Macmillan Co., 1957), p. 134. (First emphasis added.)

programs that include study groups, social events, theological discussions, social action, and so on.

Evidence that the campus ministry contains "radicals" is seen in the comparison of results from two studies, one of parish clergy, the other of their campus counterparts. The data on campus ministers were collected in the Spring, 1963 by mail questionnaire sent to all known full-time Protestant campus clergy. The return from this population universe was 79 percent for an N of 997. The parish-minister data were collected three years earlier, by mail questionnaire sent to a 10 percent random sample of eight denominations which are members of the National Council of Churches. Smaller samples were taken of two non-member denominations. The return rate in this study was 68 percent for an N of 4,077.[6]

Table 1 contains evidence of radicalism. There it can be seen that, relative to

Table 1. *Percentage of Campus Ministers and of Parish Ministers Who Agree with Various Statements*

Statement	Campus Ministers (N = 997)	Parish Ministers (N = 4,077)
Political attitudes:		
1. Strongly approve of the purposes of the United Nations	73%	57%
2. Strongly approve of the purposes of the AFL-CIO	21	11
Breadth of interest:		
3. Regularly read *Christian Century*	67	33
4. Regularly read *Christianity and Crisis*	44	6
5. Very interested in news of national and international affairs	75	62
6. Very interested in news of own denomination	35	68
7. Very or quite interested in news of other denominations.	57	68
The church and social action:		
8. Would very much like to see church-sponsored examination of major ethical issues*	66	57
9. Agree own denomination is too conservative in the field of social action	53	17
Ecumenical attitudes:		
10. Agree own denomination is not sufficiently ecumenical-minded	42	10
11. Strongly approve of the National Council of Churches	51	42
12. Strongly approve of the World Council of Churches	59	44
Miscellaneous:		
13. Agree own denomination does not have clearly defined policies	27	15
14. Have a Bachelor of Divinity degree	84	65
15. Have a Ph.D. degree	13	2
16. Choose, as closest to own belief regarding the Bible, "An infallible revelation of God's will"†	8	24

* The question to campus ministers read ". . . see greater social action by Protestants."
† Other options: "Inspired by God, but subject to historical criticism," and "a great history of religious experience, but not necessarily inspired by God." These two were chosen by 84% and 7%, respectively, of campus ministers 70% and 3%, respectively, of parish ministers.

[6]For details of sampling, see Phillip E. Hammond, *The Campus Clergyman* (New York: Basic Books, 1966).

parish ministers, campus clergy are more liberal in their attitudes toward labor unions and the UN, more critical of their denominations, more favorable toward ecumenical affairs, better educated, and have wider interests. These data are convincing. Although too cumbersome to show in tabular form, the differences are maintained across ten denominations and, within denomination, across three age groups.[7] This latter point is especially worth emphasizing because, although the "radicalism" of campus ministers might be widely acknowledged, it might also be attributed solely to their youth. Yet, in fact, campus and parish ministerial differences persist in all age groups.

Organizational Consequences of the Campus Ministry

Because of the differences between campus and parish ministers in attitudes and values, some consequences of there being a campus ministry can be inferred. Here are several which seem to have strategic importance for organized Protantism:

1. *More persons are recruited and kept in the ministry than otherwise would be.*—Probably any increase in the diversity of jobs offered by an organization will attract and hold more diverse persons, but careers in education and religion have a special affinity. The job anticipated by the second largest number of seminarians, for example (the largest number expect to be parish ministers), is teaching.[8] An investigation of 111 former ministers discovered that no fewer than 72 were "teachers or administrators in universities, colleges, or public schools."[9] Campus ministers report that, were they to leave the campus ministry, they would prefer (by a two-to-one ratio) full-time teaching over the parish ministry. Not only does the campus ministry represent a different career possibility for clergymen, therefore, but also an especially important one. An educational occupation that is contained *within* the church and that can be pursued without forsaking a "call" stands to attract and hold persons who might otherwise be in education *outside* of the church.

2. *Radicals are removed from the parish structure.*—Campus posts not only represent an *added* attraction to persons who otherwise would not enter the ministry but also serve as locations for ministers who might otherwise leave the parish. More than seven in ten campus clergy have experience in a parish setting. Leaving, of course, is not always a result of conflict, but Table 1 makes it clear that those who leave are more radical than those who stay, and radicalism does explain some of the moves. One campus minister, for example, had been a parish minister in a border state and intended to remain so. But he was "eased out" by his superior over the question of civil rights. Rather than continue with the

[7]With three age groups in ten denominations, a total of 480 comparisons are possible. Of these 480, 89 percent reveal the difference contained in Table 1 and 11 percent do not, although a quarter of this last group involves cells containing fewer than ten cases.

[8]See the study of 17,565 seminarians by K. R. Bridston and D. W. Culver, reported in *Seminary Quarterly*, V (Spring, 1964), 2.

[9]H. G. Duncan, "Reactions of Ex-Ministers toward the Ministry," *Journal of Religion*, XII (1932), 101-15.

tensions created by this man, his administrator urged him to take his denomination's ministry at the state university. Another told of his inability to communicate liberal theology to primarily non-college-educated congregations. He then asked to be assigned a campus ministerial post.[10]

Insofar as these minsters' experience is common, it suggests that liberal agents are removed from parish settings. Thus the campus ministry not only provides a "retreat" for dissident clergymen but also supplies some insulation for the larger segment of the church—insulation from potential disturbance. If the foregoing is essentially true—that an outlet is created for ministers frustrated by the constraints of the parish—then the *extent* to which this is true should differ by denomination according to their degree of constraint. Churches in which "radical" sentiment is relatively rare have greater need for an outlet. To test this hypothesis we have classified denominations by the proportions of parish ministers expressing certain liberal-conservative attitudes. This classification serves as a measure of the constraint a liberal may feel. A comparison of the answers by campus and by parish clergy to various items indicating criticism of the church reveals that in more restrictive denominations the difference is greater between the two groups. For example, in the United Church of Christ (a denomination in which liberal sentiment is common), campus ministers, compared with parish ministers, are more critical, by 15 percent, of their denomination for being too conservative in social action. In contrast, Missouri Synod Lutheran campus ministers are 53 percent more critical than are *their* parish counterparts. Table 2 supplies the evidence on three such issues for all ten denominations.

Table 2 does not indicate however, that radicalism (defined above as "inside pressures for changing the organization") is less of a factor in liberal denominations. It merely means that, for them, radicalism regarding *political-theological* issues is less of a factor in creating conflicts. Were the data available, they would probably indicate that campus ministers in politically and theologically liberal denominations are radical in other ways, perhaps in regard to ecclesiastical arrangements, salaries, or routine parish duties. The point is that a campus ministry segments "radicals," providing them with a legitimate base and insulating them from the parish.

3. *The campus ministry serves to sustain radicalism.*—If the short-run consequence of removing some persons to the campus ministry is to leave the parish structure less radical, probably the long-run effect is quite the opposite. One reason for such a speculation stems from the known differences in radicalism between academic communities and the general public.[11] The campus minister, surrounded by university personnel and having a clientele that remains

[10]Examples are from case interviews with campus ministers. A similar problem is discussed by Marshall Sklare in *Conservative Judaism* (Glencoe, Ill.: Free Press, 1955). He speaks of the difficulty faced by seminarians who are trained by the churches' best intellects only to be sent into parishes with no provision for fulfilling their intellectual aspirations.

[11]For example, compare the civil libertarianism of social scientists, community leaders, and the general public as reported in P. F. Lazarsfeld and W. Thielens, *The Academic Mind* (Glencoe, Ill.: Free Press, 1958), pp. 391-92, and S. A. Stouffer, *Communism, Conformity and Civil Liberties* (New York: Doubleday & Co., 1955), pp. 40-43.

Table 2. *Relationship between Denominational Constraint and Differences between Campus (C) and Parish (P) Clergy in Three Issues Indicating Criticism of Their Denominations*

Denominations Ranked by Degree of Constraint*	Percentage Who Criticize Their Denominations for									No. Cases		Percentage of Parish Ministers Who Strongly Approve of the	
	Being Too Conservative in Social Action			Not Being Ecumenical Enough†			Not Having Clearly Defined Policies†						
	C	P	Difference	C	P	Difference	C	P	Difference	C	P	UN*	WCC*
Least:													
United Church	22	7	15	12	6	6	27	30	− 3	71	228	61	54
Disciples	70	17	53	46	13	33	45	39	6	32	291	60	50
Episcopal	50	28	22	29	17	12	26	19	7	125	467	65	38
Presbyterian, USA	28	9	19	10	5	5	7	4	3	113	585	54	48
Methodist	37	9	28	49	10	39	27	15	12	273	1,566	57	44
Lutheran	66	16	50	54	7	47	26	8	18	79	273	57	43
American Baptist	77	19	58	70	16	54	63	25	38	68	330	49	33
Presbyterian, US	69	20	49	68	16	52	37	6	31	43	188	40	33
Southern Baptist	77	20	57	48	17	31	29	9	20	133	62	36	5
Most:													
Mo. Synod, Lutheran	71	18	53	65	14	51	3	1	2	31	87	19	2

* Denominations are ranked on the basis of *parish* ministers' combined strong approval of the United Nations and the World Council of Churches. Greatest approval = least constraint. Had different items from Table 1 been used, the ordering of denominations would change but little.

† Percentages are non-weighted averages of the three age groups (20-29; 30-39; 40+) in each denomination.

perpetually young, is in a location that nurtures and sustains intellectualism in general and perhaps radicalism (as defined here) in particular. Certainly it supplies him with a context in which questioning traditional procedures is less frowned upon. Insofar as this radicalism is linked to the "intellectualist—anti-intellectualist" conflict in Protestantism (which Niebuhr has maintained is its primary theological conflict),[12] the campus ministry may represent a strategic realignment of forces within the church. Seminaries no doubt remain the commonest battleground for this issue, but the creation of still more university-based positions might well have a radical effect on how the issue is fought.

4. *Radicalism is returned to the church through ministers who themselves return to the parish.*—The turnover of campus ministers is quite high, estimated at 14 percent annually. The majority of those who leave go back into a local parish, although some move to college teaching, hospital chaplaincies, church administration, and so forth.[13] Granted, the more conservative are more likely to return to the parish, but even these persons' answers to the items of Table 1 are far more radical than those of parish ministers. Furthermore, not only conservatives return to the parish. It is reasonable to speculate, therefore, that those resuming parish duties are more likely to serve as agents of change in the church because (1) they are more radical to begin with than ministers who never were campus ministers and (2) they come from their campus ministerial years having had that radicalism supported.

5. *Radicalism is returned to the church through campus ministers' clients who become church members.*—Given the difference between campus and parish clergy in such matters as those contained in Table 1, it probably is the case that campus ministers' influence on the church via their clients is a radical one. It is true that little is known of the effects on the clients of campus ministers. But we reason as follows: most, if not all, of the persons *who become church members* following campus ministerial contact are of two kinds. First, there are students from active church backgrounds whose attitudes will more nearly reflect a parish ministerial viewpoint. Insofar as their attitudes are altered, they will probably change in the radical direction. Second, there are persons who, because of their radical attitudes, would not affiliate with the church were it not for campus ministerial contact. Both cases represent additions to the radical sector of church membership.[14]

6. *Radicalism is returned to the church by campus ministers' greater leadership potential in radical causes.*—At mid-twentieth century, two of the

[12]H. Richard Niebuhr, D. D. Williams, and J. M. Gustafson, *The Advancement of Theological Education* (New York: Harper & Bros., 1957).

[13]Estimates are based on answers to questions asked of campus ministers regarding where they *would* go if they leave. See also Donald Bossart, "Leaving the Campus Ministry" (unpublished Ph.D. dissertation, Boston University, 1963), in which it is reported that 50 percent of former campus ministers are in parish work. This is more than double the proportion going into any other occupation.

[14]The disconfirming cases—persons made so radical by campus ministerial contact that they leave the church and others who react to campus ministers by becoming less radical—we assume are rare. This is only assumption, however.

major forces impinging on the church are the civil-rights movement and the move toward ecumenicism. Either issue stands to force organizational change. The campus ministry has been disproportionately involved in both movements, a fact not widely known among church laymen and known hardly at all by the public.

In the case of civil rights, Chaplain Coffin of Yale and Reverend Klunder (campus minister to Cleveland colleges) have been visible examples owing to the one's early arrest and the other's death under the tracks of an earth mover. These are only two instances, however; many of the clergy—Protestant and Catholic, Christian and Jew—involved in protest demonstrations are ministers on campus. The reason their activity is greater than that of parish ministers is easily understood. They are more radical to begin with, it is true, but also they are more strategically located in that they have immediate access to a major source of manpower for many demonstrations: college students. The recruitment and training of these students frequently have been under the auspices—or at least with the counsel—of the religious ministry on their campuses.

Whereas the civil-rights movement challenges the church at the level of goals, ecumenicism not only challenges goals but also is a rather direct threat to denominational integrity or organizational boundaries. That it may prove to be an organizational necessity if such goal challenges as civil rights persist only accents the leavening function of those persons in the church who are at the ecumenical forefront. In disproportionate numbers here, too, campus ministers have been active.

Visser'T Hooft, as the first (and until recently only) general secretary of the World Council of Churches, had his ecclesiastical experience in European student work, and this fact has often been noted.[15]

Less dramatic but organizationally more significant is the fact that his is no isolated case.

> It is . . . to the student Christian movements . . . that tribute must be paid for aggressive and radical ecumenical pioneering. Existing in the different countries of Europe, Britain, the United States, and the Far East . . . [they] met together on a world basis, and kept in contact with each other through their speakers and their literature. Not a part of the churches officially, the student Christian movements . . . have regarded themselves in both a spiritual and a functional sense as close to the churches, indeed as the representatives of the church on the university campuses of the world. Free from ecclesiastical control, with the imagination stimulated by the intellectual climate of the great universities and the small colleges as well, they have been able to point the way. . . . It is from the student

---

[15]"Certainly his experience in the World's Student Christian Federation stood him in good stead, giving him personal contacts and the knowledge of how to take initiative" (Mackie, in R. C. Mackie and C. C. West [eds.], *The Sufficiency of God* [London: SCM Press, 1963], p. 8). On the history of ecumenicism see also R. S. Bilheimer, *The Quest for Christian Unity* (New York: Association Press, 1952); R. Rouse and S. Neill (eds.), *A History of the Ecumenical Movement* (Philadelphia: Westminster Press, 1954); Robert Lee, *The Social Sources of Church Unity* (New York: Abingdon Press, 1960).

movements that some of the greatest of ecumenical leadership has come and continues to come.[16]

This account has the value of focusing on more than the motivation for ecumenicism; it suggests the importance of facilities such as communication networks and available candidates for leadership through which motivation can be channeled. And this, it seems, is where campus ministers have entered. They have been in a position to assume leadership, and they have had ecumenical experience and prior access to communication networks across denominations.

Some reasons for this availability and experience are clear. First, many campus ministers are chaplains to entire student bodies and therefore cannot appropriately restrict their ministry to persons of their own denominations. Second, like that of the military chaplaincy, the campus ministry's situation has spawned change in an ecumenical direction when, for example, it has felt the need to relax rules for giving and receiving communion. Third, many of the (especially monetary) concerns of parish administration are minimized because they are assumed by college administrations or regional or national offices of the denomination. Fourth, the very lack of structure for many campus ministers encourages interdenomination co-operation, for example, in negotiations with college administrators over matters such as visitation privileges in dormitories, obtaining church preference lists at registration time, and so forth.[17]

In brief, campus ministers, as seen in Table 1, are less interested than are parish ministers in news of their own denominations but more interested in and more concerned with the purposes of the National and the World Council of Churches. As in the case of civil rights, however, campus ministers not only *favor* the changes implied but their segmentation puts them in a better position to *act* on those changes.

Structural Mechanisms Involved in the Segmentation of Radicalism

Control over channels of communication in an organization are of crucial significance if that organization is to contain and use its radicalism. In the case of the safety-valve function, expression of radicalism is restricted to places and times where it is thought to be least disruptive, in other words, where communication can be allowed to go unpunished. Physical isolation—in monasteries, for example—is perhaps the clearest device of this sort. (Of course, the "isolation" must be rewarding or else it is more likely to be defined as

---

[16]Bilheimer, *op. cit.*, pp. 81-82. "By 1895 the Student Christian Movements ... had already coalesced in the World's Student Christian Federation. This was the movement which was destined to produce the great bulk of leadership of the modern ecumenical movement ..." (Rouse, *in* Rouse and Neill [eds.], *op. cit.*, p. 341).

[17]Thus, fully 70 percent of campus ministers would like to see "the merger of various denominational campus ministers on the same campus whenever possible." The propensity for the campus ministry, from its beginnings, to be interdenominational is discussed in Clarence P. Shedd, *The Church Follows Its Students* (New Haven, Conn.: Yale University Press, 1938), p. 67, chap. v.

punishment.) Provision for selective target audiences along with selectively decreasing visibility to other audiences would seem to be the structural mechanisms through which the safety-valve function operates. Examples include a monk charged with translating esoteric palimpsests, a researcher in industry or university assigned to laboratory or institute, or a campus minister permitted his radicalism in the particular company of academics and young adults. In each case, one result from the organizational standpoint is the selective segmenting of potentially disruptive communications.

But if the structural devices for providing an outlet for radicals (so their commitment is maintained and their communication is selectively directed) are readily understood and practiced by many organizations, the structural means whereby the segment leavens the whole are not. The case of the campus ministry suggests several mechanisms, however, whose applicability would seem to extend beyond church organizations.[18]

Here again the focus is on communication, but this time on its use more than on its containment. The first mechanism is quite obviously a *recruitment* mechanism. Called "co-optation" in some contexts, or quota hiring in others, the practice of attracting more heterogeneous personnel, if only by offering a wider range of positions, is one device for seeing that innovation is more likely *brought into* the organization.

A second structural device for enhancing the leavening function of radicals is implied in the term "segment"—radicals are clustered for mutual reinforcement. Among ministers on campuses with more than one minister, for example, fully 86 percent report at least weekly contact with one another. A series of separate questions relating to formal and informal relations with clergy of their own and other denominations was asked of the *parish* ministers, although here the time period was not a week but a month. Sixty-five percent reported that they met informally with clergy of their own denomination at least once a month, whereas the second highest percentage, 57 percent, was reported for informal contact with clergy of other denominations. (The respective figures for formal contacts are 51 percent for own denomination and 38 percent for other denominations.) It would seem clear that parish clergy have less contact with one another than do campus clergy.

Medieval monks were located *together* in monasteries, and research scientists typically *collaborate* in their "isolated" divisions. Whatever may be the difficulty of sustaining "deviance" alone is alleviated to some extent by regular interaction with others likewise predisposed to innovative thoughts.

The campus ministry exemplifies a third structural mechanism: the routine location of the radical segment in or alongside populations with particular characteristics. Whether intended and/or recognized or not, the alignment of radical clergymen with the university community serves to maintain the former's

---

[18]A similar discussion, although in different terms, is found in Eugene Litwak, "Models of Bureaucracy Which Permit Conflict," *American Journal of Sociology*, 67 (1961): 177-84. Litwak identifies several "mechanisms of segregation," procedures "by which potentially contradictory social relations are co-ordinated in some common organizational goals."

propensity to change. The practice of locating professional schools in universities would seem to be another example of the importance of this mechanism, as would its antithesis—the practice of isolating novitiates from any contact other than with planned echelons of the parent organization.

A fourth mechanism for increasing the probability that a radical segment will have a radical effect is the designing of a position with freedom from routine duties, which is to say freedom from the *usual* constraints impinging on other sectors of the organization. Campus ministers, like junior executives sent to training institutes, would probably object to the statement that their duties are *less*. The significance, therefore, is that the duties are *different* and may include the tasks of leading civil-rights protests or assuming ecumenical leadership. The fact, for example, that most campus ministers need not assume major responsibility for their salaries but may rely upon the denomination's support quite clearly allows them certain extraordinary freedoms that the great majority of parish ministers do not have. The effort to "serve" college populations is at least not contingent upon evoking their financial support.

The radicalism of the campus ministry is used through a fifth structural mechanism which might be called the "circulation of radicals." Granted, in the case of campus ministers, the habit of returning to the parish after a term of serving higher education is not typically anticipated by either the church administration or the campus clergyman, and yet this is the path usually followed. As such, it is structurally analogous to a corporation's practice of electing board members regularly from all its divisions, or of a university's "handing around" its administrative offices to persons from various disciplines. The chance of infusing new ideas increases with the circulation of different types of individuals.

The sixth mechanism is similar to the fifth in that carriers of radical communication are circulated. However, in this case the circulation is of the *clients* of radicals and not of the radicals themselves. The argument was presented above that the impact of the campus minister on would-be church members in most cases would have to be radical, given the differences between campus clergymen and their parish counterparts. The *content* of those differences is irrelevant to the operation of the mechanism, provided only that differences systematically exist. In similar fashion, the mechanism operates in the case of executives-in-training who circulate from department to department thereby being influenced (to the extent that they are) by agents representing various concerns within the organization, all potentially different from each other and from the concerns of current executives. Likewise, the practice of relegating children to elementary instruction from unmarried females, of Catholic young people to college instruction from members of certain orders, or professional trainees to academic rather than to practitioners in an apprentice-craftsman relationship, all exemplify the circulation of clients. The result, as in the case of the other mechanisms identified, is an increased probability that use will be made of a radical segment.

It should be clear from the discussion that the mechanisms through which the "leavening" function operates are not contingent upon particular substantive communications. If an organization typically moves in a certain direction, a "radical" element is any element that would alter that direction. The discussion of these last few pages, then, might be useful in explaining the *inability* of an organization to adapt, just as it might explain the opposite.

Conclusion

Every organization has its potential "radicals"—persons whose commitment to the organizational structure and/or its goals is unusual. Just as these persons can be disruptive if located randomly throughout the organization, so also can they be prophetic. If there exist structures for their segmentation, however, radicalism is more likely to be contained and also more likely to be used. Such segmentation not only serves as an escape valve for disruptive forces, therefore, but also may serve as a source of organizational change.

The mere isolation of the radical segment (perhaps epitomized in imprisonment) can do no more than serve the escape-valve function, however. Simple banishment, firing, or defrocking removes the radicals, but it does not allow use of their possible leavening effect. For this function to operate, certain mechanisms must be associated with segmentation so that radical communication can flow back into the organization. The campus ministry illustrates both these functions—the safety valve and the leavening—and it illustrates also a number of the mechanisms by which they operate. These include devices such as heterogeneous recruitment, mutual reinforcement, location of the radical segment alongside populations with known characteristics, freedom from usual duties, circulation of radicals, and circulation of the clients of radicals.

It is unnecessary to argue that the Protestant campus ministry is only functional, and not at all dysfunctional, for Protestant denominations. The future is contingent on other factors than just the segmentation of radicals. If the analysis here is correct, however, that future will have resulted in part from the presence of the campus ministry—a radical segment with consequences for its parent organization.

Chapter 13

Social Structure and Civil Rights Involvement: A Case Study of Protestant Ministers*

Jeffrey K. Hadden and Raymond C. Rymph

While clergymen have been on the forefront of the civil rights movement, their role in this movement has not been carefully studied. Systematic study of clergymen in the civil rights movement should be important for several reasons. First, such an investigation should lead to a better understanding of the movement. Second, the role and position of the clergy should be clarified. Third, inasmuch as the activist element of the civil rights movement is at variance with dominant public sentiment regarding the appropriate means of obtaining the objective of freedom and equality for Negroes, an analysis of ministers' participation in this movement may lead to theoretical insights in several areas including deviance, role conflict, the influence of the group on the individual, and social structural concomitants of behavior.

The purpose of this paper is to explore some of these theoretical perspectives by examining a case study in which 48 Protestant ministers assembled for a training program were faced with the decision of whether to become involved in a civil rights demonstration. For a variety of reasons which will become obvious, the data cannot be interpreted as more than suggestive of appropriate theoretical frameworks to study the civil rights movement and the involvement of ministers in it. But in spite of the limitations of the case study, it provides both the opportunity to "try out" theoretical speculation as well as generating insights which lend themselves to systematic investigation.

A study by Campbell and Pettigrew of ministers in Little Rock, Arkansas, during the racial crisis that erupted over the admission of Negro students in an all-white high school in the fall of 1957, constitutes the only systematic attempt by social scientists to understand the role of clergymen in civil rights.[1] Campbell

*Jeffrey K. Hadden and Raymond C. Rymph, "Social Structure and Civil Rights Involvement: A Case Study of Protestant Ministers," *Social Forces* 45, no. 1 (September 1966). Reprinted with the permission of the authors and *Social Forces*.

[1]Ernest Q. Campbell and Thomas F. Pettigrew, *Christians in Racial Crisis: A Study of Little Rock's Ministry* (Washington, D.C.: Public Affairs Press, 1959).

and Pettigrew found that only five of the 29 ministers interviewed were segregationists. Moreover, they found that by 1957 all of the major Protestant denominations had adopted declarations commending the 1954 Supreme Court decision on desegregation. Yet, in spite of their personal beliefs favoring desegregation and the official position of their denominations, the Little Rock ministers remained relatively inactive during the city's racial crisis.

Campbell and Pettigrew explain this paradox in terms of a role conflict theory and a reference system model. The minister is an actor in three reference systems: (1) his own personal convictions, *self-reference system* (SRS); (2) the position of his denomination, *professional reference system* (PRS); and (3) the expectations of his congregation, *membership reference system* (MRS). While his *self-reference system* and his *professional reference system* favor desegregation, his *membership reference system* is apparently committed to maintaining the status quo. If he goes against the MRS and takes a strong stand for desegregation, he may face the possibility of losing membership in his congregation, financial resources, and even his job. Thus, an aggressive stand in favor of desegregation could possibly lead to a cleavage in his congregation that would bankrupt his church financially as well as spiritually.

Faced with this possibility, his PRS may even impose sanctions on him to conform to the expectation of the MRS, for the PRS has a commitment to the preservation of the institution that probably runs deeper than commitment to desegregation. At least, it can be asserted that the denominational leaders, like the ministers, are caught in a role conflict between supporting a creed and system maintenance. Thus, it is highly unlikely that the PRS will impose negative sanctions on the ministers for not conforming to a creed, and it seems more likely that negative sanctions would come were the minister to ignore the problem of system maintenance. In Little Rock, at least, extremely strong pressures were brought to bear on ministers to conform to the expectations of the MRS, and most of them did conform.[2]

If these rather strong institutional restraints against active involvement are typical in the South, the invasion of the South by northern ministers takes on a new dimension. In order for the church to take an active role in the civil rights movement in the South, it was necessary that much of the leadership come from ministers in northern states, because southern ministers could not actively participate in large numbers without severely endangering the institutional strength of the church in the South.[3]

---

[2]Campbell and Pettigrew discuss the various mechanisms which ministers use to control the development of guilt which might ensue from compromising their SRS, but these need not concern us here.

[3]Although they have not been systematically studied, numerous examples can be cited where pressure has been exerted to keep clergymen silent on civil rights. For example, in January 1963, 28 Mississippi Methodist ministers signed a document entitled "Born of Conviction," in which they declared that they were united in affirming that the Christian tradition does not permit discrimination because of race, color, or creed. By mid-1965 only nine of these native Mississippi ministers remained in the state, and only two occupied the same pulpit as they had two and a half years previous. Furthermore, there was evidence that several of those who remained in Mississippi were still facing reprisals and would yet be forced to leave the state.

But what about the participation of northern ministers in the civil rights movements? It is becoming increasingly apparent that the North is not without prejudice and its own techniques for creating segregation in schools, jobs, and housing. Do not the northern ministers encounter difficulty in moving from the preaching of a creed to active involvement in the civil rights struggle? The answer is that quite obviously many northern ministers also face powerful constraints that limit their participation. Equally obvious, however, are the hundreds who have descended on Montgomery, Birmingham, Jackson, Selma, and other southern cities to express their convictions.

How do we account for the fact that some ministers become involved while others do not? Extrapolating from the Campbell and Pettigrew model, we might predict that ministers with congregations in which the "influentials" have favorable attitudes toward the civil rights cause will be more likely to become involved than those lacking this MRS support. This model would assume that ministers are able to fairly accurately perceive the attitudes toward the civil rights cause of their parishioners and that they act accordingly. When this model is lifted out of the context of a locally-centered crisis situation, however, the emphasis shifts from a role conflict model to a cost model. Rather than being faced with the dilemma of how to resolve role conflict, the question becomes simply: "What are the consequences (costs) of my getting involved?"

The costs of involvement are obviously related to (a) the intensity of involvement and (b) the popularity-unpopularity of the particular event. Thus, for example, probably few congregations in the Washington, D.C. area would have expressed strong opposition to their ministers milling in the crowd of 100,000 persons who descended on the nation's Capital in the summer of 1963. This would constitute relatively low intensity of involvement in an event which was receiving wide popular support including the encouragement of the President. On the other hand, many of these same congregations would respond quite negatively to their pastor traveling a thousand miles to get arrested in a civil rights demonstration in Mississippi. This behavior might well be interpreted as "prying into the other people's business, committing an act of civil disobedience, associating with persons of dubious character, and neglecting the responsibilities of his parish."

These two variables, intensity and popularity, thus do not seem to account for the fact that several hundred ministers have been intensely involved in civil rights activities that have been extremely unpopular in the North as well as the South. Who, then, are the ministers who are involved in the civil rights movement? Are they a special breed—men of courage and conviction who are willing to risk their careers and, if need be, their lives for the cause they believe in?

While the courage that many ministers have displayed in their participation in the civil rights movement should not be discredited, it would seem appropriate to examine the social structural context of their participation. In other words, do actors come forth randomly from the ranks of the church at large, or are persons in particular positions with certain other social structural characteristics more likely to become involved in the civil rights movement than others?

Ministers in Chicago

The civil rights demonstrations in Chicago during the summer of 1965 provided a unique opportunity to examine the structural concomitants of participation in a civil rights movement. During the initial days of the summer demonstrations, there were 48 Protestant ministers, all but one white, coming from 17 states and representing seven denominations participating in an intensive one month study program at the Urban Training Center for Christian Mission located in Chicago.[4] The Urban Training Center (UTC) is an ecumenical program designed to better equip clergymen to minister to the inner-city by informing and involving them in the political, economic, social, and spiritual problems of the metropolis.

While in Chicago for the training program, 25 of these clergymen elected to be arrested during the civil rights demonstrations and 23 chose not to become involved in this way. The uniqueness of this situation provided a rare opportunity to examine the concomitants of the decision to become involved in a civil rights demonstration.

The Chicago civil rights demonstrations began on Thursday, June 10, following a circuit court injunction prohibiting civil rights groups from carrying out a two-day school boycott to protest the rehiring of School Superintendent Benjamin Willis by the Board of Education. On that day an estimated 400 persons marched from Soldier Field down the middle of Outer Drive to City Hall and staged a sit-in on LaSalle Street. There were no arrests. The failure of the police to intervene in this obstruction of traffic was sharply criticized publicly by Mayor Daley. The following day, Friday, June 11, marchers again assembled at Soldier Field to march on City Hall. They complied with police instructions for the march. However, at an intersection in Grant Park police surrounded the marchers and demanded that they walk in a single lane. This was contrary to the civil rights marchers' understanding of the ground rules for the march, and in protest many of the marchers sat down and 252 were arrested. The following day the marchers were stopped at State and Madison in the Loop where 192 sat down and were arrested.

The UTC trainees were given a detailed orientation to the Chicago school

---

[4]There were a total of 54 persons enrolled for the June session of the Urban Training Center. Six have been excluded from analysis here because they were theological students. The remaining 48 are all ordained ministers serving in full-time church positions. The seven denominations and the number representing each denomination are as follows: American Lutheran church, 26; Protestant Episcopal church, 7; United Church of Christ, 6; Missouri Synod Lutheran, 4; Lutheran Church of America, 3; American Baptist, 1; and the Moravian church, 1.

While the large number of Lutherans attending the session limits denominational comparisons, many other factors also limit the interpretations and generalization of the findings. We were not able to determine, for example, how candidates were selected for the program. Some were in attendance at their own initiative, while others were present at the request of a denominational official.

Data used in this report came from three sources: (1) records from the Urban Training Center; (2) personal interviews ranging from two to six hours with 27 of the trainees plus the entire staff; and (3) a questionnaire that was mailed to them after the training session which was completed by 92 percent of the trainees.

situation on Wednesday, prior to the initial march, and were informed that the training center curriculum would be suspended on Thursday so that those who wanted to could participate in the demonstrations. While it was emphasized that each trainee should follow his own conscience, and that they did not have to participate in the march if they did not want to, participation was unambiguously approved by the staff.

All but eight of the 48 trainees appeared at Soldier Field and marched on Thursday.[5] On Friday the number of trainees who marched declined to 35. On each day the UTC director emphasized that if arrests occurred each should act according to his conscience and as individuals. If they wanted to step out of the march they should feel free to do so.

On Friday, when the first arrests occurred, the ministers were given an additional opportunity by police to get up out of the street and thus avoid arrest. Eleven of the UTC trainees who marched either did not sit down or got up when given the opportunity by police. Twenty-four of the trainees and six staff members were arrested.

On Saturday there were only 20 UTC trainees who marched. Five who had marched the previous day had elected to remain in jail. Eleven were arrested Saturday, including one who had stepped out of line on Friday.

This is a brief summary of the background of the initial Chicago civil rights demonstrations and the involvement of the UTC trainees in the arrests that occurred during those first days of demonstrating.

The uniqueness of the situation, of course, does not permit generalization to the broader context of clergymen's participation in the civil rights movement. Nevertheless, it does provide a context in which several ideas can be explored, and thus suggest avenues for more comprehensive investigation.

Implicit in our earlier comments was the hypothesis that ministers who participate in civil rights do not come randomly from the ranks of the church at large, but rather that they possess certain characteristics vis-à-vis the organizational structure of the churches which tend to "free" them to act. We will attempt to elaborate and clarify this hypothesis by developing several subhypotheses and examining them by looking at the behavior of the UTC trainees.

First of all, the action of an individual minister is probably not independent of the position his denomination has taken on the civil rights issue. If his denomination has repeatedly and consistently taken a strong stand on the civil rights issue, then his involvement would be congruent with denominational policy. Where the position of the denomination has been something less than active involvement, the involvement of an individual who is a member of that denomination is less likely to be met by denominational officials with unanimous approval than in the former case. Thus, we would predict that the

---

[5]The data presented here are subject to slight error since we did not receive the questionnaire from four of the participants. We had interviewed two of the nonrespondents extensively and, thus, are reasonably certain of their behavior and background characteristics. In the other two cases, we utilized the UTC files for background information and attempted to make informed judgments on their behavior in Chicago.

stronger the position taken on civil rights by the denomination of which the trainee is a member, the greater the probability that he will involve himself in the demonstrations to the point of being arrested.

Of the five denominations with more than a single representative at UTC, two of them, the United Church of Christ and the Episcopal church, have repeatedly taken strong stands on civil rights. The other three denominations, all Lutheran, have taken stands that have been somewhat more modest in scope and less vigorous in actual lines of activity.

While the number of cases is small, this simple dichotomy between strong and moderate denominational commitment to civil rights is clearly related to the involvement pattern of the minister-trainees. (Table 1.) Of the seven Episcopalians only one was not arrested and he was physically unable to march. Four of the six members of the United Church of Christ were arrested. One of the two not arrested was in Detroit speaking on the civil rights issue. The Lutheran denominations, on the other hand, had considerably smaller proportions arrested. If we combine the three Lutheran groups, we see that only 14 of 33, or 42 percent were arrested, as compared with 75 percent for the two more liberal denominations. Thus, the hypothesis that trainee arrest is positively associated with a strong denominational stand is supported by this simple measure.

Table 1. *Percent Arrested in Each Denomination*

	Total	Arrested		Nonarrested	
		N	%	N	%
American Lutheran Church	26	11	42	15	58
Lutheran Church of America	3	1	33	2	67
Missouri Synod Lutheran	4	2	50	2	50
United Church of Christ	6	4	67	2	33
Episcopal	7	6	86	1	14
Others	2	1	50	1	50

The Campbell and Pettigrew study as well as numerous case histories suggest that southern congregations resist the involvement of their ministers in the civil rights struggle. The reaction of non-South congregations to the active involvement of their ministers in the movement is not as well documented, but there is also evidence of resistance by congregations. Thus, we would expect to find that ministers who occupy positions in which they are not directly responsible to an all-white congregation are more actively involved in the civil rights movement than those who must account for their behavior to an all-white congregation.

In short, we would not expect to find the type of position a man occupies to be independent of his involvement in the civil rights movement. Since the official position of all denominations has been in favor of desegregation, clergymen in nonparish positions should be able to involve themselves in the civil rights movement without facing serious reprisals. Similarly, ministers serving congregations that are substantially integrated should be relatively free to involve themselves in civil rights activities. In fact, they may be expected to do so. On the other hand, ministers serving all-white suburban congregations might expect to face resistance from their laity if they became actively involved in the civil rights movement. Physically separated from the Negro community, suburbanites would probably view any form of involvement as a threat to the established patterns of ecological segregation.

In between is the minister who serves a congregation in the inner-city. Many factors influence the response of the inner-city church to the Negro. Factors such as ecological location of the church vis-à-vis Negro populations, financial status of the parish, socio-economic and ethnic backgrounds of the church membership, etc., influence the freedom of the inner-city minister to become involved in civil rights.

The behavior of the UTC trainees was examined from the perspective of the typology suggested in the discussion above. Confirmation of the prediction of involvement can readily be seen in Table 2.

Table 2.   *Percent Arrested in Each Type of Position*

	Total	Arrested		Nonarrested	
		N	%	N	%
Inner-city–integrated	4	4	100	0	0
Nonparish	9	7	78	2	22
Inner-city–token or no integration	19	7	37	12	63
Fringe or Suburban	10	1	10	9	90
Nonmetropolitan*	6	6	100	0	0

*Nonmetropolitan is defined as outside of a Standard Metropolitan Statistical Area.

There were only four ministers from integrated inner-city parishes, but all four were arrested. These four represent three denominations suggesting that this involvement is independent of denominational affiliation.

Next, we see that seven of the nine, or 78 percent of the ministers in nonparish positions were arrested. While each of these persons is responsible to denomination officials or boards it would appear that the absence of a responsibility to a specific parish membership "frees" one to act according to his conscience or some other reference system. In examining the two deviant cases, we found that one came from the most conservative denomination represented at the training center, and the other was not in the city during the marches.

Of the ten suburban ministers, nine did not get arrested in the demonstrations. The one deviant case expressed some ambivalence toward remaining in his current position. Four of the suburban church ministers did not even march in the demonstrations. The almost unanimous response of the suburban ministers strongly suggests the influence of the *membership reference system* as reported by Campbell and Pettigrew among ministers in Little Rock. Independent of their own personal views, the position of their respective denominations, the position of the UTC staff, and the views and actions of their fellow ministers in the training programs, these men would appear to have responded to this choice in terms of their congregations' expectations.

Seven of the 19, or 32 percent of the ministers in inner-city churches that are not integrated were arrested, thus occupying an intermediate position, as predicted, between inner-city integrated and suburban ministers. We asked these ministers how they felt the "influentials" of their congregation would react to the possibility of church integration. Of the 12 who were not arrested, two said that the influentials would be openly opposed to integration; five reported that the influentials would verbally go along with integration but would probably be pretty uncomfortable if Negroes actually came into the church; and three reported that the influentials would probably go along with "token integration" but would probably resist a serious attempt to develop a truly integrated congregation.[6] Of the seven inner-city ministers who were arrested, only one felt that the influentials in his congregation were opposed to church integration. Three of these men were serving congregations with token integration. Thus, it would appear that the inner-city ministers did not act independently of their congregations' views on integration, or at least their perceptions of their congregations' views. The dominant response of suburban ministers was that they did not know how the influentials of their congregations felt about integration. Thus, in the inner-city the issue appears to be more salient. Ministers think they know how their congregations feel and tend to act in a manner which is consistent with the feeling of the congregation. In the suburbs, ministers claim they do not know how their congregations feel about integration, but they do not become involved in behavior that could be upsetting to their congregations.

An unanticipated finding was the fact that all six of the ministers from the nonmetropolitan communities were arrested. Why this should be presents an intriguing question. There are several possible explanations, and it is not possible to untangle the interactions of these several factors.

An immediately plausible explanation of the propensity of the small town ministers to choose arrest is derived from the unusual situation of small town ministers receiving urban training at the request of their denominations. This may have been taken by these men as an indication that they would soon be moved by their denominations to a metropolitan situation. In other words, they may have felt that they need not concern themselves too much about the attitudes of their current congregations because they could expect an early transfer to an urban position.[7]

A second possible explanation is to be found in the demographic structure of the nonmetropolitan areas. Except for the South, these areas have small proportions, if any, Negroes. The question of civil rights, thus, remains an academic one. Therefore, their minister's participation in a civil rights demonstration is little more than an intellectual extension of their noninvolved "tolerance" for civil rights.

[6]The other two inner-city ministers who were not arrested did not return their questionnaires.

[7]One of these men was appointed to an inner-city mission parish only two months after completing the UTC training program.

A third possible explanation for the nonmetropolitan minister's behavior is based on a process of selective perception of the congregation's position. As there are probably no Negroes in the community, a civil rights sermon would probably draw little criticism from the congregation. This would lead the minister to conclude, perhaps erroneously, that the congregation supported the minister's position.

The age of the nonmetropolitan ministers offers still another possible explanation for their behavior. The average age of the nonmetropolitan ministers is 30.2 years compared with 38.0 for the total group, a difference of 7.8 years. Popular psychology and history have long linked youth to radical behavior. Thus, his behavior may reflect the independence of youth, and a more critical attitude toward the existing social structure which has nothing whatsoever to do with his parish location. He is in a nonmetropolitan parish because nonmetropolitan parishes are not the prize positions and the prize positions do not normally accrue to youth.

But independent of their personal convictions, why do they act unanimously and without hesitation? Do they not have some concern for what this may mean for their careers? We doubt that they act without concern for their careers. What this does suggest, however, is that their career aspirations lie someplace other than the suburban church. This suggestion is supported by the Bridston and Culver study of seminary students that indicates that only 33 percent of seminary students aspire to eventually be in a parish situation.[8] In other words, these men may not weigh how this experience will influence their chances of getting into a suburban parish, because they do not aspire to this type of position. If these nonmetropolitan ministers aspire to inner-city careers or nonparish careers, then far from being a detriment to their careers, the arrest may be worn as a badge of courage.

This leads us to a consideration of the relationship between age and involvement in civil rights activities. The average age of the UTC ministers who were arrested was 36.2 years compared with 39.4 years for the nonarrested. (Table 3.) This difference does not hold for all denominations, especially those

Table 3.   *Mean Age of Arrested and Nonarrested Ministers in Each Denomination*

	Arrested		Nonarrested	
	N	X Age	N	X Age
American Lutheran Church	11	35.7	15	41.6
Lutheran Church of America	1	38.0	2	34.0
Missouri Synod Lutheran	2	29.0	2	40.0
United Church of Christ	4	41.5	2	41.5
Episcopal	6	36.7	1	33.0
Others	1	31.0	1	28.0
Total	25	36.2	23	39.4

[8]Keith R. Bridston and Dwight W. Culver, *Pre-Seminary Education* (Minneapolis: Augsburg Publishing House, 1965).

with a very small number of participants. The difference is quite marked for the American Lutheran church, the largest group, where the average age difference between arrests and nonarrests is six years. In summary, arrest appears to be independent of age in the more liberal denominations while in the denominations taking a more moderate stand on civil rights, young age is strongly associated with getting arrested.

Although it was clear that the staff of the Urban Training Center favored involvement in the civil rights demonstrations, including arrests for civil disobedience, it is unlikely that this sentiment was universally shared by the ministers. Thus, one might predict that there would be a tendency for the undecided minister to turn to his peers for guidance. It is impossible to reconstruct the mental processes of the ministers at the moment of arrest, and it is nearly as difficult to determine after the event, the feelings of the participants beforehand. However, one consequence of such dependence upon peer support can be measured. If an undecided minister were seeking peer guidance, a likely candidate would be his roommate. Therefore, if ministers tend to behave as their roommates behave, the seeking of peer support is at least suggested. That roommates should be close peers seems particularly plausible considering the fact that the training session had only been in process a few days and other peer alliances had probably not had adequate time to develop.

Roommates were arbitrarily assigned alphabetically, subject to late cancellations and registrations for the program. The presence of a systematic bias in the assigning of roommates, thus, appears unlikely. Of the 50 ministers who had roommates, 32 acted with respect to arrest, just as their roommates did, and only 18 deviated from their roommate's behavior.[9] Arrestees were no more conforming than nonarrestees. These data suggest, thus, that peer identification was an important aspect of the decision-making process. Having a roommate who was getting arrested probably made it easier for those who were in doubt to also choose arrest—or possibly more difficult to avoid choosing arrest. By the same token, those who were not in sympathy with civil disobedience probably found it easier to avoid going with the crowd when their roommate shared their sentiments.

Discussion

The theoretical stance taken thus far in this paper has been that the occupancy of certain positions in a social structure entails greater freedom to act than the occupancy of other positions. In the case of the UTC trainees, ministers who were younger, in nonparish or in integrated parishes, who belong to denominations taking a strong position on integration, and who had roommates who positively evaluate arrest were *freer* to choose arrest than those who had the opposite characteristics.

---

[9]This figure includes the seminary students who were attending the training program. See footnote 4.

This is, of course, only one of several ways of viewing the data. Furthermore, the small N does not permit adequate multivariate analysis. Other interpretations may be equally plausible. Thus, in an exploratory investigation of this nature, it is appropriate to speculate about other factors which may be related to involvement in the civil rights movement as well as the meaning of the behavior observed.

While our approach is certainly not incongruent with the Campbell and Pettigrew role conflict model, clearly our interpretation might have been couched more explicitly in terms of conflicting reference systems. Elaborating on this theoretical interpretation, we would view the students and staff of the Urban Training Center as yet another reference system imposing certain expectations on its membership.

It can also be argued that the issue is not one of greater or lesser amounts of freedom to act in a deviant way, but a matter of different obligations being attached to different social positions. The positions we have described could be aligned along a continuum varying from heavy obligation to parish, on the one hand, to heavy obligation to the denominational structure on the other. Thus, a minister who serves a prosperous suburban parish that is conservative on the civil rights issue faces an entirely different set of role requirements than the minister who works for a church bureaucracy that has taken a strong position in favor of an activist approach to achieving integration. In between is the minister who serves an inner-city parish that may be partly dependent upon the denomination for support.

Lenski's study of religion in metropolitan Detroit suggests support for the proposition that the expectations coming from the professional organizational staff are different than the expectations coming from the congregation. He observed that 74 percent of the white Protestant clergymen felt that ministers should take a public stand on the civil rights issue, while only 42 percent of the laity shared this view.[10]

The hypothesis, thus, becomes obvious; the more dependent the minister is upon the denominational leaders, the more obligated he is to reflect their beliefs in action.[11] Or, viewed from a slightly different perspective, different structural positions must respond to different reference groups.

Still another interpretation might emphasize variables antecedent to positional occupancy—i.e., different types of ministers get recruited into the different positions we have described. Thus, we might hypothesize that ministers whose views on civil rights are conservative may be differentially recruited into all-white suburban parishes, while ministers with attitudes supporting the civil rights movement are recruited into integrated parishes and denominational bureaucracy. In other words, a particular civil rights stance precedes rather than

[10]Gerhard Lenski, *The Religious Factor* (New York: Doubleday Anchor, 1961), p. 315.

[11] This should not be interpreted to mean that a minister is always under obligation to liberal denominational leaders. Some circumstances may place him under obligation to leaders who are more concerned with institutional maintenance. Furthermore, the positions that denominational leaders hold within the organization may significantly influence how much attention they must give to problems of institutional maintenance.

follows positional occupancy.[12] It would be surprising if further research did not demonstrate that some selectivity is operating in filling positions. However, at the same time, it is also plausible that attitude formation does not stop with entrance into these positions, and that positions which we have called "free" affect the rate and direction of attitude change. Just as a minister in a denominational position may come to feel that he has a responsibility to become more actively involved in the civil rights struggle, so also may the minister who has been appointed to a suburban parish undergo a process of resocialization so that his views become more congruent with his congregation.

These data might further be viewed from the perspective of social deviance. Using Merton's typology from his classic paper on "Social Structure and Anomie," ministers who participate in civil rights demonstrations might be classified as "Innovators."[13] They accept the cultural goal (integration) but see the institutional means (legal process and Negro self-improvement) as inadequate to achieve the goals. Many of the UTC trainees brought with them a growing tension between what the church teaches and what the church does about brotherhood. Inasmuch as involvement may be viewed as an attempt at reduction of tension, it can be argued that these ministers brought with them a predisposition for involvement.

What happened to the ministers at the Urban Training Center would seem to fit a number of concomitants necessary for the emergence of social deviance. First, the ministers were introduced to a deviant role model. To be sure, they had been introduced to the role model through the mass media, but now they were confronting the model in the flesh. Group involvement at the UTC provided an opportunity for progressive step-by-step involvement. For those favorably predisposed toward the deviant act, each interaction with fellow trainees provided the opportunity to reinforce commitment to act. Furthermore, most of the trainees did not view arrest as an imminent possibility before they actually marched. Thus, we see evidence of progressive involvement through the process of group interaction. Also, from the perspective of progressive involvement, all 12 of the ministers who had *previously* participated in a civil rights demonstration and participated in Chicago were arrested in the June demonstration.[14] Among those who marched in Chicago but had not previously marched in a civil rights demonstration, only half were arrested.

Through selective interaction in a subculture, and because they believed that the cause was right, they gradually came to view the means as legitimate or right. While only slightly more than half of the trainees were arrested, most of them perceived that the proportion arrested was much larger. Several were noticeably disturbed to learn that public sentiment, as expressed through newspaper and

[12]The extent to which ministers who occupy different structural positions do, in fact, have differential racial attitudes is now being explored by the authors in a national sample of Protestant clergymen.

[13]Robert K. Merton, *Social Theory and Social Structure* (Glencoe, Illinois: The Free Press, 1949), chap. 4.

[14]Two of the trainees reported that they had previously participated in a demonstration but they did not march in Chicago.

television coverage, was opposed to their behavior. In other words, it would appear that there were all the ingredients of an emerging subculture acting in terms of its own norms.

Another structural variable that we have not discussed is that of participation outside one's own community. When a minister participates in a civil rights demonstration in his own community, there is always the possibility that even though his congregation is willing to tolerate his behavior, members of the power structure of the community may bring pressure upon his laity to initiate reprisals. This is less likely when the minister is participating in another community. Furthermore, it is easier for his congregation to view his behavior in a favorable light when he is not protesting against their prejudices or the injustices of their community.

Based upon observations of the Chicago demonstrations during the summer of 1965, our impressions are that the local parish ministry was not widely represented in the marches. Local ministers who marched tended to be one of three types: Negro ministers of Negro churches, white ministers of Negro churches, and nonparish ministers associated with seminaries and denominational offices.

This subjective impression of the Chicago situation is consistent with observations of civil rights activity in other areas. For example, in Little Rock during the 1957 desegregation crisis, Negro children were escorted through the hostile crowds to Central High School by seven clergymen, five of whom were from out of town. This pattern appears to be fairly typical of almost every civil rights demonstration.

Implicit in our discussion thus far has been the argument that ministers' involvement in civil rights may also be viewed from an *organizational* perspective. The connection we have seen between structural parameters and civil rights involvement raises the question of whether there have been significant changes in the structural organization of the churches which have made possible its involvement in the civil rights movement. If, in fact, it is true that those ministers who are involved in the movement occupy positions that free them from the conservative constraints of congregations, then the extent of involvement of the church is a function of the number of and desirability of those particular types of positions. Forty years ago the extent of the church bureaucracy was much smaller than it is today, and the ecumenical organizations such as the National Council of Churches were fewer in number and also smaller in staff. Thus, it is altogether possible that 40 years ago the church could not have been involved in the civil rights movement.

The same questions we have raised about organizational structure in the churches may also be raised for the society more generally. Increasing population size in congressional districts and increasing financial abundance in the nation, for example, have perhaps made congressmen less dependent upon the expectations of a select minority of their electorate. Similarly, it may be that the legal profession is less dependent upon a small minority of the population. To be sure, there is evidence that special interest groups who are concerned with the civil rights movement and civil liberties have created their own legal staffs.

But possibly even more significant is the fact that mass society does give a certain degree of anonymity to individuals as well as organizations. Thus, we may have an emerging social structure in which there is a decline in the amount of client based constraints placed on professionals, which, in turn, makes it increasingly possible for them to advocate radical social change.

Summary

In the summer of 1965 a group of 48 ministers from seven Protestant denominations attending an urban training program in Chicago were given an opportunity to participate in a civil rights demonstration. Most of them did participate and 25 chose to be arrested during the demonstrations.

Analysis of the differences between those who chose arrest and those who chose not to become involved in this way revealed several systematic differences. Arrestees tended to be younger, coming disproportionately from denominations that had taken a strong stand in favor of integration, occupied positions that were not directly responsible to all-white congregations, and tended to have roommates who also chose arrest.

The data lend themselves to several possible theoretical models including role and reference group expectations, structural restraints, social deviance, and changing organizational structures. The value of a case study of this nature is not in accounting for all the variance involved in a minister's decision to become involved in the civil rights movement, but rather to open up a range of theoretical perspectives which seem appropriate for analyzing the problem. The case study, thus, has provided an opportunity to explore some of these ideas. We would anticipate, thus, that a more comprehensive study can now proceed with a broader sense of the relevant variables to examine.

Chapter Fourteen:

Ministers as Moral Guides: The Sounds of Silence*

Rodney Stark, Bruce D. Foster, Charles Y. Glock,
and Harold E. Quinley

At least once a week pastors are preachers. For the churches the Sunday morning worship service is the primary manifestation of religious activity, and the center of the service is the sermon. The sermon is the primary means whereby the churches, through the clergy, instruct the faithful in the meaning and character of Christian thought. In terms of reaching the laity, the sermon far surpasses other media such as church periodicals, discussion groups, or radio and television programs.[1] Most church members attend church fairly often and in so doing become a captive audience for their pastor's message.

Many clergy have suggested that the sermon is not an effective means of moral and ethical communication. They say in despair that sermons seem to fall on deaf ears: people are able to compartmentalize their lives so that their prejudice, hatred, selfishness, and "sinfulness" remain unaffected by messages from the pulpit. But there is a second logical possibility: that the laity remain apparently unshaken by years of sermonizing because rarely does the sermon touch on controversial moral and ethical issues. Have the clergy been trying to lead and failing to achieve results, or are congregations unmoved because the clergy have not made any appreciable efforts to move them?

Thus far very little has been known systematically about what use the clergy make of their sermons. Probably the most accurate way to find out what the clergy are saying from the pulpit would be to assign a group of trained observer-reporters to attend a random sample of church services and record what

*Excerpted from Chapter 5 of Rodney Stark, Bruce D. Foster, Charles Y. Glock, and Harold E. Quinley, *Wayward Shepherds: Prejudice and the Protestant Clergy* (New York: Harper & Row, Publishers, 1971). Reprinted with the permission of the authors, the Anti-Defamation League, and the publishers.

[1]Rodney Stark and Charles Y. Glock, *American Piety: The Nature of Religious Commitment* (Berkeley and Los Angeles: University of California Press, 1968); and Charles Y. Glock, Benjamin B. Ringer, and Earl R. Babbie, *To Comfort and to Challenge* (Berkeley and Los Angeles: University of California Press, 1967).

is said. Of course, this would be a very expensive undertaking. However, it seems reasonable to ask the clergy themselves about the kinds of sermons they give. We recognize that such a technique could produce inflated estimates: that there may be a tendency for clergymen to report sermons they wish they had preached along with those they did preach. Still, as will be considered in detail later, the rationale by which clergymen conduct themselves in the pulpit suggests they do what they think they ought to do and thus should not be self-conscious about sins of omission.

In this chapter we shall scrutinize clergy reports of whether and how frequently they preach on the great moral and social issues which beset modern society. We shall not be concerned with what stand the clergy have taken on such issues, but only with whether or not they have had anything to say at all.

Our report is based on a survey of Protestant ministers from nine major denominations in California. All ministers serving in parish churches in these denominations were in the original sampling frame, and approximately 80 percent of them were selected randomly to receive a mail questionnaire in the spring of 1968. Appropriate follow-up mailings were sent to encourage nonrespondents to answer. A total of 1,580 questionnaires were completed and returned, constituting an overall response rate of 63 percent. A special assessment was made of a randomly chosen subsample of nonrespondents in an effort to determine what, if any, bias may have operated in the returns. This showed there was a modest tendency toward overrepresentation of younger and more theologically liberal clergymen. This means that the clergy as a whole are somewhat more conservative theologically than the tables presented in this chapter report. The biases detected work against the hypotheses we shall attempt to test, with the effect of increasing the rigor of the test if the hypotheses are supported.[2]

Table 1 examines clergy performance on three questions dealing with preaching on social and political issues. The first item makes it clear that giving sermons which deal *mainly* with controversial social or political topics is not the usual practice of the clergy. For every minister who reported having given such a sermon at least eight times in the past year (13 percent), two other clergymen said they had not even given one such sermon (25 percent). The majority came close to their totally silent colleagues than to those who devoted one out of six of their approximately forty-eight sermons during the year to controversial social and political topics. Twenty-seven percent reported giving one or two such sermons, 23 percent reported giving three or four, and 12 percent said they had done so five to seven times. Thus, 52 percent had given no more than two such sermons, and half of these had given none. Based on these self-reports, we calculate that approximately *6 percent of the sermons given in California Protestant churches during the year preceding the study were mainly devoted to social and political topics.*[3]

[2]Full details on sampling are presented in Harold E. Quinley, "The Prophetic Clergy: Social Activism among Protestant Ministers," Ph.D. diss., Department of Political Science, Stanford University, 1971.

[3]The base for computations was forty-eight sermons given per year, allowing for ministers to spend a month on vacation. This, of course, is a conservative estimate since in many denominations, especially those which are more conservative, ministers give several sermons a week.

Table 1. The Delivery of Sermons on Controversial Social or Political Topics

	United Church of Christ	Methodist	Episcopal	Presbyterian	Luth. Church in Amer.	Amer. Luth. Church	American Baptist	Missouri Lutheran	South. Baptist	Total
Number	(137)	(354)	(207)	(226)	(87)	(118)	(147)	(134)	(170)	(1,580)
Percent who *dealt mainly* with a controversial social or political topic										
8 or more times	20%	17%	19%	10%	13%	9%	10%	3%	6%	13%
5-7 times	18	16	14	17	17	5	6	5	3	12
3-4 times	22	32	24	30	21	9	26	10	15	23
Once or twice	24	24	26	29	28	25	32	26	34	27
Never	16	10	17	13	21	52	26	56	42	25
	100%	99%[a]	100%	99%[a]	100%	100%	100%	100%	100%	100%
Percent who *touched upon,* but did not deal mainly with, a controversial social or political topic										
8 or more times	56%	67%	60%	57%	68%	42%	50%	38%	35%	54%
5-7 times	11	13	11	20	10	16	18	24	15	15
3-4 times	23	13	16	19	7	21	19	21	19	17
Once or twice	7	5	9	3	9	16	8	9	26	10
Never	3	2	3	1	3	5	5	8	5	4
	100%	100%	99%[a]	100%	99%[a]	100%	100%	100%	100%	100%
Percent who have *ever* taken a stand from the pulpit on some political *issue*										
Yes[b]	72%	81%	64%	69%	63%	38%	33%	26%	47%	62%
No	28	19	36	31	37	62	67	74	53	38
	100%	100%	100%	100%	100%	100%	100%	100%	100%	100%

[a]Percentages fail to add to 100 because of rounding error.

[b]Yes combines "Yes, while in present church," "Yes, before present church," and "Yes, both present church and before."

Speaking out from the pulpit on such matters is strongly influenced by denomination: while 33 percent of the Methodists and Episcopalians preached on controversial social and political topics five times or more during the previous year, only 8 percent of the Missouri Lutherans and 9 percent of the Southern Baptists did so. Conversely, only 10 percent of the Methodists failed to give even one such sermon, while 56 percent of the Missouri Lutherans, 52 percent of the American Lutheran Church clergy, and 42 percent of the Southern Baptists found no occasion during the year to devote a sermon to such matters.

In order adequately to gauge the meaning of the fact that only 6 percent of Protestant sermonizing was devoted to social and political topics during the past year, it is important to recall that this period—late spring, 1967, to late spring, 1968—was one of the most agonizing years in American history. During the summer of 1967 Detroit and dozens of other American cities burned. The Kerner Commission was appointed, conducted investigations, and issued its monumental report on the racial crisis. In Vietnam came the crisis of the Tet offensive, while at home protest against the war became increasingly militant. The McCarthy campaign was launched. Lyndon Johnson announced his withdrawal from the presidential race and began an effort to negotiate peace. The Middle East was torn by the lightning war and followed by a bleeding peace. Biafrans starved by the tens of thousands. In Memphis, the Reverend Dr. Martin Luther King, Jr., was gunned down, and a new wave of riots followed.

In response to these crises, prominent clergy saw profound moral issues and took active roles. Such activists were admittedly only a handful of the whole clergy.[4] But one might have thought their less visible colleagues would have been prompted at least to speak out from the pulpit.

To a limited extent they were. While the many crises were often insufficient to lead pastors to devote the major portion of a sermon to social and political questions, few found it possible to ignore them utterly. As the second item in Table 1 shows, when asked how frequently during the past year they had delivered "sermons which *touched upon*, but did not deal mainly with, controversial social or political topics," only 4 percent reported never having done so. On the other hand, 54 percent reported they had done so eight or more times during the year. Clearly, it is relatively more common for the clergy to deal with such matters in a peripheral way than to make them the central topic of a sermon.

The data from questions 1 and 2 tell us nothing, however, about *what is said* when the clergy do choose to speak out from the pulpit. Considering responses to the next item, it is clear that often the clergy speak only in bland, ambiguous, and vague ways on such topics. Item 3 shows the proportion of clergymen who have ever in their entire career taken a stand on a political *issue* from the pulpit. While 62 percent say they have done so at least once in their lives, more than a third indicate they have *never* made their own position clear from the pulpit on a political *issue*. (We stress *issue*—it was also italicized in the questionnaire—to avoid confusion with taking stands on political candidates, a practice one would

---

[4]Data supporting this point will appear in Harold E. Quinley, *op. cit.*

not expect to be widespread among the clergy. Political issues, obviously, include such matters as school prayers, legislation on drugs, sexual conduct, divorce, pornography, and the like, not merely party issues. Further, political issues permit conservative as well as liberal comment.) The 62 percent of the clergy who have taken a stand from the pulpit is considerably smaller than the 96 percent who report they touched upon a controversial social or political topic in a sermon during the previous year. It is also smaller than the proportion (75 percent) who said they had devoted at least one sermon mainly to such a topic during the year. From these discrepancies it seems obvious that many clergymen manage to take up a controversial topic from the pulpit without revealing their own moral or ethical positions—to mention controversy without being at all controversial themselves.

Thus, even the relatively poor quantitative performance of the clergy in speaking out from the pulpit must be taken with considerable qualitative reservation. Many who say something say it very circumspectly.

Ministers in conservative denominations are particularly prone to circumspection. For example, while 44 percent of the Missouri Lutherans say they have preached on a controversial social or political topic in the past year, only 26 percent say they have ever taken a stand on such an issue. The same comparison among Southern Baptists is 58 and 47 percent.

In the next section we shall seek to understand why the clergy are so prone to pulpit silence. But first it will be useful to understand when the silence is broken. On the few occasions when more than a handful of the clergy do speak out, what particular social and political issues do they address?

Our findings are that it requires an issue of extraordinary urgency to break the pulpit silence. Even then a substantial proportion of pulpits remain silent.

In the spring of 1968 the issue which most troubled Americans was the war in Vietnam. Thousands of American youth had felt morally obligated to risk prison or leave the country rather than fight and thousands of other Americans risked jail to protest against the war. Bitter controversy raged over the Christian view of the war. The late Cardinal Spellman and others saw it as a holy and Christian endeavor. Other Christian spokesmen saw the war as morally abhorrent.

Among the rank-and-file clergymen the war was sufficiently important to two-thirds of them to be mentioned from the pulpit; 65 percent said they had *sometime devoted at least one sermon or part of a sermon to the war* (Table 2). For the remaining third, not even the war could break their silence. As was seen with Table 1, silence was more common in the conservative than in the theologically more liberal denominations. While 22 percent of the Methodist clergy had never mentioned the war from the pulpit, half or more of the American and Missouri Lutherans and Southern Baptists had been mute on the war.

If the Vietnam war was the most compelling national issue at the time of the study, the most debated local issue in California was Proposition 14. This was an amendment placed on the ballot to change the constitution of the state in order to repeal an open housing law passed by the legislature and to outlaw any such laws in the future. The amendment was strongly opposed by major political

Table 2.   *The Delivery of Sermons on Two Controversial Issues*

	United Church of Christ	Methodist	Episcopal	Presbyterian	Luth. Church in Amer.	Amer. Luth. Church	American Baptist	Missouri Lutheran	South. Baptist	Total
Number	(137)	(354)	(207)	(226)	(87)	(118)	(147)	(134)	(170)	(1,580)
Percent who had delivered a sermon or a section of a sermon on:										
The Vietnam War	75	78	68	68	69	47	62	47	50	65
Proposition 14	61	79	71	67	63	32	47	22	16	56[a]

[a] Percentages are based on those ministers who were serving California parishes during the time of the Proposition 14 campaign.

spokesmen from both parties and brought an outpouring of clergy opposition unprecedented in recent California history. Newspapers ran a great many ads opposing the proposition which were signed by most of the prominent church leaders—not only clerical activists but also bishops and denominational leaders not noted for public participation in social issues. (Such moral leadership was repudiated two to one at the polls as the voters abolished the open housing law; the amendment was later voided by the courts.)

So high a degree of public activity by religious leaders had its effect on the parish clergy: a majority who served California parishes at the time of the election delivered a sermon or at least a section of a sermon on this issue. But the majority was hardly overwhelming—56 percent—while from the remainder of the pulpits silence reigned. Keep in mind that the distinction here is not between being for or against Proposition 14, but between having or not having anything to say about it at all. Again silence is strongly related to denomination; 79 percent of the Methodists spoke out, while only 22 percent of the Missouri Lutherans and 16 percent of the Southern Baptists did so.

The war and Proposition 14 are exceptions that may prove the rule. Of the many other issues we investigated, the majority (and usually the overwhelming majority) of the clergy had not found an occasion during the year to devote a major portion of a sermon to any of them. This is especially remarkable, since the racial problem was one of these topics.

Each clergyman was asked to indicate for each of thirteen issues whether or not during the past year he had preached a sermon which dealt mainly with this topic.

As mentioned earlier, the past year in question was one of racial trauma, beginning with fire and death in Detroit and many other cities and ending with the assassination of Martin Luther King, Jr. Thus, it is no surprise that "racial problems" led the list among these thirteen topics on which sermons had been preached. Rather the surprise lies in the fact that the majority of pulpits (55 percent) had not been used for such a sermon: *the majority of Protestant clergymen in California—not in Mississippi or North Dakota—had not devoted a single sermon mainly to racial problems during this year of death, turmoil, and tragedy.*

From racial problems on, the extent of sermonizing on social problems declined rapidly to near nonexistence.[5]

Only 28 percent preached on World Poverty, while a mere 22 percent preached on National Poverty.

---

[5]We have eliminated data on ministers who claimed to have "touched upon" one or more of these topics during a sermon. Careful analysis showed that those who only touched upon such a topic very closely resembled those who remained utterly silent when it came to taking any other forms of action of these issues: they were unlikely to discuss them informally, to write letters to political leaders, to organize or attend study groups on these matters, and so on. Those who did do more than touch upon such matters were relatively likely to take such additional actions as well. As has already been shown, devoting a sermon mainly to these topics can mean little enough; it may include not even taking a stand. In our judgment the data show that touching upon such a topic means virtually nothing in terms of speaking out from the pulpit on such issues.

Crime and Juvenile Delinquency sermons were given from one of five Protestant pulpits in California.

16 percent delivered sermons on The UN and World Peace.

Drugs, alcohol, and sex were preached about by 14 to 16 percent of the clergy.

Black Power (7 percent), Birth Control (3 percent), Capital Punishment (8 percent), and The Conduct of Public Officials (5 percent) received mention from only a tiny proportion of pulpits.

Only 2 percent preached on Abortion Laws, despite the fact that this was a widely disputed issue at the time.

Given the fact that the average minister in this sample devoted only three sermons during the year mainly to social and political issues, it is no surprise that these specific topics were so infrequently taken up. Yet the silence itself remains enigmatic.

The Sources of Silence

Most pulpits are silent. Why?

To answer this question is also to say why some clergymen, albeit a minority, do speak out on the moral, social, and political issues that divide and anguish Americans.

Past speculation and writing on this question have concentrated on character defects of individual clergymen, such as their timidity, and on the hostility of the social climate in which they perform.[6] But a forthcoming volume based on these same data indicates that these are at best marginal factors influencing the clergy.[7] The overwhelming majority of clergymen in all denominations believe in the power of the pulpit and thus reject the "deaf ears cause frustration" explanation of pulpit silence. Yet many do not use this power. All sectors of the clergy believe that their congregations object to "relevant" sermons. But some give them anyway. There is some evidence that clergymen who believe their colleagues approve of speaking out are more likely to do so. But the effect is not large and is modified by the fact that those who believe their colleagues would not approve of such behavior do not themselves approve of clergymen speaking out. Thus, it is difficult to attribute their silence to conformity with the expectations of fellow clergymen. It could just as easily be conformity to their own conceptions of propriety.

Consequently our search for the sources of silence turned elsewhere. In examining the data we became convinced that pulpit silence is not something imposed on the clergy, but something they impose on themselves; that just as much as the clergyman who speaks out believes in what he is doing, so the

[6]See Hadden, *op. cit.*

[7]Quinley, *op. cit.*

clergyman who remains silent believes he is doing the right thing. And each bases his interpretation on his theological, social, and political beliefs.

We begin with the theological roots of silence. Table 3 shows the relationship between the many items on pulpit behavior we have examined in this chapter and a measure of how conservative or liberal these ministers are doctrinally.[8] The relationships are very strong: the more doctrinally conservative, the less likely a minister is to speak out. Thus, 93 percent of those who scored zero on doctrinalism have at some time (at least once) taken a stand from the pulpit on some political issue, while only 42 percent of the most conservative have ever done so. Sixty-six percent of the least theologically conservative had preached on controversial topics five times or more in the past year, and only 10 percent of the most conservative had done so. Indeed, nearly half (42 percent) of the most conservative had never done so, and only half of them (54 percent) had even "touched upon" such topics in one sermon out of ten during the last year.

When we come to specific issues the pattern remains much the same. Virtually all those who scored zero and 80 percent of those who scored 1 on doctrinalism preached on Proposition 14—the referendum to repeal an open housing law—while only 29 percent of those who scored 4 did so. Nine out of ten of the liberals had preached on the war; five out of ten of the most conservative clergy had not. On racial problems, three-fourths of those who scored zero and two-thirds of those who scored 1 gave at least one sermon out of forty-eight which dealt mainly with racial problems, while three-fourths of those who scored 4 did not. And thus it goes until the last four items (below the broken line in the table).

While on all other sermon topics in the table there was a strong, linear, negative relationship between doctrinalism and preaching on social and political issues, on these four items this pattern gives way to curvilinear relationships. On the issues of Crime and Juvenile Delinquency, The Use of Drugs, Alcoholism, and Sexual Conduct there is a tendency for the most and least doctrinally committed to be the two groups most likely to have preached about them. That is, reading across these items from left to right, the proportions tend to fall as doctrinal scores increase and then to reverse the trend and climb again.

When we recognize that each of these topics concerns not only social and political issues but "personal vices" in the most traditional sense, the reasons for this curvilinearity become apparent. Traditional Christianity has placed major emphasis on combating personal vices, which are defined as barriers to salvation. Indeed, a major criticism made of evangelical Christianity by liberal Christian spokesmen is the privatism and egocentricism of this inclination to define morality in purely individualistic and vice terms.[9] Thus, it should not occasion

---

[8]The Doctrinal Index score is based on how many of a set of traditional doctrines a minister claims to believe unwaveringly. Doctrines include the existence of a personal God, the divinity of Jesus, life beyond death, the literal existence of the devil, and the necessity to believe in Jesus in order to be saved. Scores range from 0 to 4; the higher the score, the more conservative doctrinally. For detailed scoring procedures, see Rodney Stark, *et al., op. cit.,* fn 5, Chapter 3, and fn 10, Chapter 5.

[9]Langdon Gilkey, "Social and Intellectual Sources of Contemporary Protestant Theology in America," *Daedalus* (Winter 1967).

surprise that the more conservative clergy mention such topics from the pulpit; perhaps it is more surprising that they are generally so unlikely to do so. Presumably, when the liberal clergy preach on these topics they tend to do so in terms of a social problems perspective rather than in terms of individual sin. We also suspect that when the conservative clergy preach on such topics it is to denounce such individual action—that the conservatives, for example, emphasize

Table 3. *Doctrinalism and Speaking Out on Social and Political Issues*

Number	Low 0 (28)	1 (134)	2 (296)	3 (467)	High 4 (568)	Total (1,493)
			Doctrinal Index			

Number	Low 0 (28)	1 (134)	2 (296)	3 (467)	High 4 (568)	Total (1,493)
1. Percent who have *ever* taken a stand from the pulpit on some political issue	93	80	79	67	42	62
2. *"During the past year, how often did you deliver sermons which dealt mainly with controversial social or political topics?"*						
Percent who did so at least *five* times	66	40	38	26	10	25
Percent who *never* did so	0	7	11	18	42	25
3. *"During the past year, how often did you deliver sermons which touched upon, but did not deal mainly with, controversial social or political topics?"*						
Percent who did so at least *five* times	88	82	78	73	54	68
Percent who *never* did so	0	0	1	3	7	4
4. Percent who *ever* delivered a sermon *or a section* of a sermon on:						
Proposition 14	95	80	74	65	29	56[a]
The War in Vietnam	89	80	75	69	49	65
5. Percent who gave a sermon *during the previous year* which dealt mainly with:						
Racial Problems	78	66	63	53	25	45
World Poverty	52	41	33	34	18	28
National Poverty	68	36	25	29	12	22
The UN and World Peace	33	27	30	18	6	16
Capital Punishment	19	18	10	8	4	8
Black Power	22	18	12	7	3	7
The Conduct of Public Officials	15	6	4	5	5	5
Birth Control	19	2	5	2	1	3
Abortion Laws	19	4	3	2	1	2
Crime and Juvenile Delinquency	30	18	18	19	24	20
The Use of Drugs	26	15	13	13	16	14
Alcoholism	19	11	13	14	17	14
Sexual Conduct	15	12	15	19	18	16

[a] Based only on those ministers serving California parishes at the time of the Proposition 14 issue.

"Thou shalt not steal" when they preach on crime, while the more liberal clergy emphasize the social causes of crime.

Support for this interpretation can be found in the fact that an overwhelming 82 percent of those who scored zero on doctrinalism advocated *weakening* the laws regulating marijuana, while an equally overwhelming 78 percent of those who scored 4 wanted to make these laws *stronger*. Similarly, only 18 percent of those who scored zero wanted to strengthen laws regulating the sale of liquor (more than wanted to strengthen laws against marijuana), while 65 percent of those who scored 4 wanted to strengthen such laws. Clearly, sermons on drugs and liquor by groups holding such opposite views would be very different indeed.

Thus we have seen that theological convictions, as measured by the Doctrinal Index, strongly influence pulpit performance. It seems obvious that theology would influence the content of what is said on social and political issues. But that is not presently at issue. *Why does theology so powerfully influence the very act of speaking out?* It is inadequate to rest our exploration of theological sources of silence simply with these findings. To say silence is produced by conservative theology is simply to deepen the mystery. We must know what it is about traditional doctrines that disposes the conservative clergy to remain silent.

A first step toward understanding the role of theology in pulpit silence is to see how it affects conceptions of what sermons are for. The clergymen were asked, "How important do you feel it is to accomplish each of the following purposes in your sermons?" The findings appear in Table 4. The first of these sermon purposes—"point out the existence of human sin"—deals directly with the differences we have already observed on sermon topics. While only 32 percent of those who scored zero and 24 percent of those who scored 1 on

Table 4. *Doctrinalism and the Purpose of Sermons*

	Doctrinal Index					
	Low				High	
Number	0 (28)	1 (134)	2 (296)	3 (467)	4 (568)	Total (1,493)
"How important do you feel it is to accomplish each of the following purposes in your sermons?"						
Percent who thought it very important to "point out the existence of human sin."	32	24	33	49	77	54
Percent who thought it very important to "illustrate the type of life a Christian should follow."	57	63	78	76	89	79
Percent who thought it very important to "apply Christian standards to judge human institutions and behavior."	72	75	75	69	73	73
Percent who thought it very important to provide "spiritual uplifting and moral comfort."	39	55	68	69	87	74

doctrinalism felt this was very important, 77 percent of those who scored 4 did so. It would be quite possible to interpret speaking out on political and social issues as pointing out human sin, but from these data one must conclude that the clergy did not regard this item from such a frame of reference. The fact that it is the conservatives who feel this is important (and who remain silent on social and political matters), and the liberals (who speak out) who regard this as unimportant, suggests that this item was understood primarily as sin in the old-fashioned hell-fire sense.

The second item—"illustrate the type of life a Christian should follow"—is closely related to the first, and eight out of ten clergymen felt it very important to accomplish this in their sermons. On this item a majority of liberals join with an overwhelming majority of conservatives (although a substantial relationship still remains). But clearly liberals and conservatives read this item differently. Since the conservatives are very unlikely to preach on social and political topics, they must define a Christian type of life on rather different criteria than do the liberals. This is further corroborated by the answers to the third item. Nearly three-fourths of the clergy (73 percent) agreed it is very important that a sermon "apply Christian standards to judge human institutions and behavior." Responses here are not affected by doctrinalism. But since we know that the liberals do preach about human institutions and conservatives rarely or never seem to do so, it seems certain that there is substantial disagreement over how this purpose of sermons is to be accomplished. Apparently, in the judgment of conservatives this is done by preaching on the weaknesses of the flesh.

Finally, we see that doctrinalism is powerfully related to what has been called the "comforting function" of religion.[10] The last item reflects this in relatively pure form: to provide "spiritual uplifting and moral comfort to those who are distressed." Most conservatives thought this was very important to accomplish in their sermons. Among those least doctrinally conservative, most did not.

Looking back over these items, it seems clear that conservatives tend to view the purpose of their sermons in terms of individual salvation and sin. And they define both in a relatively otherworldly way. Human sin, apparently, is not predominantly related to social and political issues, and salvation does not, for example, seem to depend on freeing oneself of prejudice. We shall now follow up these cues directly.

Otherworldliness and the Miracle Motif

One of the critical issues in modern religion is a conflict between a salvational conception of the mission of the church and a this-worldly, direct approach to social ills. There are several major strands to this argument. The first minimizes the importance of this world. Life is merely a time of testing during which one must establish his right to spend eternity in heaven. The proper role of the clergy is to help members ignore the trivial concerns of this world—for all these things shall pass away—and to fix their concern on preparing for life beyond the

[10]Glock, Ringer, and Babbie, *op. cit.*

grave. Furthermore, this conception of what is truly important rejects the possibility of substantially improving worldly affairs. This world is necessarily sinful to a point of depravity, and it is the most sinful sort of human pride to think otherwise. From this point of view, men should concentrate on overcoming their personal vices and committing themselves to Christ's redeeming love. "Where will you spend eternity?" is the only worthwhile concern.

The second strand in the salvational conception of the mission of the church is what in chapter 9 is called the miracle motif.

Recently, in response to critics, Billy Graham claimed to be a revolutionary. He argued that far from being unresponsive to the growing crises in human affairs—war, annihilation, inequality, hatred, and despair—he is actively pursuing a complete reconstruction of society. He believes that he differs with his critics primarily on means, not ends. For Graham, the means are a miraculous revolution through individual salvation. Graham is hardly an isolated instance. Rather the thrust of evangelical Protestantism is toward a miraculous view of social reform: that if all men are brought to Christ, social evils will disappear through the miraculous regeneration of the individual by the Holy Spirit. Thus evangelicals concentrate on conversion, and except for occasional efforts to outlaw what they deem to be personal vices, evangelical Protestant groups largely ignore social and political efforts for reform. Indeed, they also largely ignore the fact that "born-again" and regenerated Christians seem to remain noticeably sinful. Perhaps because they rely on a miracle to change their adherents, they say little about how the miraculously changed man ought to act. A possibily unintended consequence of Christian preoccupation with individual salvation is a suspicion of, and often a hostility to, social and political efforts for reform. So long as there are men who have not been won to Christ, a sinful society is seen as inevitable. Therefore, any attempts to reform society, other than through conversion of individuals to Christ, are doomed to failure.

Theological conceptions such as these could play a substantial role in the silence of the more conservative clergy on social issues. From their perspective it would seem there is nothing to say about such matters that is not said in exhorting men to give their lives to Christ. If "Christ is the answer," why talk about superficialities such as programs to ease social crises?

The more liberal Protestant clergy, of course, strongly reject these otherworldly and miraculous views. They argue that reliance on individual salvation as the sole means for ameliorating social problems is theologically wrong and impractical. Furthermore, they reject the idea that Christian morality and ethics are primarily concerned with the relationship between man and God. Rather they see them as primarily between men and emphasize loving thy neighbor as the major Christian ethical dictum.

We need give no further explication of this theological controversy. Our interest is in whether or not salvational and miraculous orientations remain common among the Christian clergy and whether or not such orientations are responsible for the silence of the clergy on major social issues.

Table 5 shows that such views are widespread, and they are powerfully related to the Doctrinal Index.

176 On Conformity and Rebellion among Religious Professionals

Table 5.   *Doctrinalism, Otherworldliness, and the Miracle Motif*

	Doctrinal Index					
	Low 0	1	2	3	High 4	Total
Number	(28)	(134)	(296)	(467)	(568)	(1,493)
1. *"If enough men were brought to Christ, social ills would take care of themselves."*						
Percent agree	7	17	35	41	77	44
Percent disagree	86	69	54	51	21	42
2. *"It would be better if the church were to place less emphasis on individual sanctification and more on bringing human conditions into conformity with Christian teachings."*						
Percent agree	93	80	73	51	19	47
Percent disagree	4	11	18	36	69	42
3. *"It is not as important to worry about life after death as about what one can do in this life."*						
Percent agree	100	93	90	76	42	68
Percent disagree	0	6	7	19	47	26

Item 1 assesses the miracle motif. Ministers were asked to agree or disagree with the statement: "If enough men were brought to Christ, social ills would take care of themselves." Over all, 44 percent of the clergy agreed, 42 percent disagreed, and the rest were uncertain of their position on this question. Thus the clergy are about evenly split on the conception of saving society by saving individual souls. Agreement, as would be expected, is powerfully related to one's religious views as measured by the Doctrinal Index. Seven percent of the lowest scorers agreed with this statement, while 77 percent of the highest scorers did so.

The second item contains elements of both otherworldliness and the miracle motif: "It would be better if the church were to place less emphasis on individual sanctification and more on bringing human conditions into conformity with Christian teachings." Again the clergy are about evenly split. Forty-seven percent agreed that emphasis should shift from individual sanctification to human conditions, while 42 percent disagreed. And again the relationship with doctrinalism is very powerful: 93 percent of the lowest scorers agreed, while only 19 percent of the highest scorers did so.

The final item is a fairly extreme assessment of otherworldliness: "It is not as important to worry about life after death as about what one can do in this life." Two-thirds of the clergy accepted this statement and thus put this world ahead of the world to come. Still, the relationship with doctrinalism remains very powerful. While *every* clergyman who scored zero on the Doctrinalism Index agreed with this statement, only 42 percent of those who scored highest did so.

Based on these findings, it is plain that the more traditional clergy tend to have an antipathy toward the affairs of this world and to believe that individual salvation will solve our social ills. Is it any wonder that they do not preach on social problems? Tables 6, 7, and 8 indicate that it is not.

If an important reason for the silence of the doctrinally conservative clergy is their commitment to miraculous and otherworldly solutions to human problems, the strong original relationships between doctrinalism and preaching on various topics ought to be substantially reduced when such otherworldliness is controlled. We do not hypothesize that this is the only linking mechanism involved, but we do hypothesize that it is an important mechanism. Thus, the reductions of the original relationship should be quite sizable, if our hypothesis is correct.[11]

The logic of this argument is that an important reason why clergymen do not address themselves to social issues in their sermons lies not merely in their commitment to traditional church doctrines, but that such doctrinal commitment leads them also to adopt an otherworldly, miraculous outlook, and this in turn makes preaching on such issues seem irrelevant.

To test empirically these suppositions, an Otherworldliness Index was constructed from the three items discussed above and shown in Table 3. Scores on the index range from none (persons who rejected all otherworldliness items) to high (those who embraced all otherworldliness items).[12] We then used this index as a control on several of the key relationships previously presented in Table 3. The results are shown in Tables 6-8.

Looking first at Table 6, it is apparent that in categories of the Otherworldliness Index the powerful original relationship between doctrinalism and *never* having taken a stand from the pulpit on some political issue is substantially reduced, that is, the percentage-point differences between lower and higher scorers on doctrinalism are smaller when scores on otherworldliness are controlled. This can most readily be seen by comparing correlation coefficients.[13] The correlation between doctrinalism and never taking a stand is .237. When otherworldliness is controlled, the resulting coefficients are reduced considerably, ranging from virtually zero to .138. The amount of the reduction can be interpreted as the extent to which the original relationship is produced by

[11]What we are arguing logically is that X (doctrinalism) causes T (Other-Worldliness) which causes Y (silence from the pulpit on social issues), or, put another way, the means through which X causes Y is T. Statistically this is called an interpretation and is revealed when the size of the original relationship between X and Y is reduced when computed separately for those with different amounts of T (Other-Worldliness). See Charles Y. Glock, *Survey Research in the Social Sciences* (New York: Russell Sage, 1968), chap. 1 for introductory discussion of logic of survey analysis.

[12]Item 1 was scored: "Strongly agree" 3; "Agree" 2; "Disagree" 1; "Strongly disagree" 0; "No opinion" respondents dropped from index; items 2 and 3 were also scored 3 through 0, but in reverse order. Thus, the full index ranged from zero through 9. Four analysis scores were collapsed as follows: 0 = None; 1, 2, and 3 = Low; 4 and 5 = Medium; and 6, 7, 8, and 9 = High.

[13] See Robert Somers, "A New Asymmetric Measure of Association for Ordinal Variables," *American Sociological Review*, 27, no. 6, (December 1962), 799-811. We have chosen to present Somers,DXY results because they proved to be the most conservative estimate of the measures computed. In all cases r, G, and Q showed higher initial correlations and greater reductions when controls were introduced. Thus we have chosen to maximize the difficulty of establishing our case, which is as it should be.

Table 6.   *Doctrinalism, Otherworldliness, and Preaching on Political Issues*

(Percent who have *never* taken a stand from the pulpit on some political issue.)

	Doctrinal Index					Correlation coefficients[a] within categories of otherworldliness
	Low 0	1	2	3	High 4	DXY
Otherworldliness Index:						
None	0	0	0	—	X	−.064
Number	(6)	(8)	(12)	(9)		
Low	11	13	13	27	48	.138
Number	(18)	(85)	(151)	(151)	(42)	
Medium	0	57	33	36	51	.110
Number	(1)	(14)	(61)	(162)	(182)	
High	X	—	—	54	64	.049
Number		(1)	(9)	(46)	(231)	
						Original correlation coefficient
Original relationship	7	19	21	33	58	.237

[a]Somers' DXY.

the fact that those committed to traditional Christian doctrines are led to ignore social and political issues from the pulpit *because they believe salvation of the individual is the only relevant solution to such problems.*

Table 7 reveals a similar reduction. Here the original relationship between doctrinalism and the proportions who did not deliver a sermon in the past year which dealt mainly with a controversial social or political topic is reexamined with otherworldliness controlled. Within each category of the Otherworldliness Index the relationship is smaller than originally. The original correlation

Table 7.   *Doctrinalism, Otherworldliness, and Giving a Controversial Sermon*

(Percent who during the past year *did not* deliver a sermon which dealt mainly with a controversial social or political topic.)

	Doctrinal Index					Controlled DXY
	Low 0	1	2	3	High 4	
Otherworldliness Index:						
None	0	0	8	0	X	.076
Number	(6)	(8)	(12)	(9)		
Low	0	4	6	15	29	.193
Number	(17)	(82)	(146)	(149)	(42)	
Medium	0	14	17	19	34	.208
Number	(1)	(14)	(60)	(159)	(181)	
High	X	0	—	30	53	.248
Number		(1)	(8)	(46)	(231)	
						Original DXY
Original relationship	0	7	11	18	43	.344

Table 8.   *Doctrinalism, Otherworldliness, and Giving a Sermon on Racial Problems and on World Poverty*

(Percent who during the past year devoted at least one sermon mainly to racial problems.)

	Low 0	1	2	3	High 4	Controlled DXY
		Doctrinal Index				
Otherworldliness Index:						
None	–	–	67	–	X	.062
Number	(6)	(8)	(12)	(9)		
Low	70	67	69	58	40	.101
Number	(17)	(82)	(145)	(144)	(38)	
Medium	–	57	44	50	30	.146
Number	(1)	(14)	(59)	(154)	(173)	
High	X	0	–	38	19	.223
Number		(1)	(7)	(45)	(211)	
Original relationship	78	67	63	52	25	Original DXY .262

(Percent who during the past year devoted at least one sermon mainly to world poverty.)

	Low 0	1	2	3	High 4	Controlled DXY
		Doctrinal Index				
Otherworldliness Index:						
None	–	–	50	–	X	.107
Number	(6)	(8)	(12)	(9)		
Low	47	43	35	39	37	.013
Number	(17)	(82)	(145)	(144)	(38)	
Medium	0	29	22	32	21	.010
Number	(1)	(14)	(59)	(154)	(173)	
High	X	0	–	22	13	.160
Number		(1)	(7)	(45)	(211)	
Original relationship	52	41	33	34	18	Original DXY .138

coefficient of .344 declines to .076, .193, .208, and .248 when the control is added. Again, the hypothesis that otherworldliness is the mechanism linking doctrinalism and silence is substantially confirmed.

Table 9 reexamines sermonizing on two specific problems: race and poverty. In both instances there is a substantial reduction in the original relationship between doctrinalism and preaching on social justice. The correlation between doctrinalism and preaching on racial problems is reduced from .262 to .062, .101, .146, and .223, while on world poverty the reduction is from .138 to .107, .013, .010, and (no reduction) .160.

Thus suspicions that a chain of theological convictions is a primary source of pulpit silence is convincingly sustained statistically. But we do not have to rest our case here. There is strong evidence available that the motives we have imputed to the clergy are recognized and accepted by the clergy themselves. In a sense, we have not uncovered a process which the clergy have failed to recognize, but only one which had not previously been empirically confirmed.

The clergymen in the sample were asked to evaluate various factors which might encourage or discourage individual ministers to "participate in social action activities." Now, admittedly, this is not exactly the same thing as preaching sermons on the questions toward which the social action activities of the clergy are normally directed, although action and preaching are very strongly related.[14] Still, it is very interesting to see in Table 9 how ministers rated their own theological views as affecting social action. Over all, two-thirds said that their own theological views *generally encouraged* participation in social action. But while 96 percent of the least doctrinally committed and 90 percent of those who scored 1 chose this reponse, only a minority—39 percent—of the most conservative clergy did so. This closely parallels the proportions who use their pulpits to speak out on social issues—at least once in a while. It also indicates that the majority of the conservative clergy find some incompatibility between their theological convictions and the appropriateness of participation in social action. We have argued precisely this point and expanded it to include preaching on social and political issues. An excellent test of whether or not we are properly interpreting the implications of Table 9 is relatively simple. If our interpretation is correct, differences among clergy in judging their theological views as encouraging or discouraging their participation in social action can be substituted for the Otherworldliness Index with similar consequences. That is, the individual clergyman's own evaluation ought to be as effective as that we have imputed to him.

Table 9.   *Doctrinalism and the Effect of Clergy Views on Social Action*

Number	Doctrinal Index					
	Low 0 (28)	1 (134)	2 (296)	3 (467)	High 4 (568)	Total (1,493)
Percent who said their "own *theological views*" generally *encouraged* their participation in social action activities	96	90	84	79	39	67

Table 10 shows that this is the case. The clergy's own views are effective replacement controls which reduce the original relationships about as well as the Otherworldliness Index did. Thus, on never taking a stand from the pulpit on a political issue the correlation coefficient is reduced from .237 to .092, .065, and .102 by adding the self-designated control. On preaching a sermon on racial problems in the past year the reduction is from .262 to .140, .145, and .195.

This interchangeability of measures is strong testimony for the validity of our inference of the otherworldly, theological source of clerical silence. We are

[14]Quinley, *op. cit.*

Table 10. *Subjective Assessment of Role of Their Own Theological Views as a Substitute for the Otherworldliness Index*

(Percent who have *never* taken a stand from the pulpit on some political issue.)

	Doctrinal Index					Controlled DXY
	Low 0	1	2	3	High 4	
Generally encourages their participation: Number	4 (27)	14 (120)	15 (249)	25 (372)	37 (223)	.092
Generally discourages their participation: Number	— (1)	— (4)	60 (25)	69 (62)	73 (229)	.065
Neither: Number	X	— (9)	47 (17)	63 (32)	69 (105)	.102
Original relationship:	7	19	21	33	58	Original DXY .237

(Percent who during the past year devoted at least one sermon mainly to racial problems.)

	Doctrinal Index					Controlled DXY
	Low 0	1	2	3	High 4	
Clergy judgments of the effect of their own theological views on their participation in social action activities						
Generally encourages their participation: Number	78 (27)	69 (117)	67 (240)	60 (360)	42 (214)	.140
Generally discourages their participation: Number	0 (1)	— (4)	33 (24)	22 (58)	14 (209)	.145
Neither: Number	X	— (9)	38 (16)	23 (30)	14 (94)	.195
Original relationship:	78	67	63	52	25	Original DXY .262

forced to conclude that a major reason why clergymen high on doctrinalism are so much less likely than their more modernist colleagues to preach about the problems of race, war, or poverty is that they see such problems as mundane in contrast to the joys of the world to come, and besides they believe these social ills would take care of themselves if enough men were brought to Christ.

There remains, however, a perhaps unlikely but nevertheless possible alternative explanation for these findings. It is held in some conservative theological circles and by some denominations that the pulpit ought to be reserved for communicating the Gospel in all its purity and that sermons ought not be derailed from this "sacred" purpose by dealing with more mundane matters of everyday life. The existence of this perspective was indicated earlier, when we examined clergy conceptions of the purposes of sermons. The responses of conservative clergy were considerably more consistent with a purely sacred view of the use of the sermon than were those of the liberal clergy.

Thus, it is conceivable that doctrinally conservative clergymen, while considerably less likely than their more liberal counterparts to speak out on the moral and social issues of the day in sermons, may be as likely or even more likely to speak out in other contexts. We were able to check out this possibility by examining responses to the question, "How frequently do you discuss public affairs with members of your congregation?"

All in all, 54 percent of the clergy reported that they do this frequently, but the most doctrinally liberal clergy are twice as likely to do so as the most doctrinally conservative clergy. The range between the extremes is from 82 to 41 percent, figures which are very consistent with those found earlier with reference to clergy performance in the pulpit.

A further indication that the phenomenon we have been examining covers more than pulpit behavior is that the most liberal clergy are also much more likely than the most conservative clergy (64 percent versus 26 percent) to say that they feel that they have a special obligation to stay politically informed.

Thus the conclusion is warranted that it is because of their religious convictions that many Protestant clergymen reject the relevance of speaking out from the pulpit or elsewhere on social issues. So long as this continues to be the case, it seems futile to expect them to change their pulpit performances. If the majority remain silent, it is because they believe in doing so.

Yet, if the majority are silent, we must acknowledge that there is also an outspoken minority among clergy. Perhaps it is both unrealistic and unnecessary to expect more than this—unrealistic because activism is almost always a minority phenomenon, whatever the context, whatever the group examined; unnecessary because the outspoken clergy may be the vanguard of far-reaching changes in our religious institutions and thus important far beyond their numbers. To conclude this chapter, we must consider this latter possibility.

The "New Breed"

Much has been written in the past few years about the rapid and widespread changes assumed to be occurring in religious institutions. It is generally agreed that we are in the midst of a "New Reformation." Furthermore, it is widely believed that a "New Breed"[15] of younger clergy have entered the churches and are the dynamic behind changes which, it is hoped, will result in a regenerated church that is relevant, responsive, engaged, and humane.

There can be no doubt that the New Breed exists. There is evidence that they have made considerable headway in campus and experimental ministries and

[15] Harvey Cox, "The 'New Breed' in American Churches: Sources of Social Activism in American Religion," *Daedalus* (Winter 1967).

even in denominational headquarters and administrative positions.[16] But, as we shall see below, our data suggest that the New Breed have made very little headway in the real organizational backbone of the church—the parish ministry. Although there are substantial numbers of what might be regarded as New Breed clergymen in some denominations, in the clergy as a whole their numbers have remained relatively small. Furthermore, there is reason to suspect that they are not growing.

The size of the New Breed depends somewhat on how one defines its membership, but, however defined, it seems to be very small. The two main defining criteria used in writings by and about the New Breed are a modernist theology and a commitment to social justice—a Christian witness in the world. Using only a theological definition, on the basis of the Doctrinal Index one could only argue that at most a third (31 percent) of the clergy could be called New Breed (scores zero to 2), but a more realistic estimate might be in the neighborhood of one in ten. Turning to the criterion of exhibiting through action a strong commitment to social justice, the estimates remain about the same: 25 percent of the clergy in this sample reported speaking out from their pulpits on controversial social and political issues as often as five times in the previous year. But, of course, some of this activity comes from theologically conservative clergymen. Thus, combining these very permissive criteria allows an estimate that no more than 12 percent of the clergy in this sample can conceivably be called New Breed. There seem compelling grounds to think that the New Breed is especially common in California and that a nationwide estimate would probably be substantially smaller.[17]

Thus, at the moment the New Breed is a tiny minority. Of course, our data apply to only one point in time and could easily miss the fact of rapid growth in progress which had not yet reached sizable proportions in an absolute sense. A single, static picture of a rapid process is necessarily misleading. Thus we run the danger of pondering immutable statistics while the rapid growth in the real world goes by unnoticed.

Yet, if this is the case there ought to be some detectable signs. Instead, in our judgment, the signs point to a lack of growth, for it seems certain that the New Breed suffers from a high rate of defection. It is hardly news that a major crisis facing the churches is the fact that so many are leaving the clergy. Ministers, priests, nuns, and seminarians are quitting in large and growing numbers each year. It has not been possible to obtain reliable statistics on the size of defections, but many church officials have estimated that withdrawals from the clergy have been about 7 percent a year recently. In the seminaries, both in

---

[16]Phillip E. Hammond, *The Campus Clergyman* (Garden City, N.Y.: Doubleday, 1966); Hadden, *op. cit.*; and Phillip E. Hammond and Robert E. Mitchell, "Segmentation of Radicalism: The Case of the Protestant Campus Minister," *American Journal of Sociology*, LXXI (1965), 133-143.

[17]A comparison between California clergymen and their colleagues nationwide can be made by reference to Hadden, *op. cit.* Such a comparison shows that California clergy in all denominations are more liberal and activist than are clergy elsewhere.

terms of declining enrollments, dropouts, and graduates who do not enter the clergy, the decline is probably considerably greater.[18] The question is: Who is leaving? There is widespread evidence that it is mainly the New Breed. For one thing, many of the most prominent original New Breed leaders have themselves left. Data show that New Breed types have long tried to avoid the parish and have flowed into administrative positions, especially campus chaplaincies, and that it is also from these ranks that many defections come.[19] Our data do not directly bear on defection. All were still in the church at the time of the study. Yet, Table 11 provides strong indication that defection is endemic among the New Breed.

All clergymen were asked to reconsider their calling: "Looking back on things—if you had it to do over—how certain are you that you would enter the ministry?" It seems a telling comment on the state of religious institutions that only just over half (56 percent) had no regrets and would definitely do it again. More important, only 14 percent of those who scored zero and 22 percent of those who scored 1 believed they would definitely go into the clergy again, while 75 percent of those who scored 4 on doctrinalism definitely would. The majority of the theological New Breed has second thoughts about their vocation. Indeed, 26 percent of those who scored zero said they definitely or probably would not do it again—only 6 percent of the whole Protestant clergy were this much disillusioned with being ministers.

If defection is high and probably on the increase while recruitment is declining, and if both of these processes mainly affect the New Breed, the New

Table 11. *Doctrinalism and Disillusionment*

	Doctrinal Index					
Number	Low 0 (28)	1 (134)	2 (296)	3 (467)	High 4 (568)	Total (1,493)
"Looking back on things— *if you had it to do over—* *how certain are you that* *you would enter the ministry?"*						
Definitely would do it again	14%	22%	45%	54%	75%	56%
Probably would do it again	39	40	32	31	18	27
Not sure	21	19	15	13	4	11
Probably would not do it again	22	18	6	2	3	5
Definitely would not enter the ministry	4	1	2	0	0	1
	100%	100%	100%	100%	100%	100%

[18]For the first time in a decade, seminary applications and enrollments rose for the academic year 1969-1970. Leading seminary deans candidly admitted, however, that this seemed wholly caused by young men wanting to avoid the draft.

[19]Hammond and Mitchell, *op. cit.*, and Hadden, *op. cit.*

Breed would seem to have been a short-lived phenomenon among the clergy and to have reflected rebellion, not revolution. The "Old Breed" greatly predominate. It seems likely to us that they will increase their dominance if only through default—while the vanguard is being decimated, the rear guard proceeds unscathed.

Evidence that it is the New Breed who are most prone to leave the ministry coincides with evidence that among the laity it is those most inclined to theological modernism and ethical commitment who are drifting into inactivity or even out of the churches altogether.[20] Since such laymen represent the potential constituency of the New Breed, the fact of their defection and inactivity should have raised serious questions about the plausibility of the New Reformation which has been so widely taken for granted. As we have shown elsewhere, the backbone of lay support for the churches remains very conservative.[21] Jeffrey Hadden has suggested that the commitment of the clergy to refashioning the churches is bound to produce a profound struggle between the clergy and the laity who oppose such change—some signs of which have already appeared in church conflicts, clergy firings, the withholding of funds, and the like.[22]

Our data partly support his conclusions. Clergymen most likely to speak out from the pulpit on human and social issues or otherwise engage in activism are overwhelmingly theologically *and* politically liberal. Thus, a conservative lay constituency is confronted with clergy activism which runs counter to their own political and social views. Consequently clergy activism has become more or less synonymous in the minds of the laity with liberal activism, and this has, indeed, created considerable conflict over the proper role of the clergy. But, as our data show, the majority of the clergy are not really in conflict with the laity. They are not activists, either in the streets or in the pulpit, and their social and political views are quite conservative. Thus, the pressure against clerical activism is borne almost wholly by the New Breed, whose influence, in our judgment, is not sufficient to produce more than superficial changes in religious institutions. They appear to find cosmetic solutions unacceptable as a substitute for real reformation. Consequently, they will probably continue to leave out of frustration.

Of course, many of the leaders of the New Breed expect that this very frustration will be the source of radically new forms of ministry and will produce a transformation in the basic organization of the churches. They do not envision the possibility of reforming a church still based on a parish structure. Rather they dismiss such a structure as anachronistic and believe that the faster young clergymen abandon it for a ministry not rooted in an institutional base, the faster a regenerated church will emerge. In our judgment, this is naïve. It assumes a church without a structure for funding itself, for coordinating its activities, or through which to involve its constituents. A church not based on

[20]Stark and Glock, *American Piety.*

[21]*Ibid.*

[22]Hadden, *op. cit.*

parishes has no way to organize its connections with the laity. Even a charismatic evangelist such as Billy Graham cannot gather his great rallies except through months of organizational effort based on the congregations in the local community. We cannot envision a church except of the most flimsy and tenuous kind not built on organized local units; and, of course, this is also true for social movements, political parties, or any other large-scale effort to mobilize people. Indeed, we believe that the New Breed have dismissed the parish church mainly because of their failure to make significant inroads in this sector of the churches. Rather than a portent of a new institutionless church, their turn to secular society and away from organized religion seems a sign of the immovability of religious institutions.

So where does that leave those who wish to enlist the churches in efforts to eradicate social evils? The only workable answer we can offer is predicated on dealing with the churches as they really are, not with some hoped-for vision of the future. Efforts must be concentrated on the silent majority. We have elsewhere commented that it is difficult to maintain a realistic view of the religious situation if one often attends conferences and symposiums on problems of peace, race, and the like in which religious spokesmen participate.[23] The majority of such clerical participants are filled with moral fervor and compassion and seek an active Christian witness on such matters. One is easily misled into thinking of them as representative of moral ferment in the churches and as certain evidence that the churches are a potentially powerful force in such matters. This is always the danger in preaching to the converted; as many important evangelists have recognized, it prevents you from reaching the heathen. Thus, in our judgment it is vital now to turn away from the comforts of dialogues with the New Breed and seek conversations with the main body of the clergy.

So long as efforts to arouse the average parish clergymen on such human issues as peace, poverty, prejudice, and justice are no more successful than they have been so far, Sunday will remain the same: the American silent majority sitting righteously in the pews listening to silent sermons.

[23]See Chapter 9.

Chapter Fifteen

New Forms of Religion in the Seminary*

Robert Wuthnow

For some time now, sociologists and others have been describing what religion in America is *not*. Traditional orthodox beliefs are not the center of faith for many religious groups; church attendance is not the mark of religiosity it once was; religion is not popular among intellectuals, nor is it serving the lower classes of the inner-city; ministers do not communicate adequately and do not challenge their parishioners; ministers are not satisfied with the traditional church; seminarians do not plan to enter traditional forms of ministry; and theologians do not advocate traditional theology.[1] But although descriptions of what religion is *not* have been abundant, systematic studies of what religion *is* or is becoming have not yet been forthcoming.

As an approach to trying to anticipate what new forms religion may take in contemporary society, a few students of religion, particularly journalists and sociologists, have recently turned to the study of religious elites, assuming that new religious beliefs and practices emerge first from religious leaders. Hadden (1969), for example, has sought to assess new directions in religion by examining current attitudes of young in contrast to older parish clergy.[2] *Time* journalists recently turned to young and vocal priests and nuns to judge the

*Robert Wuthnow, "New Forms of Religion in the Seminary," *Review of Religious Research* 12, no. 2 (Winter 1971). Reprinted with the permission of the author and the *Review of Religious Research*.

[1] Rodney Stark and Charles Y. Glock, *American Piety: The Nature of Religious Commitment* (Berkeley and Los Angeles: University of California Press, 1968); Charles Y. Glock and Rodney Stark, *Religion and Society in Tension* (Chicago: Rand McNally & Co., 1965), p. 74 and pp. 262-288; Pierre Berton, *The Comfortable Pew* (Philadelphia: J. B. Lippincott Company, 1965); *Time*, "Priests and Nuns: Going Their Way," (February 23, 1970), pp. 51-58; Keith R. Bridston and Dwight W. Culver, *Pre-Seminary Education* (Minneapolis, Minnesota: Augsburg Publishing House, 1965).

[2] Jeffrey K. Hadden, *The Gathering Storm in the Churches* (Garden City, N.Y.: Doubleday & Company, Inc., 1969).

tenor and pace of changes taking place in the Roman Catholic Church.[3] Seminarians also have been a source for discovering where religion may be going. *Time, Life,* and the *Christian Science Monitor,* for example, have all featured stories within the last year on the religious perspectives current among youth training for the ministry.

The study of religious elites cannot in itself fully predict the nature of new religious forms, but it has long been recognized as a useful place to start. Max Weber, for example, considered elites essential to his sociology of religion, devoting much of his work to comparing such groups as Confucian mandarins, the mendicant monks of Buddhism, Islamic warriors, Sufi mystics, and the itinerant artisans of early Christianity. To understand new forms of religion in contemporary society, attention must be given to studying "avant-garde" clergymen, campus chaplains, seminarians, and even the functionaries of occult groups such as Krishna and Zen. Attention should also be given to "religion" among rising *secular* elites, such as students, scientists, and political leaders. Moreover, as Weber has shown, these elites cannot be studied in isolation, but must be analyzed in interaction with the remainder of society. Predictions about new contemporary forms of religion, then, would not be complete without consideration of the dominant values of society at large.

In light of these considerations, the purpose of the present study is extremely modest. It is restricted, first, to making predictions only about new forms of *institutionalized* religion; second, it considers only religious *elites*; and third, among religious elites, only *seminarians* are examined. Since the course of tomorrow's church is largely held in the hands of today's seminary students, however, this appears to be a fruitful strategy.

The data presented here was collected from interviews with seventy-five students and ten faculty members from six seminaries affiliated with the Graduate Theological Union in Berkeley, California. The denominations (or religious orders) of the students interviewed included Episcopalian, Baptist, Jesuit, Franciscan, Presbyterian, Methodist, and Lutheran. Due to the liberal milieu of these seminaries, a special effort was made to include a number of conservative students in the sample. The interviews focused on obtaining qualitative data descriptive of the students' religious perspectives, the types of ministry that attract them, and some of the sources and consequences of their choices.

Four Types of Seminarians

In order to analyze new forms of religion in the seminary, seminarians are classified according to the types of ministry they plan to pursue. The religious perspectives of these different types of seminarians are then described and compared and implications are suggested for the church and society.

Four distinct types of seminary students can be identified according to their vocational plans. The primary dimension which distinguishes these types

[3]*Op. cit.*

of seminarians is their acceptance or rejection of parish ministry. Two types, the *Academic* and the *Activist*, reject parish ministry. The Academic plans to engage in college teaching while the Activist plans to enter a social action ministry, such as a street mission or civil rights work. The two types of students who plan to enter parish ministry are the *Traditionalist* and the *Revisionist*. The Traditionalist plans to commit himself primarily to preaching the gospel and cultivating relationships with God while the Revisionist plans to engage more in group activities and the pursuit of human relationships.

Most seminarians plan to pursue one of these four types of ministries. Of the seventy-five seminarians interviewed, only one did not plan to enter one of these ministries. Of the seminarians whom Louis Garringer interviewed for his recent articles in the *Christian Science Monitor*, approximately ninety percent fit into these four categories. It can be inferred that at least eighty-five percent of those interviewed on the Bridsten and Culver study of pre-seminarians fit into these categories.[4] Other types of ministry which attract a few seminarians include counseling, administration, chaplaincy, and missions. These, however, are not large categories and are generally similar to one of the four major types of ministry. The type of ministry which is most popular appears to be the Revisionist type; each of the other three types attracts a smaller, but approximately equal number of seminarians.

The Traditionalist

The Traditionalist is so named because he subscribes primarily to traditional religious beliefs and practices. For the Traditionalist, ministry is primarily preaching the gospel and encouraging people to find fellowship with God. In fact, the primary motif which distinguishes the Traditionalist from other types of seminarians is his emphasis upon a personal relationship with God. Only as the individual submits himself to a relationship with God does he find true fulfillment.

Since God is knowable only through personal fellowship, however, the Traditionalist is somewhat reluctant to define God. God is knowable, not through philosophy or reason or nature, but only as He reveals Himself to individuals. When the Traditionalist is asked to describe his relationship with God, however, he generally defines God as a *creative, loving Being*. God is *creative* because He is the Creator and Controller of nature. "God is in creation and the products of His creation." Since God is the Creator of the world, the world is sacred. The world has Fallen, but yet it remains God's creation and must not be tampered with. Although God created nature, the Traditionalist hesitates to say that God is "supernatural," however, because this term implies that God is foreign or removed from human experience. Rather, the Traditionalist prefers to say that God is "more than nature," although He is also "in nature." Since God created nature, He is more than nature and cannot be knowable entirely through nature. God is *loving* because

[4]*Op. cit.*

He calls individuals into intimate fellowship with Him, giving them peace and comfort, forgiving their sins, and promising them eternal life. Finally, God is a *Being* because He is personal. "God is a person we can trust in and who loves us and disciplines us." "Personal" not only means that God relates to persons, but also that He is an abstract, integrated, and superior system of personal attributes or virtues, such as love, wisdom, power, mercy, immortality, goodness, and justice. "God is the experience of peace, love, and order we have through Jesus Christ." Relating to God then, in a simplified sense, means relating to and cultivating these virtues.

Since God is knowable only as He reveals Himself, the Traditionalist attributes unique importance to Jesus Christ, defining him as God's ultimate revelation: "Jesus was God's ultimate revelation to mankind; he showed God's love and concern; he was sent by God to teach the ways of his Father." For the Traditionalist, Jesus is the divine Son of God through which God saves individuals and calls them into fellowship with Him. "Jesus isn't significant because he was a moral teacher or a good man; he was Incarnate God." He is the means by which a personal relationship with God is established. The Traditionalist is likely to reinforce his concept of Christ's divinity with beliefs in the Virgin Birth, the miracles of Christ, and the Resurrection and emphasizes the importance of trusting in him for salvation.

Because the Traditionalist places God at the center of his religious orientation, his images of man and society are dependent upon his image of God. The following statement is typical of the Traditionalist's image of man:

> Man's spirit is made after the image of God. It is possible to break fellowship with God, but the consequence is unhappiness. It's good to be a slave of God's; He's no tyrant.

The ideal state of man is personal fellowship with God. This primarily means attaining the system of personal virtues that the Traditionalist identifies with God. The individual achieves these virtues by passively denying his own will and by seeking to follow Christ, the human personification of these virtues. He is encouraged to study the Bible in order to better understand the life of Christ and to pray, relinquishing his own will and desiring these ultimate virtues, both for himself and for others. Man is totally free to control his will, so his greatest sin is to direct his will against this superior system of personal virtues. Man relates to others primarily to demonstrate that he has attained these virtues and to encourage others to attain them.

The importance of God for the Traditionalist also influences his image of society:

> The problems of society are due to basic selfishness. After the Fall man was alienated from God and from others. I believe in the total depravity of man. Man looks after his own self-interest first.

Man has substituted his own will for God's will, thereby depriving himself of a perfect world. Only as individuals deny their wills and attain the personal virtues of God can society be improved. The Traditionalist's strategy for social betterment is primarily one of working with other individuals to bring them into fellowship with God.

The purpose of the church, then, is to bring individuals back into relationship with God. Externally, the church's primary contact with society is individualistic, preaching individual repentance and fellowship with God:

> The church's outreach should be mainly through the contacts of each person in the church. They don't have to carry big banners; it is through their jobs. People identify the church with them. They don't talk church-talk, but they talk to people on their own level and then witness if the opportunity arises.

Internally, the church functions primarily as a place of comfort and refreshment for its members and as a center for the worship of God.

In summary, the dominant motif of the Traditionalist is personal fellowship with God. God is a creative, loving Being who forms personal relationships with people, giving them access to superior personal qualities. Fellowship with God fulfills the individual, improves society, and defines the roles of the church.

The Revisionist

The Revisionist is the modal type of seminarian and, therefore, appears to be most significant for determining the face of the church in the future. Like the Traditionalist, the Revisionist plans to enter parish ministry, but he revises traditional definitions of ministry, traditional religious beliefs, and traditional attitudes toward social change. He is distinguishable from the Traditionalist, not primarily by his rejection of traditional religious symbols, but by his revision of the meaning of these symbols. Whereas the dominant motif of the Traditionalist is personal fellowship with God, the dominant motif of the Revisionist is *community*, or fellowship among men.

The Revisionist's image of God is more pantheistic than personal. God, according to the Revisionist, is defined as *everything that makes up our life experience*. Other phrases that the Revisionist uses to describe God are "the on-goingness of life," "the processes of the universe," and "the force behind all life." The Revisionist's pantheism is not primarily a pantheism of nature, but a pantheism of life, particularly human life and human relationships. God is emphatically not supernatural because He is so closely related to the world. In fact, God is not only related to the world, He *is* the world, the universe, and life itself. Identifying God as all things in life does not imply that in actuality there is no God; rather, it implies that all things in life are sacred. According to this definition of God, everything takes on special value and importance, hence the Revisionist's acceptance of the basic structure of the *status quo*. God remains transcendent because He transcends the individual and the individual's knowledge of life; yet, God's transcendence is dimmed by His immanence, for He is present in all things. Since God is everything in life, the Revisionist experiences "Him" not through prayer or meditation, but in the everyday activities of life, particularly in relationships with others.

The Revisionist's image of Christ also stresses human relationships. Like the Traditionalist, the Revisionist recognizes Jesus as a revelation of God, but the primary significance of Jesus for the Revisionist is not that he exemplifies fellowship with God, but that he exemplifies fellowship with others. Phrases used to describe Jesus include: the one who crystallizes our insights into love, justice, and brotherhood; a self-sacrificing person; a person who accepted others and challenges us to lower our barriers; the one who teaches us how to relate and be accepting and open; and a person who had a good grasp on human nature. Since Jesus is defined as a link between men rather than a link with God, beliefs in his divinity are unimportant. Beliefs in the Virgin Birth, miracles, and the Resurrection, whether true or not, are important only in that they reveal the impression that Jesus made upon those who wrote about him. For the Revisionist, belief in Christ is not adhering to doctrine, but following his example of self-sacrifice and concern for others. Thus, both the Revisionist's image of God and his image of Christ emphasize human relationships or community.

The Revisionist's image of man also stresses community. Man's primary responsibility is to live openly and unselfishly toward others:

> Man should find meaning in his relationships. He should have meaningful contact with other people, dialogue, openness, and honesty with others. Man's primary responsibility is to his "supportive community." He must not close himself off to others through fear of loneliness, separation, and rejection. Christianity frees man by providing him with a "supportive community."

Man's tendency is to be selfish and turned inward upon himself, but by being more aware of others and striving for fellowship with others, he can overcome his selfishness and transcend himself. The Revisionist is not utopian about establishing relationships with others, however. He defines man's ideal state not as perfect fellowship with others, but as continual searching for reconciliation. Fulfillment is gained through striving, not through attaining.

Since God is knowable through everyday activities and relationships, life after death and hope for a better tomorrow are unimportant. Man must rather seek fulfillment through constant activity in his daily life. Continually striving to overcome selfishness and to establish accepting relationships with others is man's primary responsibility and his ultimate ideal.

This view of man determines the Revisionist's view of society:

> Problems exist in society because man is selfish and greedy. He has been hurt by others and wants to hurt back.

But since selfishness is impossible to completely annihilate, the Revisionist is not utopian about changing society. Social betterment must be attained slowly and orderly by individuals working in their own contexts:

> Society can be improved only by a bunch of guys that keep trying to make things better. We should try to reduce those factors that isolate men and keep them from being open—prejudice, hate, poverty, and self-glorification.

The role of the church must be both "a moral critic within the community and a supportive community which builds and prods people." Since the basic problems of society are attributable to individual selfishness, the church must work to overcome selfishness by providing a community in which personal relationships may be formed. Sensitivity groups, communal forms of liturgy, counseling, discussion groups, recreation, etc. are the major activities within the church. In seeking community, however,

> the church must not be above society, but be a part of it. The church has a special role to bring about betterment. This is the creative good that is never attained, but is just around the corner. The church should not be above using political pressure on things involving ethical questions. It should motivate individuals within the church to act on their convictions.

It must not engage in specific social action plans, however, or seek radical social change. Its duty is primarily to be tolerant, recognizing individual differences and encouraging individuals to live responsibly in their different situations.

The dominant motif of the Revisionist, then, is community. God is all of life and must be sought in everyday activities, particularly in human relationships. Man's tendency is to be selfish, but he can reduce his selfishness as he relates to others. The role of the church is to provide a community in which such relationships may be formed.

The Academic

The Academic differs little theologically from the Revisionist, although his vocational plans are quite different. He plans to become a college professor instead of a parish minister. Since the Academic rejects parish ministry, he is not significant directly for predicting the course of the church in the future; indirectly, however, he is of interest to the church because he forms the largest category of seminarians who are being siphoned out of the church. Moreover, this category is increasing in size and is becoming a significant new form of religious ministry in itself. Since theological differences between the Academic and the Revisionist are minimal, reasons for the Academic's rejection of parish ministry must be discovered in his own personal background. These background factors are considered in detail in the following section; suffice it here to say, however, that the most distinguishing reason for the Academic's rejection of parish ministry is his feeling of inability to cope with the social complexities of the parish.

Although Academics are more diverse theologically than are other types of seminarians, the majority of them have moderate views and appear to be developing a theological consensus similar to that of the Revisionists. Since the Academic's theological perspective corresponds closely to the Revisionist's, only a brief description of the Academic's views is necessary.

The Academic, like the Revisionist, defines God in pantheistic terms. God is all that is. Phrases defining God include "that which unites us," "the entire universe," "what you really are," "unconditional love," and "the force of order in the universe." Christ is God's revelation to man and is defined as an example of self-sacrifice and unconditional love.

The Academic's image of man also emphasizes human relationships and self-sacrifice to others. In contrast to the Revisionist's exclusive focus on self-sacrifice, however, the Academic appears to add an element of self-actualization.

> Man's responsibility is self-actualization, being in tune with our self. Also, man is inherently social, so being in touch with self causes us to be in touch with others.

The Academic and the Revisionist also converge on their images of society. Like the Revisionist, the Academic attributes the problems of society to man's selfishness.

> To change society, we need to be concerned for other people and search for community. Also we need to work on the social institutions; this is therapeutic for the individual. In order to be free from something, we must be free for something. Human relationships are most important; we need love and support.

The ministry of the church again is both social criticism and personal support:

> As for ministry, I am more concerned with providing people with meaning, with the ability to be at home with uncertainty and to know themselves, than with working on big plans to bring progress. I think progress can be achieved, but I would get discouraged if that was all I was working for.

Although there is less consensus among Academics, then, they tend to be similar theologically to the Revisionists. Community is their dominant motif, God is everything that is, man's responsibility is to be open and accepting of others and to actualize himself, society is improved primarily by overcoming man's selfishness, and the role of the church is social critic and creator of community.

The Activist

The Activist also rejects parish ministry, but plans to engage in social action work, such as urban renewal, ghetto education, revolutionary tactics, or critical journalism. Some Activists hope to stay within the broad structure of the church, but most plan to support themselves due to diminished church funds for social action ministries. The determining factor of the Activist's background appears to be close identification with a counter-culture during some period of his development. The counter-culture is often a mystical group, although it is sometimes a Marxist group or other type of activist group.

The Activist's theological position is characterized by his alienation from society. He defines ministry broadly as any activity directed toward changing society. Phrases typifying this type of ministry include "destroying conventional social fictions" and "developing alternatives for existing social structures." The dominant theme of the Activist is *social transformation.*

Since the Activist is primarily concerned with transformation, his concept of God is generally eschatological. God is defined as either *the hope of transformation and liberation* or *the mystical nature of life.* Examples of "hope" definitions include "the process of good in history that we trust in" and "that which moves before us and frees us," while examples of "mystical" definitions include "being in touch with yourself" and "man's innermost desire." The Activist's choice between these two types of definition of God appears to be related to his relative exposure to Marxist or mystical groups. The significant feature common to both of these definitions is that God is not identified with everyday life. God ultimately resides either in the future or in some mystical aspect of life which has not yet been attained in the present. While the Revisionist and the Academic define God as everyday activity, then, the Activist defines Him as a *goal* for everyday activity. Since God is removed from everyday activity, He is generally not as salient for the daily life of the Activist as He is for the other types of seminarians. God provides hope and encouragement, but does not concern Himself directly with the activities of the world.

Jesus is also defined in terms consistent with transformation. He is identified as "a man who exemplified a new way of life," "A member of the disinherited who affirmed life in spite of alienation," "a person who sets up new norms," "a person not attached to the *status quo*," "a person who discovered a rational life style," and "someone who wants us to be free and nice." Jesus' most significant role was his revolutionary role.

The Activist's image of man also contains themes conducive to revolution and transformation. The ideal state of man is "to be in balance with all things; an ecological thing." Being in balance with one's situation is not achieved through conforming to the situation, however:

> Changing society is the first priority because it is getting to the person earlier and earlier. We don't grow up in contact with our self. The only

way a person comes to self-realization is through working with society.
Man's responsibility is to educate himself. This is a very personal
thing that transcends institutionalized education. It is a life-time process.
One should be able to recognize what is going on in the physical world,
to see the things that are wrong, and to think out alternatives and try to
implement them. The ultimate goal is that everybody can have
self-realization to the point that Christ did, a unity of consciousness.

The Activist's image of society is imbued with alienation. While the
problems of society may be caused by man's selfishness, man's selfishness is
perpetuated by evil social structures:

Man is determined by educational influences, government, property, and
political manipulation. He has no freedom to make individual decisions.
He is controlled by the consciousness that is imposed by educational
influences. Man doesn't act religiously because he is obsessed with the
physical world. We need to change the political and economic structure
so that we can turn to the spiritual.

The role of the church in society is primarily a force for social change, but
"church" will have to take on a new form since the present church "has
gotten hooked up with authoritarian figures and wealth." The "church" must
be identified as any group pursuing liberation and transformation:

I think the church should try to put a human face on the world, but
this has already happened outside the church at places like Esalen. I
think there will probably be new structures similar to the churches.
   The institutionalized church will die in the long-run. In the meantime
there will be a resurgence attached to patriotism that will suppress and
deceive people. To be free, people will have to meet in small groups.
These have to be stepping stones to the revolution, to man returning
himself to God-consciousness.

All of the perspectives of the Activist, then, are directed toward social
transformation. God is removed from the present world and placed in the
future. Man must seek balance with all things. Social structures corrupt man,
so they must be revolutionized. Ministry is the act of revolution and the
church is its primary agent.

Backgrounds of the Four Types

To suggest some of the sources of the different religious perspectives
outlined above, the backgrounds of the four types of seminarians are
compared. In general, the Traditionalist, the Academic, and the Activist have
each been influenced by a particularized subculture or reference group, while

the Revisionist has lacked any such group and has identified more with the dominant values of society.

Traditionalists have generally been exposed to a conservative religious orientation and have since remained relatively isolated from situations threatening to this orientation. Their relative isolation is the trait which most distinguishes them from other seminarians. Traditionalists are most likely to have grown up in a religiously conservative family and church and are likely to have evaded liberal ideas during college while their religious perspectives were crystallizing. They are least likely of any of the seminarians to have majored in potentially threatening subjects like philosophy, English literature, or social science and are most likely to have majored in courses such as natural science, engineering, fine arts, or foreign language. They also are least likely to have been involved in potentially threatening T-groups or sensitivity groups. Moreover, the Traditionalist is most likely to have come to seminary immediately after college instead of working in the interim. Furthermore, data from sociometric questions showed that the Traditionalist generally isolates himself from exposure to other religious orientations during seminary by choosing other Traditionalists as friends and by identifying with conservative faculty members. He also tends to study traditional Biblical and historical theology rather than philosophical theology or behavioral sciences, and tends to avoid group dynamics types of classes. The Traditionalist, therefore, maintains his traditional religious orientation primarily by isolating himself from alternative views.

At the opposite end of the theological continuum is the Activist, who has also been a member of a particularized reference group. The Activist has been most exposed to situations opposed to conservative beliefs. He has generally been raised in a religiously liberal home and has belonged to a religiously liberal denomination, if any; has gone to a large university where he majored in philosophy, social science, English literature, or some other discipline in which traditional religious beliefs were challenged; has been involved in sensitivity groups where he was confronted with alternative philosophies and life styles; and has had formative contact with liberal ministers, particularly liberal college chaplains.

These liberal influences, however, are not sufficient in themselves to produce an Activist. To mold a student who is alienated from society, rejects ordinary forms of ministry, and supports revolution or other radical social transformation requires more than exposure to liberal theology. What is required appears to be identification with a counter-culture, often a mystical group. As one student said:

> I feel I must work in the world to change it, but you have to be strong to do that in American society. You need some other source of identity or you will destroy yourself. You need a counter-culture to break down the social structures that alienate. I look to an Eastern counter-culture for authority.

Identifying with a mystical group provides the Activist with a reference group whose values are alien to society at large; it provides him with a base from which to operationalize his revolutionary strategies. Within this counter-culture the liberal seminarian's alienation from society is nurtured so that he rejects institutionalized means of changing society. The mystical group, then, far from encouraging the Activist to withdraw from the world, supports his alienation and stimulates his activism.

This proposition is significant, for it appears to contradict the familiar theme of Weber and Troeltsch that mysticism is antithetical to socially relevant activity. It appears that the Weber-Troeltsch thesis still holds for some students; for example, one student who frequented a Zen temple said he thought people should contemplate to find "their innermost desire." But it appears that an increasing number of students adhere more to the position of the student quoted above who sees mysticism as a base from which to pursue radical social activities. Another student, for example, traced the stages in his development from Presbyterian, to non-church-goer, to Meher Baba enthusiast, to SDS member, to Marxist revolutionary. It appears, then, that the Weber-Troeltsch thesis has become complicated by recent forms of mysticism and radical activism which, due to their simultaneous emergence in America, have become linked so that mysticism functions as a substitute reference group for social activists.

The determining factor in the development of the Activist, then, appears to be identification with a counter-culture, usually a mystical group but sometimes a Marxist group, drug culture, or other activist group. If the Activist chooses a mystical group, he is likely to find its belief system in tension with his norms of social action. Resolution of this tension generally results in compartmentalization, wherein mystical rites function only as occasional interludes of refreshment from social activism. On the whole, therefore, mysticism appears to support social activism and encourages an Activist type of ministry.

In between the extremes of Activism and Traditionalism stand the Academic and the Revisionist. The Academic and the Revisionist have not been as isolated from liberalizing influences as the Traditionalist, but neither have they identified with a counter-culture such as that of the Activist. They have been exposed to limited liberal orientations and have developed a moderate theology.

The Academic differs from the Revisionist because he has identified primarily with an academic reference group during his college training. The Academic is least likely to have been influenced by actual contact with other people such as ministers or church groups; rather, he is likely to have identified with theologians, philosophers, and other scholars. He has been most interested in academics in college, studied most, and earned the highest grades. The Academic does not identify important religious experiences in his life with groups, meetings, or personal encounters, but with thoughts, books, and theological concepts. He has been most influenced by ideas, does not find himself stimulated by working with other people, and feels unqualified to handle the social relationships involved in parish ministry. He has come to seminary, however, because of his interest in religion and his desire to serve others. He sees college teaching as the optimum capacity in which to fulfill his goals.

The Revisionist has not been as strongly influenced by ideas and scholars as has the Academic. He has not had a specialized reference group, but has been most influenced by everyday experiences. The Revisionist has had a relatively liberal church and family background. He was active in church during his youth, but was not especially interested in doctrine or theology. His face-to-face relationships with ministers, college chaplains, and other young people appear to have been most significant in channeling him into the ministry. His interest in the church is likely to have been reinforced through holding leadership positions in college ministries, national conferences, church committees, etc. His college training is likely to have included a number of courses in the humanities and social sciences, plus some sensitivity training which reinforced his interest in working with people. The Revisionist category also includes a number of men who have worked for awhile in another occupation and found it providing too few opportunities for working with and helping people. In either case the Revisionist's religious orientations, as indicated above, give a sacred overtone to his desire to work with people and he is, thus, drawn to the parish ministry.

These conclusions, of course, are only suggestive due to the small sample on which they are based. They do, however, indicate some of the ways in which several important background variables—parents' religious beliefs, parents' denomination, college major, academic success, contacts with ministers, and differential reference group attachments—operate to produce different religious orientations among seminarians.

Consequences of the Four Types

The type of ministry most significant for the future of the church appears to be the Revisionist. Not only is the Revisionist the largest category of seminarians, it also appears to be developing the most consensus about new forms of religion. Agreement is widespread that God is the totality of life and that man's responsibility is to relate to life by relating to others. This belief also predominates among Academics, supporting the consensus emerging among the Revisionists.

The Revisionist type of ministry is also most significant for the future of the church because its beliefs appear to be generally compatible with basic social values. The reason for this compatibility lies primarily in the Revisionist's personal background. Unlike the Traditionalist who has identified with a religiously conservative reference group or the Activist who has identified with a mystical or Marxist reference group, the Revisionist has lacked any particularized reference group and has developed values which conform to predominant social values. Two examples of the conformity between the Revisionist's views and general social values indicate dramatically the saliency of the Revisionist type of ministry for the future of the church in society.

One indication that the Revisionist type of ministry is likely to appeal to society is that the Revisionist's emphasis upon groups and human relationships is consistent with the group form of social organization that prevails in society at large. This group form of social organization is clearly exemplified by the committee groups which, according to Galbraith, predominate in modern corporations. According to Galbraith,[5] "association in a committee enables each member to come to know the intellectual resources and the reliability of his colleagues." For the Revisionist, to associate with others in a group is to know God himself. Group relations which are so important to modern industry are, thus, sacralized by the Revisionist. In both the corporation group and the religious group, emphasis is upon getting along with others, contributing to the group, and aligning one's will with the will of the group. In the corporation the committee permits individuals to maximize the potential of their individual technical specialties. For the Revisionist the group provides the individual with meaning and transcendence. Thus, there is striking similarity between the imagery and organization of the modern corporation and the Revisionist type of ministry, a factor of inescapable importance for the future of the church. In fact, this group-centered alignment between religion and industry appears to be as significant as the earlier individualistic alignment which Max Weber described as the "Protestant ethic and the spirit of capitalism."

Another indication that Revisionist ministry is likely to appeal to society at large is its comforting function. Glock, *et al.*[6] have shown that the traditional role of the church has been primarily to comfort its members rather than to challenge them. It appears that the main function of the Revisionist type of ministry is also to comfort. Since God is believed to be everything in life, the present world is sacralized. People are not challenged by the Revisionist to transform their present situation, but to live within it. Since man's primary responsibility is to be open and accepting of others, the church becomes a community where individuals expect to find acceptance, recognition, and sympathy. The Revisionist type of church comforts through its groups and human relationships and, thus, is an attractive institution, particularly for those members of society who are deprived of open and accepting relationships.

The Revisionist type of ministry, then, attracts the largest number of seminarians, appears to be developing a consensus in its imagery of God and man, maintains the established comforting role of the church, and is congruent with the predominant group form of orgnization in society.

---

[5]John Kenneth Galbraith, *The New Industrial State* (Boston: Houghton Mifflin Company, 1967), p. 75.

[6]Charles Y. Glock, Benjamin B. Ringer, and Earl R. Babbie, *To Comfort and To Challenge: A Dilemma of the Contemporary Church* (Berkeley and Loss Angeles: University of California Press, 1967).

However, since the Revisionist so closely identifies religious experience with everyday activities and group relations, the problem arises, can its imagery of God and man provide the basis for a differentiated church or will the church be replaced by other institutions? According to the Revisionist, all of life is sacred. But if this is the case, there is little need for a specialized institution to promulgate sacred activities. If man's transcendence stems only from group relationships, then recreational groups, mental health clinics, and sensitivity training centers are all functional alternatives for the church. Nowhere is this inherent problem of the Revisionist's imagery of God and man more apparent than in its remedy for man's problems. As shown above, the Revisionist says that, "Man's tendency is to be selfish and turned inward upon himself, but by being more aware of others and striving for fellowship with others, he can overcome his selfishness and transcend himself." What? Man can be less selfish by being less selfish? This imagery presents itself as a "closed system" in comparison with Traditionalist imagery which is built upon objective faith in a set of sacred symbols which introduce supernatural elements into the system. In fact, it would appear that the Revisionist's bid for long-run popularity must be predicated upon developing consensual faith in a set of sacred symbols similar to that of the Traditionalists. Significantly, the Revisionists do not discard traditional religious symbols, but attempt to redefine their meaning. The symbol of "God" is redefined as the totality of everyday life, "Incarnation" symbolizes the sacralization of humanity, "Christ" is the symbol of altruism, the "Devil" symbolizes man's selfishness, and "Heaven" symbolizes man's transcendence. It appears that the degree to which these redefinitions can be made consensual and sacred is crucial for the Revisionist type of church. If the Revisionists fail at this task, their bid for maintaining the church as a viable, differentiated institution must rest on nothing more than the strength of the church's widespread organizational structure alone. This is a resource of no little consequence in itself, including fund-raising techniques, physical property, committees, recruiting and training methods, etc. It is unlikely, therefore, that the church will "die" in the near future as some have predicted. But the long-run impact of the church would appear to be severely restricted unless the Revisionists are able to develop a consensually-defined system of sacred symbols to support their imagery of God and man.

It remains to indicate the consequences of the other three types of ministry. The Traditionalist type of ministry continues to appeal to a minority of church members. It maintains its comforting function primarily in the psychological realm, promising individuals miraculous access to desirable personal attributes. The Traditionalist's themes of individuality and passivity contradict the active group-centered motif of society at large, but, increasingly, establishing warm group relationships is becoming the proper method for the Traditionalist to demonstrate the personal virtues which he has attained. The Traditionalist, therefore, appears to be converging toward the group-centered ethic of both the Revisionist and society at large, suggesting the continued saliency of Traditionalism for at least a minority of church-goers.

The Academic type of ministry supports the Revisionist type in belief, but channels a number of seminarians out of the church into the university. Its main significance for the church, then, appears to be the transference of the knowledge dimension of religion[7] into the university. Whether this transference will weaken the church's control over religious knowledge and eventually lead to significant alterations in conventional forms of religion can only be a matter of conjecture. Shifting the knowledge dimension of religion into the university permits the church to pursue more intensely its primary function of encouraging group relationships, but it also suggests the possibility of new university-centered religious movements developing.

The Activist type of ministry provides the most significant alternative to the Revisionist type. Instead of focusing on everyday activities and group relationships, it encourages revolutionary social transformation. In spite of widespread claims to the contrary, the Activist does not appear to be the dominant, emergent form of ministry, however. Neither are Activists as numerous in the seminary as Revisionists, nor is their consensus on religious beliefs as great. Since Activists have been influenced by Christianity, Marxism, and mystical traditions, belief components from all these must compete for predominance. Moreover, the Activist's beliefs are not consistent with general social values, but are opposed to them. They do not comfort the parishioner, but challenge him to adopt new ways of life. Furthermore, movements within the ranks of the Activists suggest that they are not the emerging dominant form of ministry. As Activists advance through seminary, it appears that their ranks are diminished by a significant number who become discouraged with radical social activity and shift into either a more moderate Revisionist ministry or an Academic ministry or else withdraw into mysticism.

Even though Activism is not emerging as the dominant form of ministry, it has important implications for the church and for religion. Radical activists are increasingly being channeled out of the church into government, university, or other positions. The church, deprived of its radical elements, then, continues to function primarily as an institution of comfort. The Activist perhaps has an indirect influence upon the church, calling it to more social concern, but does not involve it directly in radical social activities. It remains to be seen whether religious activists acting outside the church and obtaining their support from other sources will continue to adhere to traditional religious symbols or if they will develop a totally new religious movement based perhaps upon Marxian or mystical concepts.

In conclusion, then, the Revisionist type of ministry appears to be most significant for defining the nature of the church in the future. It believes in God as everything that makes up life and man as a social being whose responsibility is to establish human relationships. It advocates communal forms of worship, extensive networks of small groups, adherence to old symbols redefined, but only general stands on ethical issues. Traditionalism is also a viable form of religion for a minority, advocating personal virtues and

[7]Glock and Stark, *op. cit.*, p. 32.

stressing service to others as a demonstration of these virtues. Non-church forms of religion are primarily the Academic, who is important as the bearer of theological knowledge, and the Activist, whose function is to carry on religious traditions of revolution.

It should be stressed again that these conclusions are tentative and merely suggestive of the work which must follow if alternatives to traditional forms of religion are to be conceptualized and measured. Leaving aside the broader study of other religious elites and their relationships to society, a number of further steps must be taken to fully grasp new forms of religion in the seminary. Additional qualitative studies must be conducted to qualify the "types" considered here and to discover other types or forms of religiosity. Interested seminary professors and administrators who have daily contact with students and their ideas could make valuable contributions in this regard. Once general types and dimensions have been specified, considerable effort would be required to develop scales to measure and compare them. This task, of course, cannot proceed at a rate more rapid than the rate at which consensus is actually developing on new forms of religion. Finally, attention should be directed toward obtaining data representative of the general population of seminarians to provide a descriptive overview of their religious perspectives and to indicate the sources and consequences of these. A task of this nature would both benefit from and contribute greatly to the general understanding of new forms of religion provided by similar studies of other religious elites and groups.

Part Four

On the Origin and Evolution of Religious Groups

New religious groups and movements have arisen in all periods of history. Most of these have involved only small groups of people, have been short-lived, and have had little direct impact on the larger course of events. The effect has not been to discourage the phenomenon, however, and even in an age popularly described as secular, new religious groups continue to appear in amazing number and diversity.

That new religious groups and movements arise, take different forms, and survive for short or longer periods of time is obvious grist for the mill of the sociology of religion, and trying to account for their origin and evolution has been an abiding sociological interest that is made ever the more intriguing by the new forms of religious consciousness represented in contemporary movements.

The inspiration for much of the work done in this area is about a dozen or so pages in *The Social Teachings of the Christian Churches*, in which Ernst Troeltsch elaborates on a distinction, first suggested to him by Max Weber, between two forms religious movements may take—namely, church and sect.[1] A vast literature has since been devoted to refining the distinction, to establishing criteria for classification, and to theorizing about and doing research on the conditions that give rise to new sects and determine their subsequent course.

The initial distinction between church and sect and subsequent theorizing about the interplay between them grew out of investigations of Western, mostly Christian, religious groups. For the most part, those who formulated

[1] Ernst Troeltsch, *The Social Teachings of the Christian Churches* (New York: Macmillan Co., 1931), pp. 331-43.

and elaborated on the typology and who later developed theory around it were not concerned with producing a universally applicable typology or a generalizeable theory. As attention was directed to the study of religious movements in other cultures, the wider inapplicability of church-sect notions became quickly apparent. This, combined with new difficulties in applying the ideas to new religious and pseudoreligious movements in the West, has produced a growing disenchantment with the concept and increasing pressure for a new start.

No new formulation which promises to succeed church-sect theory as an overarching schema for studying religious groups and movements has yet appeared, although the matter continues to receive attention and remains a challenge. The absence of adequate theory on so vital a topic is a major gap in the sociology of religion, but its generation is likely to require better case studies of new and ongoing religious groups than we now have. Of the many major and minor groups extant in the world, only a handful have been the subject of sociological attention.

The group at Berkeley has given attention both to the larger theoretical task and to the need for more case studies. We have included four examples from this work in the present volume: a theoretical essay and three case studies. Chapter 16, the theoretical essay, suggests a reformulation of church-sect theory as a possible basis for ordering future work in the subject matter area. The three case studies are of Reformed Judaism in the United States, the Japanese religion Sokagakkai, and the Jesus people, and reports respectively by Stephen Steinberg, Earl R. Babbie, and Donald Peterson and Armand L. Mauss on these movements are included as chapters 17, 18, and 19.

Additional Reading

Harrison, Paul M. *Authority and Power in the Free Church Tradition: A Social Case Study of the American Baptist Convention.* Princeton, N.J.: Princeton, University Press, 1959. Undoubtedly still the best contemporary study in the sociology of religous organization.

Sklare, Marshall. *Conservative Judaism: An American Religious Movement.* New York: Free Press, 1958. The inspiration for chapter 17 of the present volume and a fine sociological case study of the birth and development of a religious group.

Metz, Donald. *New Congregations: Security and Mission in Conflict.* Philadelphia: Westminster Press, 1967. A report on a study of the growth patterns and pains of individual parish churches.

Wilson, Bryan. *Religious Sects.* New York: McGraw-Hill Book Co., 1970. Wilson is the world's leading sociologist of sects. This, his latest book, summarizes his thought and research on sect emergence and development to date.

Johnson, Benton. "Church-Sect Revisited." *Journal for the Scientific Study of Religion* 10:2 (Summer 1971). A critical but constructive treatment of the present status of church-sect theory in the sociology of religion.

Chapter Sixteen

On the Origin and Evolution of Religious Groups*

Charles Y. Glock

During the nineteenth century the impact of Darwinian biology on social thought led to a scholarly preoccupation with the origins and evolution of social institutions. Consequently, an enormous amount of work in the sociology of religion sought to establish how it was that religious ideas and traditions sprang up in human societies. But, as social Darwinism passed out of vogue, it was recognized that the question of how men first came to be religious is shrouded in the unknowable past, and is badly put in any event.[1] Nevertheless it has remained relevant and seemingly fruitful to ask about a process of religious innovation and development that is still with us: What accounts for the rise and evolution of new religious groups in society?

This question remains generally unanswered although it has received more attention than any other problem in the sociology of religion. In this chapter we shall review the current state of social science knowledge on the origins of new religious groups, particularly those theories which attribute these innovations to class conflicts. Then we shall propose the outlines for a more general theory which seems to overcome the limitations of existing theories, and suggest how this broader conception can also help account for the directions in which religious groups evolve.

Current thinking about the origin and development of religious groups in Western society has been largely informed by so-called "sect-church" theory. The distinction between church and sect, as formulated in the work of Max

*Charles Y. Glock, "The Role of Deprivation in the Origin and Evolution of Religious Groups," in *Religion and Social Conflict*, ed. Robert Lee and Martin E. Marty (New York: Oxford University Press, 1964), pp. 24-36. Copyright © 1964 by Oxford University Press, Inc. Reprinted with permission.

[1]An excellent critique of this work has been provided by Kingsley Davis, see his *Human Society* (New York: The Macmillan Co., 1949), especially Chapter 19.

Weber[2] and his contemporary, Ernst Troeltsch,[3] was initially an attempt to distinguish types of religious groups and not an effort to discover the conditions under which religious groups originate. Sects were characterized, for example, as being in tension with the world, as having a converted rather than an inherited membership, and as being highly emotional in character. Churches, in contrast, were seen as compromising with the world, as having a predominantly inherited membership, and as restrained and ritualistic in their services.

The sect-church distinction was later refined by H. Richard Niebuhr who postulated a dynamic interrelationship between the two types and saw in this interrelationship a way to help account for the development of new religious groups.[4] Briefly, the compromising tendencies of the church lead some of its members to feel that the church is no longer faithful to its religious traditions. These dissenting members then break away to form new religious groups. At the outset, these new groups take on a highly sect-like character, eschewing the dominant characteristics of the church they have rejected. They assume an uncompromising posture toward the world, they gainsay a professional clergy, they insist on a conversion experience as a condition for membership, and they adopt a strict and literalistic theology.

Over time, however, the conditions which gave rise to the sect change, and a process begins which leads the sect slowly to take on the church-like qualities which it had originally denied. Once it has made the transition from sect to church, the religious group then becomes the breeding ground for new sects which proceed anew through the same process.

New sects, according to sect-church theory, recruit their membership primarily from the economically deprived, or as Niebuhr calls them, "the disinherited" classes of society. Their emergence, therefore, is to be understood as a result not only of religious dissent but of social unrest as well. The theological dissent masks an underlying social protest. However, the new sect functions to contain the incipient social protest, and later, to help eliminate the conditions which produced it.

_ The containment is accomplished through a process of derailment. The sects provide a channel through which their members come to transcend their feelings of deprivation by replacing them with feelings of religious privilege. Sect members no longer compare themselves to others in terms of their relatively lower economic position, but in terms of their superior religious status.

Built into the sect ideology, however, is a puritanical ethic which stresses self-discipline. Thrift, frugality, industry are highly valued. Over time, their

[2]Max Weber, "The Social Psychology of the World's Religions," in Gerth and Mills, eds., *From Max Weber: Essays in Sociology* (New York: Oxford University Press, 1940).

[3]Ernst Troeltsch, *Social Teachings of the Christian Churches* (New York: The Macmillan Co., 1949), esp. Vol. I, pp. 331-343.

[4]H. Richard Niebuhr, *The Social Sources of Denominationalism* (New York: Henry Holt and Co., 1929).

ideology helps to elevate sect members to middle-class statuses which in turn socialize them to middle-class values. Because the economic deprivation itself has been eliminated, feelings of economic deprivation no longer need to be assuaged. As the sect members become accommodated to the larger society, their religious movement proceeds to accommodate itself too. In so doing, it makes the transition from sect to church.

This is an admittedly brief and simplified account of sect-church theory and omits the many refinements that have been made in it over the last decades.[5] However, for our purposes, it conveys the essential points of traditional theory, namely, that new religious movements begin by being sect-like in character, that they arise by breaking off from church-type bodies, that they are rooted in economic deprivation, and that they gradually transform themselves into churches.

This theory is valid for many cases. Nevertheless, in a number of ways it falls short of being a general theory of the origin and evolution of religious groups. Overlooked is the fact that not all religious groups emerge as sects. Some are churches in their original form. This was true of Reform Judaism in Europe and of Conservative Judaism in America. Most Protestant groups were from their beginnings more like churches than like sects.

Not only may new religious groups emerge in other than sect form, they need not, contrary to the theory, draw their membership primarily from the lower class. The American Ethical Union was clearly a middle-class movement from its inception, as were Unity and, probably, Christian Science.

The theory also does not take account of cults. These are religious movements which draw their inspiration from other than the primary religion of the culture, and which are not schismatic movements in the same sense as sects, whose concern is with preserving a purer form of the traditional faith. Thus, while the theory may be adequate to explain the Pentecostal movement or the evolution of such religious groups as the Disciples of Christ (The Christian Church) and the Church of God in Jesus Christ, it does not provide a way to account for Theosophy, or the I AM movement, or the Black Muslims. Nor does the theory account for religious movements which show no signs of evolving toward the church form. Finally, the theory ignores the question of the conditions which produce a secular rather than a religious response to economic deprivation.

As may be clear, our quarrel with sect-church theory is not over what it does, but what it fails to do—too many innovating religious movements fall beyond the present scope of the theory. Consequently, in attempting to formulate the elements of a more satisfactory theory of religious origins we shall not discard sect-church theory so much as try to generalize and extend it. We shall continue to regard deprivation as a necessary condition for the rise

[5]See, for example, J. M. Yinger, *Religion in the Struggle for Power* (Durham, N.C.: Duke University Press, 1946), Bryan Wilson, "An Analysis of Sect Development," *American Sociological Review*, XX (February, 1957); and Leopold Von Wiese and Howard Becker, *Systematic Sociology* (New York: John Wiley and Sons, 1932).

of new religious movements. However, the concept of deprivation seems due for a general extension and restatement.[6]

Sect-church theory conceives of deprivation almost entirely in economic terms. To be sure, in every society there are individuals and groups which are economically underprivileged relative to others, and some are always at the very bottom of the economic hierarchy. However, there are forms of deprivation other than economic ones, and these too, we suggest, have implications for the development of religious and, as we shall see, secular movements as well.

Deprivation, as we conceive it, refers to *any and all of the ways that an individual or group may be, or feel disadvantaged in comparison either to other individuals or groups or to an internalized set of standards.* The experience of deprivation may be conscious, in which case the individual or group may be aware of its causes. It may also be experienced as something other than deprivation, in which case its causes will be unknown to the individual or the group. But, whether directly or indirectly experienced, whether its causes are known or unknown, deprivation tends to be accompanied by a desire to overcome it.[7] Efforts to deal with deprivation will differ, however, according to the degree to which its nature is correctly perceived and individuals and groups are in a position to eliminate its cause.

Types of Deprivation

There are five kinds of deprivation to which individuals or groups may be subject relative to others in society. We shall call these five: economic, social, organismic, ethical, and psychic. The types are not pure; any one individual or group may experience more than one kind of deprivation. However, we can distinguish among them not only analytically, but empirically, since one type of deprivation is likely to be dominant for particular individuals and groups in particular situations.

Economic deprivation has its source in the differential distribution of income in societies and in the limited access of some individuals to the necessities and luxuries of life. Economic deprivation may be judged on objective or on subjective criteria. The person who appears economically privileged on objective criteria might nevertheless perceive himself as economically deprived. For our purposes the subjective assessment is likely to be the more important.

Social deprivation, our second type, is based on society's propensity to value some attributes of individuals and groups more highly than others and to distribute such societal rewards as prestige, power, status, and opportunities for social participation accordingly. Social deprivation, then, arises out of the

---

[6]This chapter has also been informed by Robert K. Merton, "Social Structure and Anomie," in *Social Theory and Social Structure* (Glencoe, Ill.: The Free Press, 1957).

[7]This may not be the case, however, where the value system of the society warrants deprivation, for example, the Hindu caste system.

differential distribution of highly regarded attributes. The grounds for such differentiation are virtually endless. In our society, for example, we regard youth more highly than old age, greater rewards tend to go to men rather than to women, and the "gifted" person is given privileges denied the mediocre.

Social deprivation is additive in the sense that the fewer the number of desirable attributes the individual possesses, the lower his relative status, and the reverse is also true. In our society, it is in general "better" to be educated than uneducated. But one's status is further enhanced if one is white rather than Negro, Protestant rather than Catholic, youthful rather than old.

The distinction between economic and social deprivation is akin to the distinction sociologists make between social class and social status. Designations of social class tend to be made on economic criteria. Social status distinctions, on the other hand, give greater attention to considerations of prestige and acceptance. While the two tend to go together, the correlation is not perfect. For our present purposes, we will consider social deprivation to be limited to situations in which it exists independently of economic deprivation.

Organismic deprivation comprises ways in which persons are disadvantaged relative to others through physical or mental deformities, ill health, or other such stigmatizing or disabling traits. Within this class of deprivations would be persons suffering from neuroses and psychoses or who are feeble minded. On the physiological side, it would include the blind, the deaf, the dumb, the crippled, the chronically ill, in short all who suffer physical impairment.

Ethical deprivation refers to value conflicts between the ideals of society and those of individuals or groups. Such conflicts seemingly may stem from many sources. They can occur because some persons perceive incompatibilities in the values of the society, or detect negative latent functions of rules and standards, or even because they are struck by discrepancies between ideals and realities. Often such value conflicts occur because of contradictions in social organization. For example, some persons may find themselves embedded in situations conducive to the development and maintenance of values not held by the greater society, and, indeed, that conflict with general societal values. A classic example of ethical deprivation of this sort is provided in Veblen's analysis of the role strain on engineers who are torn between their own attachment to efficiency and excellence as standards for judging their own products, and the value of maximum profits imposed on them by management.[8]

The celebrated conflicts of the intellectuals, induced to "sell out" their own criteria of excellence in art, journalism, and the like, because their standards are not shared by the public, have been used to explain the propensity of these objectively privileged groups for radical politics.[9] Such conceptions fit

[8]Thorstein Veblen, *The Instincts of Workmanship and the State of Industrial Arts* (New York: The Viking Press, 1943).

[9]Seymour Martin Lipset, *Political Man* (Garden City: Doubleday & Co., 1960), pp. 318-319.

well with current theories of revolution which specify that there must be a defection from the ranks of the elite in order that direction and leadership be provided for lower class discontent, if revolution is to occur.

Ethical deprivation, then, is basically philosophical. Many great religious innovators, such as Luther and Wesley, as well as political innovators such as Marx, seem to have been motivated primarily by a sense of deprivation stemming from their ethical conflicts with society—an inability to lead their lives according to their own lights.

Psychic deprivation occurs, not in the face of value conflicts, but when persons find themselves without a meaningful system of values by which to interpret and organize their lives. Such a condition is primarily the result of severe and unresolved social deprivations which, by denying access to rewards, cause men to lose any stake in, and commitment to, existing values.

A likely response to psychic deprivation is the search for new values, a new faith, a quest for meaning and purpose. The vulnerability of the deprived to new ideologies reflects their psychic deprivation. In contrast, the ethically deprived have a firm commitment to values, albeit values that conflict with prevailing conditions. Thus, psychic deprivation can be thought of primarily as an intervening variable, state of despair, estrangement, or anomie stemming from objective deprivations (social, economic, or organismic) that leads to actions to relieve these deprivations.[10]

We suggest that a necessary precondition for the rise of any organized social movement, whether it be religious or secular, is a situation of felt deprivation. However, while a necessary condition, deprivation is not, in itself, a sufficient condition. Also required are the additional conditions that the deprivation be shared, that no alternative institutional arrangements for its resolution are perceived, and that a leadership emerge with an innovating idea for building a movement out of the existing deprivation.

Where these conditions exist, the organizational effort to overcome deprivation may be religious, or it may be secular. In the case of economic, social, and organismic deprivation—the three characterized by deprivation relative to others—religious resolutions are more likely to occur where the nature of the deprivation is inaccurately perceived or those experiencing the deprivation are not in a position to work directly at eliminating the causes. The resolution is likely to be secular under the opposite conditions—where the nature of the deprivation is correctly assessed by those experiencing it and they have, or feel they have, the power, or feel they can gain the power, to deal with it directly. Religious resolutions, then, are likely to compensate for feelings of deprivation rather than to eliminate its causes. Secular resolutions, where they are successful, are more likely to eliminate the causes, and therefore, also the feelings.

These tendencies do not hold for ethical and psychic deprivation. In the

---

[10]Despite the enormous amount of work done on various forms of this concept under a variety of names, it has been primarily treated as an outcome of economic deprivation or as a cause of political extremism, and too few attempts have been made to place it in a context of deprivation plus action.

case of ethical and psychic deprivation, as we shall see, a religious resolution may be as efficacious as a secular one in overcoming the deprivation directly. In America, resolutions to psychic deprivation usually tend to be religious, defined in the broad sense of invoking some supernatural authority. However, radical political movements may be the outcome of psychic deprivation combined with economic deprivation.

Both religious and secular resolutions, then, may follow from each kind of deprivation. However, whether religious or secular, the resolution will be different in character according to which type stimulates it.

Organizational Resolutions of Deprivations

Economic deprivation, once it becomes intense, has in it the seed of revolution. And indeed, where the movements which it stimulates are secular, they are likely to be revolutionary. However, to be successful, revolutions require a degree of power which the deprived group is unlikely to be able to muster. Consequently, even when it is intense, economic deprivation seldom leads to revolution.

Religious resolutions to economic deprivation, while not literally revolutionary, are symbolically so. The latent resentment against society tends to be expressed in an ideology which rejects and radically devalues the society. Thus, for those in the movement, the society is symbolically transformed while actually, of course, it is left relatively untouched.

This is characteristically what sects do, and it is this form of religious organization which is likely to arise out of economic deprivation. This is in accord with what we have said earlier in our discussion of sect-church theory, and we need not elaborate further on the way in which sect members compensate for economic disadvantage by substituting religious privilege in its place. We would add, however, that the religious movement which grows out of economic deprivation need not have its theological base in the traditional religion of the society. The Black Muslim movement, for example, borrows heavily from an "alien" religious doctrine. Yet, in its strong tone of social protest and its doctrine of black superiority, it exemplifies the kind of religious movement which grows out of economic deprivation (with, of course, its accompanying social deprivation).

Social deprivation, where it exists without a strong economic component, ordinarily does not require a complete transformation of society, either literally or symbolically, to produce relief. What is at fault is not the basic organization of society, but one or several of its parts. Consequently, efforts at resolution are likely to be directed at the parts, without questioning the whole. As with economic deprivation, however, resolutions are not always possible. Once again, responses to the deprivation are most likely to be secular where its cause can be attacked more or less directly.

Many secular movements with roots in one or another kind of social deprivation have arisen in America over the last century. Earlier the woman's suffrage and now the Women's Liberation movement, the Townsend movement, the NAACP, and various professional organizations such as those for druggists and beauticians, all represent movements whose purpose has been to eliminate the social deprivation of some particular group by raising its status.

Other semi-secular groups have attempted to compensate for lack of status by supplying an alternative status system. In particular, fraternal clubs and lodges have played such a role, especially for disadvantaged racial and ethnic groups. A man may amount to little all week long, but on Friday nights he can become the Most Venerated, Consecrated, and All-Powerful Poobah of the Grand Lodge of Water Buffalo, dress in a gaudy costume, and whisper secret rites.

Social deprivations may be directly connected with religious status and hence generate religious innovations. Such groups as the African Methodist Episcopal Church and the ethnic subdenominations of Lutheranism were organized because the existing religious structure was incapable of meeting the status needs of the groups involved. While overtly a means to overcome religious disadvantages, these organizations also served to overcome sources of social deprivation.

Classic instances are provided by the Jewish Reform movement and the founding of Conservative Judaism. Both movements were launched as an effort to provide Jews with a religious connection with their heritage while allowing them to dispense with those aspects of Orthodoxy, particularly customs of dress and food, which interfered with their attaining status in secular society.[11]

The organizational form of religious groups which emerge out of social deprivation tends to be church-like rather than sect-like. This is because the basic interest of the socially deprived is to accommodate themselves to the larger society rather than to escape from it or, alternatively, to completely transform it. Consequently, they also tend to adopt those institutional arrangements with which the larger society is most comfortable.

The psychoanalytic movement, group dynamics, and Alcoholics Anonymous are examples of a secular response to organismic deprivation where the mental component of this form of deprivation is dominant. In turn, the Society for the Blind, the Society for Crippled Children, and the myriad formal and informal social groups constructed around an ailment exemplify secular efforts toward resolution where the physiological element is primary. However successful or unsuccessful are these movements, they all represent attempts to deal with a problem directly. They are revolutionary in that they seek to transform the individual either mentally or physiologically. However, they do not question the value system of the society per se.

There have been religious movements—healing cults, for example—which are organized primarily as resolutions to organismic deprivation. More often, however, we find that religious responses to this form of deprivation are not

11See Chapter 17.

the entire *raison d'être* of a religious movement, but are included as one aspect of it. We may note that a faith healing movement has been organized within the Episcopal Church. Many sects—Father Divine, for example—include a healing element as do cults such as Christian Science and Unity. Thus, religious responses seem not to be identified with any particular organizational form. We suspect, however, that where healing is the exclusive concern of the religious movement, it is more likely to be cult-like in character, such as early Christian Science, than to be a sect or a church.

Responses to ethical deprivations are more typically reformist than revolutionary, and, we suspect, more likely to be religious or secular depending on the prevailing ethos of the time in which they occur. Reformers in medieval times sought to enforce or establish religious values, while since the Enlightenment a great deal of ethical deprivation has been expressed in humanistic terms. In our own time both kinds of response flourish.

Secular movements based on ethical deprivations sometimes lead to revolution, particularly when an ethically deprived elite enlists the support of economically deprived masses. But more often ethical deprivations lead to reform movements aimed at enforcing some neglected value or changing some portion of the prevailing value system without abandoning a commitment to the general outlines of existing social organization. The American Civil Liberties Union illustrates one secular response to ethical deprivation. This group is concerned with enforcing the ideals expressed in the Bill of Rights upon day-to-day realities. Similarly the American Planned Parenthood League derives from ethical deprivation, but is concerned with establishing a general value concerning family planning, and with altering religious prohibitions against birth control. Political reform groups, both of the left and right, often are motivated by a sense of ethical deprivation. Indeed, the current right wing activity in American politics seems to stem to a great extent from the perceptions of small town and rural Americans that their traditional values are no longer predominant in American society.

Religious movements growing out of ethical deprivations can lead to religious revolutions, as in the case of the Lutherans, when the movement is both powerful and powerfully opposed. But it must be recalled that Luther did not intend to found a new faith or lead a revolution, rather he hoped to reform the Church to make it more closely correspond to its avowed ideals. More commonly religious movements based on ethical deprivations do not lead to religious revolutions, but to reform movements. The Prohibition movement in the early part of this century is a classic example, while the participation of white religious leaders in the civil rights movement is another.[12] Other examples are the Ethical Culture Union and Unitarianism, both of which seem to have been produced as a solution to the conflict felt by some persons between traditional religious orthodoxy and scientific

[12]The involvement of blacks in the Civil Rights movement obviously is based on their economic and social deprivation. However, white clergymen do not share the blacks' deprived lot, but instead are responding to the discrepancies between Christian and social ideals of equality and the actual denial of equality to blacks.

discovery. Secular counterparts may be seen in the hippie and existentialist movements.

Ethical deprivations may well be typically limited to members of society's elites, or at least to the middle classes or above. The notion of value conflicts presupposes a certain intellectualism, such as that required in theological or philosophical disputation, which is commonly regarded as an idiosyncracy of the leisured and learned classes.

Whether the movement is secular or religious, responses to psychic deprivation are generally extreme because it constitutes a rejection of the prevailing value orientation of the society. When persons have become psychically deprived in response to economic deprivations they may adopt a new ideology that embodies a revolutionary political program (whether on the left or the right). When they take up a religious solution it will typically be of the cult variety. The research reported in Chapter 5 of members of a millenarian religious group showed that all had passed through a period of "church-hopping," ultimately rejected all available religious perspectives, and passed through a period of religious despair before being converted to the new movement. The entire occult milieu is made up of persons afflicted with psychic deprivations. Movements born in this setting, such as Theosophy, Vedanta, the I AM, or the various Flying Saucer groups, are essentially religious innovations that reject dominant American religious traditions, and are classified as cults.

Deprivation need not be immediately present to stimulate an organizational response. The prospect of deprivation may produce a similar effect. The White Citizens' Councils in the South, for example, can be conceived of as organizations growing out of anticipated economic and social deprivation. The John Birch Society is a response to anticipated social deprivation. Protestants and Other Americans United is an example of a religious movement organized around anticipated ethical and social deprivation.

In sum, deprivation—present or anticipated—would appear to be a central factor in the rise of new movements. The organizational response to deprivation may be either religious or secular. In the case of economic, social, and organismic deprivation, religious responses tend to function as compensations for the deprivation, secular ones as means to overcome it. The type of deprivation around which a movement arises is influential in shaping its character in all cases except those of organismic and ethical deprivation. Generally speaking, religious movements emerge as sects where they are stimulated by economic deprivation, as churches where the deprivation is social, and as cults where it is psychic.

Deprivation and Organizational Evolution

Deprivation is important not only to the rise of new movements but to the path of their development and their potential for survival. Movements may evolve in a myriad of ways, and we have no intention of trying to cope with all of their variety. We would suggest, however, that movements tend to follow one of three basic patterns. They may flower briefly and then die. They may survive indefinitely in substantially their original form. Or, they may survive but in a form radically different from their original one. How movements develop, and whether or not they survive, is influenced by the type of deprivation which stimulated them, how they deal with this deprivation, and the degree to which the deprivation persists in the society, and therefore, provides a continuing source of new recruits.

Movements arising out of economic deprivation tend to follow a pattern of either disappearing relatively quickly or of having to change their organizational form to survive. They seldom survive indefinitely in their original form. This is because the deprivation they respond to may itself be short-lived or because they themselves help to overcome the deprivation of their adherents.

Few sects survive as sects. They either disappear or evolve from a sect into a church. Where they follow the former course, it is likely that their source of recruitment suddenly withers because of conditions over which they have no control. Thus, depression-born sects tend to have a low survival rate, lasting only as long as the depression itself. Sects also have the tendency, noted earlier, to socialize their members to higher economic status. In the process, their organizational form is transformed to conform to the changing status of their membership.

Secular responses to economic deprivation follow a similar pattern. Depression-born movements—technocracy, for example—tend to flower briefly and then die. More fundamental movements, such as revolutions, tend, where they are successful, to lose their revolutionary character and to survive as movements functioning to maintain the advantages which have been gained.

Organizational responses to social deprivation may also follow a pattern of disappearing quickly, but where they survive, they are likely to do so without radical alteration of their original form. Which of these paths is followed is largely dependent on the persistence of the deprivation which gave rise to the movement. Successful elimination of the experienced deprivation—for example, the successful attempt to gain women the right to vote—is likely to produce an early end to the movement.

It is characteristic of many kinds of social deprivation to persist over extended periods of time and to continue from generation to generation. This is because the value systems of societies tend to change slowly, and the differential social rewards and punishments of one era are not likely, in the natural course of events, to be radically altered in the next.

The ability of churches to survive in basically unchanged form is, in substantial part, a consequence of the persistence of social deprivation. Participation in a church, we would suggest, functions to provide individuals with a source of gratification which they cannot find in the society-at-large. Since there are always individuals who are socially deprived in this sense, there exists a continuing source of new recruits to the church. Furthermore, church participation only compensates for the deprivation; it does not eliminate it. Thus, in contrast with the sect, the primary reasons for the existence of the church are not likely to be dissipated over time.

The contention that a major function of church participation is to relieve members' feelings of social deprivation is made here primarily on theoretical grounds. What little empirical evidence there is, however, suggests that churches tend to gain their greatest commitment from individuals who are most deprived of the rewards of the larger society. Thus, it is the less gifted intellectually, the aged, women, and those without normal family lives who are most often actively involved in the church.[13]

Organismic deprivation produces movements whose evolution is likely to be influenced by the development of new knowledge about the causes and treatment of mental and physical disorders. Existing movements can expect to thrive only so long as the therapies they provide are subjectively perceived as efficacious and superior to prevailing alternatives. However, the survival of these movements is constantly threatened by innovations in therapy or treatment which eliminate their *raison d'être*. Under such conditions, they may simply disband—like the Sister Kenny Foundation, for example—or they may elect to chart their course along a different path, like the National Foundation.

Religious movements or submovements which are sustained by organismic deprivation may, of course, survive for a very long time, and indeed recruit new members from those who cannot find relief through secular sources. However, in the long run they too are likely to fall victim to innovations in medical knowledge. For, as Malinowski reported of the Trobriand Islanders, people do not resort to magic when they have more effective means of control.

Many movements which arise out of ethical deprivation, we suggest, have a propensity to be short-lived. This is not because ethical deprivation is not a persistent element in society; there are always likely to be individuals who feel that some portion of the dominant value system ought to be changed or reapplied. However, the ethically deprived are likely to generate strong opposition to their efforts to reform or change society and, furthermore, resolutions that seem appropriate at one time are not likely to be so at another. Consequently, ethical deprivation tends to be subject to fads, and while responses to ethical deprivations may capture attention for the moment, they tend to be quickly replaced by new solutions. The various hippie and bohemian movements are cases in point.

The exceptions—the movements of this kind which survive—do so because they provide solutions which have relevance to long-term trends in society. Such trends function to provide these movements with a continuing source of new recruits. For example, the long-term trend toward secularization in American life is, we suspect, a major factor in the survival and recent

[13]See Chapter 6.

acceleration in growth of the Unitarian movement. In general, ethical deprivation characterizes only a small minority of a population at a given time and movements which respond to such deprivation are likely—whether they survive or not—always to be minority movements.

Movements based on psychic deprivations typically follow one of two courses. Either they rise to power and transform societies, and are then themselves transformed, or they die out quickly. Since movements stemming from psychic deprivations take on value orientations incompatible with those prevalent in a society, they engender strong opposition and must either succeed or be crushed. When they take a religious form they are usually defined as cults and subject to public definitions of "evil," "demented," "dangerous," and "subversive." However, cult movements may also succeed (for example, Christianity was a cult viewed from the standpoint of traditional Roman religions), and by success find themselves faced with problems similar to those of the religion they replaced. That is, once in power a new religion is not in a much better position to resolve the endemic basis for economic, social, organismic, and even ethical deprivation than the religious institution that it replaced. Thus, while new religious movements like I AM, Theosophy, Mankind United, or Scientology, may initially provide a new meaning system to their converts, they are not able to overcome the social sources of deprivation which initially produced psychic deprivation, or despair. These are left to produce a new clientele for new movements, or to at least form a festering sore in the integration of any society.

Similarly the extremist secular movements that spring up in response to psychic deprivations are faced with massive opposition. If they succeed in overcoming such opposition, they too face the problem of being transformed by their responsibilities so they may no longer provide a suitable outlet for the psychically deprived.

Conclusions

Our aim in this chapter has been to assess some implications of an extension of the concept of deprivation for the origin and evolution of social movements, particularly religious movements. Our speculations have been informed by the assumption that religion functions to compensate persons for deprivations for which direct means of resolution are not available.

We have tried to show that the original form and subsequent development of religious movements may be largely determined by the variety of deprivation which provided them with an available clientele. A summary of our suggestions appears in Table 1.

We must, of course, acknowledge the fact that our observations on the relationship between kinds of deprivations and types of religious groups are imprecise and very provisional. This is necessarily the case since these suggested extensions of existing theory have not yet been subjected to

Table 1.   *Origins, Forms, and Development of Religious Groups*

Type of Deprivation	Form of Religious Group	Success Expectations
1. Economic	Sect	Extinction or transformation
2. Social	Church	Retain original form
3. Organismic	Healing movement	Becomes cultlike or is destroyed by medical discoveries.
4. Ethical	Reform movements	Early extinction due to success, opposition or becoming irrelevant.
5. Psychic	Cult	Total success resulting in extinction through transformation, or failure due to extreme opposition.

empirical testing. Nevertheless, no matter how greatly our notions may be altered by future analysis, it seems likely that some theoretical extension along these lines will be necessary if we are to achieve any precise understanding of the forces which give birth to and shape new religious and secular groups.

Chapter Seventeen

Reform Judaism: The Origin and Evolution of a "Church Movement"*

Stephen Steinberg

An early obstacle to systematic study of Reform Judaism is the difficulty of accommodating the Reform case to accepted sociological propositions concerning church and sect. At first glance one would surmise that the Reform group, having severed its relation with Orthodoxy, is a sectarian movement, analytically indistinct from Christian sects that arise out of schisms within established religious bodies. Yet certain elements usually associated with sects, such as literal adherence to Biblical teachings and apocalyptic ideological tendencies, are conspicuously absent. Of greater significance, while most religious movements seek to modify or transform societal norms and values, the Reform Movement is striking for its attempt to bring its norms and values into greater conformity with those of the larger society. This apparent ambiguity provides a useful point of departure for analysis of the Reform Movement, and a possible basis for the reformulation of theory. To state the question simply—is Reform Judaism a church or a sect?

This issue has been raised many times in terms of criticism of the church-sect typology as it was first formulated by Troeltsch and unsuccessfully redefined by subsequent sociologists. In a recent paper Benton Johnson offers a clear statement of the problem:

> Troeltsch's definitions of sect and church each contain a large number of characteristics, or elements . . . (many of which) vary independently of each other. . . . If elements vary independently, the classification of mixed cases becomes an almost impossible task. So far the major response to this difficulty has been to coin new types on an *ad hoc* basis as important new mixed cases present themselves. . . . The trouble

*Stephen Steinberg, "Reform Judaism: The Origin and Evolution of a 'Church Movement,'" *Journal for the Scientific Study of Religion* 5, no. 1 (1965). Reprinted with the permision of the author and the *Journal for the Scientific Study of Religion.*

with most of these newer typologies is that they have never really stipulated all of the elements under consideration and they have never succeeded in transcending the particular considerations that led to their development.[1]

Johnson proposes a refinement of the church-sect typology which he demonstrates to be both accurate and useful. I propose now to build upon Johnson's formulation by elaborating several distinctions that are undeveloped in the original scheme. These will provide a theoretical perspective that will allow comparisons between Reform Judaism and other kinds of religious movements.

The core of Johnson's thesis rests upon his one-variable definition of church and sect: "A church is a religious group that accepts the social environment in which it exists."[2] These definitions can be worded still more precisely. In Johnson's application of them, it becomes clear that the defining variable is not acceptance or rejection of the social environment, but a similar characteristic: whether or not there is a discrepancy or tension between the norms and values of the religious group and those of the surrounding society. This language is preferable because either society or the religious group may reject the values of the other, or both may occur at once. The sectarian nature of Judaism through most of its history in the Diaspora is as much a product of society's rejection of Jewish norms and values, as a calculated rejection of society on the part of Jews. Hence the concept of value tension is more accurate and more widely applicable than acceptance or rejection of the social environment. To apply this slight modification, a church is defined as a religious group that is in low tension with the social environment. A sect is a religious group that is in high tension with the surrounding environment.[3]

Consistent with Johnson's treatment, the concept of tension should be accorded both absolute and relative value. Hence, a religious group that comes into less tension is moving in the direction of becoming a church; however, if the state of tension is still high, the group must be classified as a sect. In other words, there is a continuum extending from low tension to high tension, with church and sect as the polar types. When the continuum is dichotomized, each half represents a church-like and a sect-like category. A further division

---

[1]Benton Johnson, "On Church and Sect," *American Sociological Review*, 28 (August, 1963), p. 541.

In the immediately preceding chapter, Charles Y. Glock argues in similar terms that the defining characteristics of sects are not universally applicable to new religious movements. He shows that for any characteristics, one can point to a religious group in which that characteristic is absent, but which would be classified as a sect by the other criteria.

[2]Johnson, *Ibid.*, p. 542

[3]As indicated above, these definitions do not differ substantially from Johnson's formulation. For example, Johnson states: "Since a sect tends to be in a state of tension with its surroundings, we are safe in supposing that religions that have totally withdrawn from participation in a society or that are engaged in open attack on it are likely to fall close to the sect end . . . Churches, on the other hand, are comparatively at ease with the established values and practices of a society." *Ibid.*, p. 544.

along each half establishes the cutting-point for classifying a group as a church or a sect. This conceptualization is presented schematically below:

less tension		more tension	
church	church-like	sect-like	sect

It should be added that the relative, rather than the absolute value of tension deserves emphasis. It is not of theoretical importance that "group X" is a church, but only that "group X" is in less tension with the surrounding environment than "group Y," or that "group X" is more church-like than "group Y."

The first step in elaborating Johnson's definition is to distinguish between two generic types: institutions and rump groups (schismatic groups). No sociological qualities should be attributed to either; rather, they should be defined in terms of some physical attribute, such as ownership of property. For the purposes of the present analysis, it will suffice to define an institution as a religious organization that possesses property. A rump group, in contradistinction, is a group that severs its connection with the institution and thereby forsakes its right to the property of the institution.[4] Of course, in time it may itself acquire property, whereupon it will *ipso facto* become an institution.

The relation of *both* institutions and rump groups to the larger society can be conceptualized in terms of the amount of tension between their values and the values of the dominant social system. Hence, cross-classifying these two generic types of religious groups with Johnson's criterion of church and sect, we arrive at the following calculation: both institutions and rump groups may come into either more or less tension with the surrounding environment. An institution that reduces the level of tension with society may be said to be in the process of becoming more churchly. This process is often called "institutionalization." Institutions that come into more tension with society manifest a tendency to become more sect-like. I will refer to this simply as institutional conflict. On the other side, a rump group that comes into more tension with society is a sect movement. Finally, rump groups that come into less tension with society from the time of their separation from the parent institution will be termed "church movements." The schematic presentation is as follows:

	Institution	Rump group
More tension	Institutional Conflict	Sect Movement
Less	Institution-alization	Church Movement

[4]Rump groups do not always originate as dissenting elements that voluntarily break off from the parent institution. As in the case of the Anabaptists, a group of dissenters may be declared *persona no grata* by the authorities of the institution and their relation terminated by exclusion or formal excommunication.

Social scientists have understandably focused attention on the two types that occur with greatest frequency. *Typically*, institutions are in a state of low tension with society. Through the process of institutionalization discordant elements of the religious institution become obscured before the emerging identity between fundmental aspects of the religious and secular cultures. In a stable social system, one normally finds an alliance, if not a fusion, between religious and social institutions. The religious institutions partake of and help to maintain the normative order of the larger society. Hence, most religious institutions are churches. In contrast, rump groups originate under conditions of instability and strain when the institution is not functioning to meet the needs of a significant proportion of its adherents. Hence, rump groups *typically* fall into greater tension with society as they break off from the religious institution, and are therefore sects.

However, not all institutions are churches and not all rump groups are sects. Two further possibilities exist:

First, a religious *institution* may come into greater tension with society and thereby move in the direction of becoming a sect.

Second, a *rump group* (from the time of its inception and not through the process of institutionalization) may come into less tension with society and thereby move in the direction of becoming a church. I have called this a "church movement."[5]

These will be shown to be not mere analytical possibilities, but empirical realities. My main objective is to demonstrate that the Reform Movement is an anomaly among religious movements in that it sought to modify institutional norms and values that were discrepant with those of the larger society. Afterwards, I will examine other anomalous features of this "church movement," and explore their implications for social theory. First, however, it will be helpful to briefly analyze Orthodox Judaism in order to uncover some of the social conditions that gave rise to the peculiar phenomenon of a religious movement that, in a sense, sought to eliminate those very qualities that made it a distinctive religious entity.

Orthodoxy: An Anachronism

How may a religious institution come into increased tension with the social environment? Established religions, as I have mentioned, are usually closely allied with the secular institutions. Under normal conditions they are able to adjust to changes in society. However, under conditions of rapid and extreme change in society, such adjustment may be impossible and a situation of

---

[5]This chapter has profited from Glock's discussion of the origin and evolution of religious groups in the previous chapter. Glock says: ". . . not all religious groups emerge as sects. Some are churches in their original form. This was true of Reform Judaism in Europe and Conservative Judaism in America. Most Protestant groups were from their beginnings more like churches than like sects." *Op. cit.*

greater tension will result. In this way, a religious institution whose values were once compatible with those of society may be thrust abruptly into a state of high tension with the surrounding environment.

Such was the case of Orthodox Judaism in Western Europe during the last half of the eighteenth century. During the Middle Ages the discrepancy between the traditional social system of the Jews and the norms and values of the accommodating European societies was, to be sure, of considerable magnitude. Tension was great, and according to Johnson's definition, Orthodoxy must be classified as a sect. But conflict between antagonistic elements of the two cultures was kept in bounds, ironically, by the physical and social isolation of the Jewish community. However, with the transformation of European society and the emancipation of the ghettoized Jew, the contradictions became more apparent. Tension with the (literally) surrounding society reached its crest and threw Orthodoxy into crisis. In his study of the Jewish community during this period, Jacob Katz writes:

> Traditional Jewish society ... experienced a unique development. Instead of banishment and migration, changes now took place that left the society in the same place geographically, but that shattered, or at least distorted, its framework.[6]

In short, the elevation of the Jew to national citizenship and the breakdown of the ghetto walls made Jewish religious institutions vulnerable to the pressures of the developing nation-states, and resulted in even greater tension with the dominant social system.

While it is true that Orthodoxy had successfully adapted to disadvantageous social conditions during its long history in the Diaspora, it must also be said that the Emancipation represented a threat that was unprecedented in kind. A social revolution was taking place on all sides of the ghetto *and* within its midst, for the pressures that at first were imposed from outside soon began to foment from within. Although Jews had experienced centuries of religious persecution and enforced migration, their independent status as a nation in exile had never before been seriously challenged.

It is not necessary, in view of my limited objectives, to comment further upon the disintegration of the traditional Jewish community. Let it suffice to say that the value system of Orthodoxy was so discrepant with that of the enlightened society that adjustment *in its current form* was an impossibility. Two theoretical possibilities for a collective response existed. Either Orthodoxy could further isolate itself from the larger society—to reject society as well as be rejected by it, or it could transform (even to the point of abandoning) its norms and values to conform in greater degree to those of the dominant social system. In short, Judaism could move in the direction of becoming either more sect-like

---

[6]Jacob Katz, *Tradition and Crisis: Jewish Society at the End of the Middle Ages* (New York: The Free Press, 1961), p. 227.

or more churchly. However, movement in one direction or the other was inescapable.[7]

The prospect of national citizenship, ending centuries of banishment and persecution, barred a collective withdrawal from society. In actuality, the crisis following the Emancipation precipitated a collective attempt toward accommodation. This began with the Haskala Movement in Western Europe and culminated in the American Reform Movement. These were "church movements" that aimed at greater conformity to the norms and values of secular society.[8]

The Reform Movement: An Anomaly among Social Movements

Rump groups typically originate, as Niebuhr has shown, when the discrepancy between individual and group values is a function of the institutionalization of the group to middle-class standards. As the institution adjusts its theological and social posture to conform to societal norms, it dispossesses a portion of its adherents whose values conflict sharply with those of both church and society. With the Emancipation, however, the Jewish religious institution was coming into greater tension with society at the same time that individuals were coming into less tension. This rare situation was the most important condition for an even more anomalous phenomenon: a rump group that aims at greater conformity to the values of the dominant social system. I have referred to this as a "church movement."

If the goal of the emancipated Jew was to conform to societal norms and values, why did this produce a religious rather than a secular response? Of paramount importance here was the Jew's desire to maintain some attachment with traditional culture. His hope was to venture out of the ghetto without going too far, to accept some of society's values without becoming altogether immersed in the dominant culture. Thus, the desire to remain apart was a necessary condition for the evolution of a church movement. Yet halfway integration is an ambiguous, if not precarious goal, one that would inevitably create difficulties for the emerging movement.

The European Approach to Reform

The disintegration of the Jewish community following the Emancipation was never allowed to reach the point of absorption into the surrounding society. An

---

[7]It should be made explicit that adjustment did not have to take a collective form. As often happens, individuals might realign themselves with groups whose values are consonant with their own. This, however, was not a realistic alternative for Jews, since denominationalism, practically speaking, was unknown to Judaism. The only other possibility for individual adjustment was conversion to Christianity or abandonment of religion altogether, but few Jews were willing to go this far.

[8]In contrast, the Hasidic Movement in Eastern Europe, arising out of conditions of economic hardship and political repression, was a sectarian movement that included a theologically based rejection of societal norms and values.

intellectual elite who had penetrated into the enlightened society also moved to the forefront of Jewish community life. According to Katz, the emergence of this special class was the decisive event for checking the decay of the Jewish social system:

> The social turning point . . . is revealed in the emergence of a new type, the *maskil*, who added to his knowledge of the Torah a command of foreign languages, general erudition, and an interest in what was happening in the non-Jewish world. This type became increasingly numerous beginning with the 1760's, and it soon constituted a subgroup in Jewish society. It demanded for itself not only the right of existence, but also the privilege of leadership.[9]

This general erudition included a knowledge of, and dedication to, the rationalist principles of the Enlightenment which were acquired through the acceptance of the *maskilim* into the intellectual circles of "the neutral society." These principles eventually became translated into a liberal ideology that was to prove an effective rallying point for the Reform Movement.

Two general points should be made concerning the status and the role of the *maskilim*. First, many emancipated Jews began to identify with this intellectual elite. In effect, they had "transferred their social goals to the context of the non-Jewish milieu"[10] through the intellectuals. This was an important development because once the *maskilim* achieved a degree of status within the Jewish community, their potential as a progressive leadership was enhanced.

Social status was a necessary, but not a sufficient condition for leadership. Obviously, the *maskilim* themselves had to resist the attractions of assimilation and devote their energies first to an intellectual reappraisal of Jewish tradition, and ultimately to a reconstruction of the Jewish community. While some *maskilim* defected permanently from Judaism, most followed the example of Mendelsohn, the foremost Jewish leader during this period, and "out of a sense of responsibility for the fate of Jewish society . . . agreed to undertake tasks which more or less delineated its course."[11] The *maskilim* became a distinctive element "whose identification with the values of the neutral society set them apart from the members of the traditional society, but whose attachment to the values and the culture of their original milieu did not allow them to divorce themselves completely from it."[12] This marked the appearance, virtually for the first time in Jewish history, of a marginal man who passionately sought to reconcile the antagonistic elements of his two worlds.

The *maskilim*, under some pressure from the secular authorities, set about the task of applying their rationalist principles to the traditional Jewish institutions.

[9]*Ibid.*, p. 246.
[10]*Ibid.*, p. 251.
[11]*Ibid.*, p. 257.
[12]*Ibid.*

In Western Europe the progressive elements eventually organized into the Haskala Movement which, "like the parallel non-Jewish Enlightenment movement . . . aimed not at reforming the evils of reality but at setting up a new reality in its place."[13] Progress along these lines, however, was circumscribed by the tradition-bound structure of European society. The locus for change was transferred to the American community.

The Reform Movement in America: The First Years

Although Reform Judaism is rooted in the intellectual and social transformation that occurred in Europe between 1750 and 1850, and had been transplanted, in an unmaturated form, from Germany, it first became a distinctive social movement and reached its fruition in the United States.

It should be noted that the situation in America before 1850 was not very different from that in Europe, at least with regard to the relation of Judaism to the wider society. The clash between the two value systems, even if this did not take the form of open conflict, was apparent to American Jews, most of whom had emigrated from Western Europe and had adapted in other respects to the new social environment. In addition, the American Jewish community had suffered a breakdown of the traditional system of controls similar to that experienced by its European counterpart. Writing about Jewish society around the middle of the nineteenth century, Moshe Davis concludes:

> At the end of this period, in 1840, American Jewry entered a new stage in its development. The dynamism of American life had released powerful forces . . . The older methods of fines and bans lost their punitive powers . . . Intermarriage, Jewish ignorance, and above all, the paralyzing indifference to the destiny of Judaism thoroughly upset Jewish religious institutional life. In the Colonial period, a Jew was zealously controlled from birth to death by the synagogue. Now a Jew could live or die as a Jew without regard for that control.[14]

It is not surprising that the crisis within the American Jewish community was so similar to the European pattern since the same disintegrating forces were operating in both environments.

However, one important condition was unique to America, and this helps to explain the unprecedented success of the Reform Movement. American society was structurally conducive to the advancement of rationalist principles and the reorganization of Jewish institutions. This claim is not overexaggerated. In European society the Reformers encountered unyielding opposition by the traditionalists. Not only did they face the internal sanctions of the Jewish

---

[13]*Ibid.*, p. 260.

[14]Moshe Davis, "Jewish Religious Life and Institutions in America," in Louis Finklestein, ed., *The Jews* (New York: Harper, 1949), p. 365.

community—"denunciation, punishment, and excommunication"[15]—but the traditionalist could also invoke the support of the secular authorities in suppressing deviation. In contrast, the freedom and religious diversity of American society precluded any such barrier to the mobilization of progressive elements within the Jewish community. Furthermore, the religious orientation of American society probably functioned indirectly to encourage the development of a liberal movement.

In general, the American setting was disastrous for the traditional system. Changes in American society had the effect of weakening the authority of the Jewish institutions. For example, the development of a system of state-controlled secular education deprived the synagogue of one of its chief functions. However, the sheer increase in the number of synagogues helped to undermine central authority, since synagogues were dispersed over a wide area and their memberships were socially different.[16] Finally, migration to America itself represented a breach from the past, and in his quest for social advancement, the immigrant was forced to abandon, at least temporarily, constricting social customs and religious rituals. However, his emotional attachment to Judaism endured, and this led him to seek an alternative that would allow him to retain his identification with the formal Jewish community. Thus, American Jews were psychologically prepared to accept the innovations that Jewish leaders proposed. In addition, conditions within the larger society were conducive for the development and success of a reform movement.

While there were sporadic attempts toward Reform before the influx of German Jews, it is clear that a desire simply to adapt to the American system of values was too ambiguous a goal to inspire organized action. In short, a collective movement was conditioned by the introduction of a system of generalized beliefs.[17] The unique contribution of the German intellectuals who migrated to America was that they invested this desire for social adjustment with religious significance. Once the rationalist principles of the Enlightment were applied to traditional Judaism, "the traditional position could be attacked as wrong as well as inconvenient."[18] This ideology functioned to draw many uncommitted elements of the Jewish community into a cohesive social movement.

A critical evaluation of the entire traditional system was a principal feature of the new ideology. The conclusion was that most of Jewish tradition was grounded in superstition and antiquated custom. This new attitude provided ample justification for the abandonment of much traditional ritual and belief,

[15]Katz, op. cit., p. 274.

[16]Nathan Glazer, American Judiasm, Chicago: University of Chicago Press, 1957, p. 34.

[17]My analysis of the factors that conditioned the development of the Reform Movement has been guided by Neil J. Smelser's Theory of Collective Behavior (New York: The Free Press, 1962). According to Smelser, generalized beliefs help to mobilize people for collective action and thus are a necessary condition for the occurence of a collective episode.

[18]Glazer, op. cit., p. 49. Glazer also suggests that the political and religious philosophy of the Enlightenment had special historical significance for Jews, since these ideas had freed them from medieval restrictions.

and the formulation of a new system that was consistent with the social arrangements of modern society. This was the accomplishment of the intellectual leadership. The immoderacy of the early reformers, however, is astonishing even from the vantage point of contemporary Reform.

The Pittsburgh Platform reflects the general tenet of the Reform Movement during its first years. This historic document was a statement of Reform principles that emerged from a conference of Reform rabbis. It culminated a half century of controversy between traditionalists and progressives, and, by proclaiming a formal ideology, underscored the finality of the Reform defection from historical Judaism. The following passages are revealing of the rationalist philosophical strain in Reform ideology and illustrate the Movement's objective of greater conformity to the norms and values of Western society:

> We recognize in the Mosaic legislation a system of training the Jewish people for its mission during its national life in Palestine, and today we accept as binding only its moral laws and maintain only such ceremonials as elevate and sanctify our lives, *but reject all such as are not adapted to the views and habits of modern civilization.*"
>
> We hold that all such Mosaic and Rabbinical laws as regulate diet, priestly purity and dress originated in ages and under the influence of ideas altogether foreign to our present mental and spiritual state.
>
> We recognize in Judaism a progressive religion, ever striving to be in accord with the postulates of reason.[19]

These bold statements heralded major changes in doctrine and liturgy the effect of which "was to make the social atmosphere of the synagogue that of a Protestant church of the upper and upper-middle classes."[20] The specific nature of these changes does not have to be considered here. Let it suffice to say that by 1885 Reform had completed the schism from the Orthodox institution, and by embracing principles and practices that were harmonious with the dominant value system, had substantially reduced tension with the surrounding society. It was, by my definition, a church movement.

The Later Stages of the Reform Movement

As I suggested earlier, conformity to American values and maintenance of a Jewish consciousness were, in some ways, incompatible goals especially for a social movement whose avowed method was to destroy the ancient symbols which represented and vitalized that consciousness. Could the Reform Movement follow their principles to their logical extreme without defeating their fundmental purpose of "preserving the historical identity of our great past?"[21] The issue concerning Jewish nationalism illustrates how this problem was

[19]This document is reprinted in Glazer, *Ibid.*, p. 151-152.

[20]*Ibid.*, p. 16.

[21]This, also, is part of the Pittsburgh Platform, *Ibid.*, p. 152.

resolved and the new direction of the Reform Movement in the twentieth century.

Jewish nationalism, stated in prayers and ritual as a longing for the end of the Dispersion and return to Palestine, and expressed socially by the conception of Judaism as a people as well as a religion, was the most formidable barrier to acceptance into the secular world. In Europe, Napoleon and other secular authorities had assembled Jewish leaders in order to establish whether Jews were loyal to the emerging nation-states. In addition, Jewish nationalism was contradictory to the Reform conception of Judaism as a universal and rational religion that was to join forces with modern humanism in realizing the utopia of the Enlightenment—"a Kingdom of truth, justice and peace among all men."[22] The authors of the Pittsburgh Platform were straightforward in their rejection of Jewish nationalism:

> We consider ourselves no longer a nation but a religious community, and therefore expect neither a return to Palestine, nor a sacrifical worship under the administration of the sons of Aaron, nor the restoration of any of the laws concerning the Jewish state.[23]

Even after the Zionist Movement came into existence, the official attitude of the Reform Movement was hostile to the creation of a Jewish state. Following the Balfour Declaration in 1917, the Central Conference of Reform rabbis passed a resolution which, although welcoming the Declaration as an act of good-will toward the Jews, was clear in the renunciation of the concept of a national homeland:

> We hold that Jews in Palestine as well as anywhere else in the world are entitled to equality in political, civil, and religious rights but we do not subscribe to the phrase in the declaration which says, 'Palestine is to be a national home-land for the Jewish people' . . . We hold that the Jews are and of right ought to be at home in all lands . . . The mission of the Jew is to witness God all over the world.[24]

However, the anti-nationalistic position, notwithstanding the intellectual zeal with which it was enunciated, was accepted half-heartedly. The perseverance of nationalistic sentiment can be seen in the popular and official response to the persecution of European Jews. To quote Glazer again: "The solid majority, while they claimed to be members of a religion, not a 'people,' reacted to pogroms and persecutions abroad with somewhat more feeling than would have

[22] From the Pittsburgh Platform. The entire sentence is: "We recognize in the modern era of universal culture of heart and intellect the approach of the realization of Israel's great Messianic hope for the establishment of the Kingdom of truth, justice and peace among all men." *Ibid.*

[23] *Ibid.*

[24] Quoted in Beryl H. Levy, *Reform Judaism in America* (New York: Block Publishing Co., 1933), p. 134.

been justified by concern for co-religionists alone."[25] Finally, in 1935 the Central Conference replaced the anti-Zionist clause of the Pittsburgh Platform with a resolution that stipulated a neutral position with respect to Zionism and a determination to "continue to cooperate in the upbuilding of Palestine, and in the economic, cultural, and particularly spiritual tasks confronting the growing and evolving Jewish community there."[26] This was indicative of a more general trend away from the initial radicalism of the Movement.

In 1937 the Conference produced a new platform "whereby the debates and discussions of two decades were crystallized into a compromise program."[27] The Reform Movement had moved into the moderate camp. Crucial differences remained, to be sure, but the earlier radicalism was absent. The persecution of Jews abroad was only one factor. The feeling of spiritual emptiness that pervaded the Movement was another. A third factor was the emergence of the Conservative Movement and the liberalizing tendencies of the Orthodox synagogue. These changes meant that three religious bodies were competing for the loyalties of the more tradition-oriented East Europeans who, since 1881, were immigrating at an unprecedented rate. Finally, moderate leaders, such as Mordecai Kaplan, were replacing the radical intellectuals of the first generation. Collectively, these factors led to a revival of many forgotten traditions, the reinterpretation of many Orthodox beliefs and their inclusion into Reform ideology, and a general modification of the extremism of the early Reform Movement.

This development is important from an analytical standpoint. The decline in the radicalism of Reform principles and practices signified, in effect, a corresponding increase in the discrepancy between religious values and the values of the larger society. Sects, as Niebuhr demonstrates, are in greatest tension with the surrounding society at the time of schism from the religious institution, and eventually become institutionalized to middle-class standards. The reverse pattern is found in a church movement (if it is possible to generalize from this single case). Church movements appear to be at their lowest point of tension at the time of their schism from the parent institution, and to come into more tension with societal values as their original aims are modified.

There is a logical basis for the generalization. While it is possible to conceive of a church movement which steadily reduces the level of tension with society, this is unlikely to be an empirical reality. Unlimited pursuit of its original aims would result in total integration into the secular society and were this the purpose, the movement would not have taken a religious form in the first place. Hence, a church movement is likely to confront internal conservative forces that either halt or revert its conforming tendency and thereby stabilize or increase its

---

[25]Glazer, *Ibid.*, p. 54. Glazer suggests that the commitment to Reform principles was rarely complete. "Even in the formulated positions of Reform Judaism there were interesting anomalies indicating that Reform rabbis were still held back by some kind of primal attachments to the Jewish people." It is especially significant that, despite their rationalistic overtures, the Reformists could not sanction intermarriage. *Op. cit.*, p. 55.

[26]Quoted in Davis, *op. cit.*, p. 420.

[27]*Ibid.*

tension with the surrounding environment. Indeed, it would appear that a church movement, by its very nature, contains the seeds of moderation. As in the case of the Reform Movement, however, the rump group is likely to remain more churchly than the parent institution.

The Reform Movement suggests a second characteristic which distinguishes church movements from sect movements. Reform in Germany "began as a movement of Jews of high social status who wished to dignify Jewish religious services and make them decorous."[28] The leaders, as I have indicated, composed an intellectual elite, and their followers in America were also drawn from the upper classes. One Reform leader complained in 1932:

> Judaism has been alienated from the Jewish people. Its upkeep is today the concern of a class above a certain income level rather than of the masses and by and large this class is concerned only to the point of supplying the cost of the plant and the 'spiritual leader' through whose professional expertness they may discharge their religious obligations.[29]

The Movement's trend, however, was to broaden its social base. Both out of a sense of moral obligation and out of organizational necessity, Reform leaders acted to make Reformism more palatable to the Jewish masses. This was particularly true during and subsequent to the East European migration. Hence, while sect movements are made up of "disinherited" individuals whose social and economic advancement has lagged behind that of the group, church movements originate as middle-class movements and appear to broaden their bases of support during their evolution.

Indeed, a church movement may be contrasted to a sect movement with respect to virtually all of the elements which analysts have used to characterize sects. In the beginning the Reform Movement emphasized a universal theology; with its development it became more parochial as it reinterpreted traditional doctrine and moved closer to historical Judaism. (Sects tend to move from parochialism to a position that emphasizes the universalism of the gospel.) While in the beginning the guiding principle for admitting proselytes was the Talmudic statement "Whoever renounces idolatry is a Jew," in time the requirements for converts became more rigorous. (Sects tend to restrict their memberships at first and later adopt a less discriminatory policy.) Practically the only characteristic which sect and church movements share in common is that both are rump groups. However, the circumstances of their origin and the direction of their development are antithetical.

Conclusion

That the origin and development of the Reform Movement was markedly different from the pattern observed for sects suggests that church movements

---

[28]Glazer, *Ibid.*, p. 27.

[29]From Horace M. Kallen, *Judaism at Bay*. Quoted in Levy, *op. cit.*, pp. 77.

constitute a meaningful theoretical type, one that should be included in theories concerning church and sect. It should be added, however, that the conditions that generated the Reform Movement rarely exist. While it is not uncommon for a religious institution to come into greater tension with a changing society, it rarely happens that the institution cannot adapt to the new situation, or in that event, that other institutional alternatives do not already exist.[30] In the case of Judaism, however, Orthodoxy could not quickly adjust to the sudden change, and individual Jews, unwilling to forsake their Jewish identity, had no institutional outlet for their social and religious needs. As a minority religion, Judaism had to create a new form for the Jew who wished to maintain his marginality between his religious culture and the secular order. The Reform Movement, then, is an anomalous case, and in this capacity helps to define the limits of current theory and suggests guidelines for its improvement.

[30]In Christianity, for example, individuals who want to move into closer conformity with societal values can, and often do, cross denominational lines without altering their basic identification with Christian religion. Such a convenient option did not exist for Jews around the time of the Emancipation. Lacking an institutional alternative that would satisfy their desire for social adjustment, Jews were forced to create one.

Chapter Eighteen

The Third Civilization: An Examination of Sokagakkai[1]

Earl R. Babbie

Throughout history we may note the rise of countless religious movements within social groups of various sizes and compositions. Typically, new religions are regarded by the sociologist as responses to particular problems faced by particular people in particular situations. Where the religion itself does not explicitly specify the problems which it seeks to alleviate, the observer may frequently suggest the sources of the movement as a conjecture from the apparent needs of its followers. If the adherents are all from the same social or economic stratum, from the same ethnic or national group, the sociologist may take this as a clue to the functions of the movement. The peculiar quality of *some* religions, however, is their ability to transcend such delimiting boundaries and capture a substantial following which extends across economic, social, ethnic and national lines. Perhaps the classic example of such a religion is Christianity with its international memberships composed of people from a variety of classes, races and political ideologies. It seems a fair assessment to note that few religious movements achieve such a broadly based membership, although this is not to deny that many attempt to enroll the entire family of man in their ranks.

The purpose of this paper is to suggest some of the factors involved in the rise and development of a successful world-proselytizing religion. To facilitate the examination, we shall focus on a contemporary movement of this *genre* which has gained a substantial international following. It is the Japan-based Buddhist group: *Sokagakkai*. "The Third Civilization"[2] which it seeks to establish would

Earl R. Babbie, "The Third Civilization: An Examination of Sokagakkai", *Review of Religious Research, 7,* no. 2 (Winter 1966). Reprinted with the permission of the author and the *Review of Religious Research.*

[1]The contributions of Professor James A. Dator, University of Hawaii, in the revision and updating of this paper for the present republication are gratefully acknowledged.

[2]As *Sokagakkai* has come to assert its responsible role in world leadership, it has begun calling itself "The Third Civilization" in contrast to the "Western" and "Communist" civilizations.

encompass the world. Considering its goals and current successes, *Sokagakkai* provides an appropriate case study for our discussion. Since many readers may be generally unfamiliar with *Sokagakkai*, I shall begin by briefly sketching the history of the movement.

The Origins of Sokagakkai

It is written that on the 17th of October in 1271, the dark Japanese sky covering *Tatsu-no-Kuchi* burst into a brilliance of light as a meteor was hurled across the heavens.[3] In the face of so miraculous an event, the executioner dropped his sword and sank to the ground, holding his face in trembling hands. Soldiers turned in flight, and the condemned prisoner raised his head from the execution block. With his death sentence auspiciously commuted, he was now free to continue preaching the True Faith. Announcing himself to be executed and resurrected, he could continue his unyielding attack on the heretics (those holding any other beliefs whatsoever) and maintain the continuous stream of invectives against the government. Prophet, street-preacher, rabble-rouser, probably the first absolutely intolerant Buddhist—this was Nichiren.

Who was this man who would command his executioners to stop the march to his own beheading that he might address the sacred temple of *Hachiman*, the revered god of *Monamotos*

> O Hachiman! Art thou really a divine being? When the Great Master Dengyo gave lectures on the Lotus of Truth, thou didst honor him by offering a purple robe. Now, I, Nichiren, am the one, the supreme one . . . When, tonight, I, Nichiren, shall be beheaded and go to the Paradise of Vulture Peak, I shall declare before our Lord Sakya-muni that thou, Hachiman, and the Sun-Goddess have not fulfilled your oaths. Art thou not afraid of that?[4]

Certainly this was a man of enormous conviction and self-confidence. Although we shall be concerned primarily with his importance as a religious leader, Nichiren is generally recognized as one of the finest calligraphers in history, an extreme nationalist, and one of the ten or twelve leading Japanese figures of all times.

The details of Nichiren's life are somewhat hazy, but scholars have been able to piece together bits and scraps of his history until we are able to appreciate something of the man's life and character. He was born in 1222 to a family of a samurai-descended fisherman. As a child, young Rencho (his given name) was sent to a *Tendai* monastery. Although we do not know his father's motives, it was a fairly common practice. Very soon, however, the boy demonstrated that

---

[3] The best single source on Nichiren's life is Masaharu Anesaki's *Nichiren, The Buddhist Prophet*, Cambridge: Harvard University Press, 1916. The first half of this historical discussion is singly indebted to that book.

[4] Anesaki, op. cit., pp. 56-57.

he was no common student. Rencho was possessed of an unquenchable thirst for knowledge, coupled with a high degree of brilliance. The young monk was deeply impressed by the figure of Sakyamuni, the Eternal Buddha, but was appalled by the diversity of schools and sects bearing his name.[5] Just as Lord Sakyamuni had tried all the existing Indian religions of his day, the young Rencho buried himself in the teachings of the religions of Japan. His later writings demonstrate his erudition on these matters. His aim ultimately was to unite all Buddhists; perhaps his task was hopeless. The end result of his efforts was an acceptance of the Lotus Sutra as the *most* important teaching of the Eternal Buddha. In effect, he had simply created another sect. The Lotus Sutra itself had been the source of much popular Buddhism in Japan. Central to this sutra is the doctrine of *mappo*—the Law of the Latter Days. According to this belief, the original teachings of Sakyamuni would retain their power for a period of one thousand years, to be followed by the period of the Copied Law which would maintain *its* power for one thousand years, also. At the end of the second millenium, the Copied Law would lose its power and the world would be plunged into chaos and strife. Heretical sects would multiply, and war would rage. At this dreadful time, the Buddha would reappear in a small country to the northeast of India and he would preach the Truth of the Lotus Sutra and the magic formula—*Nam-myoho-renge-kyo* (Hail to the Mystery of the Lotus Sutra[6]). The symbolism of the lotus was one of cause and effect. Just as the lotus seeds cast on the soil would give rise to flowers, the deeds of one's prior existence would give rise to one's fate in this life. The crucial element in the popularization of this doctrine was that a sure faith in the efficacy of the Law and the power of the chant would transcend the deeds of prior existences and allow one to find Enlightenment.[7]

Upon his acceptance of the Lotus Sutra, the monk assumed the name of Nichiren (Sun-Lotus). In 1253, he made his first pronouncement on behalf of the Lotus of Truth and began actively proselytizing. Nichiren later taught his followers to seek the conversion of their parents, their masters and their ruler. The first of these provided Nichiren with his first converts. He was to spend the rest of his life in a vain attempt to convert the other two.

It is important to note the historical condition in Japan during Nichiren's lifetime. If there were ever a moment in Japanese history when the country seemed to be experiencing the prophesied end of the Law, that moment

---

[5]This religious diversity was hardly a fancy on the part of the twelve-year-old monk, for Japan has long been noted for its accommodation of foreign items of culture. The country is sometimes referred to as the "graveyard of religions." In Japan, any new religion seems assured of finding at least some small following. This national tendency is confounded by the character and history of Buddhism itself. Grounded in the broad spectrum of teachings handed down by Sakyamuni, the religion has been the constant scene of splits and schisms. Each new school normally takes one particular sutra as its central doctrine. The result is a collection of extremely different religions grouped under the general rubric of "Buddhism."

[6]Anesaki translates this as "Adoration be to the Lotus of the Perfect Truth." The *Sokagakkai* translation has been presented here.

[7]This was also the case in the *Jodo* or "Pure Land" sects of Amida Buddhism which stressed the universality of salvation and the ease of attainment.

corresponded with Nichiren's appearance. The traditional structures of the society were crumbling, and a class of military families were competing for national dominance. The emperor had become little more than a ritual figurehead. The competing military families engaged in countless skirmishes, and territory shifted hands frequently. Many of the more powerful Buddhist temples supported their own armies and participated in the struggle for influence. In the face of this internal strife, an external threat appeared. The Mongol rulers of Korea had twice served notice for Japan to surrender to their authority or else an attack would be mounted against the island. The Japanese government had chosen to ignore the warnings. Nichiren, in his best-known tract—*Rissho Ankoku Ron* (Pacification of the Land Through the Establishment of the True Religion)—had warned that the country would in fact be overrun by the Mongols unless the government subscribed to his teachings and gave up its heretical beliefs. At this point, we find Nichiren, the extreme nationalist, referring to himself as the "Pillar of Japan." Normally such patriotic zeal might have been welcomed, but his outspoken pretensions and gloomy defeatism did not win him a great deal of popularity in the eyes of the government. Soon he and his followers were being persecuted—two exiles and an attempted execution were to follow.

If we are to take anything away from the original teachings of Nichiren—as an aid to understanding the later developments of the religion—the most important doctrine would be that of *San-dai-hiho*: The Three Secret Laws.

(1) *Honmon-no-Honzon*—(Chief Object of Worship of the True Teaching); *honzon* is the generic term for mandalas or scrolls. In this instance it is the graphic representation of the Supreme Being, drawn by Nichiren. It is the object of all worship. To a large extent Nichiren's teachings included many of the traditional Japanese gods—all of whom became subordinate to the *Dai-Gohonzon*. For example, the *Shoten-zenjin* (three thousand gods) are pledged to serve the worshippers of the sacred mandala. The *Dai-Gohonzon* is the medium for making contact with all the gods and Buddhas of the universe. *Go* is an honorific, and *dai* is the Japanese prefix for big or great: hence the original mandala drawn by Nichiren is the *Dai-Gohonzon*, the most sacred object of worship.

(2) *Honmon no Daimoku*—(Name of the True Teaching); this is the sacred chant: *Nam-myoho-renge-kyo*. As in many of the other popularized Japanese Buddhist schools, the chanting of the sacred incantation is considered more or less sufficient to bring the believer enlightenment or salvation. The basic ritual derived from Nichiren's teachings is the chanting of the *daimoku* before the *Dai-Gohonzon*.

(3) *Honmon-no-kaidan*—(Sanctuary of the True Teaching); this is, of course, the proper place of worship. In Nichiren's teachings, this concept changed its meaning frequently: sometimes meaning a particular sanctuary which Nichiren had designated, and at other times simply meaning that place where Nichiren was. (Even at the present day, the term may mean the head temple at *Taisekiji*, or simply the place where members gathered for worship or instruction.)

Thus, in brief compass, we have seen the general course of Nichiren's life and teachings. In his own lifetime, he succeeded in winning converts from among the peasants and had a small following among the military. However, his dream of a Japan united under the *Dai-Gohonzon* went unrealized. In 1282, Nichiren took his leave for Vulture's Peak. He died among his followers, while reading from his beloved Lotus Sutra:

> I am the Father of the world,
> The One who cures all ills and averts
>   disaster.
> Since I see the mass of men infatuated,
> I appear to die, although I am really
>   living. . . .
> I am ever watching to see whether all
>   beings
> Are faithful to the Way or not;
> And I preach to them various aspects
>   of truth,
> According to their capacities
>   and for the sake of their salvation.[8]

Prior to his death, Nichiren had established a more or less permanent sanctuary at *Mt. Minobu*. Shortly after the passing of the founder, however, disputes broke out among his followers and several Nichiren-based sects emerged. One of these was founded by Nikko Shonin[9] who allegedly carried Nichiren's bones and the *Dai Gohonzon* to a new sanctuary at *Taisekiji*, at the foot of Mt. Fuji. The sect which Nikko formed was *Nichiren Shoshu*. In view of Japan's past religious history, the group seemed destined for a purely non-Achillean existence.

The Growth of Sokagakkai

Yomiuri Shimbun, April 1, 1963:
   The powerful religious organization, Soka Gakkai, Monday decided to throw its support behind Ryotaro Azuma, the incumbent conservative governor, in the election for governor of Tokyo on April 17. . .
   About 600,000 of Tokyo's 6,497,000 registered voters are members of Soka Gakkai.

Yomiuri Shimbun, January 24, 1963:
   Osaka police authorities have become alarmed with the increasing number of policemen who have gone too far in their religious activities.

[8]Anesaki, op. cit., p. 134.

[9]The term *shonin* means religious leader or high priest. It is applied to all the high priests from Nikko *Shonin*, Nichiren's successor, to Nitatsu *Shonin*, the current high priest. Nichiren is referred to as the *Dai-shonin*.

In a recent case, a policeman who was converted to Soka-Gakkai, a newly emerging religious group, began neglecting his official duties in order to carry out his personal campaign to win new converts.

A little over one month before the appearance of this last story, the *Sokagakkai* had announced the attainment of an important membership goal—three million families of believers. The same issue of the *Seikyo News*[10] which carried the announcement also printed a picture of the 10th General Meeting of the Young Women's Division, with 25,000 *representative leaders* in attendance.

By 1969, an independent observer estimated *Sokagakkai's* membership at seven million families.[11] At the same time, *Sokagakkai's* political arm, the *Komeito* (Clean Government Party), represented the third largest political party in Japan.

What was this movement which was attracting so much attention among the Japanese people and which was coming to enroll ever increasing numbers of them in its ranks of believers?

During the 1930's, the principal of Tokyo's *Nishimachi* School began publishing a series of essays concerning "the creation of value." Tsunesaburo Makiguchi had first presented his new philosophy in 1903 in a book entitled *Geography of Life*. His system was basically a modification of Kant's notion of the cardinal values of good, beauty and truth. Makiguchi's belief, however, was that *benefit* was more meaningful to the common man than the abstract conception of truth. In 1928, he converted to *Nichiren Shoshu* and had soon incorporated his own philosophical system into his new religious beliefs. He saw the *Dai-Gohonzon* of Nichiren *Daishonin* as the source of good, beauty and—perhaps most important—benefit. Makiguchi began discussing these ideas with his friends and the essays entitled *Kachiron* (An Essay on Value) appeared. Upon his retirement from teaching in 1930, he formed a small study group called *Soka Kyoiku Gakkai* (Value-creating Education Association). Relatively little is known about Makiguchi, but the indication is that he was something of a stern disciplinarian and a rather reserved scholar. Oddly enough, even as the founder of the movement, he is of only minor importance in the present activities and lore of the religion. Justification for present activities is found in the life of Nichiren, and Makiguchi has greatly faded into the background as an historical figure for the religion.

We know considerably more about one of his first followers: Josei Toda, a teacher at *Nishimachi*. During Makiguchi's leadership of the group, Toda seems to have been a loyal disciple. He had joined Makiguchi in accepting *Nichiren Shoshu* in 1928 and been a junior partner in the formation of *Soka Kyoiku Gakkai* in 1930.

[10]*The Seikyo News* is the official English-language publication of the *Sokagakkai*. At about the time of attainment of 3 million families, it changed from a fortnightly to a weekly publication. It is one of the publications of the organizational publishing house, *Seikyo Press*, which is owned by the current president, Daisaku Ikeda.

[11]James White, *The Sokagakkai and Mass Society* (Palo Alto: Stanford University Press, 1970), p. 303.

By 1937, the group had grown to a scant 60 members. During the next five years, its membership began growing more rapidly, but the movement also began experiencing considerable pressure from the government. As part of Japan's early attempts at international expansion, strong measures were being taken to insure the internal solidarity of the country. This involved the suppression of religious freedom in the attempt to enforce subscription to State Shinto. Each Japanese family was expected to maintain a Shinto god-shelf in its home. Makiguchi and his followers refused. Toda was one of the followers who joined Makiguchi in prison for the duration of the war. Makiguchi died in prison, while Toda's faith was greatly strengthened.

At the end of the war, Toda was released. Under the Allied Occupation, religious freedom was restored. Toda attempted to reorganize the old members of the movement; the name was changed to its present form: *Sokagakkai* (Value-Creation Society). By 1951, the membership had increased to 5,000. Toda appears drastically different from Makiguchi; he was much more a man of the common people than the abstract philosopher. Although his earliest lectures reflect the mood of the founder, he later displayed a popular charisma which finally allowed him to reach the uneducated masses. By his death in 1958, Toda had increased the membership of *Sokagakkai* to 750,000 families. He had created a tightly-knit organization, based on the *setai* (household) as the basic unit and moving in an ascending order to the *Sokagakkai* Headquarters at the apex of the structure. *Sokagakkai* was a lay movement for the support of *Nichiren Shoshu*, existing parallel to the religious structure. The high priest of *Nichiren Shoshu* was and is the final source of theological doctrine, but appears to have little to say about the functioning of the secular movement. Although Prime Minister Kishi attended Toda's funeral procession, the Japanese people still regarded the movement as a curious band of fanatics—fostering an unheard-of brand of religious intolerance.

Upon Toda's death, a member of the Youth Division, Daisaku Ikeda, assumed leadership of *Sokagakkai*. In the tradition of both *Nichiren Shoshu* and *Sokagakkai*, he had been singled out by his predecessor and was later chosen by acclamation. He appears to have brought a youth and energy to the movement, strengthening its highly structured organization and increasing its membership.

Out of the post-war religious boom in Japan, *Sokagakkai* is generally acknowledged as the unique success. It alone has achieved an impressive international following, and there is little indication that it is waning. My own contact with the movement occurred during a stay in Japan from May, 1962 to June, 1963. During that time I lived among *Sokagakkai* members, attended meetings, collected literature and discussed the movement with members and nonmembers. Most of the observations in this paper derive from my personal contacts, two excellent books on the new religions in Japan,[12] and a body of *Sokagakkai* organizational literature.[13]

[12]These books are: Harry Thomsen's *The New Religions of Japan* (Tokyo: Charles E. Tuttle, 1963) and C. B. Offner and H. Van Straelen's *Modern Japanese Religions* (Tokyo: Rupert Enderle, 1963). The Thomsen volume seems the superior of the two books.

[13]In addition to issues of *The Seikyo News*, much data is drawn from *Essays on Buddhism* (Toda), *Lectures on Buddhism* Vols. I and II (Ikeda) and the anonymous book *Sokagakkai*—all published by the Seikyo Press in Tokyo.

We shall turn now to a brief discussion of the sociological literature on the origin and development of religious movements. In the light of that review, I shall suggest some elements in a theoretical model of the world-proselytizing religion. Finally, we shall return to the examination of *Sokagakkai* in the terms of that model.

A Review of the Literature

Our traditional conceptions of religious organization arose largely from the formulations of Max Weber and Ernst Troeltsch. Particularly in *The Social Teachings of the Christian Churches*,[14] Troeltsch makes the basic distinction between "church" and "sect" types of religious organizations. The former is characterized by its formalized rituals, lack of emotionalism and general harmony with the secular society. The latter is more emotional in character, less formalized and often somewhat alienated from the secular society. Another differentiating characteristic concerns patterns of recruitment—sects obtain their members through conversion, while church inherit theirs from among the children of members.

Modifications of this model have taken three forms: (1) expansions of the typology; (2) the postulated interplay between types; and (3) attempts to explain their origins. The first of these has been pursued by a number of theorists who have attempted to add precision to the dichotomous typology. The efforts of Bryan Wilson,[15] Elmer Clark,[16] and J. Milton Yinger[17] are good examples of this approach. These authors elaborate on the notions of sect and church to provide a more extensive *description* of the existing types of religious organizations.

The best known attempt at suggesting an interplay between the types of religious organizations is to be found in H. Richard Niebuhr's *The Social Sources of Denominationalism*.[18] In this work, Niebuhr attempted to demonstrate the influence of socio-economic factors on religious organization. In his examination, he described the movement from sect-organization to church-organization. Since Niebuhr dealt basically with religions arising from economic disadvantage—among "the disinherited"—he showed that such people formed emotional, proselytizing sects with institutionalized ethics of thrift and hard work. As a result, the second generation was no longer disadvantaged and the religion evolved into a church-type organization, more appropriate to other aspects of their new social positions. The assumption was that this process was more or less to be expected. More recently Yinger re-examined Niebuhr's

[14]Translation by Olive Wyon (New York: Harper & Brothers, 1960).

[15]Bryan R. Wilson, "An Analysis of Sect Development," *American Sociological Review*, 24:1 (February, 1959).

[16]Elmer Clark, *The Small Sects in America* (New York: Abingdon Press, 1949).

[17]J. Milton Yinger, *Religion, Society and the Individual* (New York: The Macmillan Company, 1963).

[18](New York: Meridian Books, Inc., 1960.)

postulate and suggested that not all religious movements begin at the sect-end of the scale, nor do all of them progress toward the church-end. This assertion was combined with Yinger's expanded typology.

Bryan Wilson was previously mentioned in connection with his elaboration of the sect-church typology. He must also be considered as one of those concerned with the dynamic interplay of organizational structures and with the explanation of the origins of religious movements. In the article cited, he not only discussed the various forms of "sects" to be treated separately, but he also suggested varying organizational histories for each type. Although his typology is neither logically exhaustive nor exclusive, it would appear that *Sokagakkai* approximates Wilson's "conversionist" sect. Much of his description of this type of sect was limited to Christian groups, but the application to *Sokagakkai* is appropriate in many instances. Rather than treat Wilson's discussion at this point, I shall consider it during the examination of *Sokagakkai* in the last section of the paper.

While Niebuhr's discussion assumed the singular importance of economic dispossession in the origin of religious groups, Charles Y. Glock, as we have just read in Chapter Sixteen, takes exception to this and suggests the importance of five types of "deprivation"—economic, organismic, social, psychic and ethical. *Economic* deprivation, it will be recalled, is essentially the same as Niebuhr's notion of "economic dispossession". The *organismically deprived* are the sick and the disabled. By *social deprivation*, Glock refers to those personal attributes a person may have which are generally down-graded by the values and norms of secular society. In the United States, being Negro or lacking a formal education would be examples of social deprivation. In a study of Episcopalian parishioners,[19] Glock examines additional attributes which he feels represent other forms of social deprivation in American society—among other things: being female, being elderly and being without a family. Persons categorized as *psychically and ethically* deprived are the "seekers" in society. The former seek a satisfactory relationship to God or to some other power in the universe, while the latter seek a satisfactory relationship to their fellow men. Each of the deprivation types represents ways in which some members of a society are deprived of the satisfactory social existence enjoyed by others around them. The poor are deprived of the benefits enjoyed by the rich, the sick are deprived of the advantages of the healthy and so forth.

Glock contends that such forms of deprivation may serve as the source of social movements aimed at their alleviation. Where persons perceive the means of resolving their deprivation through the secular society, secular movements will appear. The economically deprived may band together in labor unions, for example. If no secular solutions are recognized, however, Glock suggests religious movements will be the result. While Glock's original discussion dealt primarily with the sources of movements, he later contends that deprivations may lead people to participate in existing secular or religious organizations as well.

Glock is careful to point out that secular or religious movements need not be

[19]Charles Y. Glock, Benjamin B. Ringer, and Earl R. Babbie, *To Comfort and to Challenge* (Berkeley and Los Angeles: University of California Press, 1967).

directed at the resolution of only one type of deprivation, nor should we expect individuals to experience only one form of deprived status. However, it is often possible to suggest the most salient deprivation-type which informs the goals and organization of a particular movement.

I have elaborated on the various types of deprivation discussed by Glock because I feel they are of considerable significance in the understanding of successful world-proselytizing religions. To utilize his conceptions, however, it is necessary to carry his discussion one step further. I should contend that economic and organismic deprivation are qualitatively different from the other three forms in terms of the secular solutions available for their relief and in terms of their inherent saliency. First, economic and organismic deprivation are in competition with more extensively developed secular alternatives in a modern, industrial society. In the case of economic deprivation, participation in the economic market is an institutionalized, secular solution. While a man may be disadvantaged in finding employment for other reasons, the broadly accepted secular solution to economic deprivation is apparent to him. On the other hand, religious movements which direct their primary efforts at organismic deprivations must ultimately compete with a rapidly growing medical science and care.

Niebuhr's observations seem to suggest that both secular and religious factors effect the resolution of economic deprivation, and that no religious movement can last very long on a "disinherited" membership. Similarly, we might note the limited success of religious movements dealing strictly with organismic deprivation—the healing movements. Christian Science has never attained a wide acceptance. The Oral Roberts-type of movement has followed the pattern of tent-meeting revivalism rather than establishing an enduring denominational structure. The conclusion drawn for purposes of this paper is that economic and organismic deprivations cannot form the sole, enduring focus for the type of religion we are discussing.

To varying degrees, the same may hold for some kinds of social deprivation, depending on changes in the social structure—especially the legislative process. Civil Rights legislation for example may help to alleviate the social deprivation attached to being Black. However, the kinds of social deprivation which Glock sees as maintaining commitment to the established denominations (age, sex, family and marital status) cannot be resolved readily by legislation. They are part of the implicit value structure of society. These kinds of social deprivation, plus psychic and ethical deprivations are not nearly as amenable to secular resolutions as is true of economic and organismic.

Second, it will be contended that social, psychic and ethical deprivations are largely the privileged possessions of the economically and organismically nondeprived. This contention is not to imply these types of deprivations are not present among the economically and organismically deprived, but they are of less importance for such persons. The unemployed coalminer, for example, is undoubtedly socially deprived and feels this deprivation, but he is surely more concerned with the lack of bread than with the lack of status. Therefore, my assumption is that while economic and organismic deprivation cannot sustain a religion indefinitely, they are of utmost importance where they exist.

A Developmental Model

In light of these theoretical antecedents and the assumptions being made in their regard, I shall now suggest a model for the development of a successful, world-proselytizing religion. The model is organized around four elements: the field, the message, the initial group and the expansion phase. I have found it more useful to discuss leadership in terms of these elements rather than separately.

The Field

One of the problems involved in establishing a religion, a political rule or any type of authority is the creation of "legitimacy." There is a tendency in sociology to speak of legitimacy as something to be actively established by the leader. Parsons, however, suggests another conception of legitimacy when he discusses the fact that the norms and mores of a society are never completely reflected in reality—society never really lives up to its ideals. In this context, he speaks of a "latent reservoir of legitimation possibilities."[20] Discontent with the established order, either personal or systemic, may serve as a readymade source of legitimacy for some other form of authority. Essentially this notion closely approaches Glock's discussion of deprivation as a source of social movements.

Therefore, we should expect to find a proliferation of new religions rising out of times characterized by social, political and economic upheavals. Such situations not only create very real social and economic deprivations; but they may often depose previous authorities, secular and religious, and create authority vacuums in the social structure. As the old authorities crumble, many people may feel the need for a new organizing schema for their lives. Religion is a traditional source of such schemas.

Certainly religions arise at other times, and all those religions which are born in times of upheaval do not last—much less do all of them succeed in spreading their message around the globe. Many religions have arisen in response to some felt need, only to wane and to die at the passing of that need. The crucial factor, however, is that such periods may provide a longer duration of discontent and deprivation—hence, a more enduring source of legitimation potential.

The Message

Religious prophecies are no doubt present at all times and in all places. But the simple presence of would-be prophets is not sufficient for the formation of a movement any more than the simple existence of discontent is sufficient. Only when the prophet's message is deemed appropriate to the alleviation of deprivations for which no secular solutions are perceived should we expect the birth of a successful movement. While the personality of the prophet is indeed most important in the early formation of a movement, we shall be primarily

---

[20]Talcott Parsons, *The Social System* (Glencoe, Ill.: The Free Press, 1952), page 296.

concerned in the ways in which he directs his appeal at the specific problems of his audience and following.

The application of a religious message to a particular problem is important to the formation of any religious movement. There are two additional characteristics of the message which are necessary for its later acceptance by an international following. First, and most obvious, it must contain a proselytizing element. Rather than simply establishing an example of proper behavior, the prophet must demand that his followers go into the world seeking the conversion of others.

Secondly, the message must be flexible. There seem to be two possibilities for this. Either the message may be loosely formulated—as in an oral tradition—or extremely extensive. I shall contend later that the developing religion must change some of its most basic emphases from time to time, and it is imperative that the sacred scriptures be capable of providing legitimation for these changes. In the case of Christianity, for example, an oral tradition, plus diverse interpretations and formulations during the first centuries of the religion's history, have provided a body of sacred literature which is still capable of adaptation some two thousand years later.

The second element of the model, then, is the input of a message, perceived as effective in resolving felt-needs, and yet flexible enough to accommodate diverse groups and an ever changing situation.

The Initial Group

The initial group established by the founder will probably be relatively small, but it should be held together by some other affective bonds. For example, the religious group will be more likely to stay together if its members are additionally joined by family and friendship ties. Such affective bonds provide a constant consolidation and reinforcement of group solidarity at a time when the larger society does not recognize its legitimacy. Initial conversions are likely to proceed along the lines of "friends and relations." Lofland and Stark have elaborated on this conversion model earlier in this volume in Chapter 5.

In discussing "the field", I suggested that times of great upheaval would enhance the long-range existence of a religious movement by providing intensified and continued needs among the population. Furthermore, in the discussion of the types of deprivation, it was contended that economic and organismic deprivations were of a greater saliency to deprived persons. As a result, I should further suggest that a religious movement would stand the best chance of becoming firmly rooted in society if it were to apply itself to the problems of economic and organismic deprivation during times when such problems were widespread and were maintained for an extended period. It is not surprising, therefore, to find so many fledgling religious movements forming their initial groups around these problems.

Finally, we should expect a great deal of provincial emphasis during the early stages of any religious movement which succeeds in establishing a stable initial group of followers. The problems which it seeks to resolve are likely to reflect the specific deprivations of its members. Until such time as the movement establishes a broader acceptance within the larger society, people are likely to participate in it only if they feel it aims specifically at their own personal problems.

Thus, the third element in our developmental model is the establishment of a visible, tightly-knit initial group which lends identity to the movement.

The Expansion Phase

The expansion phase is perhaps the most critical for our model of a world-proselytizing religion. It is at this point that we note the significance of the preceding discussion of the field, message and initial group. In terms of the sociological literature, this is essentially when the "sect" becomes a "church" although we are dealing with a particular type of transition.

First, the basic desire for expansion should be fed by early successes in proselytization. A mere growth in numbers may enhance the sense of mission in the movement's leaders and early followers. To achieve its expansion, however, the group must be in a position to do so. The initial group should be located at an advantageous point in the larger communication network. Christianity and Islam, for example, first appeared along major trade routes. In the present day, it would appear that an urban-based movement is in a better position to spread its message than is a rural movement. Access to the mass media would be another advantage.

Secondly, we should expect to note many of the structural changes observed in the previous sociological literature. For example, a crystallization of leadership and formal training for the clergy should appear. In the long run, membership recruitment should shift from conversion to inheritance. However, in the early years of expansion, we should expect a change in the conversion model itself. Rather than expanding only through family and friendship networks, strangers should appear among the converts. If the movement is publicized in the media, persons may establish their initial contacts in that fashion.

Thirdly, the basic emphases of the movement should begin to shift. As the movement begins to encompass diverse memberships in differing cultures, certain beliefs and practices which are inappropriate to certain groups are likely to be modified. A variety of doctrines and prescriptions are likely to emerge at all levels of sophistication. If the movement originated with an appeal to the economically and organismically deprived, we should expect to find an emerging emphasis on other forms of deprivation: social, psychic and ethical. These emphases may be noted not only in the official promulgation of doctrines, but also they may be noted in the reasons which members give for joining and the benefits they claim to have reaped. In the final stage of international expansion, we shall see the importance of flexibility in the founder's message in permitting these several changes.

In this brief discussion, I have tried to outline some of the important elements involved in this process. Now we shall turn to the case of *Sokagakkai* to examine the model more specifically.

Sokagakkai: A Case Study

The Field

Harry Thomsen describes the field within which the new Sokagakkai appeared after World War II.

> The times of crisis during and after World War II led, on a world-wide scale, to the emergence of all kinds of religions and sects which might minister to the needs of man. The defeat of Japan, the first in its long history, left the nation in a state of moral and economic chaos. War's destruction and defeat's blow to national self-confidence combined to create for many a need for religion. Some turned to Shinto, Buddhism, and Christianity to satisfy these needs. But many more found their answer in the new religions.[21]

The members of *Sokagakkai* hotly refute the general assumption that theirs is a new, postwar religion, and, of course, it *had* its birth prior to the war. If we are to understand its growth, however, it is sheer blindness to neglect the consideration of a postwar environment which has given rise to some 171 new religious groups.[22] Japan's defeat in World War II was a classic example of social, economic and political upheaval. The war itself had been preceded by a period of rapid industrial growth in a traditionally agricultural society. The loss of the war only compounded the strains inherent in rapid industrialization. Certainly the Emperor's renunciation of divinity further necessitated the reordering of life in post-war Japan. It seems dangerous to under-estimate the importance of this symbolic loss of meaning and order. The *East Asian Co-prosperity Sphere* was envisioned as a means for lending order to a confused and disorganized world. All peoples of the world were to be organized under the Japanese nation, at the top of which was the Emperor. With the end of the war, the hierarchical social structure was without an apex. The economy had collapsed, and the land was under the control of a foreign power for the first time in the country's history. Out of the rubble of buildings and cities came religion.

What were these religions like? Joseph Spae describes their founders:

> Their deportment is folksy, their speech is direct and even uncouth in its carefully nurtured dialectal brogue. At all times they keep close to the common man whose ailments they transfer upon themselves, whose hidden aspirations they voice, whose yearning for safety and deliverance they incarnate. They travel much; they preach relentlessly; they live luxuriously. They bask in adulation and even anthropolatry. Several of

[21]Thomsen, op. cit., page 18.

[22]This figure is taken from the Ministry of Education's "Year Book of Religion," cited in Thomsen, op. cit., pp. 16-17.

them claim to be theophanies, unerringly led by divine inspiration. Others, more modest, are satisfied with the role of prophet or medium. All are proficient in spiritual science. Mystical experiences are common with them. For they commune with gods, demons and ancestral spirits.[23]

Although there are exceptions, the major emphasis of the new religions in Japan is on the resolution of economic and organismic deprivation. In addition to promises of wealth, healing movements are numerous. Offner suggests that much of the success of the curing religions is due to the retarded state of medical science in Japan—both in diagnosis and treatment. There seem to be a number of cases where physicians, confronted with baffling symptoms, suggested that the cause *might* be tuberculosis—a common and feared disease in Japan. The frightened patient then fled to the nearest curing religion where he was assigned religious duties and provided assurances which relieved the psychosomatic origins of his symptoms. Later he would be declared free of tuberculosis, confirming his faith in his new religion.

This was the field within which *Sokagakkai* reappeared: rapid industrialization followed by the loss of the war, bringing with it economic chaos and a restructuring of authority.

The Message

Conducive though this situation was for the rise of popular religions, it was hardly the place for a dignified philosopher and scholar such as Tsunesaburo Makiguchi. Yet he seems to have maintained this posture throughout his leadership of the group. Following the example of his predecessor, Josei Toda's earliest appeal was also on a fairly sophisticated plane. He spoke of the "quintessence of Buddhism," argued theology and condemned the rising tide of popular, postwar religions. In the earliest speech of President Toda translated into English (July 10, 1949), he warned.

> Superstitions are rampant in the present-day religious world. Priests brazenly advertise that people will be cured of sickness and the poor will become rich through incantations and prayers. The divine favors they advertise are of low grade.[24]

Nonetheless, the more we read about Toda and his later leadership, the more he appears to fit Spae's description. He became more a man of the common people. His deportment became more "folksy"; his speech was "direct and even uncouth." It was Toda who could easily slip into the Lutheresque analogies of his wife breaking wind, Toda who chided his followers by joking about their morality or lack thereof. We can only assume that Toda gave up the dignified

[23]Joseph J. Spae, "The Religions of Japan," *The Japan Missionary Bulletin*, Vol. X, No. 2 (March, 1956), page 127; reprinted in Offner, op. cit., page 30.

[24]Josei Toda, *Essays on Buddhism*, (Tokyo: Seikyo Press, 1961), pp. 3-4.

example of his predecessor and perhaps gave vent to his own personality. Thus on July 18, 1954, we find an interesting contrast with Toda's earlier diatribe against the "cheap favors" of other religions.

> The reason why I recommend this faith is because I wish each of you to enjoy a happy life wherein it is unnecessary to experience any inconvenience in your next life, being able to live at least in a house as large as this hall; possessing everything from piano to jewelry; your mother being a beauty; you being born with intelligence, fortune, and in excellent health; growing up and marrying a woman of noble character, who will bear you a blessed child. This is why I am zealously encouraging this faith.[25]

A content analysis of Toda's speeches during the period from July 10, 1949 to April 1, 1958 indicates that this quotation does not represent an isolated statement, but rather, a definite trend. By classifying each of the paragraphs of Toda's speeches, we find the following fluctuations in references to direct benefits (e.g., good health) to be gained from adherence to the teachings of *Sokagakkai*.

Period[26]	Percentage of paragraphs stressing direct benefits[27]
10 July '49-10 Sept. '51	6%
1 Nov '51-1 Nov '54	16%
1 Jan '55-1 Feb '56	67%
1 June '57-1 April '58	32%

Although these figures reflect the emphasis on a variety of benefits to be gained from *Sokagakkai*, a considerable portion of the references are to the healing power of a faith in *Gohonzon*. The enduring statement on this matter is found in Toda's *Gobyo* lecture on April 1, 1955.

> There are six causes for disease.
>
> (1) Irregularity of *Shidai* (the four elements of earth, water, air and fire). Man suffers from various illness due to a disturbance in any one of the four elements (cold, heat, vitamin deficiency, etc.)
>
> (2) Immoderate eating or drinking (overeating or drinking, malnutrition, or unbalanced diet, etc.)

[25]Quoted in *Sokagakkai* (Tokyo: Seikyo Press, 1962), page 99.

[26]The breakdown of periods for this table partly reflects the distribution of lectures available for analysis, but primarily I have attempted to show when the shift in emphasis occurred. The gaps which exist between periods result from the fact that no lectures were available in English for the missing periods.

[27]See Bellah's unpublished paper; "Some Suggestions for the Systematic Study of Religion." The integrative function clearly includes the notion of benefit. Bellah himself includes theories of disease and curing.

(3) Lack of uniformity in daily life (excessive or insufficient exercise, lack of sleep, exhaustion, etc.)

(4) A demon taking advantage of one's weakness (germ-carried diseases, such as cholera, dysentery, infant diarrhea, etc.)

(5) A demon's behaviour becomes the cause of disease (disease of unknown causes)

(6) *Go* (a man's deeds in his former life) becomes the cause and its effect appears as *Gobyo* in this life.[28]

In case the implication were not clear enough, Toda continues to explain that physicians can cure the first three, and with luck the fourth and fifth causes of disease. Only the True Religion can cure the sixth cause. How does one know the cause of his disease? If the physician cannot cure the illness, the cause is certainly *go*, or the *karma* of previous lives. From this formulation (from Nichiren), the message became: "If the doctor can't help you, come to *Sokagakkai*."

During the period starting in the middle of 1954, therefore, the table indicates a shift in doctrine, emphasizing a type of message which our model suggests would enhance the religion's chances for early success.[29] What happened to membership after this shift?

> ... by 1951 five thousand members were gathered behind the new president, Josei Toda. The next year the membership increased to eleven thousand households. In 1956, the number had increased to four hundred thousand households. ...[30]

Perhaps we can safely discount the early growth of *Sokagakkai* in light of the fact that almost all religions were growing somewhat—largely due to the traditional Japanese refusal to settle for only one religion. As William P. Woodward has noted:

> Consequently, according to the Ministry of Education, the total number of adherents of all religions in 1959 (133,811,316) exceeded by about forty million the total population of the country (93,419,000).[31]

The important fact is the increase in the *rate* of growth by 1956. It seems reasonable to assume that *Sokagakkai* had succeeded in establishing a firm base among the economically and organismically deprived.

The postulated developmental model included two other characteristics of

[28]Toda, op. cit., page 63.

[29]Later, we shall consider the implications of the decline in emphasis on the integrative function in the 1957-58 period.

[30]Thomsen, op. cit., page 85.

[31]William P. Woodward, "A Statistical Survey of Religions in Japan," *Contemporary Religions in Japan*, Vol. II, No. 4 (December, 1961), pp. 34 f, 46; reprinted in Offner, op. cit., page 19.

the message. We shall examine the flexibility of *Sokagakkai's* message in depth when we discuss the more recent development of the religion. The *proselytizing* element was certainly present in Nichiren's preaching; it was no less present in Toda's. Two terms, taken from Nichiren's writings, were used by Toda to provide the expansionist ethic for the movement. *Shakubuku* refers to the aggressive conversion of non-believers; *Kosen-rufu* refers to the conversion of the world. Toda's emphasis on *shakubuku* and *kosen-rufu* appears later in his career, as did the emphasis on worldly benefits. Near the end of his career, he wrote a book entitled *Shakubuku Kyoten*: a handbook on conversion methods. The book is organized around the various types of resistance which a member may meet. Toda's last lectures available to the English reader were delivered to the Youth Division, inculcating an evangelistic sense of responsibility for becoming the *avant-garde* of the Japanese nation and the Third Civilization.

The Initial Group

It has already been suggested that the initial, prewar group which was formed by Makiguchi and Toda consisted of close friends of the cofounders. The earliest converts were relatives and friends of members. The organizational literature and the testimonials of members seems to indicate that this was the conversion model even during the rapid growth late in Toda's life. During the rapid growth in membership, the relationship between leader and followers began undergoing a definite change. This change was reflected in the beginning of Toda's July 18, 1954 speech (quoted above).

> Although I am to give you a talk, I do not wish to speak as if delivering a lecture. Perhaps some of you here have just become new members. I really feel sorry, because I now seldom have the opportunity to talk with you. As for the old-timers, I could talk with them personally, listen to their stories, and give them necessary advice. Therefore I hope you will listen to me just as if we were face-to-face having a conversation.[32]

This situation may have been at least partly responsible for the tightly knit organization which seems to have existed from the early days of the movement. One feature of this organization was the practice of assigning the new convert to the *kumi* (squad) of the member who had converted him. This practice provided face-to-face reinforcement which Toda was no longer able to offer.

Although Toda had begun, in the manner of Makiguchi, by directing his broad and sophisticated appeal to a reform of the entire world, he later came to stress the importance of converting the Japanese population. Increasingly, the goal of *kosen-rufu* was Japan rather than the world. His teaching became more provincial in this regard. The term *"Sokagakkai"* seems to have taken on a particular, national meaning. Throughout his career as leader of the group, Toda

[32]Toda, op. cit., page 97.

spoke less of Buddhism and *Nichiren Shoshu*, and more of *Sokagakkai*. A content analysis of his speeches shows a steady tendency in that direction.

Period	Percentage of references to the movement as *"Sokagakkai"*
10 July '49-30 March '53	19%
20 May '53-1 Aug '55	21%
1 Sept '55-1 April '58	49%

We shall return to this point later to examine the effects of an international appeal in the more recent days of the movement.

In summary, then, the initial group was based on an appeal in terms of economic and organismic deprivation, primarily. Conversion took place mainly among friends and relatives. As it became impossible for Toda to maintain face-to-face relations with all followers, an organizational structure was established to serve the same function. It is debatable whether the religion had succeeded in creating value as Makiguchi had intended, but it must be conceded that it *had* created certain facilities: a visible group of believers, an organizational structure, and a specific identity: *Sokagakkai*.

The Expansion Phase

The final section of this analysis will deal with that phenomenon which captured the imagination of Niebuhr and so many theorists since. We have noted the sect-like beginnings of *Sokagakkai* and have analyzed certain elements which would allow it to grow and develop. We know that it has grown; now let us see how it has changed.

It was suggested in the discussion of the developmental model, that an expanding religion should be located on the larger communication network. This was certainly the case in postwar Japan. Her economic redevelopment was a serious concern of the United States and other countries after the war. The Japanese people themselves responded to the challenge, and today Japan is an important import-export nation. Additionally, Japan was considered a strategic defense location and is populated by a large complement of foreign military personnel. Although there are no reliable statistics, it is generally felt that *Sokagakkai* has been primarily an urban phenomenon. It has largely availed itself of the victims of rapid industrialization and urbanization. Perhaps because the appearance of the American military personnel both symbolize and compound those problems, the *Sokagakkai* seem especially strong in those areas around American military bases. It becomes evident, then, that *Sokagakkai* has been in an excellent position to reach out to a larger population than that of native Japan. It is hardly surprising that the bulk of foreign converts have been American servicemen. Most of these conversions involved a Japanese girl-friend or a Japanese wife who was a member. This pattern has held true, not only with regard to American conversion, but also for other non-Orientals. Some of the converts have been merchantmen putting into port in Japan, but even these have been effected primarily through Japanese wives and girl-friends.

Wilson's article implies that this stage of *Sokagakkai's* development should be marked by a formalization of leadership roles and by a decline in member participation. The process of religious education and examination which has been institutionalized in the movement confirms his first expectation, but it has tended to deny the second. The leaders of *Nichiren Shoshu* are still trained and chosen in the traditional manner, but the lay leaders of *Sokagakkai* are chosen largely on the basis of periodic examinations. The requirements for leadership positions are definite and rigorous, and the responsibilities are carefully specified. If anything, however, they represent a continuation of member participation. In January, 1963, when the membership of *Sokagakkai* had just reached three million families, some 500,000 members took examinations for leadership positions. It should be noted that this fact does not mean simply that many people showed up for an examination, but, rather, that some half million members devoted a considerable amount of effort and study in preparation. The author was greatly surprised to find groups of members gathering three or four times a week for study group meetings in preparation for the examinations. This phenomenon hardly fits the accepted picture of a religion getting larger and losing the real commitment of its members.

The continued high level of member participation clearly contradicts Wilson's model and it provides a definite exception to what appears to be the normal transition from sect to church organization. *Sokagakkai* seems to have accomplished this deviation through its highly integrated organizational structure (see the earlier discussion of the history of the movement). Rather than simply growing larger at all levels of organization, *Sokagakkai* has maintained its primary-group character in its *kumi*. Rather than enlarging, the *kumi* have multiplied. Therefore even when the organization is several million strong, each member belongs to an active *kumi* of fourteen or fifteen coreligionists. Rather than losing himself in the "audience" characteristic of most Christian congregations, the *Sokagakkai* member finds himself meeting with and responsible to a small group of friends and relatives who are aware of his actual religious activities. Though the call to proselytize may originate from above, individual efforts and successes are reviewed and noted within the face-to-face *kumi*. Certainly the highly integrated organization of proselytization is crucial to the continued growth of *Sokagakkai* among Japanese, but we shall see later that the whole process has generated special problems for its American members.

Our developmental model further suggests that during the expansion phase, a world-proselytizing religion must begin to break down its original provincial character. This breakdown is not simply a matter of publishing materials in foreign languages, though that practice enhances such a shift. It was suggested earlier that under Toda, the name *Sokagakkai* had taken on a specifically Japanese connotation. With this in mind, it is interesting to note the speeches of Daisaku Ikeda, the third and current president. When we analyze the latter's speeches in terms of the types of reference terms used to refer to the movement, we find a shift in just the opposite direction from that of Toda.

Period	Percentage of references to the movement as "Sokagakkai"
9 May '60-23 Sept '60	58%
31 Oct. '60-1 Jan '63	54%
15 Feb '63-16 Sept '63	46%
7 Oct '63-25 Feb '64	34%

If, in fact, the term *Sokagakkai* had become primarily associated with the Japanese movement, we can now understand a return to its identity as *Nichiren Shoshu*, True Buddhism, etc.

Parallel to this shift in identity, the nature of Ikeda's lectures have changed also. Far from being aimed at rebuilding a new Japan, they take the world as their object. A brief perusal of the titles of his lectures in the recent *Seikyo News* is indicative of this change.

"True Buddhism for All People"—11 Feb '64
"Peaceful Revolution Sweeping The World"—4 Feb '64
"World Propagation of Buddhism Is Natural Trend of Universe"—16 Sept '63
"True Buddhism Embodies Principles of Democracy"—19 Aug '63

Similarly, the banner headline of the August 12, 1963 issue: "Sokagakkai Seeks World Peace And Happiness Of All Mankind." Oddly enough, this approach is virtually the same one used by Toda in his earliest years as head of the movement, but, as I have contended, the situation was not right for such a message at that time. Today, this type of proclamation lends legitimacy to the religion's international expansion, rather than marking it as pretentious.

It was asserted earlier that economic and organismic deprivation could not sustain a movement for very long. As the *Sokagakkai* moves through its expansion phase, we should expect to find a shift in the types of deprivations resolved by the movement. It is not possible at this time to present good statistical evidence of this shift, but the reader of the *Seikyo News* can scarcely help noticing a new breed of testimonials. In addition to the regular type of healings and financial windfalls, there have appeared a series of testimonials dealing with a new range of problems. The following are a few examples from the *Seikyo News:*

I worked hard at my job, but was constantly in a state of unhappiness. (March 31, 1965)
I lost all desires to do the evil things that thrilled me before. I began to enjoy life again. (January 21, 1964)

> I have tried practically almost every religion you can imagine, but many of them did not satisfy me, and since I converted to Nichiren Shoshu I have found what I have been looking for for a long time. (December 24, 1963).

As a final example of the shift in emphasis, we turn to the editorial summary accompanying the headline: "Widow of Russian Birth Finds Confidence in Life."

> Most women who are generally called "widows" have parted from their husbands by death or divorce. If there is no child, loneliness deepens and life becomes aimless unless they have particular object worth living for. Once Mrs. Alice Mashurzeff was among such women but since she accepted belief in Nichiren Shoshu and knew the essence of existence by learning the teaching of Nichiren Daishonin, she changed her life to be of confidence and hope for the future. (January 1, 1964)

This quotation contains virtually every item which Glock considers in his discussion of social deprivation with regard to American church members. Although Alice also discarded her wheel-chair after embracing *Nichiren Shoshu*, it is interesting to note the benefits which are singled out for editorial comment.

Traditional sect-church theory postulates a change in recruitment patterns which, in part, marks the transition from one form of organization to the other. Churches inherit their members from the second generation. Our developmental model further suggested that as the religion began expanding and attempting to capture an international following, converts would be found through other than the face-to-face conversion model. It is a little early to test the traditional notion, although there is no reason to presume that it will not hold true. However, it is possible to find evidence that the new pattern suggested by the model is already appearing. While a September 10, 1963 *Look* magazine article on *Sokagakkai* by Richard Okamoto[33] should have instilled nothing but fear and alarm in the hearts of readers, the results were not always in that direction.

> I was a Roman Catholic. But I had been searching for religion which would make my life meaningful. . . . Yes, when I read two lines of the *Look* article, I was convinced very definitely that the article was so distorted that I could not believe all those things mentioned about the Sokagakkai were true. Then, I made up my mind to know more about the Sokagakkai. . . . (February 25, 1964)

[33]This "Japan issue" of *Look* magazine carried Mr. Okamoto's article under the subtitle: "A booming economy has spawned a militant new religion with 10 million adherents bent on dominating the world." Although the author mentions discussions with *Sokagakkai* leaders, his article is a work of thinly guised alarmism and is often erroneous. His most blatant error lies with his bizarre translation of the chant *Nam-myoho-renge-kyo* as "I am the Supreme Power." I can only assume that Okamoto has confused *Sokagakkai* with *Ananaikyo*, founded in 1949 by Nakano Yonosuke and based on the study of spiritualism and astronomy. During the *Chinkon* ritual of this latter group, believers sit cross-legged on the floor staring at a black stone through the hole formed by their closed fists, concentrating on some thought such as "I am God."

This middle-aged American musician is not the only member to have written directly to the *Sokagakkai* after hearing about it through the media. The original pattern of making contact through friends and relatives is still the predominant one, but we should expect to find more and more of this new pattern appearing in the future.

A common indictment against religion in America today is that it is continually adapting to society and no longer exercises a definite influence over social behavior. It is frequently suggested that such a tendency toward accommodation is a necessary feature of the sect becoming a church, in that membership rules must become less stringent in order to maintain the second generation which has not joined out of religious zeal. It is only natural to expect that if the religion comes to recognize the legitimacy of the secular society, some mechanisms must be created to reduce the dissonance existing between the two orders. We have already suggested that the same problem holds true for the religion which attempts to create a membership extending across national, ethnic and social boundaries. Not only must the religion reduce its disparity with a given set of secular norms and values, but it must accomplish this reduction with regard to a number of societies and diverse views of the same society. Thus, we should expect certain beliefs and practices of *Sokagakkai* to be modified as the movement expands to different social levels and different nations. Even in this seemingly fanatic and intolerant religion, such has been the case.

My first realization of this trend came during an American meeting in Japan. The Japanese discussion leader was answering questions. One member complained that the incense to be burned at the family altar irritated his asthma. The Japanese leader conceded that he could omit the burning of incense until his faith had cured his asthma. In answer to the seemingly petty complaint that Americans were not accustomed to the rather tiring Japanese kneeling position, the leader recommended that the members alternate between kneeling and sitting on a low stool until they became accustomed to the traditional position.

The most astounding accommodation, however, has been in the concept of proselytization. We have discussed the practice of *shakubuku* at length. The aggressiveness of this procedure cannot be stressed too strongly. And once a person has joined, the same tactics may be used to keep him faithful. To quote from the December 7, 1962 edition of the *Yomiuri Shimbun*:

A newspaper dealer in Tenjincho Hamamatsu, who left the aggressive Buddhist religious sect Soka Gakkai last October, complained to police last night that nine local Soka Gakkai had tried to lynch him.

It should be noted that the *Yomiuri* has never given the *Sokagakkai* a very favorable press, but the story is probably true. The author has noted this type of religious fervor in his contacts with many *Sokagakkai* members. One of the perennial problems of American members, however, is the hesitance to express such zeal. With some exception, the American members have been willing to pray to *Gohonzon* and to keep the faith, but they have been generally unwilling to carry the message fervently to their friends. The generally negative attitude of the U.S. miliary has undoubtedly added to this problem. Such a situation presented the *Sokagakkai* with something of a dilemma.

The March 17, 1964 issue of the *Seikyo News* carried as its lead article, a piece written by General Director Koji Harashima under the headline: "Method of Propagation Differs Outside Japan." Another article on page one bore the title: "No Shakubuku Abroad, President Ikeda says." The heading of Vice-General Director Hiroshi Hojo's question and answer section was: "Flexible Application of Buddhism is Necessary in Overseas Area." The glossary of Buddhist terms, a regular feature, contained a new term.

> SHOJU
>
> Shoju is a mild way of propagating the Buddhism, that is to introduce the true religion to people admitting the false doctrines of the inferior religions or sects. In the period of Mappo (2,000 years after the death of Sakyamuni) Shoju is used in the country where there has not been the influence of Buddhism.

Shoju appeared in the glossary sections of the next two issues. In the March 24, 1964 issue, President Ikeda reiterated the distinction.

> When general ignorance of Buddhism prevails in a country, Shoju should be adopted ... when slanders against Buddhism permeate a country, Shakubuku should be used....

How different this is from Toda's pronouncement, thirteen years prior.

> The Daishonin strongly preaches that a man should practice Shakubuku, and unless he practices Shakubuku, he will not be able to attain enlightenment. What strong words they are—whether he be a priest or a layman, one will fall into hell if he does not practice Shakubuku! He declares that a man will positively attain enlightenment when he practices Shakubuku.[34]

Fortunately for the expansion of *Sokagakkai*, Nichiren had indeed mentioned these two methods, but *shoju* had gone unnoticed until this time.

The final example of recent accommodations is to be found in Sokagakkai's view of other religions. This issue is a particularly crucial one with converted memberships. *Sokagakkai* has compounded the problem by its inductive approach to conversion, encouraging people to *try* the religion and to experience its benefits. If the new member does not reap the promised rewards, he is assured that he may leave with no difficulty. A problem exists, however, with regard to the "provisional" member's relationship to his old religion, and particularly with respect to the religious articles which he may possess. What does a Christian do with his cross and Bible during this period of testing? The

[34]Toda, op. cit., page 76.

accepted solution in the past has been to destroy them. Tearing up his Bible was a sure sign of commitment to the test. If the prospective convert was unwilling to do this, the missionaries were not. This practice has not enhanced *Sokagakkai's* image in the press. In response to the growing resistance to this practice on the part of the international membership, these articles are no longer "satanized" but are simply secularized. To quote Hiroshi Hojo in the same question and answer section:

> In every religion, there may be several religious materials: amulets, cross, the Bible, Buddha's image or idol. New converts may keep them if they wish. .... However, they will soon realize that the Gohonzon is the only object that can give true happiness to every worshipper.

If this were not sufficient accommodation, he goes on to point out that *Sokagakkai* is not really "Anti-Christian," but simply "Non-Christian."

> According to the teaching of President Ikeda, the very substance of God, which Christian believers pray to, is nothing more but the supreme law of Nam-myoho-renge-kyo, the gist of Buddhism, which was materialized in the form of the Gohonzon for believer's daily prayer.

This is the current status of *Sokagakkai*, the bearer of Nichiren's message. Nichiren—street preacher, rabble rouser, the first intolerant Buddhist; Nichiren who announced to a shocked Japan:

> The Jodo School is hell; Zen is devil; Shingon will cause national collapse, and Ritsu is an enemy of the country.[35]

As Director Hojo translates this message:

> If there is an absolute and inflexible pattern of life for a believer in Nichiren Shoshu, almost all of ten million Sokagakkai members can hardly practice the Buddhism of Nichiren Daishonin.
> Therefore, Nichiren Daishonin permits the flexible application of Buddhism for believers in specific social conditions or in foreign countries where customs and manners are quite different from Japan.

Summary

The preceding has been a brief look at what may go down in history as an internationally successful religious movement. We have used this case study to examine some of the factors which may affect the ultimate success of this or any other world-proselytizing religion. As nearly as one may determine, *Sokagakkai*

---

[35]Quoted from Vergilius Ferm (Ed.), *Encyclopedia of Religion* (Paterson, New Jersey: Littlefield, Adams and Co.,) page 105.

arose largely out of the chaotic wake of post war Japan, directing its appeal at economic and organismic deprivations. Its initial group of followers was recruited largely from among friends and relatives. In these respects, it is not significantly different from countless other movements in Japan.

During its current expansion phase, however, it has exhibited at least three tendencies which seem critical to its success. First, while growing larger, it has nonetheless maintained the primary group characteristic of its *kumi*. Second, it has lessened its emphasis on economic and organismic deprivations and has included an appeal to the socially, psychically and ethically deprived. Finally, it has renewed its direct appeal to any international community, de-emphasizing the provincial characteristics of its earlier days and accommodating the social and cultural differences of the people it seeks to enlist.

I have attempted in this paper to suggest some of the important variables involved in the study of world-proselytizing religions. Hopefully the examination of *Sokagakkai* will stimulate new attention to the problem and lay the groundwork for further analysis.

Chapter 19

The Cross and the Commune
An Interpretation of the Jesus People*

Donald W. Peterson and Armand L. Mauss

> And it shall come to pass in the last days, saith God, I will pour out of my
> Spirit upon all flesh: and your sons and your daughters shall prophesy, and
> your young men shall see visions, and your old men shall dream dreams.
>
> (Acts 2:17)

Late in the 1960s the youth movement of that tumultuous decade produced
a surprising spin-off: hippies with religion. American adults had only recently
become somewhat accustomed to regular hippies and had developed fairly
standard responses to them based on mixed attitudes of reluctant tolerance,
amusement, and contempt. Hippies were drop-outs from respectable society,
which was shameful enough, but at least they were gentle and were not
trouble-makers like the young campus militants and political agitators of the
same period. Because they rejected and withdrew from most of the institutions
of the Establishment, the hippies were thought to be unchurched and probably
atheists as well. Certainly the libertine life of drugs and free sex attributed to
hippies was an affront to traditional religion. What an anomaly, then, were
youngsters who *looked* like hippies but who *talked* like fundamentalist and
pentecostal preachers![1]

The development of the Jesus movement (participants are called Jesus people
or Jesus freaks) is so recent that very little scholarly literature exists. Journalistic
accounts proliferate, and social scientists have produced some descriptive work

*This is the first publication of this article. All rights reserved. Permission to reprint must
be obtained from the publisher and authors.

[1]The research on which this article is based was made possible in part through the facilities
and equipment of the Seattle Urban Research Station of the Department of Sociology,
Washington State University.

on the movement,[2] but questions about the conditions that activated the movement and have sustained it, about who is recruited and by what motivations, and about the movement's possible long-range consequences for its adherents and for the larger society remain to be answered.

We intend to inquire into these larger issues, especially the sociopsychological questions that apply to recruitment and adherence to the movement. The chapter is based partly on a review of some journalistic and descriptive literature and also reports the results of an empirical study of the Jesus people that was conducted during late 1971 and early 1972 in Washington and Idaho.[3] The senior author, long haired, bearded, and modestly fluent in the "hip" argot, spent seven days in a Seattle commune, three days in a rural commune in northwestern Idaho, and a hundred or so hours working the streets with freaks and "rapping" at their I Am Coffee House in Spokane, Washington. Informal interviews were conducted with some fifty members of the various communes. In some instances these mainly involved listening to lengthy testimonies and case histories of commune members. Frequently, however, it was possible to engage in dialogue with individuals about their movement, their beliefs, their perceptions, their aspirations, the meaning of biblical passages, and the like. In

[2]The Jesus *people*, who are the subject of this chapter, can be viewed as a part of the larger Jesus *movement*, which also includes youth groups such as Campus Crusade for Christ, Youth for Christ, and others. The various segments of the larger movement have in common a fundamentalist and evangelical content and probably similar social and age compositions as well. The chief differences appear to be those of *style*; the Jesus people (or Jesus freaks) exhibit a left-wing, hippie style, in great contrast to the more restrained, "straight," intellectual style of, say, the Intervarsity Christian Fellowship. One could perhaps arrange all of the segments of the Jesus movement into a continuum of style and demeanor. The term *Christian World Liberation Front* is used in some parts of the country, particularly around Berkeley, to refer to roughly the left half of this hypothetical continuum, with its miscellany of freaks and communes. These left-wing groups are of recent origin, but the youth groups on the right (for example, the Campus Crusade) have in some instances been around for decades but have only recently begun to grow and increase in vitality. (See the references in footnote 3, below.)

[3]See, for example, L. Baker, "Holiday Hiatus at a Commune," *San Francisco Chronicle*, November 25, 1971, p. 5; B. Graham, "Something for Youth to Believe," *Reader's Digest* 94 (June 1969): 77-81; J. Nolan, "Jesus Now: Hogwash and Holy Water," *Ramparts* 10 (August 6, 1971): 20-26; N. V. Peale, "We Need Their Faith," *Reader's Digest* 99 (December 1971): 138-141; E. Plowman, "Pacific Northwest Revival in the Underground: Street Christians in Spokane," *Christianity Today*, January 29, 1971, pp. 34-35; E. Plowman, "Jesus Presses are Rolling: Underground Newspapers," *Christianity Today*, April 9, 1971, pp. 3-8; R. Ruppert, "The Children of God" (and related articles), *Seattle Times*, October 17, 1971, pp. A-1, B-6, and B-10; W. Stimson, "The Jesus Revolution," *Spokesman-Review Sunday Magazine* (Spokane), January 30, 1972, pp. 6-11; (no author) "The Jesus People," *U.S. News and World Report* 77 (March 22, 1971): 97; D. M. Williams, "Close-up on the Jesus People," *Christianity Today*, August 27, 1971, pp. 5-7; and the following articles (no authors given) from *Time*: "Street Christians: Jesus as the Ultimate Trip," August 3, 1970; "The New Rebel Cry: Jesus Is Coming!" June 21, 1971; "Fellow-Traveling with Jesus: The Way and the Process," September 6, 1971; and "Whose Children?" January 24, 1972. For an official chronicle and interpretation of the movement by a sympathizer, see Edward Plowman, *The Jesus Movement* (Spokane, Wash.: Voice of Elijah [publisher of *Truth*], 1972). As we were finishing this chapter we became aware of a recent sociological account: Ronald Enroth et al., *The Jesus People* (Eerdman Publishers, 1972). Although we have not yet had a chance to study this work carefully, it appears to emphasize description more than analysis.

addition, twelve issues of *Truth*, the main publication of the movement in the Northwest, were subjected to content analysis as a supplementary source of data and as a check on the observations and interviews.[4]

We begin our report with a brief description of the Jesus people and subsequently analyze our data to illuminate the questions of to whom the movement appeals and why. We also have occasion to test the applicability and utility to our data of some of the theoretical ideas set forth in chapter 16 of this volume.

Overview of the Movement

Published accounts and reports from many of our own informed respondents in the movement indicate that the Jesus people began to appear perhaps as early as 1967, primarily along the West Coast but also in Texas.[5] The details of the movement's genesis are not well known, but apparently the origin was concurrent with the growing disillusionment about the hippie way of life that marked the closing years of the sixties. In the Haight Ashbury, in the Village, and in other well-known hippie territories murders, rapes, disastrous drug trips, and many other incidents eventually destroyed the mystique of love and gentleness that once surrounded the "flower children." One of our respondents, who is now an elder in a Spokane communal house, expressed the problem with compelling succinctness: "When I felt that I had to start carrying a knife around in the Haight, man, I knew that the whole hippie trip was over."[6] Shortly thereafter he joined a band of Jesus freaks (which they came to be called by 1970 and which they accept fully and even use among themselves).

---

[4]Although the Jesus people are found in various parts of the nation (and even abroad), they are primarily a phenomenon of the western United States and are especially strong in urban areas along the West Coast. The Washington contingent is active and numerous. It is tied to other branches along the coast by some mobility and rotation on the parts of members and by exchanges of news stories with the Christian underground newspapers in other states. As far as we can judge from our research, the Washington Jesus people are similar enough to their counterparts elsewhere to make our account reasonably generalizable to the movement as a whole.

[5]It is important for the reader to understand the restraints imposed upon our observations and interviews. In the absence of prior knowledge about the Jesus people, structured a priori interview schedules or observational guides would have been contrived and pretentious. Also, it was difficult to find the seclusion necessary to complete interviews. In a familial setting like a commune or street group, surveillance, even if unintended, is constant. Some subterfuges were used in order to get down some notes on conversations and observations reasonably close to the times when they occurred. Mainly, however, the notes from a day's observations and conversations would have to be written from memory at the end of the day. Although our interviews were intensive and our observations prolonged, our data were compiled more in the form of what Lofland calls "jotted notes" and "field notes" than in the form of carefully constructed schedules or guides (J. Lofland, *Analyzing Social Settings* [Belmont, Calif.: Wadsworth Publishing Co., 1971], chap. 5). Thus the conversational excerpts quoted in this chapter are only virtual quotations, but we are confident that they reflect both the substance and the style of our respondents' remarks fully enough to be taken as actual quotations recorded on the spot.

[6]Plowman, 1972, and the *Time* articles cited in footnote 3.

[7]Respondent no. 34.

How and why these hippies' disillusionment and reassessment suddenly turned to Christianity is one of the interesting and unresolved questions we have encountered about the movement. (Some—namely the Hare Krishna cult—accepted Buddhism.) The historical Jesus had been something of a folk hero among hippies for some time; posters and poetry from the early sixties had carried the Jesus-as-hippie motif. There is some evidence that the turn toward Jesus may have been brought about partly by the early efforts of some "straight" young evangelists from Pentecostal churches who began promoting Jesus as an antidote and substitute for drug addiction.[8] The overwhelming impression from our interviews with freaks, from the accounts of other investigators and journalists,[9] and from numerous testimonials printed in the underground newspapers of the movement is that recruits to the Jesus people are disproportionately former hippies, many of whom have been drug addicts or heavy users and nearly all of whom have drifted for a period. The apparent success of the movement in keeping converts off drugs has in fact helped to gain the unsolicited approval of such Establishment evangelists as Billy Graham and Norman Vincent Peale,[10] an approval regarded as the kiss of death by freaks who are trying to maintain their identity separate from organized religion. Allusions to a former drug-using tradition are common enough in the Jesus people publications to justify the belief that the movement self-consciously presents itself as an alternative to the drug culture. For example, one sees such slogans and headlines as "Youths High on Christ," "Get Addicted to God," and the like.[11]

In addition to their hippie and/or drug-using backgrounds, the Jesus people have other common characteristics: they are very young (average age twenty-one); they come from a predominantly middle-class (even upper-middle class) background, although they include many working-class members as well; they come from all types of religious and non-religious backgrounds, with perhaps disproportionate representations of Catholics and Jews; they tend to be strongly Anglo-Saxon in composition, with occasional Chicanos and Indians (in the Northwest) but only rarely any Negroes, and almost all are dropouts from college or even from high school.

The first five years or so of the movement's history have seen rapid growth and dispersion and the usual pattern of disorganization, schisms, and defections. The fortunes of the movement have varied considerably from time to time and from place to place, depending on sources of recruits, the support of "outside" friends, and the availability of talented and charismatic leadership. The movement as a whole has been very loosely tied together; numerous little bands organize their own communes or houses around gifted leaders, or elders. The size of the movement's membership is very difficult to estimate, partly because of its

[8]*Time*, 1970; Ruppert, op. cit.

[9]Ruppert, op. cit.; *U.S. News and World Report*, op. cit.; and *Time*, op. cit.

[10]B. Graham, op. cit., and N. V. Peale, op. cit.

[11]*Truth* (official organ of the Spokane and Seattle Jesus people, published by the Voice of Elijah, Inc., Spokane, Washington), December 1971.

loose, decentralized nature and partly because of the fairly high rate of defection and turnover, estimated at 50 percent per year by a Seattle elder.[12] Estimates of membership range up to "many thousands," most of whom are living throughout North America in communes or "Christian houses," which may number as many as 600 (200 in California alone) and which have an average of perhaps fifty residents each.[13]

One endemic problem of new social movements is their tendency to separate into factions. This tendency derives in large part from the differential needs of the membership and leadership and from the diversity of ways in which they respond to the constant pressures of cooptation and repression from the larger society.[14] We have learned of many schisms from our informants, but most of them seem to be localized and rather small. The most important division has probably been the break-off of the Children of God faction in the late summer of 1971. Our interviews and those of Ruppert indicate that the chief issues were relationships with the larger society (especially the churches) and discipline within the movement.[15]

The Jesus people have the "hang-loose" style of the hippies and a friendly, effervescent approach to proselyting. One is greeted on the street or in the coffee house with loving salutations, of which "Jesus loves you" is perhaps the most frequent. An indifferent or unfriendly response almost always brings from the "street freak" a friendly withdrawal and departure rather than an offensive persistence, particularly if one is quick to buy a copy of the local Christian underground newspaper. The hang-loose ethic also expresses itself in the comings and goings of commune residents and in the high turnover rate already mentioned. Discipline is rarely pushed to the point of causing arguments.

[12]Ruppert, op. cit.

[13]Ruppert, op. cit.; *Time*, op. cit. (all articles); Plowman, January 1971 and April 1971; and L. Kinsolving, "The Children of God Stomp up a Storm," *San Francisco Sunday Examiner and Chronicle*, March 26, 1972, p. B-6.

[14]R. Turner and L. Killian, *Collective Behavior* (Englewood Cliffs, N.J.: Prentice-Hall, 1957), part four.

[15]Ruppert, op. cit.; Kinsolving, op. cit.; and *Newsweek* (no author given), "Days in the Life of the Children of God," March 30, 1971, pp. 59-65. The so-called Children of God are an extremist or militant faction *within* the Jesus movement. Like the rest of the Jesus people, they maintain a hippie demeanor, live in communes, and "work the streets"; they also share the same general theological outlook. However, they take a rather grim and ascetic stance toward the world and toward organized religion in particular. They may offer expressions of God's love in their street preaching, but they are likely to parade about in the biblical sackcloth and ashes, carrying signs about imminent doom. They have even invaded the services of the "worldly" churches with that demeanor. They glory in persecution, and their witnessing style is definitely hard sell. Even more than the rest of the freaks, the Children of God live a fully communal existence; all incoming property from the converts is turned over to the communes (including such items as automobiles). Their separation from the world is symbolized by the new single names which they take from the Bible to replace their own family and given names. They have grown rapidly since their schism from the rest of the freaks began in the summer of 1971, and they claim a dropout rate of no more than 15 percent, due to the greater degree of commitment and discipline required of recruits from the first. The Children of God are interesting as a classic example of the tendency of new movements to divide and as a manifestation of the Jesus people par excellence. We have therefore included observations about them in our analysis, taking care to indicate where distinctions are necessary between them and the rest of the freaks.

In its relatively short history the Jesus movement has developed a surprising number of institutions and enterprises, one of which is publications, particularly (but by no means only) newspapers, such as *Truth* in the Pacific Northwest, *Right On!* in the San Francisco Bay area, and the *Hollywood Free Paper* in southern California. The format and content of these papers are very similar; circulation ranges from 100,000 to 400,000.

Another important institution is the coffee house, which serves both as a socializing milieu for the freaks and as an "outreach" device for making contact with young people who are "searching for something." The atmosphere is conducive to low-pressure proselyting in the form of "raps" with people who drop in, set against "Jesus rock" background music blaring from juke boxes or stereo systems. Coffee is usually free. In midafternoon, when visiting begins in earnest, the place is filled with animated conversation, testimonies, and interjections of "Praise God!" or "Jesus Loves You!" and the like. The mystique of the coffee house is enhanced by the name, which tends to be a highly poetic or allegorical reference to biblical or Holy Land lore—for example, I Am, House of Joshua, House of Amos, Cave Adullam, House of Elijah.

The institution at the heart of the movement, though, is the commune, or Christian house, which may take the form of an actual house (large or small) or even a hotel. The commune group is a combination of family, work group, and congregation. Sexual segregation is carefully maintained, with males and females living in different parts of the house or hall (married couples are usually able to get separate rooms). The routine is similar to that found in cooperative dormitories on college campuses. The "elders" (sometimes individual men or women, sometimes married couples, sometimes committees) provide leadership and supervision, functioning partly as "resident parents" and partly as spiritual leaders. Rules governing chores, street work, personal conduct, and the comings and going of members are observed with a minimum of pressure and regimentation. The daily routine usually calls for Bible study classes in the mornings before the members set out for street work (proselyting) and prayer meetings in the late afternoons and evenings. The latter function as worship services in every essential respect; they have a strongly pentecostal atmosphere and include praying, testifying, preaching, instrumental music, dancing and wiggling about, and interjections of "Praise God" and the like.

A Theoretical Interpretation of the Jesus People

The Jesus movement illustrates particularly well the need for the corrective elaboration on the sect-church theoretical tradition that has been undertaken in recent years. The earliest formulations of this theoretical tradition by Weber, Troeltsch, and Niebuhr (drawing in part also upon Marx) placed undue emphasis on the factor of *economic* deprivation and status differences in accounting for the rise of new sects. Later scholars have pointed out that other needs may also give rise to a sectlike religious style.[16] Most recently, Glock (in chapter 16 of

16See, for example, B. Wilson, *Sects and Society* (London: William Heinemann), and J. M. Yinger, *The Scientific Study of Religion* (New York: Macmillan Co., 1970), chap. 13.

the present volume) has postulated at least *five* different types of "deprivation" which may result in the rise of new sects (at the societal level) and/or in the susceptibility to new sects (at the individual level). Attempts to resolve these various kinds of deprivation may take *either* religious or secular form; in their religious form they characteristically result in the emergence of new sects. This conceptualization is particularly important in the case of the Jesus people, who because they have a largely bourgeois social base would not fit well with the traditional view of sect membership as economically deprived. At the same time, there is evidence of various other kinds of deprivation from the Glock taxonomy.

The central notion of the Glock elaboration on the sect-church tradition is expressed in the following paragraph.

> We suggest that a necessary precondition for the rise of any organized social movement, whether it be religious or secular, is a situation of felt-deprivation. However, while a necessary condition, deprivation is not, in itself, a sufficient condition. Also required are the additional conditions that the deprivation be shared, that no alternative institutional arrangements for its resolution are perceived, and that a leadership emerge with an innovating idea for building a movement out of the existing deprivation.[17]

Glock discusses the five types of perceived deprivation that may issue in new sects or cults, and he goes on to suggest some of the contingencies and typical organizational forms through which each type of deprivation may be expressed.[18] As far as the Jesus people are concerned, we have already noted the doubtful appropriateness and relevance of the *economic* type of deprivation in understanding the roots of their movement. We also note in passing that a second type of deprivation, called *organismic* by Glock, might have some applicability to the Jesus people, because many of the members have experienced some severe physical, mental, and nutritional problems as a result of their earlier experimentations with drugs and the hippie style of life in general. We offer this observation only as a suggestion, since our data on this point are not thorough. The three remaining types of deprivation, *ethical, psychic,* and *social,* all seem to have contributed to the genesis of the Jesus movement. The first two of these are especially likely to take *religious* (as opposed to secular) forms.

Ethical deprivation, typically a middle-class (or even an elite) phenomenon, is basically philosophical in nature. It arises from "value conflicts between the ideals of society and those of individuals or groups" or from the perceived discrepancies between ideals and social realities. A broad "anti-Establishment" stance on a variety of issues is one of the most conspicuous features of the Jesus

---

[17] See chap. 16 of the present volume.

[18] There are some interesting parallels between the deprivation theory of Glock and the theory of personal needs discussed by G. W. Allport, *The Individual and His Religion* (New York: Macmillan Co., 1950), pp. 9-27.

people (as of the hippies before them), and established religion receives special condemnation:

> The Straight Christians are the solid citizens who support the murder in Viet Nam, racism, pollution, and everything that's killing this country. They're the people who drive big pig cars, live in gaudy houses, rip off the poor, and go to church a couple of times a year to hear how pure and holy they are![19]

> Man! That's all you gotta do to get cut off is just tend to your own business! Don't get involved. Yes, just go to Church every Sunday morning and ignore the people all around you; let the rest of the world go to Hell, and Jesus said you'll be right there with them, in Hell.[20]

Almost every issue of *Truth* has at least one cartoon (seldom very clever) commenting on the hypocrisies and paradoxes in established religion. One, for example, shows two businessmen (or other "straight" types) sitting together in a pew. One turns to the other and says, "Sure, our church is filled with apathy, but who cares?"[21]

Apocalyptic jeremiads about impending disasters often accompany such condemnations:

> America is on the road to Hell! The conditions described in Revelation and in Acts paint a pretty clear picture of America today.[22]

> The country is gone; there's no way of saving it. What's terrible is that it's dragging the rest of the world down with it![23]

> America's going down for the third time, man; there's no question about it![24]

Unlike ethical deprivation, *psychic* deprivation is akin to *anomie*—that is, it is not so much a matter of value *conflicts* as a matter of value *ambiguity*. It is expressed in a "search for new values, a new faith, a quest for meaning and purpose," and it is an *intervening* variable accompanying social or economic deprivation as often as it is an independent variable. Glock does not explicitly include the *search for identity* (or for a new self-concept) under psychic deprivation, but it seems reasonable to do so, although, to be sure, problems of self-concept are perhaps as much a manifestation of social deprivation as of psychic deprivation.

[19]Respondent no. 32.
[20]*Truth*, February, 1972, p. 7.
[21]Ibid., p. 8.
[22]Respondent no. 21.
[23]Respondent no. 28.
[24]Respondent no. 36.

In the argot of the Jesus people, a new self-concept means *rebirth*, one of the most prevalent themes in their conversation and literature (this is true of most pentecostal groups). The idea and the process of rebirth carries a special appeal for Jesus people with hippie backgrounds and also, perhaps even more notably, for those who have been stigmatized by a period of deviant behavior or even crime. Testimonials from young prisoners occur frequently in *Truth* and emphasize the new identities which the prison converts have obtained as a result of their rebirth:

> I am just sorry that it took me so long to find out that Jesus is real, and what He will do for you once you just give up and decide to let Him run the show for you. . . . I haven't had anyone (in the prison) look down on me because of my decision to pack my old ways in and let Jesus show me a new way of life. I think that I was afraid of what people around the prison would say about me at first, but Jesus took care of that for me, too, so as long as I have Him on my side, what could possibly happen to me now? . . . [Now] I am allowed to go outside of these walls once every six weeks on the lifer-to-dinner program and spend 8 hours with my sponsor and his family and my girl.[25]

> Though I myself am behind these prison walls I am free. My daily prayers go out to all my brothers and sisters in Christ out there as well as my brothers in here, in hopes we can all live in unison in Christ. I'm through breaking man's laws. I'll take Jesus. Praise the Lord. . . For months I have been praying for the courage to go out among my fellow residents here and relay the wonderful blessing of knowing Jesus Christ . . . . I went back to my cell and prayed for the answer. I found it in the scriptures. . . . From that day on, I've gone out into the population allowing my Lord and precious Savior to guide me to those searching for the Answer.[26]

The first prisoner shows a sense of a new-found pride and identity as a "good maverick" within the prison and a new identification with the "straight" world outside. In the second quotation we can see a transformation of identity from "convict" to "evangelist" and the use of the concept *freedom* to mean primarily a *freedom from one's past identity* (a common use of that concept among Jesus people). Among the Children of God faction the new identity is in fact symbolized by the taking of new names from the Bible.

The experience of "rebirth" is a discussion topic of probably unsurpassed frequency among the freaks, and the "rebirth page" is a common feature of the *Truth* newspaper. The theme is usually one of a "spoiled identity" which is transformed by the conversion process:

> This is reality, man. There's no religion to it, . . . especially if you've been too BAD to be a Christian before. Like if you've tried and you couldn't

[25]*Truth*, February 1972, p. 5.
[26]Ibid.

make it. Now, Jesus is inviting all the BAD people. Forget your hang-ups; let Jesus take care of them.[27]

Some of the featured rebirths involve people who have been in prison, but most have not been to prison; most have just experienced the sordid side of life enough to have developed a spoiled identity and to welcome the chance for redefinition. One convert featured in *Truth* (at the age of nineteen) had a long history of drinking, drugs, homosexual involvements and labeling, and occasional confinement in juvenile institutions. The rebirth destroyed his dependence on the earlier (stigmatized) identity and put him in touch with peers who refurbished his self-esteem:

> Five days later, a hippy with long scraggly hair, who didn't look worth anything, said to me on the street, "God bless you." That freaked me. I had never heard that before. But the clincher was that he meant it and showed love. He told me that Jesus loved . . . even a faggot. And I believed him because I could see all those things in that kid's eyes and I could feel the love. That night Jesus came into my heart. . . . The desire for speed and booze was taken away. And thanks to God I no longer need to have sex with a guy or have that hunger for love. . . .[28]

In the same general vein are the remarks of a young sister for whom conversion had meant a new identity as a person of inherent worth rather than as a sex object:

> Before I got into the "family" guys were always talkin' about how much they loved me. Sometimes they were really convincing, but it always ended up that they really wanted me in the sack. But my Christian brothers are not like that. I'm a person, with a soul; I'm their sister in Christ.[29]

Another expression of psychic deprivation akin to the search for a new identity is the *search for meaning*. As Glock points out, when the search for meaning takes a religious form it is typically of the cult variety, and a history of switching from one cult or religion to another is usually involved. The observation that members of a certain millenarian religious group "had passed through a period of 'church-hopping,' ultimately rejected all available religious perspectives, and passed through a period of religious despair before being converted to the new movement"[30] is equally true of many members of the Jesus people. A common biographical sketch of a Jesus freak is recounted by

[27]Ibid., p. 9.

[28]*Truth*, May 1971, p. 16.

[29]Respondent no. 20.

[30]Glock, chap. 16 of the present volume.

this recent convert:

> I was into Buddhism, Hinduism, astrology, Scientology, and even witchcraft. But I just went around in circles. Each one made more questions than answers. I was into these trips while I was going to San Diego State, where I went for three years. But college was even more of a waste of time for me. It seemed like the profs were more interested in disproving theories than in proving anything. And when they did say something important, it was only a theory, you know. . . . [A]fter awhile I got really hungry for something I could hang on to. Like I got tired of questions; it was time to find some answers.[31]

Another convert's experiences were very similar:

> He studied philosophy. Then he experimented with drugs in an attempt to find some reality and escape the meaningless boredom around him. This led to a dead end, and then he began an extensive exploration of Eastern religions while lecturing on mysticism at the Free University of Montreal. . . .[32]

A prospective convert at the I Am Coffee House in Spokane put the search for meaning another way:

> "I've been searching," he said, "I've been trying to find a balance. . . . I agree wholly with the way Jesus said to live, but as far as living it in this world, that's something else. I just can't seem to find the balance. . . ."[33]

The search for meaning expressed above is accompanied by another, closely related, theme that is also often observed in the movement's publications and in conversations with the Jesus people, and which gives us still another indication of psychic deprivation—the *search for closure and simplicity.* "I just went around in circles. Each one made more questions than answers," as the problem was expressed above. When the search for simplicity is finally resolved by joining the Jesus movement, a sense of immense relief is often expressed by the convert:

> "It's so simple! You can't figure it out!" [he said]. He really had a childlike peace about him. He was just sitting in the chair shaking his head. . . . "It's so simple," he kept saying.[34]

> The utter simplicity and down-to-earth reality of what Jesus said just blew our minds![35]

31Respondent no. 27
32*Truth*, December 1971, p. 15.
33Ibid., p. 3.
34Ibid.
35*Truth*, November 1971, p. 6.

All of a sudden I could see it—two roads, a right way and a wrong way.[36]

The simplicity involved in conversion is seen by the freaks in at least two dimensions, ritual and belief, or in other words, the *conversion process* and the *belief system*. Conversion is the acceptance of Jesus, taking him into one's heart, letting him guide one's life plan, letting him make the important decisions. There are no elaborate rituals (baptism is optional), no forms to fill out, no tests, no study courses. As expressed by one prominent believer in an interview for *Truth*:

> I said, "God, I give it up; I turn my whole life over to you. You're it. You're the only one, and if that means being a missionary in Tibet, or teaching school in Georgia, or pumping gas in Pomona, or whatever you want with my life, you just take over from here. It's yours."[37]

Belief encompasses an equally simple world view: "We believe in the Bible, word for word, page for page. . . ."[38] From what we saw in practice in the communes, however, the chief emphasis was on discussion of and belief in four New Testament books—Luke, John, Acts, and Revelation. Now and then something was quoted from elsewhere in the New Testament and from Jeremiah in the Old Testament, but the biblical basis for the beliefs of the freaks appears (as is typically the case with sects) to be selective rather than comprehensive.

A search for simplicity, almost by definition, carries with it an *anti-intellectual posture*. Many freaks are unfulfilled and even deeply troubled by their academic experiences. The competing theories and the unresolved ambiguities encountered in college (or even high school) courses, together with the emphasis on success in formal education as "the way to make it," produce an intense cognitive dissonance in many youth, especially to young people who are in quest of meaning and closure. Anti-intellectualism combined with a simple faith is an effective way of resolving the dissonance.

> By my junior year, I began to lose confidence in my intellect and in intellectuals, because the more I learned, the further I got from the truth about anything. Everyone had a theory, and all defended their side of the story with every mind-trick they could muster, but no one ever proved anything. . . .[39]

> The cure for [our inability to love] can neither be taught nor learned. It cannot be arrived at rationally, nor can it be analyzed. It takes no particular training or intelligence to get it. It is the gift of God. . . .[40]

[36]Baker, op. cit.

[37]*Truth*, May 1971, p. 7.

[38]Baker, op. cit.

[39]*Truth*, December 1970, p. 3.

[40]*Truth*, January 1971, p. 9.

My head is so stuffed with chemistry, trigonometry [etc.] that it almost hurts, but Jesus is the way. . . . I know it! I know it![41]

Other evidences of an anti-intellectual posture can be seen in the frequent reference to biblical passages that seem to denigrate formal learning (for example, John 7:15-18, where the simple Jesus confounds his learned adversaries), and in the ridiculing of the theory of evolution.[42]

The anti-intellectualism of the freaks gives rise to one of their most derogatory names, the "head-tripper"—that is, one who tries to subject the teachings of Jesus to rational analysis, explanation, or deduction. Indeed, one of the hazards of being a participant-observer, we learned, is the risk of being labeled a head-tripper if in the process of drawing out a freak in conversation one seems to be posing problems of reason. Even the appearance of debating or arguing must be avoided. On one occasion, after an extremely cordial conversation with a freak in the living room of a communal house, one of us reflected on a seeming paradox in the conversation. The freak was asked how he could say he was *free* in Christ and then talk about leaving it up to Christ to guide his life in predetermined paths. The respondent fixed a straight and intense glare and replied with a mixture of disdain and surprise:

Man, you're a head-tripper! If you want to head-trip, do it someplace else. We could sit here from now until doomsday rapping about head-trips. If you want to know about Christ, the Savior, that's cool. But I'm not going to sit here and get into any asinine head-trips. They don't go anywhere.[43]

On a similar occasion the reaction was somewhat more friendly, with an expression of pity and sorrow:

Wow! I used to be into those mind-trips. They went around and around and came out nowhere. It blew my mind. You're going to be searching all your life if you stay on that route. Like, one just leads to another, and you just (you know) end up more confused than when you started. It's a bummer. I know; I've been there.[44]

Psychic deprivation, then, seems to express itself among the Jesus people in the forms of anomie, a search for a new identity or self-concept, a search for meaning, simplicity, and closure, and a disillusionment with "futile" intellectual pursuits.

There is thus a prima facie case for ethical and psychic deprivation among the Jesus people, but there is also much evidence that converts have a sense of *social deprivation* as well. Glock conceives of this kind of deprivation as a simple

41 *Truth*, March 1971, p. 11.

42 *Truth*, May 1971, p. 20.

43 Respondent no. 35

44 Respondent no. 25.

consequence of "society's propensity to value some attributes of individuals and groups more highly than others, and to distribute such societal rewards as power, status, and opportunities for social participation accordingly.... [Furthermore], social deprivation is additive in the sense that the fewer the number of desirable traits a person possesses, the lower his relative status, and the reverse is also true."[45] A sense of social deprivation might be partly a function of economic deprivation, but it differs in that it is based on one's perceptions about his *prestige and social acceptance* compared to other people's. Thus "[t]he distinction between economic and social deprivation is akin to the distinction sociologists make between social class and social status."[46] Because people derive their prestige and social acceptance only from memberships in certain groups, it follows that a lack of such membership or a lack of affiliations would be the most fundamental source of perceived social deprivation. Elsewhere Glock and his associates use this concept as the basis for a general theory of religious involvement, and they show that this manifestation of social deprivation can be successfully operationalized, measured, and used to predict the likelihood of religious involvement.[47]

Perhaps the most conspicuous expression of social deprivation among recruits to the Jesus people is the theme of the *search for belonging* that runs through their testimonies. Our discussion (for example, of the rebirth process) has included examples of such testimonies. The communal style of living, with its pseudofamilial characteristics and references, is an obvious expression at the organizational level of the search for belonging. A systematic sampling and survey analysis of Jesus freaks has not yet been done, but we were strongly impressed by the frequency with which our informants revealed that their family backgrounds were fraught with turmoil and conflict. Indeed, it has been rare to meet a freak who did not feel that his own family life had been very unhappy. It may be facile and not totally warranted to conclude that the new "family" of "brothers and sisters" in the communal houses functions as a substitute for a "normal" family life, but that impression is hard to escape; and it is confirmed by watching the filial deference and affection paid by the younger freaks to the male and female elders in charge of the houses, who relate to them very much like fathers and mothers. In the words of one young evangelist (age twenty-four) who had seen many conversions to the movement: "The kids are searching for authority, love, and understanding—ingredients missing at home."[48] A number of observers of the movement have noted that when the youngsters are converted they frequently cut off contact with their parents altogether (especially in the case of the more militant Children of God). In response, a group of alarmed parents in California and Texas reportedly have formed an organization called "the Parents' Committee to Free Our Children from the

---

45Glock, chap. 16 in this book.

46Ibid.

47C. Y. Glock et al., *To Comfort and To Challenge* (Berkeley and Los Angeles: University of California Press, 1967), chap. 5.

48*Time*, June 21, 1971, p. 59.

Children of God.[49] From the case histories we have encountered, however, we would suggest that the ruptures in communication with families had effectively occurred for most freaks long before their conversions.

The search for belonging (which might also be called the need for affiliation or the quest for *gemeinschaft*) derives not only from unfulfilling family life experiences but also from the "doping and drifting" syndrome through which many have passed since they left home. By the time a youngster has encountered a band of Jesus people, he/she typically has spent a period of months or even years with one hippie group after another, sharing few real primary relationships although perhaps a great many drug experiences. This is the story that recurs in the printed testimonials of *Truth* newspaper and in our conversations at the communes and coffee houses.

> I doped for quite awhile and I began to forget what I was looking for, so I decided to quit everything for about a month, doing absolutely nothing for anybody, including myself; and I started to go nuts again because I was so lonely. To fight off this loneliness I went downtown and looked for someone to talk to. About five minutes after I got downtown, some guy came up to me and said, "Jesus loves you, and He wants to set you free." I thought about what he said when I got home and found that I couldn't sleep. Then I did something I thought I could never do. I gave up to Jesus, and He really set me free. This was three months ago, and I found what I was looking for, love.[50]

One of our respondents, a fourteen-year-old girl, told a story in the same basic vein:

> I used to hang out at The Place [a hippie and "head" hangout]. I really got bummed out on the scene, because nobody seemed to care about you. Everybody was on their own trip. I felt like that if I had died right there, nobody would even notice. They'd just step on me on their way to the pool table. One night I got really bummed out, so I came over here [the I Am Coffee House run by Jesus freaks] to just kind of see what was happening. As soon as I walked in the door, Linda (a really good friend of mine now, who's kind of my spiritual big sister) came up to me and asked if she could help me. She could see I was bummed out, and she put her arms around me and said, "I love you." All night long the other kids talked to me and told me of Christ's love and of their love for me. It was really far out. I felt so good. I knew right then that this was a really groovy thing they were getting on.[51]

---

[49]*Time*, January 24, 1972, and Ruppert, op. cit.

[50]*Truth*, October 1971, p. 6.

[51]Respondent no. 33.

For many Jesus freaks the amelioration of social deprivation is the very essence of their new religious experience and commitment:

> When I got into Seattle I was on a real downer—like, it seemed I was invisible. I mean, there were all these people around, but they were all in a hurry to do their thing and get home. I was really lonely—just needed someone to rap with. I came to this corner and I saw these freaks, about ten to twelve of them, singin' and havin' a good time. It was like a party right there on the corner! They said to me, "Hi ya brother!" and asked me to join with 'em. They were smilin' and laughin' and really happy, man. It was really far out. Since I found the Lord, I know that this is a sign of the Lord at work. The joy of knowing Christ, ya know, just flows out from your face. Man, it's really heavy![52]

On one occasion, during a conversation in one of the communal houses, we tried to see if we could get our freak respondent to separate in his own mind the religious from the social element in his thinking. We asked him if he thought it was possible for a person to come to know Christ through his own study, meditation, and prayer. His reply made it clear that social ties were critically important to his definition of his religion:

> Sure, you could, but you'd be missing the whole idea. Anybody can read for himself, but the thing that makes our relation with Christ so groovy is our relation with each other. We're all God's children, and when you love each other, man, you're loving God. . . .[53]

In addition to whatever lack of social involvement the freaks may have felt before their conversion to the movement, there is reason to believe that they have also felt the kind of social deprivation Glock and Stark addressed more explicitly—that is, a sense of *status loss or deprivation*. The social base of recruitment is exclusively youthful; virtually all the converts are in their twenties. And in our society the late teens and early twenties constitute a period of life that is relatively *powerless* and involves considerable *role strain*, as many commentators on the youth scene have noted.[54] Whether we regard the alienation that so frequently occurs between youth and their elders as endemic and psychologically immanent, as does Feuer,[55] or whether we see it as situational and a function of social structure, along with Keniston, Flacks, Friedenberg, and others, it was a motif in the youthful uprisings of the 1960s and a factor in the genesis of the New Left, of which many freaks have once

[52]Respondent no. 37.

[53]Respondent no. 24.

[54]K. Keniston, *Young Radicals* (New York: Harcourt Brace Jovanovich, 1968), and E. Friedenberg, *The Vanishing Adolescent* (New York: Dell Books, 1959).

[55]L. Feuer, *The Conflict of Generations* (New York: Basic Books, 1969).

been part.[56] The youth element is probably the principal status-diminishing factor among the Jesus people (and is significant enough in itself), but there is also evidence of strong representation from other categories that are discriminated against in our society: Chicanos (but rarely blacks), Jews, Catholics, and the working-class.[57] One is struck particularly by the prominence given to the conversions and activities of Jewish freaks in the national press and in the movement itself.[58] Still, because the present research on the freaks is unsystematic, it would be premature to argue strongly that any factor but youth is significant in the subjective status loss we attribute to converts.

Concomitant with the sense of status loss, especially for the very young, is another important idea from Glock—that new religious movements can help to mitigate that sense of status loss by providing adherents with an *alternative status sytem*. Such a function is apparent among the Jesus freaks in at least two senses: (1) Membership in the movement means joining an entirely new community with a new status system based on new criteria and new kinds of legitimation. This is of general importance for the membership as a whole, but it is *particularly* important for recruits who have a tarnished self-concept, for those who have had trouble "making it" in the Establishment system (which for many youth means the academic system), and for those who have climbed to leadership positions via the new status system.[59] (2) The alternate status system of the new movement legitimizes the rejection of and even rebellion against the key institutions of the Establishment, particularly the traditional family, the school, and the church, all of which come under heavy attack in Jesus freak literature and conversation. Interestingly enough, as though by a tacit division of labor, the Jesus people "arm" of the radical youth movement has focused its attack mainly on these traditional "basic institutions," leaving their more politicized peers of the New Left proper to specialize in attacking political institutions, economic institutions, and universities.[60]

As has been indicated, the case histories of Jesus freaks abound with stories of maladjustment to schools, colleges, and universities but this by no means indicates that freaks have lower intelligence levels than successful students. Trouble in academic pursuits can stem from many causes, including family problems, unpopularity with peers, and poorly developed skills. Joining the Jesus movement seems to help "straighten out" some students by giving them a new sense of social acceptance and a motivation in life, but for others the

[56]A. L. Mauss, ed., *The New Left vs. the Old*, published as the *Journal of Social Issues* 27, no. 1 (1971), and E. Sampson, ed., *Student Activism and the Decade of Protest*, published as the *Journal of Social Issues* 23, no. 2 (July 1967).

[57]Ruppert, op. cit.; *Time*, June 21 and September 6, 1971; and G. W. Cornell, "Jesus People Accuse Methodists in California of Anti-Semitism," *Palouse Empire Shopper* (Associated Press syndicated column), March 27, 1972.

[58]See, for example, Cornell, op. cit., and "Jesus Freak Kosher Style," *Truth*, February 1972, p. 3.

[59]Cf. E. Hoffer, *The True Believer* (New York: Harper & Row, 1951), part 4.

[60]Cf. footnote 56.

movement functions to legitimize their protest and rebellion. Among the Jesus freaks the rebellion reaction is more likely to be found in high schools, where attendance is mandatory, than in colleges, where a disaffected student can simply drop out. Rebellious behavior, highly praised in the Jesus movement press, usually takes the form of nuisance actions such as prayer circles on the floors of the corridors and cafeterias, giving oral and written responses that are of a proselyting and propagandistic nature instead of giving the correct answers in classroom work and so on.[61] The discomfiture of the teachers delights the freaks, who with the backing of their adult leaders threaten the school authorities with court suits and other community actions if there is any interference with their "constitutional rights" of free religious expression. One wonders how much of this is bona fide witnessing and how much is youthful protest that is legitimated by a religious motif which the teachers find hard to gainsay.

The alternate status system hypothesis seems to fit especially well the case histories we have compiled of several elders, or leaders of communal houses. All of them (including the occasional female leader) are in their late twenties or early thirties (compared to the average age of twenty-one among the rest of our respondents); all of them have been heavy drug users (and even dealers), and have lived the hippie lifestyle for some years; all have had moving religious experiences which have converted them from that lifestyle; all are energetic, talented, and articulate but are college dropouts; all are strict in their observance of communal rules and have more endurance than their followers in fasting, prayer, and other observances; and all are known and admired for their aggressiveness and success in proselyting. In other words, they are clearly Jesus freaks par excellence, as we might expect. Their attitudes and attributes give them a charisma that is usually found among leaders of new cults and sects, and it is doubtful that the particular set of attributes which they have would give them any status anywhere else in the society.

It would seem, then, that there is ample reason for attributing to the Jesus people various forms of probable social deprivation before they joined the movement. These forms include nonacceptance or nonaffiliation, with a consequent search for belonging; a sense of status loss or lack mainly because of their extreme youthfulness; and a need for an alternative status system, especially for the leaders and for the recruits who were having difficulty "making it" in the Establishment, primarily the academic system.

The prospects for this rather remarkable movement are difficult to forecast, which is typical of new cults and movements. We have discussed elsewhere the kinds of assimilationist pressures in our society which make it extremely difficult for any radical movement to survive long and keep its radicalism.[62] Extrapolating from the theoretical perspective we have employed here, we would expect the prospects for the Jesus people to be related largely to the ebb and flow of the institutional forces which generate the kinds of deprivation that

[61]See *Truth*, December 1971 and February 1972, for accounts of such activities.

[62]A. L. Mauss, "On Being Strangled by the Stars and Stripes," *Journal of Social Issues* 27, no. 1 (1971).

feed the movement. Also important, of course, is the availability of alternate expressions for ameliorating perceived deprivations. A key factor for the future—especially because the constituency is young—will be the acquisition of the requisite organizational skills to match and marshal the founding fervor and elan, for as Yinger has expressed it:

> If the youth of today have not developed a glorious religion, we should not be surprised nor dismayed. Not surprised, for the task is inherently, supremely difficult; not dismayed, for many of them are at least searching, which is the first necessary step.[63]

[63] Yinger, op. cit., p. 534.

Part Five

On the Future of Religion

The future of religion has been a subject of intermittent sociological interest. Marx made the topic salient by raising the possibility of society without religion. In the last century, when evolutionary theory was having a major impact on sociological thought, it was natural to include religions in predictions about social evolution. Structural-functional theory also made the topic pertinent through its proposition that religion is a necessary condition to the maintenance of social order. And cyclical theories of human history, of which Pitirim Sorokin is the major sociological representative, also included religion as an element in prognostications about where society was headed.

The topic is again exciting attention, this time stimulated less by new theoretical innovations than by the empirical thrust of events. The happenings at Vatican Council II, the widespread proclamation of the death of God, the reversal of the religious revival, new forms of religious consciousness among youth, and rebellion among the clergy have raised the possibility that we may be in a period of profound religious change and have turned sociologists once again to pondering religion's future.

Prediction in any field is risky, but it is most successful where projections can be based on solid information about what is happening in the present and what has happened in the past. The sociology of religion has been notably without empirical information about the course of religious consciousness in the world's populations. Even within societies with more advanced data-collection systems, there has been a sensitivity about inquiring into religion, so that at best only very superficial information has been collected. Institutionalized religions have not contributed much to filling the gap; they collect very little information on their constituencies and they generally do it poorly.

The absence of information has made prediction about the future of religion highly speculative. Indeed, that sociology has managed to proceed through as many theories as it has without arriving at any consensus is a sign that no theory has had a solid empirical base. There is now some prospect that we are moving into a new phase. Periodic data collected routinely by nation-states does not appear to be in the offing; over the last several decades, however, our empirical knowledge of the state of religious consciousness in different societies has been vastly improved simply because individual social scientists have begun to conduct cross-sectional studies on the topic. This trend will not be a substitute for more systematically and regularly collected data, but at least the information being accumulated will represent a vast improvement over no information at all.

Recent sociological work on the future of religion has begun to take advantage of the increasing amount of available empirical information. Because the data base is still not strong, there continues to be more speculation than solid substance in this work. Certainly a stage of consensus about the future of religion has not been reached. There is neverthless a discernible qualitative change from past speculation and the possibility that research on the topic will be considerably more cumulative than before.

Trying to predict the future of religion has not been a primary goal of the Berkeley program, and no research which has prediction especially in mind has been pursued. As data from a larger number of studies accumulated, however, it gave rise to contemplation about what may be implied for the future of the church as we have known it in the West. Because some predictions foresaw the eventual demise of the church, what can be expected to take its place, if anything, also became a topic for meditation. To illustrate this work, two essays have been selected for this final section of the book. Chapter 20, by Rodney Stark and Charles Y. Glock, is addressed to the narrower question of what is in the cards for the future of Christianity. Chapter 21, by Charles Glock, takes on the larger and more formidable task of offering an assessment of what may be expected beyond Christianity.

Additional Reading

Greeley, Andrew. *Religion in the Year 2,000*. New York: Sheed and Ward, 1969. A view somewhat at odds with those presented in chapters 20 and 21.

Berger, Peter. "A Sociological View of the Secularization of Theology." *Journal for the Scientific Study of Religion* 6:1 (Spring 1967). An insightful examination of current theological trends and prospects for the future.

Luckman, Thomas. *The Invisible Religion*. New York: Macmillan Co., 1967. Luckman takes and defends a Durkheimian view of religion's potential for survival.

Bellah, Robert. "Religious Evolution." *American Sociological Review* 29:3 (June 1964). Bellah sets the question at issue in impressive historical perspective.

Stark, Rodney. "On the Incompatibility of Science and Religion." *Journal for the Scientific Study of Religion* 3:1 (Fall 1963). An empirical confrontation of the proposition that religion and science offer competitive rather than complementary perspectives.

Chapter Twenty

Are We Entering a Post-Christian Era?*

Rodney Stark and Charles Y. Glock

Perhaps at no time since the conversion of Paul has the future of Christianity seemed so uncertain. Clearly, a profound revolution in religious thought is sweeping the churches. Where will it lead? Is this a moment of great promise, or of great peril, for the future of Christianity?

Some observers believe we have already entered a post-Christian era—that the current upheavals are the death throes of a doomed religion. Yet many theologians interpret these same signs as the promise of renewed religious vigor. They foresee the possibility of a reconstructed and unified church that will recapture its relevance to contemporary life. A great many others, both clerics and laymen, are simply mystified. In the face of rapid changes and conflicting claims for the future, they hardly know whether to reform the church, or to administer it last rites. Probably the majority of Christians think the whole matter has been greatly exaggerated—that the present excitement will pass and that the churches will continue pretty much as before. Our own research, however, suggests that *the current religious revolution is being accompanied by a general decline in commitment to religion.*

The fact is that in the current debate about the future of Christianity there has been an almost total lack of evidence. The arguments have been based on speculation, hope, and even temperament, but rarely on fact. Mainly this has been because so few hard facts about contemporary religion have been available. Our own findings do not entirely fill this vacuum. Still, what we have learned provides a number of clues about the trends in religious commitment, and permits a cautious assessment of the direction in which Christianity is headed. We have reached two main conclusions: that the religious beliefs that have been

*Rodney Stark and Charles Y. Glock, *American Piety: The Nature of Religious Commitment* (Berkeley and Los Angeles: University of California Press, 1968), pp. 204-224. Reprinted with the permission of the authors and the publisher.

the bedrocks of Christian faith for nearly two millennia are on their way out; and that this *may* very well be the dawn of a post-Christian era.

While many Americans are still firmly committed to the traditional, supernatural conceptions of a personal God, a Divine Saviour, and the promise of eternal life, the trend is away from these convictions. Although we must expect an extended period of doubt, the fact is that a demythologized modernism is overwhelming the traditional Christ-centered, mystical faith.

Of course, rejection of the supernatural tenets of Christianity is not a strictly modern phenomenon. Through the ages men have challenged these beliefs. But never before have they found much popular support. Until now, the vast majority of people have retained unshaken faith in the otherworldly premises of Christianity.

Today, skeptics are not going unnoticed, nor are their criticisms being rejected out of hand. For the modern skeptics are not the apostates, village atheists, or political revolutionaries of old. The leaders of today's challenge to traditional beliefs are principally theologians—those in whose care the church entrusts its sacred teachings. It is not philosophers or scientists, but the greatest theologians of our time who are saying "God is dead," or that notions of a God "out there" are antiquated. And their views are becoming increasingly popular.

Erosion of Orthodoxy

Although only a minority of church members so far reject or doubt the existence of some kind of personal God or the divinity of Jesus, a near majority reject such traditional articles of faith as Christ's miracles, life after death, the promise of the second coming, and the virgin birth. An overwhelming majority reject the existence of the Devil. This overall picture, however, is subject to considerable variation among the denominations. Old-time Christianity remains predominant in some Protestant bodies, such as the Southern Baptists and the various small sects. But in most of the main-line Protestant denominations, and to a considerable extent among Roman Catholics, doubt and disbelief in historic Christian theology abound. In some denominations the doubters far outnumber the firm believers.

We are convinced that this widespread doubt of traditional Christian tenets is a recent development. What evidence there is supports this assumption. For if there has been an erosion of faith, we would expect many people to have shifted from denominations with unswerving commitment to that faith to denominations with more demythologized positions. Our data show that this is exactly what has happened. Because these denominational shifts indicate changes in religious outlook only indirectly, they do not *prove* our point. But they are very consistent with it.

More direct evidence of an erosion in orthodox belief is provided by the contrasts in the percentages of orthodox believers in different age groups reported earlier in chapter 6. Among people fifty years of age or older, age made very little difference, it will be recalled, in the percentage subscribing to traditional beliefs. Similarly, among those under fifty, orthodoxy differed little by age. But Christians over fifty are considerably *more* likely than younger people to hold orthodox views. The difference occurs in every denomination and is quite substantial.

These findings suggest that there has been an important generational break with traditional religion. The break consistently occurs between those who have reached maturity since the beginning of World War II—those who were 25 or less in 1940—and those who were raised in a pre-war America. In this as well as in many other ways, World War II seems to mark a watershed between the older America of small-town, rural, or stable-urban-neighborhood living, and the contemporary America of highly mobile urban living.

Recent Gallup Poll findings indicate that the decline in American church attendance that began in the late 1950's is accelerating.[1] This decline has been particularly sharp among young adults. The number who attend every week dropped 11 percent between 1958 and 1966. Furthermore, the Gallup interviewers found that Americans overwhelmingly believe that religion is losing its influence in contemporary life. In 1957 only 14 percent of the nation's Christians thought religion was losing its influence and 69 percent thought it was increasing; ten years later, 57 percent thought religion was losing ground and 23 percent thought it was gaining. This would seem to mark an enormous loss of confidence in religion during the past decade.

Aside from this statistical evidence, there are numerous more obvious signs that a religious revolution is taking place. The radical changes in the Roman Catholic Church flowing from the reforms of Pope John XXIII and Vatican II are perhaps the most dramatic indications. Of equal significance is the ecumenical movement. Prevailing differences in doctrinal outlook still impede the unification of Christian denominations. But though such differences seemed to preclude all prospects of unification several generations ago, today doctrinal barriers have broken down enough so that some mergers have already taken place, and clearly more are in the offing.

The mergers are taking place among denominations with the least residual commitment to traditional faith. More traditional denominations still resist the prospects of ecumenism. Thus it seems clear that a loss of concern for traditional doctrine is a precondition for ecumenism. And this in turn means that the success of ecumenism today represents a trend away from historic creeds.

These major signs of the depth and scope of religious change are accompanied by a spate of minor clues: the popularity of Anglican Bishop John A. R. Robinson's *Honest to God* and Harvey Cox's *The Secular City*; the widespread discussion of the "death of God" theology in the mass media; and the profound changes in the Westminster Confession recently adopted by the Presbyterian Church. All of these are compelling evidence of ferment. Nor is this exclusively a Protestant phenomenon. Almost daily the press reports nuns leaving their orders because they believe they can pursue their missions more effectively outside the church. Priests advocate "the pill." The number of Catholics taking up religious vocations has dropped sharply. Catholics ponder Teilhard de Chardin as seriously

---

[1] American Institute of Public Opinion, press release of April 11, 1967.

as Protestants reflect on Dietrich Bonhoeffer, the German theologian imprisoned and executed by the Nazis. A leading Jesuit theologian is quoted in *Newsweek* as admitting, "It is difficult to say in our age what the divinity of Christ can mean."

Demythologizing the Church

The seeds of this revolution were planted a long time ago. Since Kierkegaard, the "death of God" has been proclaimed—although subtly—by the theologians who have counted most. It is only because what they have been saying privately for a long time is now being popularized that the religious revolution seems such a recent phenomenon. For example, during the attempts to try him for heresy prior to his death, the then Episcopal Bishop James A. Pike defended himself by saying he had merely told the laity what the clergy had taken for granted for years. Moreover, the majority of Episcopalian church members hold theological views quite similar to Bishop Pike's. This presents an ironic picture of Sunday services in many churches. Both pastor and congregation reject or at least doubt the theological assumptions of the creeds they recite and the rituals in which they participate, but neither acknowledges this fact.

The heart of the religious revolution is the demise of what has been proclaimed as the core of Christian faith for nearly 2000 years: a literal interpretation of the phrase "Christ crucified, risen, coming again." Now, in many theological circles both the fact of the current revolution and its demythologizing character are considered obvious. But what many consider obvious is, in this instance, terribly important—perhaps vastly more important than contemporary churchmen recognize.

In most of the commentary on the major transformations of our religious institutions, the key terms are change, renewal, and improvement. Churchmen view the massive change in belief that is taking place not as a transition from belief to unbelief, but as a shift from one form of belief to another. The theologians who are leading this procession do *not* regard themselves as pallbearers at the funeral of God. It is *not* the end of the Christian era that they expect, but the dawn of a new and more profound period of Christianity.

The subtleties of what is being proposed in place of the old beliefs seem elusive, however. As sociologists, we find it difficult to imagine a Christian church without Jesus Christ as Divine Saviour, without a personal God, without the promise of eternal life. The "new breed" of theologians, as we understand them, are telling us we are wrong—that we rigidly identify Christianity with an old-fashioned fundamentalism that modern Christianity has long since discarded. Still, we find it difficult to grasp the substance of their alternatives. Conceptions of God as ultimate concern, as love, as poetry, as the divine essence in all of us—the ground of our being—have powerful esthetic and rhetorical appeal. But how do they differ from humanism? And more important, how can such conceptions induce the kind of commitment necessary to keep the church, as an organization, alive?

For some contemporary churchmen, the new theology does mean the eventual abandonment of today's church and its replacement by a still vaguely defined spiritual community. But the vast majority of clerics expect no such thing. They expect the new theology to be effectively accommodated in the present church. They recognize that this accommodation will require some changes in the church's present organization and modes of operation, but they think that these changes *can* be made.

So far, the new theology has not altered the basic structure, form, or functioning of the institutional church. The churches continue to predicate their structure and activities upon a conception of a judging, personal, active God, whether or not the theological views predominant among clergy and laity still conceive of God in these terms. Historically, the central concern of the churches has been the relationship between man and God. Part of their efforts have been directed to propitiating this active God, to teaching what must be done to escape his wrath and obtain his blessings. Such common religious terms and phrases as "praise," "worship," "seeking comfort and guidance," "bringing the unconverted to faith," and "seeking forgiveness for sins" all presuppose the existence of a conscious, judging God who intervenes in human affairs. An elaborate conception of God and his commandments is the *raison d'être* for church worship services, mission societies, adult Bible classes, baptism, and communion.

Admittedly, there have been some superficial alterations. There have been various liturgical experiments. Sometimes the mass is recited in English rather than in Latin. Pastors have made some changes in the content of their sermons. But, by and large, the churches are still organized and conducted as they have been in the past. The traditional creeds are still recited—"I believe in God the Father almighty, maker of heaven and earth . . ."—and the old hymns regularly sung—"I Know that My Redeemer Liveth." There has been no substantial change in the sacraments. And, with some rare exceptions, there are no loud, or even soft, cries from the pulpit that Christ did not walk on water or that God does not see and hear all.

Restraints on the Clergy

The general absence of institutional change does *not* mean that the clergy is more committed to traditional tenets than the laity. On the contrary, rejection of traditional Christian supernaturalism is perhaps even more widespread among the clergy than among the laity and follows essentially the same pattern of variation by denomination. A recent study comparing findings on church members with national samples of clergy showed that laymen and clergymen in a given denomination are nearly identically distributed on questions of belief.[2] For example, while 34 percent of Methodist laymen and 92 percent of Missouri Synod Lutheran laymen accept the virgin birth, 28 percent of Methodist clergy and 90 percent of Missouri Lutheran clergy accept this article of faith.

However, even if liberal ministers would like to alter the forms of the church

---

[2]Jeffrey K. Hadden, "A Protestant Paradox: Divided They Merge," *Trans-Action* (July-August 1967).

on the basis of their new theology, they are not likely to find their congregations ready to permit it. This is because in all denominations supporters of the old theology still persist. What's more, they are likely to be their churches' most active laymen.

Thus the liberal pastor faces formidable restraints. His religious convictions might dispose him to reforms—to deleting, for example, references to traditional supernaturalism in the worship service, or to preaching the new theology from the pulpit and teaching it in Sunday school. But he is unlikely to have a congregation that would tolerate such changes. Even in congregations where orthodox members are in the minority, such changes are unlikely. The minority will oppose them vigorously, while the plain fact is that the more liberal members are not likely to care much one way or the other.

This discrepancy between institutional inertia and theological revolution presents the churches with growing peril. Can the old institutional forms continue to draw commitment and support from people whose theological outlook is no longer represented in these forms—or at least maintain support until the theological revolution becomes so widespread that institutional changes are possible? More serious, can a Christianity without a divine Christ survive in *any* institutional form?

The data on the sample of California Protestant and Roman Catholic church-members described in Chapter 6 were examined to see if they might afford an answer to these questions.[3] They provide no final answers but do contribute clues as to what will happen should future developments follow the present course. Evidently belief in traditional Christian doctrines, as they are now constituted, is vital to other kinds of religious commitment. While the churches continue to be organized on the basis of traditional orthodoxy, people who lack the beliefs that are needed to make such organization meaningful are falling away from the church. Today, the acceptance of a modernized, liberal theology is being accompanied by *a general corrosion of religious commitment.*

Orthodoxy and Commitment

Among both Protestants and Roman Catholics, orthodoxy is very strongly related to other aspects of religious commitment. (See Table 1.) The highly orthodox are much more likely than the less orthodox to be ritually involved in the church, and they far surpass the less orthodox on devotionalism (private worship, such as prayer), religious experience, religious knowledge, and particularism (the belief that only Christians can be saved). Only on ethicalism among Protestants—the importance placed on "loving thy neighbor" and "doing good for others"—is the pattern reversed.[4] By a slight margin, it is the least orthodox who are most likely to hold the ideals of Christian ethics.

---

[3] P.51.

[4] See Stark and Glock, *op. cit.*, for detailed descriptions of method of construction of these indices.

Table 1.   *The Impact of Orthodox Belief on Other Forms of Religious Commitment*

	Orthodoxy Index		
	Low	Medium	High
Percentage high on ritual involvement			
Protestants	19%	39%	71%
(Sample)	(595)	(729)	(705)
Catholics	19	36	55
(Sample)	(64)	(115)	(304)
Percentage high on devotionalism			
Protestants	20	49	79
Catholics	18	58	80
Percentage high on religious experience			
Protestants	25	57	86
Catholics	29	49	70
Percentage high on religious knowledge			
Protestants	15	19	46
Catholics	0	5	7
Percentage high on particularism			
Protestants	9	25	60
Catholics	15	28	40
Percentage high on ethicalism			
Protestants	47	46	42
Catholics	48	48	56

Granted, it could be convincingly argued that devotionalism, religious experience, knowledge, particularism, and perhaps even ritual involvement are not intrinsically necessary to the existence of Christian institutions. The fact that these forms of commitment decline as traditional belief declines could be interpreted as reflecting changes in modes of religious expression, rather than as an erosion of religious commitment. After all, the new theology implies not only a departure from old-time supernaturalism, but from religious practices that reflect supernaturalism. The clergy of the new reformation can hardly expect their adherents to break out "speaking in tongues."

But it is implausible to speak simply of change, rather than of decline, unless religious institutions retain a laity committed in *some* fashion. The churches cannot survive as formal organizations unless people participate in the life of the church and give it financial support. Without funds or members, the churches would be empty shells awaiting demolition.

This could just happen. (See Table 2) Among both Protestants and Catholics, church attendance is powerfully related to orthodoxy. Only 15 percent of those Protestants with fully modernized religious beliefs attend church every week, as opposed to 59 percent of those who have retained traditional views. Among Catholics, the contrast is 27 percent versus 82 percent. Similarly, the table shows that membership in one or more church organizations is strongly related to orthodoxy. Furthermore—and perhaps most important—financial support for the churches is mainly provided by those with orthodox views.

Table 2.   *The Impact of Orthodox Belief on Organizational Support*
*for the Church**

	Orthodoxy Index		
	Low	Medium	High
Percentage attending church every week			
Protestants	15%	31%	59%
Catholics	27	60	82
Percentage belonging to one or more church organizations			
Protestants	46	61	72
Catholics	14	24	46
Percentage contributing $7.50 or more per week to their church			
Protestants	17	23	44
Catholics	2	4	8
Percentage of Catholics who contribute $4 or more per week to their church	13	19	26

*With trivial variations all computations are based on the number of cases shown in Table 1.

These findings show how the institutional church, predicated as it is on traditional theological concepts, loses its hold on its members as these concepts become outmoded. Consequently, if the erosion of traditional beliefs continues, as presumably it will, the church—as long as it remains locked in its present institutional forms—stands in ever-increasing danger of both moral and financial bankruptcy. The liberal denominations are particularly vulnerable because the demise of traditional theology and a concomitant drop in other aspects of commitment is already widespread in these bodies.

In coming days, many conservative Christians will undoubtedly argue and work for an about-face. But it seems clear to us that a return to orthodoxy is no longer possible. The current reformation in religious thought is irrevocable, and we are no more likely to recover our innocence in these matters than we are to again believe that the world is flat.

Is there any way the impending triumph of liberal theology can be translated into the renewed church that liberal clergymen expect? Or must liberalism lead inevitably to the demise of organized faith? It is here the future is most murky. The alternatives to orthodoxy being advocated by the new theologians and their supporters are still rather formless. It is too soon to know just where they will lead. However, it seems clear that their central thrust is toward the ethical rather than the mystical.

Shift toward Ethicalism

This shift is more than a change in emphasis. The ethics of the new theologies differ sharply from the old. No longer are Christian ethics defined as matters of personal holiness or the rejection of private vices. They are directed toward social justice, toward the creation of a humane society. As theologian Langdon Gilkey put it recently, there has been a "shift in Christian ethical concern from personal holiness to love of neighbor as the central obligation. . . ." In the new ethical perspective, the individual is not neglected for the sake of the group, but the social situation in which people are embedded is seen as integral to the whole question of what is ethical. The long Christian quest to save the world through individual salvation has shifted to the quest to reform society.

Consequently, the new theology is manifested less in what one believes about God than in what one believes about goodness, justice, and compassion. A depersonalized and perhaps intuitively understood God may be invoked by these theologies, but what seems to count most is not how one prepares for the next life—the reality of which the new theology seems to deny—but what one does to realize the kingdom of God on earth.

Among some modern Christians, ethicalism *may* provide a substitute for orthodoxy. Ethicalism is most prevalent in denominations where orthodoxy is least common. Furthermore, individual church members whose religious beliefs are the least orthodox score higher on ethicalism than the most orthodox.

But from an institutional point of view, is ethicalism a satisfactory substitute for orthodoxy? Can ethical concern generate and sustain the kinds of practical commitment—financial support and personal participation—that the churches need to survive?

If the churches continue their present policy of business as usual, the answer is probably No. The ethically oriented Christian seems to be deterred rather than challenged by what he finds in church. The more a man is committed to ethicalism, the less likely he is to contribute funds or participate in the life of

Table 3.　*Orthodoxy, Ethicalism, and Contributions to the Church*

	Ethicalism Index		
	High	Medium	Low
Protestants–Orthodoxy Index	Percentage who contribute $7.50 or more per week to their church		
High	38%	43%	58%
(Sample)	(304)	(240)	(111)
Medium	18	25	43
	(333)	(321)	(44)
Low	18	20	12
	(241)	(251)	(34)
Catholics–Orthodoxy Index	Percentage who contribute $4 or more per week to their church		
High	27	45	*
	(150)	(122)	(4)
Medium	16	18	*
	(48)	(56)	(4)
Low	7	21	*
	(30)	(28)	(1)

*Too few cases for a stable percentage.

the church. We suspect that, in the long run, he is also less likely to remain a member.

Tables 3 and 4 show the joint effects of orthodoxy and ethicalism on financial contributions and church attendance. Table 3 shows that, among Protestants, the more a church member is committed to ethics, the less likely he is to contribute money to his church, regardless of his level of orthodoxy. The best contributors are those of unwavering orthodoxy, who reject the religious importance of loving their neighbors or doing good for others. A similar relationship exists among Roman Catholics. Regardless of orthodoxy, the higher his score on the ethicalism index, the less likely a parishioner is to give money to the church. Member commitment to Christian ethics seems to cost the churches money.

Table 4 shows the joint impact of ethicalism and orthodoxy on church attendance. Here again, among Protestants, it is clear that the higher their ethicalism, the less likely they are to attend church regularly. The best attenders are the highly orthodox who reject ethical tenets. Among Roman Catholics, it is unclear from these data whether or not ethicalism has any effect at all upon church attendance.

These findings were rechecked within liberal, moderate, and conservative Protestant groups, and within specific denominations as well. Invariably, a concern with ethics turned out to be incompatible with church attendance and contributions. Furthermore, these same relationships held true for participation in church organizations and activities.

Today's churches are failing to engage the ethical impulses of their members. Regardless of whether they retain orthodox religious views, to the extent that people have accepted Christian ethics, they seem inclined to treat the church as

Table 4. *The Impact of Orthodox Belief on Organizational Support for the Church*

	Percentage who attend church every week Ethicalism Index		
	High	Medium	Low
Protestants–Orthodoxy Index			
High	55%	58%	67%
(Sample)	(328)	(247)	(113)
Medium	29	31	52
	(347)	(331)	(44)
Low	19	22	10
	(255)	(165)	(39)
Catholics–Orthodoxy Index			
High	82	82	*
	(161)	(124)	(4)
Medium	65)	60	*
	(51)	(57)	(4)
Low	30	27	*
	(30)	(30)	(2)

*Too few cases for a stable percentage.

irrelevant. Obviously, this bodes ill for the future of the churches. It means that the churches have to find a substitute for orthodoxy that will still guarantee their organizational survival. And while *some* form of ethicalism might work as a theological substitute for orthodoxy, clearly the existing efforts along this line have not succeeded.

Sooner or later the churches will have to face these facts. This will require a forthright admission that orthodoxy is dead. Furthermore, it will also require—and here's the real hurdle—a clear alternative. It will require a new theology, ethically-based or otherwise, and radical changes in forms of worship, programs, and organization to make them consistent with and relevant to this new theology.

But even successfully fulfilling these tasks will not ensure the survival of the church. Indeed, the immediate effect will almost certainly be to alienate those members committed to old-time orthodoxy and thus to sharply reduce the base of support on which the churches presently depend. The gamble is that these people can be replaced by renewing the commitment of those members whose interest in the church is presently waning, and by winning new adherents among those who do not now belong to any church.

Clearly, among the conservative churches such a radical change of posture is not likely. The impact of modernized theology on these bodies has so far been indirect, in the loss of members who switch to more liberal denominations. To the extent that these losses remain endurable, the conservative clergy and laymen can continue to ignore the current crisis.

Reclaiming the Dormant Christians

If institutional reforms are to come, the liberal churches must lead the way. Our findings suggest that not only are the liberal churches in the best position to make such changes, but that their existence may very well depend on their doing so.

At present, the liberal bodies are functioning as way stations for those who are moving away from orthodoxy, but who are still unwilling to move entirely outside the church. These new members may prove to be only a passing phenomenon, however, unless the liberal churches can find a way to *keep* them. And the churches' current organizing practices are clearly unequal to this task. For it is the liberal churches that are currently in the poorest organizational health.

As can be seen in Table 5 in contrast to conservative denominations, the majority of members of liberal bodies are dormant Christians. They have adopted the theology of the new reformation, but at the same time they have stopped attending church, stopped participating in church activities, stopped contributing funds, and stopped praying. They are uninformed about religion and only a minority feel that their religion provides them with answers to the meaning and purpose of life, while the overwhelming majority of conservatives feel theirs *does* supply such answers. The liberal congregations resemble theater audiences. Their members are mainly strangers to one another, while

Table 5. *Denominational Patterns of Religious Commitment*

	Members of liberal Protestant churches[a]	Members of moderate Protestant churches[b]	Members of conservative Protestant churches[c]	Members of Roman Catholic parishes
Percentage high on orthodoxy	11	33	81	61
Percentage high on ritual involvement	30	45	75	46
Percentage high on devotionalism	42	51	78	65
Percentage high on religious experience	43	57	89	58
Percentage high on religious knowledge	17	25	55	5
Percentage who feel their religious perspective provides them with the answers to the meaning and purpose of life	43	57	84	68
Percentage who attend church weekly	25	32	68	70
Percentage who have 3 or more of their 5 best friends in their congregation	22	26	54	36
Percentage who contribute $7.50 or more per week to their church	18	30	50	6

[a]Congregationalists, Methodists, Episcopalians.

[b]Disciples of Christ, Presbyterians, American Lutherans, American Baptists.

[c]Missouri Synod Lutherans, Southern Baptists, Sects.

conservative congregations are close-knit groups, united by widespread bonds of personal friendship.

In the light of these facts, the liberal churches do not seem organizationally sound in comparison with the conservative ones.

Although all these signs point to the need for a radical break with traditional forms in the liberal churches, it seems quite unlikely that this will happen any time soon. For one thing, there is no sign that the leaders of these bodies recognize the situation that confronts them. Here and there one hears a voice raised within the clergy, but such spokesmen are a minority with little power to lead. What's more, leadership is not the only thing lacking. There is no clearly formulated blueprint for renovating the churches. The critical attack on orthodoxy seems a success, but now what? The new theologians have developed no consensus as to what they want people to believe, or as to what kind of a new church they want to build.

What we expect is that all of the Christian churches will continue a policy of drift, with a rhetoric of hope and a reality of business as usual. There will be more mergers and more efforts to modernize classical interpretations of the faith, but these will go forward as compromises rather than as breaks with the past. Perhaps, when the trends we see have caused greater havoc, radical change will follow. Institutions, like people, have a strong will to survive. But institutions *do* die, and often efforts to save them come too late.

Only history will reveal the eventual fate of Christianity. As matters now stand, there seems to be little long-term future for the church as we know it. A remnant church can be expected to last for a time, if only to provide the psychic comforts that are currently dispensed by orthodoxy. But eventually substitutes for even this function are likely to emerge, leaving churches of the present form with no effective rationale for continuing to exist.

This is *not* to suggest that religion itself will die. As long as questions of ultimate meaning persist, and as long as the human spirit strives to transcend itself, the religious quest will continue. But whether the religion of the future will be in any sense Christian remains to be seen. Clearly it will *not* be, if one means by "Christian" the orthodoxy of the past and the institutional structures built upon that orthodoxy. But if one can conceive of Christianity as a continuity in a search for ethics, and retention of certain traditions of language and ritual, then perhaps Christianity *will* survive.

The institutional shape of religion in the future is as difficult to predict as its theological content. Conceivably it may take on a public character, as suggested recently by sociologist Robert Bellah, or the invisible form anticipated by another sociologist, Thomas Luckmann. Or it may live on, in a form similar to the religions of Asia, in a public witness conducted by priests without parishes. Quite possibly, religion in the future will be very different from anything we can now expect.

The portents of what is to come could easily seem trivial today. William Butler Yeats, in a poem celebrating the slow death of ancient paganism and the coming birth of a still unformed Christianity, asked a question that we may well ask of our own religious future:

> And what rough beast, its hour come round at last,
> Slouches towards Bethlehem to be born?

Chapter Twenty-One

Images of "God," Images of Man, and the Organization of Social Life*

Charles Y. Glock

Since the world began man has contrived a great variety of forms of social organization. There have been hunting and fishing societies, caste and feudal societies, capitalist and socialist societies, communal and communistic societies. Some forms of social organization have flowered briefly and died. Others have survived over extensive periods of time, sometimes in substantially their original form and other times in drastically modified form. No form of social organization of the past has proven immortal, and no present form, it is suspected, will prove so either.

The origin and evolution of forms of social organization have been given a lot of attention by sociologists in one way and another. It was a major theme in the now classic literature of sociology, and almost every major figure of the past—Marx, Weber, Durkheim, Pareto, Sombart, Comte—touched on it to a large degree. And of course questions pertaining to social organization are perhaps the major questions being addressed by contemporary social theorists.

But despite all the work which has been done, we still seem to be missing an agreed-upon way to order forms of social organization at the conceptual level and an agreed-upon accounting of the conditions governing the life cycle of old forms and giving rise to new forms of social organization at the theoretical level. Indeed, not only are we missing a satisfactory general theory but we experience considerable difficulty in gaining consensus around explanations of the origin of particular forms of social organization—for example, witness the continuing debate about the sources of Western capitalism.

This chapter has no pretensions of trying to provide comprehensive answer to major questions about the birth and life cycle of social organizations. It is concerned, however, to advance a perspective from which such questions might

*Charles Y. Glock, "Images of 'God,' Images of Man, and the Organization of Social Life," *Journal for the Scientific Study of Religion* 11, no. 1 (March 1972). Reprinted with the permission of the author and the *Journal for the Scientific Study of Religion*.

be freshly addressed. At this juncture the perspective is presented on highly speculative grounds. The intent, frankly, is to see whether these speculations strike a sufficiently responsive chord to warrant further effort to build upon them and to extend them and eventually to subject them to empirical test.

To set the stage I must begin with some rather common-sense and patent observations about social organization: first, that it is rooted always in a rather extraordinary number of ideas. Constitutions cannot be drafted, forms of government invented, laws and rules of conduct promulgated, the nature of economy and polity decided unless there are ideas to guide how these things are to be done. Ideas are important not only to the invention of a form of social organization but to warranting it. No form of social organization can evolve unless it can be made acceptable to those who are obliged to live under it. Acceptance of a sort may be achieved by force and oppression—those in power may simply impose their will whether those out of power accept it or not—but to survive over the long run rather than the short run, social organization requires the acquiescence of its constituents. There has to be some modicum of agreement that the form of social organization is just and reasonable.

To be effective, the ideas which seek to warrant social organization—that is, hierarchial forms—have a mighty task to perform. Certainly utopian societies have been postulated which would provide for total equality, and on rare occasions and for short periods of time small, isolated groups have managed to approach the utopian dream. But the forms of social organization which have prevailed are characterized by inequality rather than by equality in the distribution of desirable role assignments and of the rewards which pertain to their performance. Indeed, in most instances the most desirable roles and rewards are in very short supply and are effectively denied to the majority of populations.

Under these circumstances material self-interest is perhaps sufficient to warrant a form of social organization for those who are highly rewarded by it. Material self-interest obviously cannot be expected to persuade the less rewarded, especially those at the bottom of the social ladder, to conform *and* to do so uncomplainingly. Here, clearly, some rationalization of their social fortunes or—better—misfortunes that is acceptable to them is clearly required if conformity without complaint is to be achieved.[1]

Ideological rationalizations are probably never sufficient in and of themselves to produce the conformity necessary to the survival of a specific social organization. Even in simple, isolated, and homogeneous societies it is unlikely that the myths which justify the social order will be powerful enough by themselves to ward off all dissent and deviant behavior. Rationalizations of social order are never completely successful. Consequently, other means have to be employed to complement ideology as a means of social control. Sanctions constitute one such means and compensations another.

---

[1]These remarks are not meant to imply that self-interest is not an important element in maintaining social control. Indeed, the precise task of ideology is to convince everyone that it is in their self-interest to conform. However, for the deprived the appeal to self-interest is likely to be in a form other than material rewards.

Sanctions may range from social pressures imposed by the group on its members to force and suppression imposed by those in power on those who would thwart their will. Sanctions, in effect, are the ways that societies adopt to reward conformity and punish dissent. Compensations are a means to derail dissent rather than to suppress it directly. Those in society who might otherwise be expected to be nonconformist because conformity affords them so little direct reward are offered alternative rewards which effectively contain deviant propensities. Religion, sports, and drugs are possible compensating mechanisms.

Societies differ in the relative extent to which ideology, sanctions, and compensations are means of social control. The character of the mix is a sign of how much social solidarity exists and of how stable a society is. Social solidarity and stability can be expected to be high where the ideological rationalization of the social order is universally internalized and accepted and where there is high consensus that the way things are is the way things ought to be. In such a society everyone would be satisfied with his lot and would uncomplainingly play the role which society has seen fit to assign him. When the ideology is not so powerful, compensating mechanisms are likely to be the first means employed to contain dissent. Where these are unsuccessful, a resort to sanctions and increasingly oppressive ones is likely to follow. All three types are exemplified in contemporary history.

It is to be recognized, however, that even in the most oppressive police state ideology will not be absent. Only those in power may be persuaded by it, but it can be expected that they will have internalized some justification of why it is proper that things are the way they are and that they will bend some effort to persuade those who are being suppressed to accept the ideology and, in turn, their suppression.

Ideology, as has been frequently pointed out, is likely to be of greater importance during periods of social change than in periods of relative social stability. At such times, those who favor the status quo and those who favor change will both be concerned to explain why their position is right and to win adherents to their point of view by ideological argument. Periods of social stability, in contrast, are likely to be characterized by a weak status of ideology. Habit and custom are sufficient to maintain conformity in a stable situation without reference to the ideology rationalizing them. In the absence of alternatives, simply the fact that this is the way things always are done is sufficient to sustain them.

If, as is being suggested, ideas are important to the invention of new forms of social organization, as they were once to the invention of old ones, and if ideas are also important to warranting the inventions, both as a means to their adoption and to their maintenance following adoption, it becomes legitimate to ask where these ideas come from. What is the source of the conception of new forms of social organization and from whence come the ideas legitimating them? A distinction should probably be made between conceptions which would entirely upturn an existing social order and those which would only modify it—between conceptions of revolution and reform. However, upturning conceptions rarely stem from a single source or emerge fully all at once. Indeed, in contemporary society social change which may seem classifiable only as a modification may be the harbinger of more radical and upturning change to come. This is a point to be illustrated later. For now, major attention will be focused on the innovation of clearly more radical and holistic forms of social organization.

Briefly stated, the central proposition I wish to advance is that the organization of social life is importantly related to prevailing imagery about 'god' and imagery about man.[2] Such imagery contributes to shaping the form of social organization and to rationalizing it, and it becomes crucial to the maintenace of social solidarity and stability. Moreover, when prevailing ideas about "god" and the nature of man change, the form of social organization can also be expected to change, sometimes profoundly so. Indeed, a subsidiary theme and claim of the chapter is that a change of profound proportions is currently in progress.

Fundamental questions of creation and purpose have confronted man throughout history. The existence of the world, the sun and stars, nature, man—his birth, life and death—all are phenomena demanding some kind of explanation, even in the most primitive societies. And in every society some effort at accounting has been made. Inevitably the accounting has included a conception of transcendent forces controlling and constraining the affairs of the world of man.

These images of "god" may take rather different forms. Sometimes the otherwordly force is depicted as divinity. This has been the common pattern in the West, at least since the time of the ancient Egyptians, where images of "god" have been cast in an anthropomorphic mold. But divinity may not be central or even present at all in otherworldly conceptions. They may take the form of eternal principles or laws of creation, sacred in the sense that they are seen as inviolate and as set in motion by an otherworldly force. Such conceptions are more frequently found in the East and are illustrated by the ancient Chinese belief in a natural harmony of order in the universe or in Hindu ideas of *nirvana* and the law of *karma*. We mean also to include as images of "god" conceptions which deny the supernatural, as do Marxism and some interpretations of modern science, for example. If economic determinism or the propositions of science concerning eternal regularities are believed in, they constitute forces transcendent of man with which man must contend.

Imbued in every past image of "god" has been some explanation of the purpose of life and a setting forth of goals consistent with this purpose to which men ought aspire. Not only ends but means have been specified; proper ways to believe and to behave have been set forth and in every overarching imagery, sanctions have been introduced to reward conformity and punish deviance.

In turn, ideas about "god's" intention and purpose for man always imply an image of what man is like. Images of man differ radically in what they include in their concepts of man. Universally, however, all have addressed themselves to the

[2]By prevailing is meant that imagery which at any given time and place informs the thinking of the masses of men—not imagery which may dominate in particular elites.

question of whether and under what conditions man can be held accountable for what he thinks and what he does.

The philosophical controversy over whether man is wholly determined or possessed of free will has still to be resolved, if it can be resolved at all. Throughout history, however, some resolution of the controversy has been a practical matter in human affairs. The organization of social life has required some common understanding of what man is like and particularly what can reasonably be expected of him. The need for a resolution is not manifestly recognized, of course. Practical men of affairs have not sat down to decide what image of man is to guide the formulation of public policy. Yet some image of man is as universal an element of social life as is an image of "god."

Until now, the image of man which has prevailed in all images of "god" is that man is neither totally free nor wholly determined. Man is conceived of as possessing always at least a modicum of free will, but in all images there is also an element of determinism, sometimes larger, sometimes smaller. In all conceptions certain conditions and limitations are imposed on human experience. Some things are established as "god"-given and therefore beyond man's capacity to change. Whether men will it or not, the natural harmony of order in the universe, the law of karma, the will of Allah, economic determinism, the regularities of science will prevail.

But within the framework of these eternal verities some room is left for man to decide for himself. Thus, even in as fatalistic an imagery of "god" and man as is contained in Islam, where man's very being and existence is thought of as fated by Allah, there is still an injunction on man to do Allah's will and therefore an assumption that man is free to choose whether to do so or not.

The importance of images of "god" and of man for social structure is that the former at least warrant and sanction the latter and are almost always the source of sanctions and compensating mechanisms. Images of "god" and man may also be instrumental in the invention of forms of social organization. Imagery warrants a social order by proclaiming it to be sacred, affording an explanation of its sacredness, and imposing an obligation on man—whatever his position in that social order—to think and to behave as that social order dictates.

The proclamation of a social order's sacredness may be explicit in the prevailing image of "god." In medieval Europe, for example, there was an extended period in which the feudal organization of society was believed to have been ordained by God. The caste organization of ancient India was also conceived as inspired by "god." The imagery of "god" in Marxist thought proclaims the Communist organization of society as sacred. Some circles, perhaps more so in the past than in the present, have proclaimed capitalism as a form of social organization to be "god's" intention for man.

Proclamation alone, however, is never sufficient to warrant sacredness. In all imagery proclamation is reinforced by explanation—there is some effort to account for the form of social organization, to indicate why it takes the form it does and why the inequality it produces is proper. Medieval feudal social structure, for example, was accounted for as being functional to the performance of required social roles. Caste in India was explained as the result of the operation of the law of *karma*. Inequality in America is the result of the fact that some people are willing to work harder than others—to do more with what "god" has bestowed on them.

Explanation, in turn, leads to prescription. Given the sacredness of a form of social organization and "god's" reasons therefore, it follows inevitably that "god" intends man to conform. Medieval man, for example, was expected to be complacent about his lot and to perform uncomplainingly the role assigned to him by virtue of his birth. There are similar injunctions in Islam and in Hinduism. Under communism, one is called upon to conform so that a classless society can be achieved more quickly, and under capitalism conformity is called for because it is the best way to get ahead.

It is in prescription, of course, that the assumption of man's possession of free will is contained. To say what man ought to do is to imply that he may elect not to do so. In all imageries there is the call upon man to make the "right" choice, but also the recognition that ideology alone may not be sufficient to the task. All imageries add sanctions—that is, rewards and punishments—to the leverage of ideology. The sanctions contained in different imageries are not, of course, the same. Where the imagery contains a conception of an afterlife, as in Hinduism, Islam, and Christianity, then the system of sanctions tends to operate in that afterlife. Conceptions which postulate no afterlife also impose sanctions, but in this world rather than in the next. Whichever form they take, sanctions—rewards for conforming behavior and punishment for deviance—are part of all imageries.

All imageries also include a compensating mechanism of some kind—a means to derail dissent and to produce acceptance of their lot, particularly on the part of those who are most deprived by a social order. Promises of eternal rewards in another life constitute one mode of compensation. Where the imagery contains no conception of another life, as in Marxism, for example, persons are encouraged to feel rewarded by the sacrifices they are making for the next generation.

Like the philosophical debate over determinism and free will, the sociological controversy about the determinants of forms of social organization continues to rage. It has still to be settled whether changes in ideology are the sources of change in social organization or whether an ideological rationale is the product of the need for social change. Were the idea of *nirvana* and the law of *karma* the precursors of the Indian caste system or were they invented as its rationalization? Was the Protestant Ethic a cause or a result of the rise of capitalism?

Although controversy about which comes first remains, there is probably consensus by now that ideology and social structure are intimately related and that changes in one cannot occur without changes in the other. I intend by these observations to support this proposition, but to extend it by specifying that the ideological changes involve a revision in what "god" and man are understood to be like. I am also inclined to support Max Weber in his contention that a change in imagery may precede rather than follow a change in social structure.

To demonstrate the viability and generalizability of these propositions would require the examination of the universe, or at least a sample of the forms of social organization which man has contrived and about which there are available records. It would have to be established that these forms of social organization are indeed rooted in an ideology of "god" and man. Moreover, it would have to be demonstrated that the decline and disappearance of old forms and the rise of new forms of social organization have always been accompanied by a decline in one imagery and the innovation of another. Such an enterprise clearly is too ambitious to be undertaken lightly or by one person. Yet a collective effort might be warranted if there were enough consensus about the potential of the basic propositions. In this chapter I should like to make a case for this potential by applying the perspective to an examination of gross social change in the West.

Since the middle ages there have been a great variety of ways in which the meaning and purpose of the universe has been understood and in which "god" and man have been depicted. But much of this variety has characterized only small numbers of individuals and despite a possible potential for doing so, has never secured the wide base of public support to become the grounds for organizing or rationalizing a nation-state. Indeed, of the great variety it is suggested that only three sets of images of "god" and man and three basic forms of social organization have held sway in the West since medieval times. To the sets of images may now be added an emerging fourth set which promises to hold sway in the future but whose impact on existing social order has been to modify rather than to upturn it until now.

Max Weber's classic work, *The Protestant Ethic and the Spirit of Capitalism*, and his comparative studies of religion, together with Emile Durkheim's *The Elementary Forms of the Religious Life*, are the sources and stimuli of many of the ideas expressed in this paper.[3] Weber's contrasting analysis of the beliefs and values underlying the feudal and newly emerging capitalist society in the West and classic Chinese and Indian society in the East first suggested the idea that images of "god" and of man are importantly related to social structure. Weber does not use this terminology, of course, but sometimes explicitly and sometimes implicitly he frequently addresses himself to the questions of what man postulates about the forces beyond this world and what these conceptions signify for man's social life on earth.

Weber does this explicitly in his analysis of the ideology warranting medieval society. The feudal organization of society, he points out, is declared to be sacred by virtue of its having been ordained by "god." This is not a capricious act on "god's" part; on the contrary, by indicating that society be organized in a hierarchial way, that men be born to different stations in life, and that they perform uncomplainingly the role that that station dictates, "god" is behaving in an eminently reasonable way and in the interest of ensuring that social life proceed in an orderly fashion. After all, social life requires government, industry, and servitude, and isn't it appropriate that in his wisdom "god" has seen fit to

[3]Max Weber, *The Protestant Ethic and the Spirit of Capitalism*, translated with an introduction and new preface by Talcott Parsons (New York: Scribners, 1930). Emile Durkheim, *The Elementary Forms of the Religious Life*, translated by Joseph W. Swain (London: George Allen and Unwin, n.d.)

supply men in the quantity and with the qualifications to perform these different tasks?

The imagery, in addition to warranting the social order, imposes sanctions and affords compensations to reinforce the dicta to conform. There are to be rewards in heaven for those who conform, and although to do so may mean sacrifices in this life, there is also the compensation of better things to come. Within the system, the assumption is made that man is possessed of free will and has some control over his destiny. His control, however, is effectively limited to his fate in the next world, not this one. The latter has been determined for man by "god" and therefore is beyond man's ability to change. Being possessed of free will, it becomes reasonable to impose responsibilities on man and to judge and reward or punish him for how responsibly he behaves. In the medieval context, behaving responsibly meant accepting and acting in conformity to the social fate "god" had willed.

In combination, then, medieval images of "god" and man warrant and sanction the hierarchial organization of feudal society and thereby provide a means to persuade men to accept the particular form of inequality that society imposed. The inequality, it is especially to be noted, is in this instance of "god's," not man's contrivance. The shift from a feudal to a capitalist form of social organization was accompanied, as Weber and others have documented, by a radical change in rationalizing ideology, including a marked alteration in the prevailing imagery about "god" and man. The effect of the structural changes from feudalism to capitalism was not to eliminate inequality but to radically alter its character. The new imagery of "god" and man warranted, explained, and sanctioned the new basis of inequality and provided compensations for those who were its victims.

In the emerging ideology "god" continued to be personified, but there was a marked shift in the control he was thought to exercise over this world and specifically over the social structure. There was also a decided change in what "god" was seen to have determined for man and how much of man's destiny he granted man to decide for himself. It was no longer held, as it was in the medieval period, that any social order is explicitly ordained by "god." The theocracy which Calvin sought to establish in Geneva presumably followed from his interpretation of "god's" intentions. But the emerging secular capitalism was not considered to be the inspiration of "god," at least not directly. Its warrant was contained more in what came to be a new consensus about the nature of man.

In the medieval period man was conceived of as exercising some control over his destiny in the next world, with his fate in this world being effectively sealed by "god's" ordination. During the rise of capitalism this imagery was reversed. Man's eternal salvation came to be thought of as predestined, but his fate in this world was effectively his to decide. "God" had created man in his image but had then left man free to carve out his own destiny on earth. To be sure, there was an injunction for man to work for "god's" glory, but this did not impose on him an obligation to accept his lot in life. Indeed, it came to be that man was enjoined to improve on rather than to merely accept his social origins, in marked contrast to the medieval period.

Over time, as Weber has pointed out, the idea that "god" had predestined man's eternal fate came to be watered down. First it came to be thought that there were signs by which man could know the fate "god" had assigned to him. Later the idea gained wide acceptance, judging from its survival in contemporary times, that man could influence "god" in his favor or against his favor through his actions on this earth. The result was an image of man which conceived of him as having the power to control his destiny in this world and to influence it in the next.

Man as master of his fate became central to rationalizing the particular form of inequality capitalism created. There was an assumption to begin with that in "god's" eyes all men are created equal. Inequality then became a creation of man generated by the fact that men differ in how responsibly they exercise their freedom. Some men, as is evidenced by how well off they are in this life, are exercising their freedom wisely. Those who fail to succeed have no one to blame but themselves, because it was in their discretion to have opted otherwise. What came to be thought of as good and bad choices is highly important to the rationalizing process, of course. Here, as Weber points out, hard work, diligence, thrift, prudence, and other puritan virtues constituted one set of signs that good choices were being made, and the product of these virtues—material success—was another effective sign.

There is no firm evidence to say how powerfully these ideas in and of themselves contained dissent. Contemporary data suggest, however, that the ideas still have considerable power and provide presumptive evidence that earlier their power was still greater.[4] But the ideas did not have to carry all the weight, of course; for the deprived there were alternative compensations to material success in which to take comfort.

The explanation of inequality changed radically in the shift from feudal to capitalist society, but compensating mechanisms did not, and one finds nearly the same compensations in one society as the next. This is most forcefully evident in religion. With its retention of an anthropomorphic "god," a belief in an afterlife, and the possibilities of eternal bliss in heaven, religion continued to be a comfort to relieve the trials and tribulations of life.

Aside from helping to account for inequality, prevailing assumptions about the nature of man provided a rationalization for and played a part in shaping major institutions of capitalist society. The organization of the economic order was highly consistent with an image of man as free and therefore responsible, as were the law and the legal system created to administer it. The image also afforded a rationalization of prevailing punishment practices. Because the criminal commits a crime at his own option, it is right and just that society hold him responsible for his act and punish him for it.

Man as master of his fate was also the image of man that permeated social welfare practices of capitalist societies. The poor, it was thought, are poor because they choose to be poor, and having made their bed, they ought to be

---

[4]In a survey of the adult population of the United States conducted in 1966, for example, 67 percent of the white respondents agreed that "Negroes who want to work hard can get ahead as easily as anyone else." See Gertrude J. Selznick and Stephen Steinberg, *The Tenacity of Prejudice* (New York: Harper & Row, Publishers, 1969), p. 171.

satisfied to lie in it. This attitude did not warrant the total neglect of the poor, but charity was an act of mercy rather than a responsibility, and charitable giving was a sign of the righteousness of the affluent rather than an acknowledgement of merit in the poor.

Other institutions whose organizations were highly consistent with this individualistic image of man were politics, education, medicine, and the family; indeed, in all spheres of life, man conceived as free but responsible became a pervasive influence in deciding institutional organization, role assignment, evaluation of performance, and the distribution of scarce reward.

Socialism, as it emerged under that name in the eighteenth century, afforded no immediately effective challenge to entrenched capitalism; such a challenge became real only with Karl Marx's revolutionizing of socialism in 1848. Then, by questioning some of capitalism's fundamental assumptions about "god" and man, socialism began a process—still continuing—of reducing the viability of capitalist-inspired forms of social organization.

Until Marx, socialism produced no articulate or agreed-upon imagery of "god." Forms of Christian socialism coexisted with forms which adopted an agnostic or outright atheistic position. However, early socialist thought was agreed on an imagery of man which rejected two shibboleths of capitalist thought: (1) that however created, man was created equal in anybody's sight and (2) that man's destiny was largely his to decide. Socialist thought recognized "god" as the source of inequality, but it was no longer as clear that this was the work of an anthropomorphic "god" rather than the result of historical and social forces to which man is subject. In medieval thought inequality in capacity was seen as justification for parallel inequalities in the distribution of rewards. Under socialism there is no warrant for man being rewarded or deprived for what "god" has done. The principle which ought to apply is "from each according to his abilities, to each according to his needs."

That man is possessed of free will is implicitly assumed, but it is not nearly so unbounded a free will as under capitalism. Man cannot through his own efforts transcend his capacities; he is free, however, to choose whether he develops these capacities. Early socialism articulated a model of social organization which was consistent with these assumptions about man. By the time of Marx, however, the occasion had not arisen to put the model to a test, and Marxist thought very sharply modified its parameters and the imagery of "god" and man underlying them.

Marx's attack on capitalism constituted more than a denial of the validity of capitalism's assumptions about "god" and man, of course. These are seen primarily as epiphenomena used by those in power to suppress those out of power. Yet Marx found it necessary to invent his own epiphenomena both to inform and to warrant the form of social organization he advocated as an alternative. Marx's imagery of "god" is much closer to the Eastern model of eternal principle than to Western divinity. Marx rejected the idea of an anthropomorphic God, of course, but he firmly believed that there are forces at work which are transcendent of man, which are purposeful and goal oriented, and to whom man is called to be subject. These forces, while they inevitably direct man toward the ultimate point of culmination—a classless society—are highly benevolent and enable man to achieve his highest potential. In Marx's view therefore they are "sacred," and thus man owes his allegiance to them.

Man, as in other conceptions, is seen as free to choose for or against "god." However, until a classless society has been achieved, man's freedom of choice is limited. He can help to accelerate or he can impede progress toward a classless society. There is nothing man can do, however, to change the course of history: the ultimate achievement of a classless society is inevitable.

Marx saw success as socially determined by relations to the means of production rather than by individual virtue. In this regard Marx adopted essentially the earlier socialist view that men have no control over how they are created and therefore that there is no justification for inequality. Indeed, inequality constitutes an aberration of what is naturally intended for man and therefore ought to be eliminated, as it eventually will be in a classless society.

In sum, Marx's imagery establishes what the social order ought to be like and why and outlines a means for its achievement. As in other conceptions, both man's possession of free will and his obligation to use it responsibly are acknowledged, and acting responsibly is specified as doing "god's" will. Marxism differs from other conceptions, of course, in ideas about the nature of "god" and "god's" intention for man. However, the ingredients are consistent with the proposition that images of "god" and man are importantly related to social organization.

In his analysis of capitalism Marx was acutely aware of the role compensations and sanctions play in derailing and containing dissent. Such mechanisms would no longer be necessary once a classless society has been achieved under communism. No longer would there be occasion for revolutionary dissent. Marx recognized, however, that sanctions, if not compensations, would be required along the way, and his predictions in this respect have of course been borne out.

Contrary to his expectations, however, the revolution of the proletariat did not occur first in highly industrialized capitalist societies but in countries closer to the feudal model in their form of social organization. This has been accounted for largely as the result of the fact that capitalism in its advanced stages failed to produce the pronounced separation of classes that Marx predicted. The fact that Communist mythology conflicted so sharply with the remnants of capitalist imagery is also thought to have been a major factor. It may also be that communism has not won out, because the viability of its imagery is already being challenged, particularly in the West, by an emerging new imagery.

The new imagery has its roots in the new understanding of "god" and of man contributed by modern science, including social science.[5] Science's imagery of "god" is that there is no God, at least not as past imageries would have it. There are, to be sure, forces transcendent of man to which he is subject. Unlike in past imageries, however, there are no underlying assumptions or forthright claims that these forces have a purpose for man or that they are benevolent, inscrutable, and beyond man's control. On the contrary, foundation stones of

[5]Marx, of course, was an early contributor to this imagery.

science are that such forces are knowable, within still undetermined limits controllable, and innately benign. It is accepted by some scientists that there may be a purpose for man that can be gained by the understanding science produces. There is no consensus yet as to what this purpose might be or whether it will emerge at all.

In its understanding of man, science is also grounded in a different set of assumptions than imageries of the past. Science does not accept as given that man is possessed of free will. The basic assumption governing scientific inquiry on man and his behavior is deterministic. What man is and how he behaves are decided for him, not by him. The deterministic posture of science is heuristic; it provides a point of departure for guiding inquiry, not a personal faith for scientists. There is no expectation that it can ever be established whether man is wholly determined or not. Assuming so, however, is crucial to enabling and sustaining scientific inquiry.

Acting on its deterministic assumptions, science has been able to demonstrate that man's being and behavior, if not wholly decided by heredity and environment, is highly circumscribed by them. What man is at birth is clearly decided for man, not by him. In turn, what he becomes and does during life is conditioned by what he is at birth and by how and in what context he is socialized. Science's understanding of how heredity and environment function to affect man is highly incomplete. There are vast areas unaccounted for and controversy about the modest claims science is now capable of making. Nevertheless, science has succeeded in demonstrating the partial validity of its deterministic assumptions.

Because the determinism is not established as complete, science does not deny directly the claims, implicit if not always explicit, in old imageries that man is possessed of free will. What *is* made problematic are the additional claims of old imageries that there is an identifiable range of man's behavior over which he exercises control and for which, consequently, he can justifiably be held responsible. Scientists disagree about the possibility of gaining the knowledge someday to allow such distinctions to be made. For the moment and for the foreseeable future, man can be exempted from responsibility for the things that science is able to establish are decided for him, not by him—for example, that he is not accountable because of insanity. For the rest, however, it will be ambiguous when responsibility can be reasonably imposed and when it cannot. The possibility will always remain that aspects of human behavior now assumed to be man's free choice may not be after all.

Unlike old imageries, science neither advances a new blueprint for the organization of social life nor affirms the validity of any existing form. Rather, by being agnostic about "god's" intentions for man and ambiguous about the extent of man's responsibility for himself, science denies effectively that there exists an ideological basis for social order—that is to say, a social order in which consensus about the reasonableness of social arrangements rather than sanctions and compensations is the primary source of social control.

It is conceivable, although at this time it seems highly unlikely, that science will someday learn enough to identify a purpose for man and to establish the extent of man's freedom. Until it does, what can be expected with increased diffusion and internalization of scientific perspectives is the erosion of old imageries and the social structures they support, accompanied by an extended period of social disintegration, as men with different visions of what scientific understanding implies for social organization struggle for power.

The diffusion process will proceed more rapidly and its effects will be felt more quickly, it can be expected, in societies which are the main producers of scientific knowledge and which offer the fewest obstacles to its dissemination. This means for this generation the nation-states of the West—most notably, the United States. Indeed, in the United States the diffusion and internalization process has proceeded far enough to have already produced some dislocation of existing social arrangements and considerable ambiguity about what the future portends.

It has been asserted, probably fairly, that science cannot establish the existence or the nonexistence of God. The findings of science can and do test the credibility of particular conceptions of "god," however, and under scientific scrutiny the imagery of "god" which has been dominant in American culture has not fared very well. Scientific explorations of space have made suspect the three-story depiction of the universe characteristic of the old imagery of "god." Scientific discoveries about regularities in nature have raised serious questions about the literalness of biblical miracles. And social scientific investigations of other religions have produced doubts about the claim that the Christian "god" is the only true "god."

That "god" is dead is not a message which the majority of Americans have accepted yet, but the process of erosion appears set on an inevitable course, and "god," anthropomorphically conceived as residing in heaven and exercising dominion over this world, seems destined for residual status and perhaps for oblivion. In itself the erosion of belief in an anthropomorphic "god" does not constitute a threat to the traditional organization of American society. By raising doubt and disbelief, science probably reduces the ability of the old image of "god" to be a compensating mechanism for derailing dissent. By now, however, imagery of "god" is no longer central to the ideological rationalization of inequality in America or to warranting the validity of American institutions. Such warrants derive much more from traditional imagery about man than about "god," but that imagery is also threatened by science and in ways which are already proving a stimulus to social instability.

Perhaps the most visible sign of the threat is the weakening in the power of the old imagery of man to rationalize inequality. It is no longer as clear as it once was that the poor are poor because they choose to be poor or that blacks and other disadvantaged minorities could succeed as well as anyone else if only they would try. There is no agreed-upon alternative to these old understandings. Just as scientists are disagreed about the relative role of different hereditary and environmental factors in producing poverty and inequality between races, so too there are alternative and frequently conflicting explanations in various publics. Cultural, social, psychological, and genetic explanations compete alone and in combination in the marketplace of ideas. Nevertheless, binding those who are now committed to alternative explanations is the abandonment of the imagery that inequality is the result of differences in the way that individuals, left free by "god" to control their own destinies, choose to exercise that control.

With the weakening and gradual abandonment of this imagery has come an increasing unwillingness on the part of the disadvantaged to accept their situations passively and an increasing guilt on the part of the more affluent that deprivations exist. These changes in attitude have stimulated and allowed a growing militancy on the part of the disprivileged. They have also produced a growing effort on the part of public and private agencies to alter the social arrangements that the old imagery helped to sustain. These efforts—among them the poverty program, desegregation, compensatory education, busing, legislation against discrimination in housing, employment, and education—are all characterized by a rejection of the idea that individuals are largely responsible for their own fate.

There is no clear, unified imagery advanced to replace the old, however, and consequently no clear vision of what new social arrangements ought to substitute for past ones. There is a sense that if only man could be freed of constraining social conditions he would indeed be free to guide his own destiny. It remains ambiguous, however, as it does in science, exactly when and where conditioning ends and freedom begins. In all the ameliorative activity just cited, this ambiguity is reflected in the lack of consensus among policy makers and between policy makers, their clients, and taxpayers as to how much help ought to be extended and at what point the disadvantaged ought to be expected to help themselves. In the absence of consensus there is no possibility of formulating policy which will satisfy everyone and no hope for producing ideological agreement about the justice of any social arrangement in which inequality *or* equality prevails.

The diffusion of scientific imagery is also having an impact on the assignment of responsibility in American law. In a system of law informed by the imagery that man is in control of his own destiny, it was considered entirely reasonable and just that anyone who commits a crime be held responsible and accountable for his action. By being unclear about how much control man does have over his actions and by denying effectively that there is a way to recognize when man is in control and when he is not, the new imagery substitutes ambiguity for the explicitness of the old. The ambiguity has not as yet been so widely recognized as to result in the abandonment of the traditional concept of responsibility in American law. Increasingly in American courtrooms, however, judges and juries are experiencing difficulty in assigning responsibility to those who either acknowledge and/or have been found guilty of committing a crime. As with regard to inequality, there is disagreement as to whom or what is to be assigned responsibility if the individual is not. It is the fault of genes for some and for other deficiencies in the socialization process or the immorality of social arrangements. Here laymen reflect the imprecision of science about what the determining agents are. For increasing numbers, however, the old explanation that the individual is at fault no longer applies unequivocally.

The drift toward the welfare state is another sign of the effects of the diffusion. That individuals become sick or disabled, grow old, and die was not attributable to individual deficiency, by and large, even under the old imagery. These were things decided for men, not by him. Nevertheless, under the old imagery it remained a matter of individual responsibility that such contingencies be prepared for and taken care of, and in America's past, medicine, insurance, and even funeral arrangements were organized accordingly. The innovation of Social Security, the adoption of Medicare, the growth of group practice in medicine, of group insurance, and of funeral societies, and the increased pressure for socialized medicine reflect a substantial change from the old attitude—a change indicative of growing public recognition that man's ability to be responsible for himself is not entirely his to decide.

The shift in imagery is also an element, I would aver, in contemporary student unrest, in new forms of religious consciousness, in the increasing pluralism of American life, and indirectly in the public's response to the Vietnam war, the new interest in ecology, the women's liberation movement, and other manifestations of disenchantment with the way things are and have been. As might be expected, the explosion of a myth not only generates the breakdown of the social arrangements it supported directly but creates a threat to the entire structure as well.

I do not mean to imply by these observations that American society is in danger of imminent collapse. The abandonment of the old imagery has not proceeded that far, and old imageries, we are learning once again, are more readily given up than the fruit they produced. Moreover, until there is more agreement than there is now about alternatives, any radical upturning of social arrangements is not likely to occur. Nevertheless, the situation is considerably more in flux than it was when the old imagery prevailed, and as has been suggested earlier, it will probably continue to be so until either science learns enough so that its imagery of "god" and man becomes explicit enough to allow a consensual basis for social order or, as seems more likely, enough support is generated for a particular vision to allow its implementation by imposition. The publication of B. F. Skinner's *Beyond Freedom and Dignity*[6] as this book went to press is a sign that the competition has begun.

[6] B. F. Skinner, *Beyond Freedom and Dignity* (New York: Alfred A. Knopf, 1971).

About the Contributors

As the following brief biographical sketches testify, the contributors to this volume are now dispersed far and wide around the world of academe, but they share their contributorships and also some attachment—past or present—to the Research Program in Religion and Society of the Survey Research Center, University of California, Berkeley. Organized in 1962, that program affords a setting for faculty, graduate students, and visiting scholars at the University and the neighboring Graduate Theological Union to pursue research on the role of religion in modern society. The program is presently engaged in an extensive study of new forms of religious consciousness among American youth.

Earl R. Babbie

Babbie is currently director of the Survey Research Office and associate professor of sociology at the University of Hawaii. He is the author of *Science and Morality in Medicine* and *A Survey Research Cookbook and Other Fables* (forthcoming) and is coauthor of *To Comfort and to Challenge*. He was at Berkeley from 1963 through 1968.

Bruce D. Foster

Foster is presently a research fellow in sociology at the University of Aston in Birmingham, England, where he is working on a study of the organizational structure of churches and completing his doctoral dissertation on class styles of religious commitment. Foster was in residence at Berkeley from 1968 through 1970 as a graduate student in sociology and as a postgraduate research sociologist at the Survey Research Center.

Charles Y. Glock

Glock is professor of sociology and director of the Research Program in Religion and Society, University of California, Berkeley. He has coedited, with Phillip Hammond, *Beyond the Classics?: Essays in the Scientific Study of Religion* and is coauthor, with Rodney Stark, of *The Poor in Spirit: The Sources of Religious Commitment* (forthcoming). Glock has been at Berkeley since 1958.

Jeffrey K. Hadden

Hadden is professor of sociology and urban studies at Tulane University. He is author of *The Gathering Storm in the Churches* (1969) and is editor of *Religion in Radical Transition* (1971). He was a resident scholar at the Survey Research Center at Berkeley during the summer of 1967.

Phillip E. Hammond

Hammond is professor of sociology, University of Arizona. His latest monograph, written with K. M. Dolbeare, is *The School Prayer Decisions: From Court Policy to Local Practice*. He is currently coordinating and cowriting an introductory sociology text. In 1964-65 he was a research associate at the Survey Research Center at Berkeley while on a postdoctoral fellowship.

Travis Hirschi

Hirschi is professor of sociology, University of California, Davis. He is the author of *Causes of Delinquency* and with Hanan C. Selvin wrote *Delinquency Research: An Appraisal of Analytic Methods*. He was in residence at the Survey Research Center at Berkeley from 1960 through 1969.

John Lofland

Lofland is professor of sociology, University of California, Davis. His publications include *Analyzing Social Settings* and *Deviance and Identity*. Currently he is editor of the journal *Urban Life and Culture* and general editor of the Wadsworth series in analytic ethnography. He was in residence at Berkeley as a graduate student from 1960 through 1964.

Gary T. Marx

Marx is a lecturer in sociology at Harvard University and faculty associate at the Joint Center for Urban Studies. He is the author of *Protest and Prejudice* and the editor of *Social Conflict: Tension and Change in American Society*. Currently he is making a comparative study of police in Europe and the United States. He was in residence at Berkeley from 1960 through 1967.

Armand L. Mauss

Mauss is associate professor of sociology at Washington State University. He is the author of *Mormons and Minorities* (forthcoming). His work has been mainly in the areas of the sociology of religion, race relations, and deviant behavior. His articles and reviews have appeared in the *Journal of Social Issues, Social Problems,* the *Pacific Sociological Association Review*, and other journals. He received the Ph.D. degree in sociology from the University of California, Berkeley, in 1970.

Robert E. Mitchell

Mitchell is executive director of the Institute for Social Research at Florida State University. Formerly director of the Survey Research Centre, Chinese University of Hong Kong, he is author of *Family Life in Urban Hong Kong* and *Levels of Emotional Strain in Southeast Asian Cities*. While at Berkeley from 1962 through 1966, he served as director of the International Data Library and Reference Service and as a contributor to the Research Program in Religion and Society.

Donald W. Peterson

Peterson is an advanced graduate student in sociology at Washington State University. His chief interests are social psychology and the sociology of religion.

Harold E. Quinley

Quinley is assistant professor of political science at Brown University. He is the author of *The Prophetic Clergy: Social Activism among Protestant Ministers* and coauthor of *State Officials and Higher Education*. He received the Ph.D. degree from Stanford University and was a postdoctoral fellow at Berkeley from 1969 through 1970 under a grant from the Social Science Research Council.

Raymond C. Rymph

Rymph is an associate professor of sociology at Purdue University. He is currently on leave doing research in religion and nationalism at Biagarzici University, Bebek, Istanbul, Turkey.

Rodney Stark

Stark is professor of sociology at the University of Washington. He is the author of *Police Riots* and coauthor of *Religion and Society in Tension, Christian Beliefs and Anti-Semitism, American Piety*, and *Wayward Shepherds: Prejudice and the Protestant Clergy*. Stark was a charter member of the Research Program in Religion and Society and continues his association, although now at a distance.

Stephen Steinberg

Steinberg is assistant professor of sociology at City University of New York. He is coauthor with Gertrude J. Selznick of *The Tenacity of Prejudice: Anti-Semitism in Contemporary America*. Among his recent publications is "How Jewish Quotas Began," *Commentary*, September 1971. He received his Ph.D. in sociology from the University of California, Berkeley, in 1971 and was in residence at the Survey Research Center from 1963 through 1971.

Robert Wuthnow

Wuthnow is a graduate student in sociology at the University of California, Berkeley, and a research assistant at the Survey Research Center, where he is conducting research on new religious consciousness among American youth. He is coauthor of *Adolescent Prejudice* (forthcoming).